Christine de Pizan and the Categories of Difference

MEDIEVAL CULTURES

SERIES EDITORS
Rita Copeland
Barbara A. Hanawalt
David Wallace

Sponsored by the Center for Medieval Studies
at the University of Minnesota

Volumes in the series study the diversity of medieval cultural histories and practices including such interrelated issues as gender, class, and social hierarchies; race and ethnicity; geographical relations; definitions of political space; discourses of authority and dissent; educational institutions; canonical and non-canonical literatures; and technologies of textual and visual literacies.

For other books in the series, see p. 287

Christine de Pizan and the Categories of Difference

✣

Marilynn Desmond, editor

Medieval Cultures
Volume 14

University of Minnesota Press
Minneapolis
London

Published by the University of Minnesota Press
111 Third Avenue South, Suite 290
Minneapolis, MN 55401-2520
http://www.upress.umn.edu

Library of Congress Cataloging-in-Publication Data
Christine de Pizan and the categories of difference / Marilynn
  Desmond, editor.
     p.   cm. — (Medieval cultures ; v. 14)
  Essays originally delivered at Binghamton University in October
1995 at a conference entitled Christine de Pizan:
texts/intertexts/contexts, sponsored by the Center for Medieval and
Early Renaissance Studies.
  Includes bibliographical references and index.
  ISBN 0-8166-3080-1 (hc : alk. paper). — ISBN 0-08166-3081-X (pb :
alk. paper)
  1. Christine, de Pisan, ca. 1364–ca. 1431 — Criticism and
interpretation — Congresses.   I. Desmond, Marilynn, 1952–   .
II. State University of New York at Binghamton. Center for Medieval
and Early Renaissance Studies.   III. Series.
PQ1575.Z5C47   1998
841'.2 — dc21   97–44280

10 09 08 07 06 05 04 03 02 01 00 99 98   10 9 8 7 6 5 4 3 2 1

Contents

❖

Contents

Acknowledgments

❖

The essays in this volume were originally delivered at Binghamton University in October 1995 at a conference entitled "Christine de Pizan: Texts/Intertexts/Contexts," sponsored by the Center for Medieval and Early Modern Studies with support from the Women's Studies Program. I would like to thank Barbara Altmann, Nadia Margolis, Pamela Sheingorn, and Nancy Jones for their assistance in planning this conference; likewise, I would also like to acknowledge the seventy scholars who made presentations at the conference and who provided an extraordinarily rich forum for critical exchange. The papers here represent only a small portion of that dialogue. Lisa Freeman at the University of Minnesota Press, along with Rita Copeland, Barbara Hanawalt, and David Wallace—the editors for the Medieval Cultures series—were enthusiastic and supportive throughout the publication process, and it is a pleasure to record my debts to them. In addition, I would like to thank Helen Solterer and Cristelle Baskins for their careful reading of this collection and their suggestions for revisions. Likewise, Rhonda Knight undertook the extraordinary task of compiling the bibliography and the index; her attention to scholarly detail and her good cheer made the production of this book a joy. Robert Clark and Deborah McGrady kindly looked over my translations from the *Avision*. And Gerald Kutcher provided endless support and encouragement throughout the planning for the conference and the work of this volume. This book as a whole emerges from the collective and cooperative spirit that continues to dominate Christine studies specifically and feminist scholarship more generally. The contributors in this volume made the work of the conference and the work of this volume a priority in their professional lives, which made the book come together so rapidly. Throughout the editorial process I have had the privilege of a sustained dialogue with each contributor, and the publication of the book marks an end to many stimulating discussions. In all respects, *Christine de Pizan and the Categories of Difference* and the conference that preceded it represent a most gratifying professional experience, one that I bring to a close with some regret but with great satisfaction that the collective efforts of so many scholars will now be shared with the larger academic community.

Figure 1. Christine inscribes her manuscript. Frontispiece to the *Mutacion de Fortune*, first decade of fifteenth century. Munich, Bayerische Staatsbibliothek, MS Gallica 11, fol. 2r.

❖

From Book-Lined Cell to Cyborg Hermeneutics

Marilynn Desmond

Car en haulcant mes yeulx avisay voulant entre yceulx une grant ombre femmenine sanz corps sicomme chose esperituelle de trop estrange nature / Et quelle fut merveilleuse lexperience prouvoit. Car celle chose veoye estre une seule ombre. / mais plus de .cm. millions voire innombrables parties / les unes grandes les autres mendres autres plus petites de soy elle faisoit . . . car il nest corps de creature humaine ne destrange beste oysel monstre de mer serpent ne chose que dieux formast oncques voire des plus hautes choses celestielles et de tout quanque pensee puet presenter a la fantasie dont ny eust la fourme.

[Lifting my eyes I perceived flying between them a large female shadow without a body as if it were a spiritual thing of strange nature. Experience proved it to be supernatural. I saw this thing to be a single shadow, but she made herself seem a hundred thousand, indeed, innumerable parts, some large, others small, others smaller than herself. . . . For there was no body, whether human, strange beast, bird, sea monster, serpent or anything that God created whether of the highest heavens or anything imagined in fantasy whose form she did not take.][1]
— *L'Avision-Christine* 2.2

A cyborg is a cybernetic organism, a hybrid of machine and organism, a creature of social reality as well as a creature of fiction. Social reality is lived social relations, our most important political construction, a world-changing fiction. . . . The cyborg is a matter of fiction and lived experience that changes what counts as women's experience in the late twentieth century. This is a struggle over life and death, but the boundary between science fiction and social reality is an optical illusion.
—Donna Haraway, "A Cyborg Manifesto"

Donna Haraway's cyborg myth points to the "transgressed boundaries, potent fusions and dangerous possibilities" of technology in the late twentieth century: "we are living through a movement from an organic, industrial society to a polymorphous, information system" (*Simians* 161). Since we will become increasingly defined by our electronic relations to the "informatics of domination," this shift has inescapable implications for our social, economic, and cultural constructions as readers. Our hybrid identities will eventually be constructed through electronic textuality and the technological possibilities of hypertext and virtual reality.[2] The human organism grafted onto the electronic network will constitute the cyborg reader of the next century. That texts and textuality—like gender and sexuality—will become more protean is one of the "dangerous possibilities" for the cyborg reader (see Sue-Ellen Case). In the second part of her *Avision-Christine*, Christine visualizes Dame Opinion as ever-changing shadows flying in the air (2.2); these shadowy information systems must be negotiated as part of the road of study that leads to her encounter with Philosophy in the third part of the *Avision* (see Laennec; Skemp). Just as Christine contends with the shadow-filled vision that is Dame Opinion, the cyborg reader will face a shape-shifting textuality that challenges interpretive authority. Electronic textuality may well return us to a proliferation of texts and commentary strikingly similar to medieval textuality. Indeed, electronic networking already returns us to a collaborative and collective experience of writing that is closer to medieval than modern concepts of authorship and text production (see Sue-Ellen Case; Bolter; Simone; Woodmansee).

The cyborg reader of the next century might establish network contact with Christine's vision of Dame Opinion through an electronic hypertext that will simultaneously provide access to multiple textual traditions and digitized images of the manuscripts of the *Avision-Christine*. The ideal cyberspace archive will also provide immediate access to the miniatures and decorations in the manuscripts of this text and in other texts in the Christine corpus, as well as related texts and images in other textual traditions (Laidlaw, "From Scriptorium"; Ferrante 167–68). Like the vision of Dame Opinion as a great bodiless shadow, electronic textuality will constitute a plenitude so vast that the cyborg reader may find herself echoing Christine's comment that no creation, thought, or fantasy was absent.

For Christine studies, the electronic possibilities of the global library and cyberspace hypertextuality offer tremendous advances over the research resources of the twentieth century. Electronic editions and hypertext may finally make the complete corpus of Christine's texts available in a scholarly format. Despite the sustained interest in the texts of Christine de Pizan throughout the century (an interest promoted in large part by feminists),[3] the history of Christine studies in the context of medieval studies demonstrates the extent to which these texts have been constructed as different from the canonical norm. The masculine priorities of the humanities have excluded serious study of texts signed by women until the recent challenges of the feminist critique. While Christine's exclusion from the canon is similar to the fate of most women writers in the Western tradition, her own rhetorical awareness of authorship makes her status as an "author" itself a challenge to the masculine categories of authorship, whether medieval or modern.

In addition, the Christine corpus is vast and tremendously diverse. It includes poetry and prose (and one text, the *Epistre Othea*, that is both— and more). Christine produced texts in a range of genres, some of which are all but unique to her: lyric poetry, debate poetry, allegory and dream visions, political biography, political autobiography. Some texts, such as the *Avision* or the *Othea*, defy generic classification, thereby problematizing the concept of genre as a critical tool. In addition, the manuscript tradition of the Christine corpus is visually rich, and a large number of luxury manuscripts — often with complex programs of illustration — survive. Since Christine herself was intimately involved in the production of her books (Laidlaw, "Publisher's"), her scribal activities and her intervention into the word-image relationships of her texts often trouble the distinctions between writer, scribe, rubricator, and artist. The study of Christine's manuscripts consequently points to larger questions about medieval texts and the authorial shaping of texts as artifacts, as well as the collaborative nature of textual production (Alexander, "Art History").

One measure of the difference of the Christine corpus within the discourses of medieval studies is the history of critical editions and related scholarly apparatus. The Christine corpus has yet to be edited in its entirety, although great progress has been made during the past few decades (see *Le Livre des trois Vertus*; Fenster and Erler; *Cité*, ed. Richards), and several critical editions are currently in preparation that should appear in the near future.[4] Nonetheless, at the turn of the century, several texts will remain unavailable in modern critical editions. Moreover, despite the breathtaking quality of the visual component of the manuscript tradition, the modern reader has almost no access to this aspect of Christine's oeuvre.[5] For instance, the *Othea* is a unique text in medieval culture; it consists of a cinematic juxtaposition of images and textual material — prose and poetry, French and Latin, epistle and allegory (Desmond and Sheingorn; Parussa; Ignatius). The text of the *Othea* cannot be understood in isolation from its visual program, nor can its images be adequately "read" apart from the text. However, no facsimile of any early manuscript of this highly popular text has ever been undertaken.[6] For such a text, the electronic capabilities of hypermedia may provide a more workable format for modern scholarly presentation; indeed, the medieval *ordinatio* of the *Othea* is extremely difficult to render in standard print technology, so much does it differ from the literary norms of textual construction as understood by conventional textual studies. Only with the hypermedia possibilities of electronic technology will the modern reader find reasonably easy access to the interpretive complexity of the *Othea*.

By creating entirely new formats for presentation of textual materials and by making much more material more widely available, the electronic hypertext will transform the subject positions available to the modern reader. The electronic subjectivity of the cyborg reader will derive, in part, from the transference between human reader and electronic machine/text. The proliferation of texts and the reader's electronic dependence may well expose the fictions of interpretive mastery and replace them with a critical awareness of partiality and alterity. The act of reading as a confrontation with textual alterity is a central fiction in the narrative texts of the Christine corpus. These allegorical narratives repeatedly depict a specific scene of reading: as a solitary, contemplative reader, the Christine-narrator finds herself "avironnee de plusieurs volumes de diverses mateires" (surrounded by many volumes on various topics) (Curnow, *"Cité"* 1.1.2) as she describes the setting of her dream vision in the *Livre de la cité des dames*. Alone with her books, she is completely absorbed in her reading. Such textual depictions construct the narrator as a learned woman, a "fille descolles" (schooled daughter), which is the way the "Ombre" addresses her in the *Avision*. Likewise, the pictorial images that function as author portraits in Christine manuscripts often represent Christine alone with her books; such visual author portraits reinforce the textual construction of the narrator in establishing the authority of Christine-author (Altmann; Zühlke). The frontispiece to the allegory of the *Mutacion de Fortune* (see Figure 1) in the Munich manuscript, for instance, situates Christine at a table strewn with other books. As author and narrator, reader and scribe, she inscribes the book before her.

Such scenes represent the liminal experience of reading as it shapes the allegorical narrative that follows (see McRae). But such scenes also vividly depict the material conditions and cultural expectations negotiated by the learned woman of the early fifteenth century. In a discussion of Italian female humanists of the same era, Margaret L. King vividly characterizes the anxiety provoked by the learned woman, who was invariably seen by male contemporaries as an extraordinary anomaly, marked by a "distorted sexuality" (79). In King's terms, the female humanists were relegated to chaste isolation as "fierce goddesses in book-lined cells" (80). As humanist portraits (Willard, *Christine* 163), the authorial images of Christine reading in isolation suggest the cultural paradoxes she negotiated. These images speak to the extraordinary status she occupied as a "fille descolles" and the implicit restrictions attendant on that status (see Figure 2). Susan Groag Bell points specifically to Christine's "painful estrangement from society resulting from the fact that she was not merely a scholar, but a female scholar; not merely studious, but a studious woman" ("Christine" 183). These author portraits situate her in the conventional role of reading and writing that is culturally reserved for a male author such as Boccaccio or Petrarch, yet her gender marks her difference in this context. These author portraits visualize the fact that the reception of her work was particularly marked by her audience's awareness of the author's gender. As she notes in the *Avision*, her first audience saw in her poetry the novelty of female authorship: "la chose non usagee que femme escripse comme pieca ne avenist" (For a long time it had not been a common thing for a woman to write) (ed. Towner, 165).

Figure 2. Christine de Pizan reading a manuscript book in a bedroom filled with books. From the *Livre des faits d'armes et de chevalerie,* mid–fifteenth century. Brussels, Bibliothèque Royale, MS 9009–11, fol. 118v.

If the visual and textual depictions of Christine emphasize her isolation as an anomalous learned woman within the categories of late medieval vernacular humanism, her texts nonetheless record her presence in contemporary political discourse. As Sandra Hindman's study of the political context of the *Othea* demonstrates, Christine often deployed the poetic intertextuality of word and image in an attempt to intervene in contemporary affairs. Joël Blanchard likewise depicts Christine as a poetic mediator whose engagement with historical texts might work to interpellate her royal readers and encourage ethical and judicious conduct ("Raisons de l'histoire," "Tradition," "L'Entrée"). Throughout her career as a writer, from the time of her widowhood until she withdrew to Poissy, Christine had to negotiate and renegotiate suitable patronage for her works and her livelihood (Willard, *Christine* 155–71). Eric Hicks observes, "On pourrait dire q'elle a débuté dans la littérature en chantant, seulette en sa chambre, et qu'elle a fini par crier sur la place publique" (One could say that she began her literary career by singing, alone in her room, and she finished by shouting in the public square) ("Femme" 234).

Christine in her "book-lined cell" offers only a partial portrait of the subject positions Christine occupied as author.

Indeed, many scholarly portraits of Christine from a generation ago are limited to a view of her as the author of only a portion of her corpus, but that partial view was frequently presented as the whole picture. For instance, Daniel Poirion located Christine among the "maitres" of courtly lyric, a judgment based obviously on her poetic texts to the exclusion of her prose (*Poète*). By contrast, D. W. Robertson and John Fleming characterize her only by her role in the *Querelle de la Rose* (the Debate of the *Rose*); Robertson dismisses her as an "irate woman" (364), and Fleming repeats Montreuil's attack: "Her arguments and her manner show the acumen ... of 'the Greek whore who dared to write against Theophrastus'" (47). More recent scholars have been concerned to situate the texts of Christine within medieval categories of difference, and their portrait of Christine is richly particular; they include Nadia Margolis's exploration of Christine's discourse on Judaic history, identity, and social context ("Christine de Pizan and the Jews"); Christine Reno's consideration of Christine's understanding of gender at the intersection of class ("Christine"); and Helen Solterer's placement of Christine in the tradition of disputing women. In addition, a long-standing critical discussion points to Christine's critique of the categories of courtly romance from the perspective of the female reader and participant in the discourse (Willard, "*Cent ballades*"; Krueger, *Women Readers* 217–46; Bornstein, "Ideal"). Such approaches acknowledge that the Christine corpus is animated by a variety of subject positions and authorial perspectives.

The essays in this volume exploit the categories of difference as a critical tool; these essays exemplify how a cyborg hermeneutics might address categories of difference, not as contradictions to be resolved, but as the productive play of textual alterity. The Christine corpus simultaneously explores the constructed nature of the categories of difference and yet appeals to the "difference" of such categories. The authorial narrator often acknowledges the performative and contingent nature of difference, and yet just as frequently appeals to cultural norms as though they were fixed categories that the reader should vigilantly maintain, whether that reader is identified as the (fictional) addressee of Christine's epistles or the courtly audience implied in her allegories and lyric poetry. In addition, the Christine corpus purposefully deploys the ideological and rhetorical use of categories of difference in a political context.[7] Indeed, there even lurks an awareness of difference in the category of the universal: in its appeal to the universal category of women, the *Cité des dames* anticipates the theoretical claims of twentieth-century French feminists, who, in Naomi Schor's terms, create "the opportunity to speak the universal while not relinquishing their differences." (27). The self-conscious negotiation and deployment of the categories of difference throughout the Christine corpus illustrate the efficacy of premodern textual cultures for postmodern accounts of difference.

At the beginning of the *Avision-Christine*, Christine-narrator notes that she was "transgloutie ou ventre" (swallowed into the belly) of the image of chaos, where she meets a crowned figure who identifies herself with France and French culture. The essays in Part I, "The Belly of the Monster," attend to the ways in which Christine's texts depend on the received categories of French culture in the early fifteenth century and nonetheless work to intervene in those categories. In an analysis of chivalric discourse, Charity Cannon Willard shows how Christine's texts repeatedly deploy received notions of military conduct—for princes, knights, leaders, and the military as a whole—as an educational and political strategy intended to shape the military decisions of the day. In her military treatise, the *Fais d'armes* (1410), Christine draws her rhetorical authority, not from any sort of "experience" on the battlefield or in the army, but from her learned engagement with a wide range of texts and her observations as a participant in court culture and the discourses of chivalry. Chivalry is a category known to Christine as a language—whether written or performative—that she might appropriate through translations, citation, revision, and compilation. In addition, Willard points to the silent inheritance of this treatise by later military leaders, whose strategic decisions testify to the extensive influence of the *Fais d'armes* on later military practices and the development of codes of conduct.

The educational institutions and practices of the early fifteenth century excluded Christine de Pizan almost as thoroughly as the military institutions of the day. Nonetheless, from her "book-lined cell" Christine skillfully and effectively negotiated a program of self-education. Roberta Krueger explores the resulting anxiety of this educational self-consciousness in the didactic rhetoric evident in the works Christine produced until 1405. As student and teacher, reader and writer, the narrator of Christine's texts betrays a moral anxiety about the efficacy of didactic performance. In the process, Krueger demonstrates the significant differences in the didactic shape of texts aimed for male and female readers; Krueger notes Christine's complicity in the oppressive categories of patriarchal thinking and considers the extent to which such complicity is the result of the social contract and the cultural expectation that didactic discourse not challenge the normative categories of gender or class within the social order. Diane Wolfthal turns to the visual performances of the exuberant textual cultures of the Valois court in order to consider how the texts of Christine—both word and image—refuse the foundational category of woman as the vulnerable object of predatory sexual assault. Wolfthal's discussion uses images and narratives from Christine's texts to show the extent to which sexual violence was a language that could be critiqued and revised by texts that depict "otherwise."

These three essays, taken together, testify to the afterlife of Christine's texts in later institutions and discourses associated with the development of international codes of warfare, in the emergence of a class-based regime of conduct, and in late medieval visual interpretations of sexual violence. Mary Anne C. Case further contextualizes this trajectory by reading Christine's discourse on difference against the contemporary discussions by feminists and critical race theorists. From the perspective of legal history, Christine de Pizan and the *Querelle des femmes* tradition can be seen to participate in defining the categories of difference that continue to shape discussions on gender and sexuality. Although Christine's attempts at cultural interventions are often complicit with the dominant discourse of her world, Case demonstrates the legacy of Christine's cultural negotiations in the history of textual interventions "in the belly of the monster," as Haraway designates the "late industrial, militarized, racist and male dominant societies" (*Simians* 188; see also "Promises").

The number and range of texts surviving under the signature of Christine de Pizan are diverse and complex; taken together, these texts resist closure under the identity of a unified authorial subject. Individual texts from the Christine corpus are productive examples of "limited location and situated knowledge" in Haraway's terms (*Simians* 190). The essays in Part II,"Situated Knowledges," exemplify a critical approach to the Christine corpus that privileges a "partial perspective" and emphasizes the ways in which these texts construct "partial, locatable, critical knowledges" (Haraway, *Simians* 191). Thelma Fenster analyzes the rhetorical politics of Christine's prose style as an example of vernacular poetics within the location of French humanism and its privileging of Latin. Although critical approaches have tended to disparage Christine's prose style and point to its secondary status as a vernacular discourse within a humanist context, Fenster focuses instead on the role prose could occupy in Christine's situated discourse. Benjamin Semple further locates Christine's vernacular discourse within the categories of philosophy and theology. Through an analysis of Christine's critique of knowledge in the *Avision*, Semple demonstrates how Christine constructs the subject position of the "simple person" as a means to negotiate and subvert the hierarchies of knowledge. The limited location of Christine's simple person allows her to acknowledge the uncertainty and the situated status of all intellectual constructions.

In a discussion of illustrations in manuscripts of the *Chemin de long estude*, Mary Weitzel Gibbons explores intervisual meanings of one image, *The Bath of the Muses*, as an interpretive twist on the representation of learning as embodied knowledge. Gibbons shows how *The Bath of the Muses* pictorially revises the masculine traditions of learning for Christine as narrator, who must visit the locations of knowledge on her road of long study. Indeed, it is the image, not the text, that has revisionary force in the *Chemin.* Monica Green's essay on the *Secrés des dames* and the "Trotula" demonstrates how the references to medical knowledge in the *Cité des dames* record a highly situated recognition of the complex traditions of understanding the female body in its sexual and reproductive capacities. For Christine, the figure of "Trotula" as a learned woman would appear to be compromised by the misogynistic tradition of that learning. The limited location of each of these discourses illustrates Christine's rhetorical awareness of her subject position as "embodied other" in the face of master narratives.

Throughout the fifteenth century, the author function responds to a range of social structures, such as the cultural status of learning, royal and noble patronage, the emergence of print technology, and shifting political alliances. Judith Kellogg examines Christine's appropriation of Ovidian mythic authority to revise Ovidian misogyny. Kellogg demonstrates the significance of these two intertextual maneuvers to the emergence of Christine's subject position as a female *auctor.* In her codicological study of the discourse of authorship in the context of textual production and circulation, Deborah McGrady juxtaposes the emergence of authorship in the modern sense to the declining importance of the patron as the singular individual responsible for the production of the text. Although Christine might manipulate a changing patronage economy to claim an authorial identity for herself during her lifetime, the social processes of book production would later appropriate that identity. Cynthia Brown surveys the various representations of authorial identity in printed versions of texts from the Christine corpus. While the entrepreneurial printers in the fifteenth and sixteenth centuries initially erased Christine as the author of her texts, later French printers restored Christine's authorial identity to printed versions of her works. Brown's discussion points to the shifting status of authorship as a category in early modern France and England. In an analysis of the rhetorical significance of John Talbot's choice of Christine's *Fais d'armes et de chevalerie* as part of a text he commissioned and then presented to Margaret of Anjou as a wedding present in 1445, Michel-André Bossy explores the competing functions of author and book producer in the layout of a text designed to circulate as a diplomatic conduit. Although this version of the *Fais* is attributed to Christine's authorship, that authorial identity is displaced by the significant role Talbot claims as patron whose gift anthology emphasizes the homosocial bonds of king and soldier. These essays demonstrate that the nature of the "author function" goes beyond signature and cannot be studied as a category entirely distinct from *compilator,* patron, printer, or diplomat; the contextual relations of all these roles have left highly visible traces throughout the texts produced under the gendered signature of Christine de Pizan.

The shifting perspectives in this collection highlight the categories of difference that Christine negotiated as author and that a cyborg reader might exploit. Christine has often been defined by her seemingly paradoxical or contradictory status: as a vernacular poet who situates texts in relation to humanist themes, an Italian by birth who elaborates on a vision of French nationalism, a poet adept at prose treatises as well as didactic poetry, a female poet who self-consciously adopts the masculine subject position required to write. Christine's autobiographical narratives emphasize that social class is an uncertain category for women: as a wife, she enjoyed a range of class privileges that were withdrawn upon her widowhood and that she could only partially reclaim through her manipulation of systems of patronage. Christine's subject vividly relates her experience of what Haraway terms the "unequal parts of privilege and oppression that make up all positions" (*Simians* 187). Christine has been embraced by modern readers for her difference, critiqued for not being different enough, and generally categorized by her difference. These categories of difference should enable a readerly engagement with the Christine corpus that privileges process, partiality, and critical interventions. While the studious woman of the fifteenth century such as Christine was seen as a "fierce goddess in a book-lined cell," the studious woman of the twenty-first century will be a cyborg reader whose electronic self will negotiate a network that refuses spatial enclosure as much as interpretive closure. The possibility of cyberspace archives presents enormous potential for the reader of Christine de Pizan: access to texts, intertexts, and contexts beyond the walls of any single library or archival collection and beyond the scholarly limitations of the twentieth century (Chartier, "Libraries"). A cyborg hermeneutics allows us to approach the situated knowledges of Christine de Pizan as the words and images of a "world-changing fiction."

I would rather be a cyborg than a goddess. —Donna Haraway

Notes

1. The text of the *Avision* is from Towner's edition; the translations are my own. For a full translation, see McLeod.
2. See Chartier, *Forms* 1–24; Landow; Lyotard 1–9; Miller. For a powerful discussion of cyborg history, see Biddick; for cyborg theory, see Sandoval.
3. Willard notes the "spate of feminist theses across Europe pointing out Christine's value as a woman writer" early in the twentieth century (222); see Rigaud; Laigle; Richardson; Pinet, *Christine.* For bibliographic guides, see Kennedy.
4. The following editions should appear shortly: Barbara Altmann, ed., *Debate Poems*; Christine Reno and Liliane Dulac, eds., *Advision Cristine* (Champion); Gabriella Parussa, ed., *Epistre Othea*; Charity Cannon Willard, ed., *Fais d'armes*; Zimmerman, *Les Heures de Contemplacion.*
5. Both Hindman (*Christine*) and Meiss (*Limbourgs*) provide black-and-white reproductions of some of the *Othea*; although valuable, these images do not provide the opportunity to study the images in context.

6. A microfiche facsimile is now available for a 1455 Flemish version of the *Othea* (Erlangen-Nürnberg, Universitätsbibliothek, MS 2361); see Lengenfelder. Indeed the text of the *Othea* has not been presented in a critical edition, although Gabriella Parussa is currently preparing one.

7. For a discussion of the larger theoretical and political tensions inherent in theories of difference, see Grosz; Scott, Introduction to *Feminism and History*.

PART I

The Belly of the Monster

Sexe femenin si fus semblablement que les autres soubdainement transgloutie ou ventre de cel ymage.

[I was made in the feminine sex and like the others I was suddenly swallowed into the belly of this image.]

—Christine, *Avision 1*

CHAPTER 1

❖

Christine de Pizan on the Art of Warfare

Charity Cannon Willard

The series of letters written by Christine de Pizan during her participation in the quarrel over the *Roman de la Rose* call attention to her relations with government employees, notably the royal secretaries with whom her husband had been associated during his lifetime. Little attention, however, has been given to the knights and military men with whom she rubbed elbows early in her career, probably at the court of Louis d'Orléans, except for those who are known to have belonged to the Court of Love founded in 1402, or to the Dame Blanche à l'Ecu Vert, the order founded by the Maréchal Boucicaut in honor of women.

There is no doubt of Christine's association with a number of military men early in her literary career, for their names and qualities are to be found mentioned even in her early poems. Already in her Ballade 2 she complains that military accomplishments (*fais d'armes*) and valor are not appreciated as they were in ancient Rome, where chivalry was thought to have originated:

> Princes, par Dieu c'est grant dueil et grand rage
> Quant les biens fais ne sont guerredonné
> A ceulx qui sont, au dit de tout lengage,
> Digne d'estre de lorier couronné.
> (Oeuvres 1:3, lines 25–28)

> [Princes, it is great grief and great dismay
> That good deeds are not rewarded
> For those who are in any language
> Worthy of being crowned with laurel].

Ballade 64 is also addressed to knights, speaking of the qualities they should represent. This, of course, announces the theme she would develop in the *Epistre Othea*, and in a more limited fashion in the *Chemin de long estude* and the *Livre du corps de policie*. On this occasion she says they should be "En fais d'armes enterprenans et fiers" (In deeds of arms enterprising and proud) (*Oeuvres* 1:65). In Ballade 92 she praises an individual knight whom she does not name, but she speaks of his accomplishments in "maintgrant païs et mainte forteresse" (many countries and many a fortress) in a way that suggests Jean de Chateaumorand, of whom she would have more to say later.

In the second series of ballades, the "Autres Ballades," one finds evidence of her admiration of Charles d'Albret, who became Connétable de France in 1402 (*Oeuvres*, "Autres Ballades" 16, 1:225). From history one does not gain the impression that he was an outstanding military leader, and he was one of the victims of Agincourt. However, he was an important figure at the French court and was the subject of "Autres Ballades" 2 and 3. She further greeted him at the New Year in Ballade 16 (Brussels, Bibliothèque Royale, MS 11034) and subsequently presented him with a copy of her *Débat de deux amans* accompanied by still another ballade.

The point in giving him the debate poem is, of course, that in it she compared at some length contemporary knights with historic and literary predecessors. So it is that, among others, she speaks of such men as Louis de Sancerre, also constable of France, who had taken part in the French victory at Rosebecque; Othe de Granson, a poet as well as a knight; Jean de Chateaumorand; and Jean de Werchin, seneschal of Hainaut, in whose praise she had already written a ballade and to whom she would dedicate her *Livre des trois jugemens*, asking him to decide the true meaning of *loyauté* in the cases described in the poem (Willard, "Jean de Werchin" 595–603).

One notes with interest that Christine was less impressed by the military capabilities of these men than by their qualities as gentlemen, but it was no doubt her contact with them that influenced her ideas on *chevalerie* as expressed in the *Chemin de long estude* written only a short time later, finished before March 1403. In this longer work, when Christine and her Cumaean Sibyl guide arrive in the "fifth heaven," they are present at a debate among the four queens "who govern the world"— Sagece, Noblece, Chevalerie, and Richece, presided over by Raison. These goddesses discuss the character necessary for the man worthy to govern the world. At the conclusion of the debate Christine is, of course, appointed to carry their message back to the French princes so that they can decide the problem. It is the comments of Christine that are of particular interest here.

In a section of the poem entitled *Les Condicions que bon chevalier doit avoir selon les dis des aucteurs* (181–95), it becomes evident that Christine was already familiar with several authors of whom she would make extensive use later—first of all Vegetius, from whose *Epitoma rei militaris* she cites specific references. She also cites the *Policraticus* of John of Salisbury, Valerius Maximus, Saint Augustine, all of whom would be important sources for later writings. She ends this section of the poem by praising the accomplishments of Chateaumorand, who, at the time she was writing, had returned to Paris from defending Constantinople against the Turks, in order to accompany the ruler, Manuel Paleologus, in his quest for more European help. Maréchal Boucicaut, founder of La Dame Blanche à l'Ecu Vert, and Chateaumorand were the prime supporters of this mission, and this was the inspiration for Christine's praise on this occasion, rather than their attitude toward women, however much she may have valued that.

It was about this same time that Christine's writing underwent a change of direction. This may have been brought about by her son Jean's return from England after the death of his patron there, Sir John Montague, earl of Salisbury, who had been killed by a mob in January 1400 because of his support for the deposed King Richard II. Henry IV had offered his protection to the youth and had even invited Christine to his court, but she would have none of it, making every effort to get her son returned to France. But then she was faced with the necessity of reestablishing him. This led her to write a ballade to the duke of Orléans asking him to find a place in his household for the youth (*Oeuvres* 1:232–33). Her efforts apparently met with no response. In the end it was the duke of Burgundy who found a place at his court for Jean. This would appear to be the inspiration for the praise of the Burgundian court in a ballade written in 1403 (*Oeuvres*, "Autres ballades" 38, 1:251). There is no dependable evidence that she dedicated anything to the duke of Orléans after this date. It was to the duke of Burgundy that she offered the first copy of her *Mutacion de Fortune* at the beginning of 1404. This, of course, led to the duke's commissioning of the biography of his brother Charles, the former king.

From then on Christine wrote primarily in prose, devoting herself increasingly to the problems of France, which were plentiful, but also to the education of the dauphin, in addition to her concerns about women.

The second part of her biography of Charles V is entitled "Chivalry" (*Fais et bonnes meurs* 1:105–244). There Christine's primary purpose was to show that Charles V, a man not noted for his physical courage and also the victim of poor health, could nevertheless qualify as a military leader. Christine thus undertook to demonstrate that intelligence in directing military operations is more important than physical prowess in battle. She speaks of four qualities that characterize true chivalry: good fortune, good judgment, diligence, and strength, a standard established in Rome by Romulus. Her ideas about the origins of chivalry were influenced by Honoré Bouvet's *Arbre des batailles*, dedicated to Charles VI in 1387, a work of which she would make abundant use later (Ouy, "Honoré Bouvet" 255–59; Bouvet).

A particular point is made of Charles V's unwillingness to lead troops in battle, as his father, John II, and Edward III of England had done. He was, of course, fortunate in having the services of such a talented leader as Bertrand DuGuesclin, but it is undoubtedly true that more was accomplished by the king's diplomacy than would have been by his presence on the battlefield. There was also the recollection of the disaster brought on by John II's capture by the English at Poitiers, for which the whole country had suffered. Charles V's diplomacy succeeded in restoring a good deal that France had lost, all regarded by Christine as examples of his good judgment.

In another chapter of this second part Christine speaks of what various authors had said about chivalry, as it is necessary for military men to have some instruction in their undertakings. This leads her to an interesting explanation of why she considers herself competent to discuss such matters herself. First she speaks of the accusation that she is merely quoting others. To this she replies:

> Tout ainsi comme l'ouvrier de architecture ou
> maçonnage n'a mie fait les pierres et les
> estoffes, dont il bastist et ediffie le chastel
> ou maison, qu'il tent à perfaire et où il labeure,
> non obstant assemble les matieres ensemble,
> chascune où elle doit servir, selon la fin de
> l'entencion où il tent, aussi les brodeurs, qui
> font diverses divises, selon la soubtivité de leur
> ymaginacion, sanz faulte ne firent les soyes,
> l'or, ne les matieres, et ainsi d'aultres
> ouvrages ... il me souffist seulement que les sache
> appliquer à propos, si que bien puissent servir à
> la fin de l'ymaginacion, à laquelle je tends.
>
> *(Fais et bonnes meurs* 1:191)

> [... as the architect or mason has not made
> the stones from which he attempts to perfect the castle or mansion
> on which he labors, although he assembles
> the materials, putting each object where it belongs
> according to the plan he is trying to carry out;
> likewise the embroiderers, who create various
> designs according to the subtlety of their
> imaginations, but do not create the silk,
> the gold or the other materials they use.... It is
> sufficient for me merely to know how to apply
> all this to my purposes, so that it may serve
> the inspirations that I am trying to fulfill.]

With regard to the accusation that this is presumption on her part, she replies that the doctrine that is set forth is more important to the person who can make use of it than the person who expresses it. This echoes the sentiment expressed at the end of the *Epistre Othea*, attributed in both cases to Hugh of Saint Victor in his *Didascalion*. In the biography of Charles V she ends by citing the example of Minerva, who would, of course, serve as her mentor in composing the *Livre des fais d'armes et de chevalerie* (*Fais et bonnes meurs* 1:191–92). Another interesting chapter near the end of this second part is devoted to Charles V's desire to develop a navy (*Fais et bonnes meurs* 1:239–42). In this project he enjoyed the support of Henry of Trastamara and his excellent Spanish fleet. By 1377 there was a French navy capable of dominating the English Channel and even of capturing the English coastal town of Rye. Christine quotes the advice of Vegetius on the construction and provisioning of battle-craft. It is perhaps not surprising that a native of Venice should show an interest in naval power, but Charles V was almost unique among early French kings in understanding its value. This would not be repeated until the reign of Francis I.

It should also be noted that one of the concerns of the duke of Burgundy in commissioning the biography of his brother was to provide a model of kingship for the dauphin, Louis de Guyenne, who would soon marry his granddaughter Marguerite. The madness of Charles VI made him quite useless in this respect, and Louis was all too frequently the victim of ambitious nobles trying to solidify their power and influence at the unstable French court. Although these chapters are perhaps not of major importance to the biography of Charles V as a whole, they are useful for explaining Christine's willingness to undertake a book on the art of warfare and also her concern for the education of the French dauphin, for it was to him that she dedicated her *Livre du corps de policie*, written in 1407.

Christine had first shown an interest in the dauphin when she included him in her *Oroyson Nostre Dame*, where she wrote:

Paix, bonne vie et bonne fin
Donne a mon seigneur le Daulphin
Et science pour gouverner
Le peuple qui de bon cuer fin
L'aime, et vueilles qu'a celle fin
Apres le pere il puist regner!
                    (*Oeuvres* 3:3–4)

[Peace, a good life and a good end
To my lord, the young dauphin, pray send,
With wisdom to rule with good fame,
Over the people whose love extends
To him loyally, and so to such ends,
Like his father, long may he reign.]

Christine shared her concern for the dauphin's future with several of her contemporaries: Nicolas de Clamanges, Jean de Montreuil, and Jean Gerson, in particular.[1] Of course the formation of the "perfect prince" was a favorite concern of early humanistic writers, and these men were already influenced by new ideas from Italy. They were also in close contact with the prince's tutor, Jean d'Arsonval. Christine saw fit to add her advice to that of these others in the *Livre du corps de policie,* based on the concept of the body politic, of which the knights and the military were the protecting arms and hands. Christine had already made use of this simile in the *Chemin de long estude.*

In November 1405 Jean Gerson had also developed the comparison in a sermon entitled "Vivat Rex," which probably served as an inspiration to Christine, for there are echoes of the sermon in her writings (Gerson, *Oeuvres,* 1137–85). Both speak, for instance, of the need to pay French armies regularly so that they do not plunder the civilian population, and both make use of numerous examples drawn from the recent translation of the *Facta et dicta memorabilia* of Valerius Maximus.

It is part 2 of Christine's book that is devoted to those who must protect the country. She describes these with numerous examples of Roman leaders drawn from Valerius Maximus and also from Livy. They should love the profession of arms and devote themselves wholeheartedly to perfecting their skills. They should be brave and of such courage that they would never flee from battle or sacrifice their country to save themselves. They should be prepared to encourage each other and to inspire their companions to make their best effort; they should be truthful and faithful to their given word; they should cherish honor above all worldly things; they should be wise and wary not only in dealing with the enemy, but in all other military undertakings as well. These would certainly be qualities expected of a good military man of any era.

The second part of the *Corps de policie* would provide the basis for the *Livre des fais d'armes et de chevalerie,* which Christine composed in 1410, but one may well ask what inspired her to write as she did in the earlier work. It is of interest that it is more or less contemporary with Jean de Montreuil's treatise *A toute la chevalerie* (*Opera* 2:91–149). The first version, in Latin, was presented to Louis de Guyenne, who was offered an extended French version several years later. Some of his objectives were similar to Christine's, but in addition to a certain number of references to Roman military accomplishments, he dwells at length on episodes from French history, some of which Christine had included in her biography of Charles V. It would appear that both writers felt a need to rally the morale of the French armies, then in a regrettable state of stagnation. These earlier works provide some understanding of Christine's willingness to undertake a book on military art in 1410. She was more qualified to do this than has generally been thought, but nevertheless she appealed once more to Minerva for guidance:

> O Minerve, deese d'armes et de chevalerie,
> qui par vertu d'eslevé entendement par sus
> les autres femmes trouvas et instituas, entre
> les autres nobles ars et sciences qui de toi
> nasquirent, l'usaige de forgier fer et d'acier

armeures et harnois propices et convenable
a couvrir et targier corps de homme contre les
coups des dars nuisibles trais et lanciéz en
bataille, et fais d'armes, heaulmes, escus,
targes et autre hernois deffensibles de toy
premierment venus. Instituas et donna maniere
et ordre d'arenger batailles et d'assaillir et
combatre en maniere arree. Dame et haulte
deesse, ne te desplaise ce que moy, simple
femmelecte, si comme neant envers la grandeur
de ton renommé savoir, ose presentement
emprendre a parler de si magnifié office que
est cellui des armes, duquel premierement en
la dicte renommee contree de Grece tu donnas
l'usaige, et en tant te plaise me estre
favorable que je puis estre aucunement
consonnante a la nacion dont tu fus, en ce que
comme adonc fust nommé la Grant Grece le pais
d'oultre les Alpes qui ores est dit Puille et
Calabre en Ytalie ou tu nasquis, et je suis
comme toy femme ytalienne.
  (Brussels, Bibliothèque Royale, MS 10476, fol. 4)

[O Minerva, goddess of arms and of chivalry,
which by virtue of your understanding beyond
all other women, you founded and instituted
among other noble arts and sciences because
you initiated the habit of forging arms and
harnesses of iron and steel. . . . Lady and high
goddess, may it not displease you that I,
a simple woman in no way comparable to your
greatness in reputed knowledge, should dare
to speak of such an institution as that of
arms, which you first established in Greece.
May it rather please you to be favorable to me
because I am somewhat connected with the nation
into which you were born, which then was called
greater Greece but is now Apulia and Calabria
in Italy, for I am like you, an Italian woman.]

The earliest manuscripts show Minerva appearing to Christine in her study (see Figure 3).

The immediate reason for the book, however, is to be found in the problems of France around 1410. The king was the victim of ever more frequent spells of insanity, a situation that had brought about a deadly

Figure 3. Christine de Pizan and Minerva. From the *Livre des fais d'armes et de chevalerie,* 1434. London, British Library, Harley 4605, fol. 3. By permission of the British Library.

struggle among his relatives to dominate the government. Matters had worsened after the death of the duke of Burgundy, Philip the Bold. Since 1405 the country had been on the verge of civil war, and at the end of 1407 the new duke of Burgundy, John the Fearless, had contrived to bring about the murder of the duke of Orléans. After admitting his complicity in this affair, Burgundy had fled from Paris, but he lost no time in contriving a return to power there. After scoring a resounding victory over rebellious citizens of Liège at the Battle of Othée in October 1408, he was well on his way to achieving his goal. By the end of 1409 he had returned to Paris and succeeded in establishing his influence over the French queen. In addition to controlling the French government he had himself put in charge of the education of the dauphin.

The victory at Othée had demonstrated that John the Fearless was one of the few men in French circles with a talent for military strategy. This was no doubt largely the result of his youthful experience at the French defeat at Nicopolis in 1396, where he had been one of the few French survivors and had been able to return to Europe only after a time as a prisoner of the Turks. War was no mere game to him. It is also true that the Burgundians were among the first European armies to understand the evolving importance of artillery, which was already changing the nature of warfare.

On taking charge of the dauphin's education, the duke immediately surrounded him with advisers in whom he had confidence and who were favorable to the Burgundian ambitions. It seems certain that it was he who thought the young prince should have some education in military leadership. There exists a letter written around this time by Jean Gerson, chancellor of the University of Paris, to the prince's tutor, outlining a program of reading for that education. The list includes Vegetius, the *Stratagems* of Frontinus, and the Roman history of Valerius Maximus. It scarcely seems to be mere chance that these, along with Honoré Bouvet's *Arbre des Batailles*, should have been the principal sources for Christine's *Fais d'armes et de chevalerie* (Pannier 209–25).

It was the duke of Burgundy who had Louis de Guyenne appointed captain of the royal château of Creil, to provide him with experience in command and to encourage him to engage in physical activity, for which he had previously shown no enthusiasm. It was probably the duke who saw to it that Christine received a payment of two hundred *livres* from the royal treasury on May 11, 1411.[2] By 1412 the young prince had apparently developed enough skill to accompany the duke on two successful military expeditions. He was also beginning to show promising qualities of leadership, but unfortunately all this met an untimely end with his death, at the age of eighteen, in November 1415. He is known to us almost exclusively through Shakespeare's unfortunate portrayal of him in *Henry V.* The fact of the matter is that he was not at Agincourt as represented in the play.

Christine's *Fais d'armes et de chevalerie* has all too often been assumed to have pilfered from Vegetius, but it should be borne in mind that no other source would have been available to her. Furthermore, some hundred and fifty manuscripts of Vegetius dating from the tenth to the fifteenth centuries, including three French translations, existed (Meyer 401–23; Wisman, "L'Epitome" 13–31). Christine was by no means alone in undertaking to show how some earlier ideas were still applicable and useful. To the medieval mind the whole concept of chivalry was thought to have originated in Rome. Moreover, her intention was not merely the instruction of the dauphin or of the knights at court, for she makes it clear that she is speaking to all military men, some of whom would be incapable of reading either Vegetius or her book for themselves, but might hear her text read aloud to them. In this regard it is noteworthy that Christine makes a distinct effort to simplify her sources and to present her material in a way to hold the attention of her readers or listeners.

Undoubtedly one reason for the disregard of Christine's efforts is that few modern readers are familiar with Christine's actual text. It is usually read or cited by way of Caxton's English translation, published in 1489, for this is the only version of which there is a modern edition (Bossy, chap. 12 in this volume; Mahoney). Occasionally Antoine Vérard's French edition of 1488 is quoted. Both printers felt free to adapt Christine's text to their own purposes, Vérard trying to suggest that it was his own translation of Vegetius, omitting all mention of Christine's name. It has been in the hope of making Christine's own text available that my husband Sumner Willard and I have worked for some years on both an edition and an English translation. The translation is now finished and the edition nearing completion.

As it happens, the first eight chapters of Christine's book have nothing to do with Vegetius. They are devoted to the concept of the "just war," a matter that had occupied churchmen in particular from the time of Saint Augustine. In the late Middle Ages it was engaging the attention of legal experts, but it was unusual to find someone without a professional concern expressing views on the subject. It was, however, Christine's contention that a just war could be waged only by a king or a legitimate head of state, not as an individual but as one responsible for the welfare of his subjects. It is noteworthy that Christine extends the traditional definition slightly to include not only kings but "others who are principal lords of secular jurisdictions." It seems clear that Christine was undertaking to include the duke of Burgundy in her definition—further evidence that he was behind her undertaking to write the book. Furthermore, a lawful war could be waged only to obtain justice, or against oppression or usurpation; wars of aggression were in no way legitimate. Before undertaking a war a ruler should first seek to settle his grievances by arbitration. One of the principal objectives was to curb private wars.

The immediate source for Christine's ideas on the just war would have been Bouvet's *Arbre des batailles*, where the matter is discussed at length. Both would have been influenced, however, by the *Tractatus de bello* of John of Legnano (Wright 25–26; John of Legnano). This important Italian jurist and Christine's father would have been contemporaries at the University of Bologna, where both had studied and taught. Legnano had married into the family of another Bolognese legist, Giovanni Andrea, whose daughter Novella was praised by Christine in the *Cité des dames*. It is unlikely that Christine would not have been aware of Legnano's work, for she speaks elsewhere of the civil strife in Bologna around 1350 that inspired it. The fact that neither Christine nor Bouvet mentions Legnano by name can be attributed to the fact that he was an outspoken supporter of the Roman pope, whereas the French court was allied with his rival in Avignon.

Following these introductory chapters, Christine discusses the qualities needed by a good military leader, expanding what she had said in the *Corps de policie*, based in large measure on Vegetius, but common to all ages. She insists particularly on the point that the ideal commander need not be a king or prince. She also dwells on certain other points that she felt should be called to the attention of her contemporaries with regard to differences between Roman armies and the practices of the early fifteenth century, which showed a disturbing lack of discipline and leadership. She describes the proper training for young boys, who should become accustomed to austerity and sobriety, rather than being indulged by easy living. One can discern here a discreet criticism of the upbringing of the overindulged Louis de Guyenne.

As Christine continues to distinguish between Roman customs and the shortcomings of her own day, it is especially interesting that, following Vegetius, she warns against the deployment of an army too large for the space available on the battlefield. As this was a major cause of the French defeat at Agincourt some five years later, French military men would have done well to take this work seriously. It is noteworthy that the duke of Burgundy was roundly criticized for not taking part in that battle, nor would he permit his son, Philip, to be there. One may suspect that he was all too aware of the shortcomings in French tactics.

An especially impressive part of book 2, which is based in general on the *Stratagems* of Frontinus, is a series of chapters on siege warfare, once more comparing Roman and contemporary practices. There she actually provides lists of arms, ordnance, provisions, tools, and workmen needed to provision a castle or city against a siege. Comparable information is then provided for those who would undertake the siege. Here there is important information concerning old weapons and new missiles, apparently used side by side. Especially interesting is the presence of the word *peletteto,* referring to ammunition provided for newly developed artillery. These were made of lead, in contrast to the earlier cannonballs of stone used for earlier *bombardes* and *ribaudiquins.* This passage was repeated in great detail by the eminent military leader Jean de Bueil in *Le Jouvencel,* written around 1470 (Coopland 143–181).

One may well wonder how Christine acquired such technical knowledge. In chapter 21 of part 2, she speaks of help given her by wise knights, experts in military techniques, who did not wish to be named. She also refers to a paper containing a plan that was worthy of being saved, as it might still be useful. A consultation of the history of the period, notably the *Chroniques* of Enguerrand de Monstralet, provides the information that a siege of Calais was proposed with royal approval by the Burgundians in the fall of 1406. For some reason it was called off by the king when it was about to take place (Enguerrand 45). It would appear that Christine had access to these plans, probably through Burgundian advisers.

The third and fourth books are concerned with legal questions related to the so-called Law of War. It is in these parts that Christine makes the most extensive use of Bouvet's *Arbre des batailles.* Although she refers quite openly to her source, she does not actually name Bouvet. It is not difficult to identify, however, the wise old man who appears to her in a dream and with whom she discusses such matters as capital punishment, the payment of troops, and the treatment of noncombatants and prisoners. As she is unalterably opposed to the slaying of prisoners taken in battle, one can imagine her dismay at the slaughter of the French prisoners at Agincourt, especially as several friends of hers were among the victims.

In the final chapters of the book there are discussions of safe-conducts, letters of marque, and judicial combats, to which Christine was firmly opposed. A reference to the banning of these combats at the French court four years earlier, as Christine says, establishes the date of composition of this book as 1410. Presenting the rather dry legal matters as dialogues between Christine and her adviser was a clever way of dealing with such legal questions. In comparing Christine's chapters with her source, one is impressed by the fact that hers were not only less ponderous, but also better organized than her source. She did not forget that some of her readers would be young and others might need to have the book read to them. It was not necessarily directed to those who might read Bouvet for themselves. Her principal purpose was to promote the idea that in warfare all combatants should be bound by certain generally accepted rules of conduct — the ultimate basis for International Law.

The evidence shows that Christine's book was indeed widely read. In addition to two French imprints and the Caxton translation and imprint, a number of manuscripts still exist, including some rather handsome early ones and some later paper copies that give evidence of hard use. Some of these later copies, curiously, omit all references to Christine, as does the Vérard imprint. It has, of course, been suggested that this is because of antifeminine prejudice, but it is also possible that they were copied long after Christine had disappeared from the scene so that there was no recollection of who she was, although the book was nevertheless regarded as useful.

An especially interesting chapter in this history has to do with the reform of the French army under Charles VII around 1455. One of the king's principal advisers in this undertaking was Arthur de Richmont, one of the top commanders of the army that finally expelled the English from France (Cosneau 355–76). Taken prisoner at Agincourt, his release had been facilitated by Louis de Guyenne's widow, Marguerite, who eventually became his wife. This was, of course, the princess to whom Christine had dedicated her *Livre des trois Vertus*. Richmont had been a youthful companion of Louis de Guyenne at the time Christine's *Fais d'armes et de chevalerie* would have been presented to the prince. At this later time Richmont contributed significantly to the organization of the first truly French army by bringing into hand the undisciplined freebooters and by insisting on proper leadership and discipline, all qualities recommended by both Vegetius and Christine.

A modern military historian makes a particular point of Richmont's contribution to the "reappearance of military professionalism in Western warfare after more than a millennium," but he also praises Christine's contribution, making the point that one example of this reappearance of professionalism was the resumption of theoretical studies of warfare, almost unknown since Vegetius, citing in particular the *Fais d'armes et de chevalerie* as an early outstanding example (Dupuy and Dupuy 400).

After some five hundred years, Christine's efforts are finally receiving the appreciation they merit. None of this, of course, is intended to detract from the interest and value of Christine's writings for women. There is no question of their appeal and their importance, but it is also valuable to understand the variety represented by her talents and her versatility. This ability to deal with a number of issues important to the France of her day is perhaps her true contribution to French history and literature.

Notes

1. See Thomas.
2. Paris, B.N. Coll. Dupuy, vol. 755, fol. 97v cited by Solente, *Fais et bonnes meurs,* introduction, xxii–xxiii.

Manuscripts Cited

Brussels, Bibliothèque Royale, MS 11034
Brussels, Bibliothèque Royale, MS 10476

✤

CHAPTER 2

Christine's Anxious Lessons
Gender, Morality, and the Social Order from the *Enseignemens* to the *Avision*

Roberta Krueger

The Education of the Subject

In the midst of her autobiographical portrait at the end of the *Avision-Christine,* Christine tells how Nature inspired her to strike the anvil with her own "outils" as productively as she had formerly engendered with her womb and how, between 1399 and the time of writing the *Avision* in 1405, she wrote fifteen major works (*L'Avision-Christine,* ed. Towner, 163–64). Her activity during this period is remarkable not only for the quantity of texts she produced, but also for their variety and their complexity. The works include two books of moral dicta (the *Enseignemens* and *Proverbes moraux*); a moralized mythology (the *Epistre Othea*); the letters debating the sexual ethics of *Roman de la Rose*; three allegorical dream visions, of which one has a debate frame (the *Chemin de long estude*), one presents universal history (the *Livre de la mutacion de Fortune*), and another traces a voyage through historical turmoil and philosophical error that leads to the contemplation of God (*Avision-Christine*); a letter, dated October 5, 1405, to Queen Isabeau de Bavière; and finally, a feminist revision of misogynist literary history (the *Livre de la cité des dames*) and a book of practical *enseignements* for women of all classes (the *Livre des trois Vertus*)—to say nothing of works such as the *Dit de la Rose* and the *Livre du duc des vrais amans* that critically analyze "courtly" and uncourtly modes of conduct.

Christine's works from this period tell one of European literature's most significant stories about the education of the author and her instruction of others, about learning and teaching. Although that story is well known within medieval and Renaissance studies, thanks to the efforts of an international group of editors, translators, and commentators, Christine's life and works have yet to become fully incorporated into the history of education or into studies of the emergence of autobiography—as have, by contrast, the *Confessions* of Augustine or the *Historia* of Abelard. Unlike the male vitae, Christine's life is not recounted in a single retrospective narrative by a fully authorized speaker; those works in which Christine portrays herself do not strictly constitute autobiography.[1] Her self-portrait surfaces in fragments throughout her works, in brief cameos, in fuller autobiographical interventions, or in assertions that are filtered through the voices of allegorical figures.

The fragmentary nature of her life story and the way in which it emerges through her practice of reading, compilation, revising, and teaching, moreover, form an integral part of the story itself. The fragmentation results from Christine's exclusion from higher education because of her gender and her progressive discoveries as an autodidact; it ensues from her travails as a female head of household who struggled to defend her inheritance and support her family after her husband's death. Each time Christine tells a part of her story through a different body of materials, often citing earlier versions, she adds new perspectives to a self-narrative that grows, in the manner of a crystal, around a core of experience. Christine's works not only recount the stages in which she encounters and revises the medieval canon, they also inscribe the praxis of espousing moral and political order in a tumultuous social and political climate, in the years of contested royal counsel during the intermittent psychological illnesses of Charles VI, before the assassination, in 1407, of the king's brother Louis d'Orléans.

Critical accounts of Christine's work during the period 1399–1405 have emphasized the author's initial marginalization and the process of her intellectual emergence: she moves from being "poetess to historian" (Margolis, "Poetess"), and she enters the "champ politique" as a moral adviser (Blanchard, "L'Entrée"); she is a "laïc au pays de clercs" (Blanchard). Kevin Brownlee has traced the emergence of a female clerkly author throughout the *Rose* debate and in the *Mutacion de Fortune* ("Discourses," "Image of History"), and Helen Solterer demonstrates how Christine comes to embrace the ethical imperative of "sapiental writing" in the *Chemin de long estude* (150–75). Joël Blanchard has portrayed the troubled journey of Christine's authorial persona through the vicissitudes of Fortune in the *Mutacion,* past the disasters of History and the errors of Opinion to an understanding of God in the *Avision* ("Raisons de l'histoire"). Liliane Dulac traces the evolution of a female authorial voice from the biography of Charles V to her later political works ("Figure de l'écrivain," "Authority"). Renate Blumenfeld-Kosinski ("Misogynistic Tradition"), Maureen Quilligan, and Marilynn Desmond have shown how Christine forges her female authority through encounters with misogynistic literary traditions. For these readers and many others, Christine creates her female authority by self-consciously reflecting on her self-education, her own practice of learning and writing.

A Feminist Pedagogy? Or, The Pitfalls of Teaching

Christine's works from 1399 to 1405 tell not only of her struggle to educate herself and establish her authority; they also recount the difficulties of teaching others. Christine's role as a teacher within royal and ducal households has long been recognized (Willard, "Teacher"; Gabriel), as has the conservative nature of the program she advocates for men and for women (S. G. Bell, "Christine"). By defending women against the charges of moral and intellectual deficiency levied by medieval misogynists, Christine clears the way for women's education, which remained a contested domain in 1400, even as opportunities for female instruction increased. The idea that women's intellectual inferiority and spiritual weakness render them incapable of and unfit for learning has deep roots in medieval culture. That Christine refutes these arguments so vehemently in the *Cité des dames* proves their persistence in her day; the debate about female culture extends well into the Renaissance and early modern period, as Timmermans has documented. But, as Bell notes, Christine does not advocate her own regimen of humanistic scholarship for other women; she seems to respect the traditional distinction between educating men for public service and women for active participation in the household, which might include managing the estate and teaching children to read. However impassioned her promotion of women's worth may have been in her day, her pedagogical practice may not not strike us as particularly "feminist" by contemporary standards.[2] She aims to reform individual morality rather than to *transform* the sociopolitical order.

Yet critics have not accounted fully for the extent to which Christine reflects upon and critiques the process of teaching. Her works of this period not only portray the conflicted gender roles of a woman who seeks to educate herself and others, they also thematize the uncertain reception of moral doctrine by male and female readers and often inscribe the *failure* of moral instruction to reform the social order.

When Christine writes to or at the command of her royal and noble patrons or dedicatees—among them Louis d'Orléans, Charles VI, Philip III of Burgundy, Isabeau de Bavière, Marguerite of Burgundy, Louis de Guyenne, Jean de Berry—she assumes the position of a moralist who imparts ethical wisdom to her reader. As such, she participates in the movement of translation and vulgarization of Aristotelian political theory initiated by Charles V and continued under Charles VI, which produced a theoretical discourse that attempted to bolster the monarchy even as the regime faltered.[3] It is not difficult to demonstrate Christine's political conservatism and her espousal of traditional female roles.[4] In the years 1400 to 1405, Christine was not willing to give up the social position she had struggled to maintain (let us not forget that political turmoil forced her to retire from court life after 1418). Her ideals of reform focus on the ethical qualities of those who would advise a mad king, rather than on the interests of a particular political party or program.[5] Yet in the context of the political instability, internecine rivalries, and personal extravagance that prevailed at the court of Charles VI, her concern with moral probity, prudence, and the need for education and wise counsel demonstrates a certain political engagement.[6] Christine's educational works not only impart the traditional verities expected by her patrons; they also — and with an increasing sense of urgency — critique the social order and question the efficacy of teaching itself. Her works lead the reader not only to contemplate a moral or philosophical truth but also to encounter — as Blanchard has described the process in the *Avision* — an aporia, a profound doubt about history and human nature ("Raisons de l'histoire" 428).

In the didactic works written from 1400 to 1405, Christine often scrutinizes the teaching process and invites critical reflection on the very categories and values she imparts. This occurs first in author portraits that highlight the conflicts in her intellectual nature, her corporeal femininity, and her domestic social role. In addition, through allegorical figures and exempla, Christine presents a gallery of female scholars and teachers who often figure the transmission of knowledge as an imperfect or even dangerous process. Her works emphasize the necessity of good counsel and wise political advisers, and she portrays the consequences of not heeding such advice. In a number of ways, Christine inscribes the troubled relationship between students and teachers: she often portrays the failure of moral teaching to effect any change in its recipient. As Christine's sense of authority grows throughout the course of her apprenticeship as scholar and teacher, so, too, does her consciousness of the difficulties of imparting her acquired knowledge within an unstable social world.

From the *Enseignemens* (1399–1400) to the *Avision-Christine* (1405), Christine's pedagogical strategies and her reflections on the processes of learning and teaching become increasingly complex. The *Enseignemens* (*EM*) contain 113 moral dicta, expressed in quatrains, written in the second-person familiar by Christine for "Jehan de Castel, mon filz." The maternal speaker offers traditional moral advice without comment. There is no authorial portrait, although the counsel that one should not "diffame" women (*EM* 47) or read Ovid's *Ars amatoria* or the *Roman de la Rose* (*EM* 77) distinguish the *Enseignemens* as Christine's. The difficulty of teaching those who will not listen is expressed as conventional wisdom: "Car pour neant son oreille euvre / Homs a ouïr sans mettre a oeuvre" (The man who listens without applying himself uses his ear for nothing) (*EM* 112). The *Proverbes moraux* (*PM*), a collection of 101 distichs, echo this traditional concern of educators: "Belles raisons qui sont mal entendues / Ressemblent fleurs a pourceaulx estendues" (Beautiful reasons that are poorly heeded resemble flowers strewn before swine) (*PM* 87); "Trop petit vault bons exemples ouÿr / A qui ne veult contraire meurs fouÿr" (Listening to good examples is worth little if one does not intend to avoid bad behavior) (*PM* 99). As popular as the *Enseignemens* and the *Proverbes moraux* may have been in their time,[7] these homiletic books strike us today as Christine's most straightforward, least problematic didactic works.

The *Epistre Othea,* written circa 1401–02 and dedicated to the king's brother, Louis d'Orléans, is a much more complex undertaking that reflects the seriousness and the difficulty of imparting wisdom to a troubled court. At the time the *Othea* was composed, Louis d'Orléans represented the court's hope that he would be the governor able to stabilize political life in the midst of Charles VI's illness. When Christine completed subsequent manuscripts of *Othea* (from 1408 to 1415, according to Hindman, *Christine*), Louis d'Orléans had been assassinated and the conflict between Burgundians and Armagnacs intensified into civil war.

Othea's letter to Hector is, like the *Enseignemens,* a collection of quatrains given by a female teacher to an adolescent male. Its one hundred exempla drawn from classical mythology present conventional moral lessons. Judging from the number of extant manuscripts and from the existence of translations and printed editions, the book enjoyed great success (Mombello, "Quelques Aspects"; Campbell, *"L'Epître Othéa"*45–47). But Christine's *Othea* does more than popularize classical mythology in a moral frame. The gloss and allegory appended to each quatrain also invite the readers' critical interpretation (Noakes 110–134). Furthermore, as Sandra Hindman has shown, the choice of exempla and accompanying illuminations urge the reader to reflect on the nature of good government and good counselors at a time when these problems are especially pertinent.[8] By the time of circulation of the later editions, wherein the program of illuminations has been lavishly expanded, the madness of Charles VI plagues the court; the queen, Isabeau de Bavière, has proven to be extravagant and incapable of rule; the king's brother Louis d'Orléans has been assassinated; and the dauphin Louis de Guyenne has not yet reached majority.

The *Epistre Othea* examines critically both the role of the teacher and that of the pupil in transmitting and learning principles of good government. In the prologue, the moralist/narrator describes her own education as deficient. Christine is a "femme ignorant, de petite estature" (Loukopoulos line 19), whose meager authority derives from what crumbs — "mietes" — she has been able to glean from the table of her father, the former "philosophe et docteur" to Charles V. Within the exempla, however, Christine transcends these initial limitations and asserts the power of female pedagogy by depicting strong women teachers, such as Othea and Minerva (Chance 121–33). Cassandra is present here as a "moult... bonne dame et devote en leur loy" (XXXII, 200), a good, obedient lady who does not lie. The text concludes by reminding readers that it pays to listen to a woman's counsel, as did Augustus Caesar to the Cumaean Sibyl (C, 288–89). By ending Othea's epistle with a woman's prophetic voice, Christine highlights the sibylline teacher who will be a major force in her works and valorizes her own teaching.[9]

Memorable as these female counselors may be, a central irony pervades the *Epistre Othea.* Hector, the principal *destinataire* and the model for princes to follow, fails to heed the advice of Andromache, who has a prophetic dream about his death and warns both him and his father not to fight (see Andromache, LXXVIII, and Hector, XC-XCI).[10] Instead, propelled by *convoitise* for Polybetes' armor, he bends over to strip his enemy's body and is slain by Achilles. Thus Othea's letter to the fifteen-year-old Hector inscribes the certainty of the pupil's transgression against the father's law, his moral flaw, and his subsequent death: "Hector, noncier m'esteut ta mort, / Dont grant doulour au cuer me mort" (Hector, I must announce your death which strikes me with sadness in my heart) (*Othea* XC). Even as the *Epistre Othea* instructs the reader in moral interpretation and in the application of ethics to politics, it dramatizes the potential failure of such moral instruction.

As if to underscore the theme of teachings that fail to reach their audience, Christine's penultimate lesson warns against speaking beautiful words before those who will not understand them: "Tu ne dois belles raisons tendre / A qui bien ne les scet entendre" (Do not hold forth good reasons to those who are incapable of understanding them) (XCIX). She evokes, *in malo*, the wicked stepmother Ino, who sows "ble cuit" (cooked wheat) to deceive her husband. This exemplum calls into question both the motivations of the sower and of he who would seek to reap. Ino complicates the picture of the benevolent female teacher in the dominant frame: her seed will not germinate since it is part of a wicked plot to deprive her stepchildren of their birthright.

Through its complex layering of image, text, gloss, and allegory, the *Epistre Othea* dramatizes the problematic transmission and reception of moral doctrine. A central emblem in the text is the enigmatic figure of Hermaphroditus, whose male body has become melded with the female body he refused and whose story exemplifies the figurative language employed by the philosophers to appeal to the uneducated (LXXXII). The *Epistre Othea* is a multilayered, hermaphroditic text that yokes together classical and French imperial history, popularized mythology, patristic exegesis, and female prophetic visions. These diverse forms of instruction converge upon a fundamental doubt — the author's uncertainty about her ability to transform either the sociopolitical order or the mind of the reader.

The Cumaean Sibyl who counsels Augustus at the end of *Othea* becomes Christine's guide in the *Chemin de long estude* (October 5, 1402–March 20, 1403), a work dedicated to Charles VI whose title inscribes an educational journey. This work restages the story of Christine's own incomplete education, in greater detail than in the *Othea* preface. In the *Chemin*, the opening scene presents us with an early portrait of Christine in her study, surrounded by her books, seeking consolation from her sorrows through learning (lines 170–76). At this moment, in the midst of her debate with defenders of the *Roman de la Rose*, Christine has achieved authority and notoriety as teacher. She not only defends the rights of women to speak but indeed adopts the ethical imperative that women *must* speak to defend the common good (Solterer 171–75). But the role of a teacher is not easy. Her initial mentor Boethius is described as a scholar who was exiled for having wisely counseled and helped the common good: "Et a tort fu exillié / Por avoir bien conseillié / Et au bien commun aidier" (And he was wrongly exiled for having counseled wisely and helped the common good) (*Chemin* lines 219–21). The Cumaean Sibyl who guides Christine is an ambivalent image of female pedagogy. On the one hand, the Sibyl is positively described as representing a tradition of female learning: she's an "ameresse de sapience" from a woman's "college," a "colliege de grant science / Des femmes qui prophetiserent" (lines 669–70). But we are also told that her prophetic gifts arise from a curse stemming paradoxically both from her refusal of male desire and from her thirst for life. When Phoebus attempted to seduce the Sibyl, he promised her any gift and she unwisely—"comme mal enseigniee"— picked up a thousand grains of sand that condemned her to live for as many years, but without force or strength. The Sibyl's sapiental wisdom is thus also a burden, a gift for which she has had to repent: "Si fus si foible et envieillie, / Ains que ma vie fust faillie, / Que du don je me repenti" (And thus I became so feeble and old before my life ended that I repented of the gift) (lines 583–85).

Christine soon contemplates another intriguing image of education, a more powerful men's school, in the "fountaine de Sapience" where the nine Muses, "toutes nues" and imbued with great authority and wisdom (lines 813–17), bathe in a fountain that is visited by numerous famous philosophers, including Christine's father. As Andrea Tarnowski has suggested, Christine transforms the *Roman de la Rose* fountain from a scene of erotic desire to one of intellectual longing ("Maternity" 119–20). Indeed, this passage echoes one in her final 1402 letter to Pierre Col where Christine slyly refurbishes the *Rose* garden as a *locus intellectus* from which she can pluck "little garlands" from the lower branches of learning to offer to her readers (Hicks, *Débat* 148). But, even as Christine recasts the fountain as source of knowledge, it remains a site of exclusive male privilege: only male philosophers are named in the text, although, as Mary Weitzel Gibbons points out in chapter 7 in this volume, the manuscript illustration of this scene emphasizes the embodiment of female intellect in its visual representation of Christine, the Sibyl, and the female Muses. But, in the text, this "haute escole" is a male homosocial world from which Christine is pointedly excluded: she must content herself with dipping into the streams that run down from the fountain, as the Sibyl consoles her:

Mais s'estre de si haulte escole
Ne pues, tout au mains a seaux
Puiseras dedens les ruissiaux;

Si t'y baigneras a ton aise,
A qui qu'il plaise ou a qui poise.
     (*Chemin* lines 1084–88)

[But if you cannot belong to such a superior school, at the very least you can dip with buckets into the streams; there, you may bathe at your ease, no matter who is pleased or bothered.]

If the *Othea* problematizes the reception of moral instruction through Hector's death, the conclusion of the *Chemin* raises doubts about the enactment of its moral lessons. Its allegorical debate about kingship is left unresolved within the poem. Instead, the Sibyl gives Christine the responsibility of bringing the debate about the nature of a good king back to earth, to the "grans princes françois" (lines 6323–46). The book appeals to the moral judgment of the *reader* to choose among nobility, riches, chivalry, or wisdom as the quality most important for the king. The *Chemin*'s pedagogic strategy is thus interactive rather than prescriptive. Will Christine's royal and noble readers judge wisely, and will they then enact the chosen principles in their governance? In 1403, the question was a timely one for Charles VI and his counselors.

Gender and the Teacher: Conflict and Transformation

As readers have not failed to note, the tension between male and female identities and modes of learning is acute in the *Livre de la mutacion de Fortune* (completed in 1403). The predicament of the female cleric is recast as exclusion from higher learning, as a struggle between father and mother, and as the assumption of male gender. Once again, Christine legitimates her position as teacher by telling the story of her education. We revisit the father, here shown drawing precious stones from a fountain at the foot of Parnassus, where the nine Muses delight in entertaining "maint vaillant escolier'" (*Mutacion* lines 219–20), a description that seems to place contemporary schoolboys in a timeless, classical frame.

The masculine plural term "escolier" need not exclude girls; indeed, lay education for girls was increasingly common at the turn of the fifteenth century. But Christine refers evidently to the privileged domain of higher knowledge, the study of philosophy and theology, topics of study at the university, where women were excluded. Because maternal Nature decreed that she be born a girl and not a boy, custom — rather than natural right — dictated that she could not inherit the wealth she has taken "en la fonteine de grant pris" (line 418). Her narrator thirsts at the fountain like a disappointed courtly lover; all that she has been able to amass she has "stolen" as "racleures," "paillettes," "petis deniers," "des mailletes," which have fallen from the abundance of her father's knowledge (lines 452–61). From her mother, she has inherited moral qualities that have the quality of strengthening in the face of adversity. As Tarnowski has shown, the allegorical personification of mother as Nature and father as a "real-life" figure intensifies the division that the author feels between patriarchal and feminocentric modes of instruction, between intellectual knowledge and moral and spiritual qualities ("Maternity"). That division finds its most extreme embodiment when Christine announces that, after the death of her husband, she changed into a man in order to assume the duties of the household: "Com vous ouëz, encor suis homme / Et ay esté ja bien la somme / De plus de XIII ans tous entiers" (As you have heard, I am still a man and I have been one for more than thirteen whole years) (lines 1395–97).

We might be tempted to read Christine's period of male identification described in the *Mutacion* as a temporary stage, an imperfect one, en route to the assertively *female* personae of the *Cité des dames*, the *Livre des trois Vertus*, and the *Avision*. Yet the tension between patriarchal authority and maternal corporeality, and between intellectual aspirations and social duty, recurs throughout the works of this period. In the gender-shifting scene of the *Mutacion,* as has been pointed out, Christine continues to wear her mother's crown (Tarnowski, "Maternity"). She also longs for the days when she was a married woman: "Mais mieulx me plairoit plus du tiers / Estre femme, com je souloie / Quant a Ymeneüs parloie" (But I would far rather be a woman as I used to be, when I spoke to Hymenus [i.e., was married]) (lines 1398–1400). The *Cité des dames,* where the profemale voice seems be strongest, also retells the story—very near the midpoint—of how Christine's mother attempted to thwart her daughter's natural inclination for study (Curnow, "*Cité*" pp. 875–76), but she does not, for that, deny the role of her mother (Blumenfeld-Kosinski, "Misogynistic Tradition"; Quilligan). Just prior to this self-narrative of education, Christine describes how the learned Novella, daughter of Giovanni Andrea, read lessons of law in Bologna to replace her father and how Novella hid behind a curtain so as not to incite desire in her pupils (Curnow, "*Cité*" pp. 874–75). In these and other instances, female scholars and teachers confront the demands of social custom and the constraints of the body.

Conflicted gender roles for the female scholar and educator persist in the *Avision-Christine.* As we have seen, Christine uses the very feminine metaphor of engendering (along with the male figure of tools striking the anvil) to describe her literary production. Yet this is precisely the time in which Christine said in the *Mutacion* that she had changed into a man (and Dame Philosophy recalls this transformation later in the *Avision,* ed. Towner, pt. 3, p. 181).

To live in history as a woman is to be subject to vicissitudes and change; gender roles may shift according to the "mutations" of fortune.[11] As Christine recounts her own submission to a reluctantly assumed male role in the *Mutacion,* it is significant that she recounts three Ovidian transformations, of which two—those of Tiresias and Iphis—involve gender shifts (Richards, "Rejecting Essentialism" 109). The story of Tiresias seems especially compelling, since he is a seer, like Christine's female prophet figures, who changes sex and back again (Margolis, "Poetess" 369). In the *Mutacion* and elsewhere, Christine emphasizes the mutability and conflicted nature of the female teacher's gender roles. The discourses of male and female authority seem to be shifting subject positions that the speaker can adopt strategically and through which she must negotiate. Christine will not fail to speak in the voice of the "seulette" when she feels that it will be useful or to appeal to the queen *as a mother* to save France.[12] But she also reminds her readers of the ways in which social expectations and domestic responsibilities thwart the aspirations of women who would develop their "natural" intellectual capacity.

At the end of the *Mutacion's* extensive narrative of universal history, Christine delivers a strong warning to France's present rulers:

Vous, princes de la haulte tour,
Considerez un peu, au mains,
Se a grant seurté les humains
Sont, qui servent a tel dongier!
Pueut on la seurement logier?
Consideré les choses dictes,
Sont ses mutacïons petites?
Se doit homs donques orgueillir
Pour tel bien, qui tost peut faillir?
        (lines 23610–18)

[You, princes in the high tower / consider at least a little / if humans are in great security / who serve in such dominion. / Can one be safely lodged there (in Fortune's castle)? Considering all that has been said, / are its mutations minor ones? / Ought man pride himself / in such worldly good, which just as soon could fail?]

Christine has seen with "clairvoyant eyes" ("de mes plus clersveans yeulx," 23587–88) the vicissitudes of the princes of her realm in Fortune's castle and warns them against pride and complacency; she has also delivered pointed *lessons* on the vices of the nobility (*Mutacion* lines 5131–504) and in particular on the evil effects of bad counselors (lines 5505–760) and of bad teachers of princes (*Mutacion* lines 5761–862); these points have been made in *Charles V* and will be made again in the *Livre du corps de policie* and the *Livre de la paix* (part 1, chaps. 9–12). When Christine retreats to her study at the end of this lengthy production in order to ward off misfortune, seeking "paix" and "solitude voluntaire" (23635), she establishes a critical distance between herself and her audience.

Instructing the Princes of the Realm

Christine's appeal to the princes' wisdom in the *Mutacion* found at least one receptive reader in Duke Philip of Burgundy, who subsequently commissioned her to write a laudatory biography of Charles V, the *Livre des fais et bonnes meurs du sage roy Charles V.* The work was likely also intended for the dauphin Louis de Guyenne, who was soon to marry Philip's granddaughter, Marguerite of Burgundy.[13]

As in the *Chemin* and the *Mutacion,* the female teacher must establish her authority: the topos of feminine intellectual insufficiency permeates the opening pages; the author presents herself as "moy, Cristine, femme soubz les tenebres d'ignorance au regart de cler entendement" (I, Christine, wandering in the shadows of ignorance before those with clear understanding) (*Charles V* p. 5). This uncertain pose is soon offset by a remarkable scene in which Philip and his son summon Christine to the Louvre (*Charles V* pp. 7–9), an account that both legitimates her authority and infuses this biographical work with Christine's distinctive voice.[14] Far more than a biographical history, *Charles V* is a mirror for princes that manages to deliver, through steady backhand swipes, a powerful indictment of Charles VI's court, which so obviously fails to measure up to the standards of the father's.[15]

For example, when Christine praises Charles V's instruction in Latin, she laments the lack of learning in her contemporaries, who must resort to strangers to read the law to them, because of their laziness and lack of effort: "et tout par paresce d'un petit de temps souffrir l'excercitacion et labour d'estude" (and all because of laziness about enduring for a short time the exercise and labor of study) (*Charles V* p. 17). One senses the frustration of a woman who has traveled "le chemin de long estude" in adversity, alone, against all odds in the face of those with the advantage of birth, sex, and leisure who waste their time.

Charles V also contains a lengthy digression on adolescence, which differs considerably in tone from the pedagogical principles espoused in Giles of Rome, Christine's source.[16] Giles repeats Aristotle's image of the soft wax tablet and reminds us of the "mollece" of youth's soul, the necessity for good company, the inclination to do evil—all "reasons" enumerated in the logical sequence of a list of precepts to be implemented (2.14, pp. 215–16). Christine likewise portrays the years from seven to fourteen as imbued with "fragilitez" and fraught with peril (*Charles V* p. 23) because of youths' "chaleur" and their natural lawlessness. Adolescents are driven by sensual passions that blind them, and they disdain the very medicine that would correct them.[17] Christine then launches into a lengthy present-tense lamentation about the difficulty of correcting young people and the numerous pitfalls of tempestuous behavior, bad judgment, lack of foresight, and stubbornness that may befall them— introduced by a despairing "O Dieux!" (*Charles V* p. 24)—and appeals to the experience of her readers for instances of youths who have ruined themselves and distressed their parents. Christine is careful to point out that not all adolescents are reckless (p. 26), and later cautions parents not to despair about their children's future but rather to forgive, to show the charity of correction, and to trust in a natural process of aging, as exemplified by bad wine that improves with age (pp. 29–30). Christine's lengthy digression (which ends with "retournant à nostre matieere," p. 36) has less to do with the particular case of Charles V than it does with her interest in the highly volatile nature of adolescence in the inherent resistance of the subject to correction (which may bear more directly on the youth of Louis de Guyenne). She ends the section on a personal note by marvelling, "me suis aucune fois moult esmerveillée" about many old men who regret (in the sense of looking back fondly upon) the follies of their youth; what they miss, says Christine, is their ability to enjoy the "deliz" of youth. This suggests to Christine that they esteem "la fragilité de delit de char" far more than the perfection of understanding and that, in spite of their years, they have not become "sages." Many people, it would seem, remain perpetual adolescents, preferring sensual pleasures to intellectual governance, shunning even in maturity the principles that would make them wise.

Christine's interest in the intractability of adolescence does not just represent a warning to the governors of the young Louis de Guyenne and to the dauphin himself; in 1404, he would have been seven and just entering the tender age.[18] Christine also comments on the failure of many of her contemporaries to achieve or value "perfaitte clarté de cognoiscence." In any case, history was to bear out the necessity of wise counsel for the dauphin: the duke of Burgundy, who originally commissioned the work in January 1404 and who was the self-appointed adviser to the future king, died as *Charles V* was in progress (on April 27, 1404). Christine found a new patron in Jean de Berry, to whom the work was offered on January 1, 1405.[19]

Teaching the Female Subject

In the works we've discussed thus far, Christine uses figures and personae of female pedagogues to instruct male sovereigns or young princes. She continues to produce mirrors that espouse ethical ideals and attack current malpractice. In the later *Livre du corps de policie* (1406–7) and *Livre de la paix* (1412–13), female pedagogy is again the vehicle but not the object of her study; the "subject" relationships she analyzes are those of the male sovereign and his general "subgiez." However, in the *Cité des dames* and the *Livre des trois Vertus* (both completed in 1405), Christine focuses exclusively on the female subject and her education. First, in the *Cité* she shows how female nature has been misconstrued within male misogynistic discourse, and she vindicates women as intelligent, moral beings who are capable of being educated and of making significant social and political contributions. Then, in the *Trésor de la cité des dames*, or *Livre des trois Vertus*, she offers what is ostensibly a handbook for the ethical construction of female subjectivity within the current social order.

Critics have not failed to note the striking strategic and rhetorical differences of these two works. In the *Cité des dames*, Christine celebrates exemplary lives and revises her sources to highlight female agency in an ideal world, a "feminist" utopia.[20] In the *Trois Vertus*, she turns to the real world, where the constraints of society mean that women must learn to negotiate their limited powers and resources with skillful speech, respectful maintenance of court etiquette and vestimentary codes, and Machiavellian domestic diplomacy.[21]

The stylistic differences between these works are no less striking. The *Cité des dames* is a richly compiled work, offering a plethora of exempla and strong rereadings — in an antiphrastic vein — of misogynist literary representations. The *Trois Vertus*, by contrast, has relatively few exempla, compared not only with Christine's other didactic works but also with other works of female conduct such as the *Livre pour l'enseignements de ses filles* of the Chevalier de la Tour Landry or the *Ménagier de Paris*. In fact, the most prominent piece of compilation is one of Christine's own texts: the letter of Sebille, Dame de la Tour, from her *Livre du duc des vrais amants*, is repeated in the *Trois Vertus*. But its autoreferentiality and its detailed, realistic portrayal of women's lives in the various social classes combine to make this work one of Christine's most personal and original compositions, as has been noted (Wisman, "Aspects" 27; see also Tarnowski, "Autobiography").

If the *Cité* seems to celebrate female agency, the *Trois Vertus* advises female circumspection, a difference that manifests itself rhetorically. The multiple voices of the *Cité* are actively in dialogue: now hortatory, now argumentative, now outraged, now dramatic. The *Trois Vertus* focuses on the constraints of daily life rather than on heroic action and is more uniformly prescriptive in tone, but it is punctuated by interesting eruptions of first-person internal narration (Dulac, "Representation"; Tarnowski, "Autobiography"; Wisman, "Aspects"). Through the female figures of the *Cité*, Christine indignantly disputes charges against female inconstancy and insufficiency and makes a stunning show of her own learning, her skill in disputation, and her artful compilation and adaptation. The Virtues in the *Trois Vertus* enumerate "enseignements," "points," and "principes" that describe in close-up how daily life should be ordered for each of the classes of women.

Yet, for all their differences, the domestic and social constraints that govern female conduct in both works are the same. The *Cité des dames* argues that the example of so many virtuous women in the past and present disproves the claims of misogynists, and it exhorts women to avoid dishonor by embracing virtue. The *Trois Vertus* spells out how that ideal virtue—chastity and marital fidelity, energetic fulfillment of one's appointed social role—can be attained by women of all classes. Women should love and obey their husbands, should remain steadfastly within their families, and should maintain their station in life. Christine upholds the same difficult ideal to women who find themselves married to cruel and perverse husbands in both the *Cité* and the *Trois Vertus:* you must live and die with him, whatever he may be like.[22]

Christine's arduous task as a teacher is to educate women into this difficult, necessary precept in the context of forces that continually threaten to undermine it. Her role is not only to convince men that female virtue is possible; it is also to convince women that virtue is desirable, however constraining the ideal may seem. Small wonder—given the impossible situations in which women find themselves called upon to act virtuously, given the natural desires of the body, given the inclinations of youth—that the teacher's job should be so hard. Both the *Cité des dames* and the *Trois Vertus* inscribe a complex *problématique de l'éducation féminine* for women who would learn and for those who would teach them. Teachers and students are often in conflict.

The opening author portrait in the *Cité* restages Christine's alienation from male tradition not as a wishful dream but as a fearful hallucination. When she comes to realize that virtually everything she has read by all the great "philosophes" contains antifeminist sentiments, Christine falls into a self-deprecating trance. The "fountain of knowledge" is recast as the rush of memory—"une fontaine resourdant" (Curnow, "*Cité*" p. 619)— of the "grant foyson" of misogynists, an internalized torrent of antifeminism. She imagines the entire female sex as "monstre en nature" (monstrous in nature) (Curnow, "*Cité*" p. 620).

Once again, wise and eloquent female teachers appear to aid the scholar. Armed with the powerful tool of antiphrasis, Christine transcends her self-loathing to construct a forceful vindication of female intelligence and honor. But the anxieties of the female scholar and teacher pervade this book.

Throughout the *Cité des dames,* and especially in book 1, women are presented heroically as scholars and teachers. We meet the wise Empress Nicole, noted for her literacy and her learning, who brought law to her people (Curnow, "*Cité*" p. 666); Queen Zenobia, as adept in Greek and Latin as she was in battle, who instructed her children with strong discipline (p. 760); and Lile, who taunted her son, Theodoric, to win in battle (pp. 712–13). These women are followed by "femmes enluminees de grant science" (723): Cornificia, whose learning surpassed her brother's (p. 724); Proba, who translated Scripture into verse (pp. 725–28); Sappho, whose poetry Plato had on his deathbed (pp. 728–30); and Carmentis, who wrote the first Roman law and alphabet (pp. 734–39). The linguistic gifts of Carmenata and the military, domestic, and agricultural arts of Minerva, Ceres, and Isis are more important, says Christine, than all the philosophy of Aristotle and the other thinkers (p. 752). Female teaching is the foundation of European culture and continues to inform it.

Yet, despite Christine's heroic feminist rhetoric and her celebration of female agency, a tragic irony pervades the *Cité des dames*. Men have failed to learn from the lessons women have offered them; they have not gotten the message because they have continued to repeat faulty antifeminist arguments. Christine is all too aware of this when she says, in essence, "Shame on you" to men who have overlooked the efforts of Carmentis. When she chides "clercs medisants," as a teacher might scold schoolboys who fail to appreciate the "maistresce a l'escolle" who taught them their "nobles lettres du latin," Christine seems to remind her readers of the role women continued to play in the education of children:

> Or se taissent, or se taisent d'or en avant, les clers medisans de femmes, ceulx qui en ont parlé en blasme et qui en parlent en leurs livres et dittiez, et tous leurs complices et confors, et baissent les yeux de honte de ce que tant en [ont] osé dire a leur diz, considerant la verité qui contredit a leur diz, voyant ceste noble dame Carmentis, laquelle par la haultesce de son entendement les a apris comme leur maistresce a l'escolle—ce ne pueent ilz nyer—la leçon de laquelle savoir se treuvent tant haultains et honnourez: c'est assavoir les nobles lettres du latin! (p. 751)

> [May they be silent, may they be forever silent, those calumniating clerks who have blamed women in their books and writings (along with all their accomplices and colleagues) and may they lower their eyes in shame for all that they have dared to say in their writings—considering the truth that contradicts them, namely that this noble lady Carmentis in the superiority of her knowledge taught them like a schoolmistress (and they can't deny this!) the lesson of which they are so proud and honored: that is, the noble Latin alphabet!]

Men are often unwilling or ungrateful recipients of women's teaching, as we learn in several exempla. Among the men who have failed to heed or recognize the value of female instruction or advice, there are Brutus (pp. 844–45), Caesar (p. 849), Pompey (p. 850), and Hector (p. 851), who did not listen to their wives; Tarquin, who at first refuses to pay Almathea for her book (p. 793); and the father and brothers of Cassandra, who lock her up rather than follow her advice (pp. 798–99). The sufferings inflicted on women who impart divine truths by men who refuse to understand their words are evoked most poignantly in book 3, where martyrs such as Saint Christine attempt to convey lessons to their tormentors as they undergo painful dismemberment.

Nor are moral and spiritual lessons imparted easily to women, who must not only understand the notion of female virtue but continually live it out. At several points, the Virtues acknowledge that not *all* women display those excellent qualities whose presence in some invalidates the claims of misogynists. As Droiture explains: "Amie chiere, tu dois sçavoir que toutes femmes ne sont mie saiges et semblablement ne sont les hommes" (My dear friend, one must admit that not all women are reasonable, no more than all men) (p. 843); and later, "Je t'ai dit devant que toutes femmes ne sont mie saiges" (I've already told you that not all women are reasonable) (p. 849).

The rhetorical sword of the *Cité des dames* is double-edged for women. Even as the book offers seemingly irrefutable proof that the generalizations against women are wrong because many women have been learned, faithful, devoted, industrious, and self-sacrificing, so too does it portray the "ideal" of the virtuous woman as a painful necessity. Like the Sabine women who must bond with their rapist husbands in order to save their children (pp. 863–68), women under patriarchy construct their moral selves in seemingly impossible situations. The teacher who transmits that bitter truth to other women bears an onerous responsibility. The sufferings of Saint Christine, patron saint of the author, who continues to speak "mieulx que devant et plus cler" (better and more clearly than before) (p. 1008) when her tongue is cut by her tormentor and then severed at the root, figure the trials of the teacher as painful dismemberment.

The chaste heroines and virgin martyrs of book 3 offer striking examples not only of women's ethical agency, but also of their constraints under patriarchal authority. The *Cité des dames* ends with a direct appeal to women to be virtuous, to accept the constraints of their marriage, and to avoid the devious ways that men have devised to entangle women by "engins estranges" (strange tricks) as one would trap "les bestes aux laz" (animals in nets) (p. 1035). As the longest apostrophe to an external audience in the book, this passage reveals the difficulties that face the teacher who instructs women in casting off the deceptive "nets" of male discourse. It also directly foreshadows Christine's next work, the *Livre des trois Vertus* or the *Tresor de la Cité des dames*, a conduct book for women that was written in 1405 for Marguerite of Burgundy, who was eleven when she married the dauphin Louis de Guyenne in 1404.

The *Livre des trois Vertus* presents one of Christine's most explicit explorations of the anxieties of teaching. The author portrait at the beginning of *Trois Vertus* elaborates on what we might call *les affres de l'instruction des femmes*. For once Christine portrays herself not as an eager *fille d'estude*, but as one who is idle — worn out from her accomplishments, tired in her body, and in need of rest (*Trois Vertus* p. 7). This stance not only acknowledges the enormity of her labor in writing the *Cité des dames*, it also acknowledges the author's own struggle against moral and intellectual *paresse*. She who would instruct women in the arduous paths of virtue is herself a reluctant servant. The *Trois Vertus*

Prologue portrays the stubborn opposition of the body to the project of constructing virtue and the difficulty of being constructed as virtuous. The Boston Public Library manuscript of the *Livre des trois Vertus* portrays Christine in bed, pulled to her feet by the vigilant Virtues to resume her writing.

Reason, Justice, and Droiture—familiar teachers from the *Cité*—chastise Christine for her laziness and insist that she return to work: like a knight to the battle, like a chambermaid to her tasks. The metaphor they use to describe the next step of Christine's project reveals the burden of being virtuous. Now that Christine has erected the City, she must work like a wise birdcatcher to lure ladies and other women into it: by means of tricks, traps, and nets. Moreover these "roys beaux et nobles" are "ouvrez a neux d'amours"—laced with love-knots. Ironically, Christine deploys Ovidian motifs—trapped birds and nets of love—into service *against* lovemaking.[23] Women in the *Cité* were urged to avoid the deceptive nets of courtly discourse. Here Christine portrays herself as laying sweet nets to ensnare the readers—particularly, as she says, the ones who are "farousches et dures a dominees," wild and indomitable women (*Trois Vertus* pp. 8–9). The prologue to the *Trois Vertus* inscribes the resistance of teacher and female pupils to the construction of Virtue.

The stumbling block of resistance pervades book 1. Even as the section addressed to princesses brims with practical advice for social survival, it inscribes at beginning and end the figure of the reluctant pupil and of the failed teacher. The first book opens with the portrait of a princess who reclines comfortably on her luxurious bed, beset by temptations, surrounded by servants who are ready to leap at her command (p. 12): this vignette is a conscious echo of the prologue and perhaps a slur on royals noted for their indulgent sleep habits, or worse.[24] The princess, like Christine, is roused from her indolence and learns from Prudence Mondaine how skillfully to manipulate speech, negotiate peace, maintain courteous relations with in-laws, manage her money, and supervise the education of her sons and daughters. Christine offers sound, practical advice that shows how noblewomen can learn to work effectively within constraints, limitations, and misfortunes. At times, her counsel on the art of circumspection and strategic hypocrisy seems Machiavellian *avant la lettre*.

Yet the conclusion of book 1 inscribes another cameo of troubled student-teacher relations. The last four chapters discuss the delicate task of instructing newly married princesses. The recipient of advice shifts suddenly mid-chapter from the princess to the governess who would supervise her daughter: "Entre ses dames doit avoir une dame ou damoiselle assez d'age, prudent, bonne, et devote à qui on aura baillié par grant fiance le gouvernement de la joenne dame" (Among her ladies-in-waiting, she should have a lady or young woman of sufficient age, prudent, good, devoted, to whom one will have entrusted the government of the young lady [i.e., the princess's daughter]) (p. 92). Then the text describes how this good governess must keep her young charge so well governed that nothing dishonorable will be said about her, even as the governess remains in the pupil's good graces, two delicate assignments that are difficult to carry out at the same time, as Christine explains: "lesquelles deux choses, c'est assavoir donner correction et enseignement a joenne gent et avoir ensemble leur amour et grace, est souvent moult fort a faire" (which two things — that is to say, give correction and instruction to young people *and* retain both their love and grace — are often very hard to do) (p. 92).

In the *Charles V*, as we saw, Christine reflected upon the volatile state of adolescence, its passions, its pitfalls. In the *Trois Vertus*, the moralist shows her understanding for the precarious development of the young princess (we'll remember that Marguerite of Burgundy was only twelve when she would have received this book), who is compared to a house that might catch fire (p. 92), to a branch whose shape must be gently bent but not broken when it is young (p. 93). The text elaborates in some detail strategies by which the governess can win the young person's favor — by offering trinkets, by telling stories, by gently admonishing her. It deftly outlines how she can foster love between the young princess and her new husband, especially when the governess senses that a lover may be present. If a young lady remarks that she enjoyed dancing with someone, tell her how much more handsome and gracious you think her husband is (p. 98). Take the would-be lover aside, if he presses too adamantly, and tell him that he is wasting his time (pp. 99–100). Chapter 25 offers a step-by-step guide to the avoidance of scandal, a sort of feminine *Remedia amoris* on how to prevent *fole amour* and the appearance of love.

But, as we have seen before, Christine's *enseignements* also inscribe their failure to reach at least some members of the intended audience. Chapter 26 takes up the case of men and women who are so "perverse" that no matter what good advice they are given they will always follow their "fole ou mauvaise inclinacion" (p. 104). It describes the breakdown of student-teacher relations: the pupil rebelliously throws off the yoke of instruction (feeling that she no longer needs correction) and begins to mock, or worse, to plot against, her teacher. When these things occur, the teacher has no other recourse, says Christine, but to leave. "Car impossible est de garder personne qui ne se veult d'elle meismes garder" (For it is impossible to take care of/protect someone who does not wish to take care of herself) (p. 106). It is at this point that Christine inserts the advice of another sibyl — Sebille de la Tour, whose cautionary words appeared in the *Livre du duc des vrais amans*. In that lyrical-narrative courtly poem, the Dame de la Tour's letter had only a temporary success in separating the lovers (Krueger, *Women Readers* 232–40). The appearance of a letter that fails to persuade its *destinataire* against *fole amour* at the end of a book of moral instruction for princesses highlights the disjuncture between theory and praxis, construct and subject, indoctrination and resistance.

To be sure, Christine continues to teach in the *Trois Vertus*, but to a new audience. Books 2 and 3 are written for women of the lesser nobility and women of the bourgeoisie, artisans, peasant wives and even prostitutes. I have suggested elsewhere that in these latter books of the *Trois Vertus*, Christine's ethical and economic lessons are less conservative than they may at first appear to be (Krueger, " 'Chascune' "). Although she ostensibly upholds the traditional social hierarchy, rails against the dissolution of class boundaries, and analyzes various kinds of social disorder and their causes (Wisman, "Aspects"), she also appeals to the industrious ethics of the new bourgeois reader whom she will reach in paper manuscripts and early printed editions of this work (Willard, "Manuscript Tradition"). That reader, through diligent application of Christine's precepts, through clever manipulation of the social system, through resourceful management of the household economy, can shore up her own material and moral *trésor*. The *Trois Vertus* was an important book for royal women of the fifteenth and sixteenth century: it was certainly read by Anne de France, Louis XI's daughter, who used it as the source for her book of *Enseignemens* written for her daughter Suzanne in 1504 (Willard, "Anne de France"), and it circulated as manuscript, printed book, or translation among the royal families of France and Portugal (Willard, "Manuscript Tradition"). But Christine's stated desire in the epilogue that her work "multiply" itself in many realms throughout and beyond these nobles circles to reach other classes of women (*Trois Vertus* p. 225) appears to have been fulfilled. If Christine seeks to "correct" her noble readers and make them heed God-given social responsibilities in *Trois Vertus*, she also, albeit perhaps unwittingly, invites the social advancement of those bourgeois readers who will profit in later generations from this and other works of female instruction.[25]

To return to 1405, however, and to conclude, I would like to come back full circle to the *Avision-Christine* to consider a final, tragic figure of the teacher. In the midst of book 1, the Dame Couronnée, the voice of France's history, reveals to a horrified Christine the *plaies* (wounds) in her side that have been inflicted by the bitter fights between her own children, France's rulers (*L'Avision*, ed. Towner, 86–87). Her lengthy allegory of France's political turmoil and of the vices that plague the country ends with a complaint by the beleagured lady that surely echoes Christine's own frustration:

Hahay mais pour quoy ne a qui dis ie ces paroles quant je scay que nen seray pas creue. car ne pourront entrer es corages endurcis sicomme on dist le fol ne croit jusques il prent / mais abondance de voulente le me fait dire / comme tendre mere a ses enfans mais ce me desconforte que ia me semble en y a dentrez en obstinacion qui trop est chose perverse helas iay grant paour que semblable ie soye a cassandra la sage fille du roy. (*L'Avision* 106)

[Alas, but why or to whom do I say these words when I know that they will not be believed? For these words cannot enter into hardened hearts just as they say that the fool does not believe until he takes something. I greatly wish to speak, however, as would a tender mother to her children, although it greatly distresses me that there seems to be such obstinacy, which is a very perverse thing. Helas, I fear greatly that I resemble Cassandra, wise daughter of King Priam.]

The Lady describes her obligation to teach as the strong longing of a tender mother who cares for her children. She compares herself with Cassandra, whose warnings about the Fall of Troy were not believed. Finally, she enjoins Christine to convey these lessons to her children as a mother would provide "sweet milk" and warns her that they may well suck her breast down to the blood: "mais vueillent si espargner ses doulces mamelles quilz ne la succent jusques au sang" (108). The assimilation of history to the unfortunate Cassandra, of Cassandra to a tender mother devoured by her own offspring (with its Christian overtones), and of both these figures to Christine, the writer who has been boldly created out of the common order of women to take up her *plume* to write, presents a powerful image of the anxiety of instruction, of the dangers of casting pearls before swine. The maternal prophet whose milk may turn to blood stands not only as symbol of Christian sacrifice but also as a corporeal image of the conflicted role of the female teacher who seeks to intervene to transform the moral and social order.[26] Positive hopes and negative consequences are conflated. The milk of nourishment recalls the Roman lady who breastfeeds her imprisoned mother in the *Cité des dames* and the maternal Nature who breastfeeds Christine as an infant in the *Mutacion de Fortune*. The commingling of milk and blood echoes the sufferings of Saint Christine, whose breasts run with milk when she is tortured (1008), and echoes the exchange of milk for blood in the deaths of Saint Catherine (982) and Saint Martine (987). The image also echoes Christine's appeal to Isabeau de Bavière as a "mere conforteresse de ses subgiéz et de son peuple" (mother comforting her subjects and her people), who would prevent her children's bloodshed and the drying up of milk through famine in poor women who nurse their young (Christine, "Isabelle of Bavaria" 147–48).

Christine the voyager may move well beyond this point in the *Avision*, but not without first encountering Opinion, who is responsible for diverse views that men defend, often vehemently. After the *Avision* self-portrait, Christine's longest, the autobiographical voice of the teacher and scholar is less prominent. But Christine will continue to write major political works and to attempt to persuade the rulers of her adopted country to exercise prudence and engage in moral actions. If her social program is avowedly conservative, her "mirrors" do not fail to attack the vices of their recipients and, in some way, to point to the tragic failure of their moral indoctrination.

History fulfilled Cassandra's dire predictions. Assassination prevented Louis d'Orléans from exercising good government as counselor; the death of Louis de Guyenne in 1415 prevented him from reigning as king. Marguerite of Burgundy was never queen, and scandals continued to brew within the court of Isabeau de Bavière. In a further ironic twist of literature and history, the narrative voice of the *Livre de la paix* of 1412–13 was twice interrupted by the Cabochian insurrection. Breaks in the narrative figured the silencing of the teacher. In 1418, political turmoil muffled Christine's prophetic voice for the next ten years, until she celebrated the glorious, if ephemeral, victory of Jehanne d'Arc.

The thematics of failure in Christine's didactic works from 1400 to 1405 might be seen to foretell the tragic outcome of noble and regal historical aspirations—as does Andromache before Hector or Cassandra before the Trojans. The struggle between maternal and paternal modes of instruction figure the ongoing gender tensions of the female teacher as an intellectual, social, and embodied subject. Christine refutes the misogynists' charges of women's intellectual deficiency and proves by historical example that women have been and can be learned teachers and virtuous models of good government. But she also shows how women's teachings have often tragically failed either to transform human perceptions or to influence historical events. In Christine's gallery of neglected founding mothers, unheeded wives, marginalized female prophets or scholars, rejected governesses, and saintly martyrs we may see reflections of her tenuous, sometimes painful position, as a moralist whose own disciplined life, transcendence of suffering, and deep concern for human relations doubtless differed from the less restrained existence of some members of the royal and Burgundian courts. Self-education and the instruction of others are processes that are fraught with social and personal anxiety throughout Christine's work.

It would be wrong to conclude, however, that Christine's didactic works conveyed nothing but a sense of doom and disaster or that they were never beneficial, or consoling, to the readers. Her works from 1399 to 1405 impart numerous beneficial exempla and sound principles of conduct for men and women. The enormous popularity of these works and their dissemination—as Christine herself hopes at the end of *Trois Vertus*—not only throughout the noble households of France but also to England, Flanders, and Portugal, attest to their ultimate success in finding favor with readers who may have profited, in many ways, from their practical advice and spiritual counsel. As the audience for her works grew to include not only royal and noble women readers but also bourgeois women who may have sought material as well as moral enhancement from their exemplary tales and cautionary words, Christine's didactic works participated directly in the spread of female lay literacy. Her writings on female conduct and on the dangers of "courtly love" influenced the lessons of Anne de France in her book for her daughter (Willard, "Anne de France"; C. Winn, "*Dignitas mulieris*"; Berriot-Salvador; Krueger, "'Chascune'"), and may also have inspired the moral teachings of Marguerite de Navarre, who sought, like Christine, to vindicate female honor as she rewrote Bocaccio in her *Heptameron* (Sommers).

Christine's anxious lessons — offered by uneasy teachers to often recalcitrant pupils — invite us to reevaluate her pedagogical theories and practices. Her didactic texts never attempt merely to impose moral or political doctrine, however conservative her teachings may at first appear to be. From Christine's first dicta about the difficulties of instruction in the *Enseignemens* to her eloquent expression of the prophet's distress in the *Avision*, Christine voices uncertainty about whether the teacher's truths will transform the lives of her pupils or will effect the *bien commun*. As she retells the conflicted history of her own privileged autodidacticism, she portrays the obstacles, philosophical and social, to women's education. Although her works for women appear to reinforce the twinned hierarchies of class and gender and to maintain "chascune dans son estat," they also invite all women to embrace an ethic of moral and social self-improvement. Christine's self-narratives of education reveal both the female subject's complicity with the culture that has constructed her social identity and that subject's resistance to her cultural construction. Christine's didactic works from 1399 to 1405 inscribe the teacher's growing awareness of both the urgency and the impossibility of indoctrinating subjects, of teaching moral lessons to transform the social order.

Notes

I would like to thank Thelma Fenster and Edward Wheatley for their helpful comments on earlier drafts of this paper.

1. The classic definition is that of Philippe Lejeune, who sees autobiography as a "récit rétrospectif en prose qu'une personne réelle fait de sa propre existence, lorsqu'elle met l'accent sur sa vie individuelle, en particulier l'histoire de sa personnalité" (a retrospective prose narrative that a real person makes about his or her own existence, while accenting his individual life and, particularly, the history of his personality) (*Le Pacte autobiographique* 14). For a reconsideration of theories of the production of self-narrative from the perspective of the female subject, see Leigh Gilmore.

2. For assessments of Christine's feminism, see Joan Kelly, "Early Feminist"; F. Douglas Kelly; Beatrice Gottlieb. Although Christine passionately defends women's intellectual merit, she does not advocate the transformation of gender or class roles through pedagogical practice, as do contemporary feminists such as bell hooks.

3. On the rise of political literature from 1380 to 1440, see Krynen, *Idéal du prince*; for a study of the ideal of the prince as it emerges in earlier mirrors for princes, see Born, "The Perfect Prince." On Christine's development as an increasingly political writer, see Blanchard, "L'Entrée." Sherman's *Imaging Aristotle* examines the illuminations of translations made by Nicolas Oresme for Charles V.

4. As has been done, most emphatically, by Delany, " 'Mothers.' " For a more nuanced view, see the response by Reno, "Christine," and Delany's subsequent reply in "History." Other discussions that do not deny Christine's conservatism but stress the complexity of her thought include that of Quilligan 7–10, 260–73, and my own remarks on Christine and the reproduction of the class system in *Women Readers* 217–46.

5. As has been argued by Gauvard, "Une Pensée politique?" She shows how Christine deftly negotiates her support of Philip of Burgundy, Jean sans Peur, and then Jean de Berry as fitting counselors for the king, even as she condemns the failings of Louis d'Orléans. An early rather heroic assessment of Christine's role in the political quarrels and civil war is provided by Thomassy; Gauvard's more sober assessment of Christine's role is echoed by Lucas, ed. *Le Livre du corps de policie,* who sees Christine as a moralist rather than a political theorist (xii) and who notes the "conventional, even reactionary" tenor of social ideals (33). Yet, critics concur that Christine does not hesitate to proffer stern moral advice to those who would counsel the king. See Hindman, *"Epistre Othéa"; Livre de la paix,* ed. Willard, 28–34.

6. As Judith Ferster has written of the dangers for Gower and other writers of political advice in an equally politically incendiary arena, late-fourteenth- and early-fifteenth-century England, "Someone who wanted merely to play it safe would not have written a mirror for princes at this time" ("O Political Gower" 35). See also her *Fictions of Advice.* For an excellent overview of the political engagement of writers during the reign of Charles VI and of their ultimate failure to reform either church or state, see Claude Gauvard, "Christine de Pizan et ses contemporains."

7. The *Enseignemens* survive in twenty manuscripts; the *Proverbes* were translated into English by Anthony Woodville, Earl Rivers, governor of the royal princes, and printed by Caxton in 1478; see the remarks by Willard, "Teacher" 133. All translations of Christine's works in this article are my own.

8. A subtheme running throughout the collection is that of the necessity of rulers' exercising good judgment (Paris [68], Midas [26]), of the dangers of revealing secrets (Semele [62]), and of the importance of listening to good counsel (Helenus [77], Ceyx and Alcyone [79], and Troilus [80]). See Hindman, *"Epistre Othéa"* 33–55, and, on how this reflects in the illuminations, 123–28.

9. In medieval tradition, the Sibyl foretells the coming of Christ and is also associated with the prediction of political disaster and the end of dynasties; see McGinn. For an analysis of the importance of the sibyl to Christine's work, see Margolis, "Poetess" 363. See also Brownlee, "Structures of Authority"; Nichols.

10. On the affinity between Andromache, Othea, and Christine, and on the importance of Hector's death in the sequence of stories, see Hindman, *Christine* 56–58. In Hindman's analysis of the program of illuminations, Andromache represents Isabeau de Bavière, and she is flanked by her son Louis de Guyenne (*Christine* 130–34). For a complementary reading of the significance of Hector's death to the didactic aims of the work, see Noakes 127–28.

11. An extended discussion of Christine's notion of gender roles is offered by Richards, "Rejecting Essentialism."

12. In her letter to the queen imploring peace, Christine says that every good queen should be a "mere conforteresse de ses subgiéz et de son peuple" (mother comforting her subjects and her people) and laments that any stone-hearted mother could bear to see her children destroy themselves; see Christine, "Isabelle of Bavaria" 147.

13. As suggested by Solente in her introduction to *Le Livre des fais et bonnes meurs du sage roy Charles V* (xxvii–xxviii). Gauvard also suggests that the work may demonstrate her shifting loyalties from Louis d'Orléans, who receives scant mention, to Philippe le Hardi, the duke of Burgundy. See Gauvard, "Christine de Pisan, a-t-elle eu une pensée politique?" 423. The duke, however, died on April 27, 1404, in the midst of Christine's redaction of *Charles V,* which was offered to Jean, duke of Berry, on January 1, 1405.

14. Dulac has shown how this scene constructs Christine's legitimacy as an author (Dulac, "Figure de l'écrivain" 117–18); Blanchard has shown how Christine seeks legiti-

macy—but also a personal difference—in the portraits of herself and the king that pervade the *Charles V* (Blanchard, "Une Laïque.")

15. On several occasions, Christine's professed admiration for the wisdom of Charles V and the order of his court conveys at the same time a criticism for the ignorance, laziness, and disorder in the present. As remarked by Gauvard: "Si les critiques faites au gouvernement d'Isabeau de Bavière et duc d'Orléans demeurent extrêmement voilées, elles apparaissent en contrepoint du gouvernement idéal de l'époque de Charles V" (If the criticisms made of the government of Isabeau de Bavière and the duke of Orléans remain quite veiled, they appear as counterpoint to the ideal government of the era of Charles V) (Une pensée politique" 424. For example, her nearly incredulous description of the order of the queen's court can only evoke the disorder of Isabeau's retinue: "Dieux! Quel triomphe! Quelle paix! En quel ordre, en quel coagulence regulée en toutes choses estoit gouvernée la court de tres noble damme, la royne Jehanne de Bourbon" (God! What a triumph! What peace! How well ordered in every respect was the court of the very noble lady, Queen Jeanne of Bourbon) (*Charles V* 1.53). It may be significant, given the lack of authority that Charles VI had over Isabeau de Bavière, that Christine insists at several points that it was Charles V's dominion that so ordered the court of his wife: "En tel maniere le sage roy gouvernoit sa loial espouse" (In such a way did the wise king govern his loyal wife) (1.57). In their translation of *Charles V*, which appeared when this article was in press, Hicks and Moreau suggest that the duke of Burgundy recommended to Christine the critical orientation that her biography should have (*Charles V*, ed. Hicks and Moreau, 16).

16. As maintained by Solente in her edition of *Charles V* (22 n. 1). Solente cites from the Latin *De regimine principum*, but Christine may well have known the French translation by Henri de Gauchi; see Giles of Rome (Egidio Colonna), ed. Molenaer, 122–29, 188–223.

17. A similar passage on the heated passions and defective temperaments of young people is found in Giles of Rome 126–28.

18. Louis de Guyenne was born on January 22, 1397. Louis de Guyenne developed into a lazy scholar who had a passing knowledge of Latin and French and spent most of his day sleeping after nocturnal revelry; see Willard's comment on his description in the *Journal* of Nicolas de Baye, in her introduction to The *"Livre de la Paix" of Christine de Pisan* (30).

19. See the discussion by Solente in her introduction to *Charles V* (xxix–xxx).

20. On the feminist revision of (often misogynistic) literary sources as a strategy in the *Cité des dames*, see Curnow, *"Cité"* 65–238; Quilligan; Desmond 195–228.

21. The rich social history of fifteenth-century women evidenced in the *Trois Vertus* has been analyzed, from various perspectives, by Laigle, *Le Livre des Trois Vertus*; Willard, "View," "Feminine Ideal"; Wisman, "Aspects socio-économiques"; and Lorcin, "Pouvoirs," *"Le Livre des trois Vertus," "Les Echos."* On women's agency expressed in speech acts, see Dulac, "Representation." On the conservative sexual and domestic ideology of this and other late medieval and Renaissance conduct works, see C. Winn, *"Dignitas mulieris," "Des mères."*

22. In the *Cité*, Christine praises the loyalty of wives, contemporaries that she dare not name, who have stayed by the side of wicked husbands, enduring beatings and poverty, despite the protestations of their families, saying "Vous le m'avez donné, avec luy vivray et mouray" (You gave him to me, with him I will live and die) (Curnow, *"Cité"* 841). Compare this with the words that the wife of a wicked husband utters to herself in the *Livre des trois Vertus*: "Il faut que tu muires et vives avec lui, quel qu'il soit" (You must live and die with him, whatever he may be like) (*Trois Vertus*, ed. Willard and Hicks, 55).

23. Christine's use of the wise birdcatcher also effects an interesting reversal of the medieval tradition that characterizes Satan as a fowler who traps wayward souls; see Koonce. Thanks to Edward Wheatley for bringing this motif to my attention.

24. Laigle places the composition of the *Trois Vertus* in the period just preceding the public scandal that broke out concerning Isabeau de Bavière's reputed liaison with her

brother-in-law, Louis d'Orléans, and the queen's subsequent punishment of several ladies-in-waiting; she characterizes the tone of the *Trois Vertus* as offering "de discrets avertissements plutôt que de franches remontrances, une prudente et courtoise réticence plutôt qu'une protestation indignée" (discreet warnings rather than frank remonstrances, a prudent and courteous reticence rather than an indignant protest) (23).

25. Kathleen Ashley has considered the broader audiences of conduct literature in "Medieval Courtesy Literature" and in several presentations of her forthcoming work on an upwardly mobile Burgundian family who possessed a copy of the thirteenth-century *Miroir de bonnes femmes*, source of the *Livre du Chevalier de la Tour Landry pour l'enseignement de ses filles*. See also Riddy.

26. The image of the mother's tears appears also in "Christine de Pisan to Isabelle of Bavaria" and in the *Lamentacion sur les maux de la France*.

CHAPTER 3

"Douleur sur toutes autres"

Revisualizing the Rape Script in the *Epistre Othea* and the *Cité des dames*

Diane Wolfthal

Roy Porter recently argued that rape was not on the minds of preindustrial women and that feminist scholars should not project their concern with rape onto the past (221). Indeed, Johan Huizinga's classic account of late medieval culture, *Herfsttij der middeleeuwen* (*The Autumn of the Middle Ages*), seems to lend support to Porter's assertion that rape was not a problem for fifteenth-century women. Huizinga's book mentions all sorts of violence—execution, war, torture, assault, persecution, brigandage, and even dwarfs confined with iron collars—but omits any reference to sexual violation (1–29).

But rape was an issue for fifteenth-century women. Speaking of herself in the third person, Margery Kempe voiced her fear of sexual violation and outlined her strategy for avoiding it:

> on nyghts had sche most dreed oftyn-tymys, & perauentur it was of hir gostly enmy, for sche was euyr a-ferd to be rauischyd er defilyd. Sche durst trustyn no man; whedir sche had cawse er non, sche was euyr a-ferd. sche durst ful euyl slepyn any nyth, for sche wend men wolde a defylyd hir. Þerfor sche went to bedde gladlich no nyth les þan sche had a woman er tweyn wyth hir. (Kempe, ed. Meech and Allen, 241)
>
> [At nights she was most often afraid. She was always afraid of being raped or violated. She dared trust no man, whether she had reason or not. She did not gladly go to bed any night unless she had a woman or two with her.] (Kempe, trans. Windeatt, 130)

And rape was also a concern for Christine de Pizan, who described it in the *Livre de la Cité des dames* as "douleur sur toutes autre" (the greatest possible sorrow) (Christine, *City* 161; Curnow, "*Cité*" 885). Her clear condemnation of rape, which she sustained over several consecutive passages in the *Cité des dames,* has often been noted (Richards, Introduction xxxiii), but her interpretation of sexual violence remains unexplored. As we shall see, Christine disrupts the traditional rape script, first by refusing to imagine women as victims of sexual violence and then by visualizing them as forceful avengers.

Mieke Bal has called the word *rape* "an obscuring term," observing that it "fails to address the cultural status of the event." She cautions: "Ethical norms differ according to time and place, yet the language in which we write about other cultures is also time and place bound." Furthermore, Bal persuasively argues that the word *rape* is really a metaphor for a narrative event, which may be interpreted differently by each participant in the event as well as by the narrator (37–38). If we explore the conception of rape in Christine's culture, we find a range of interpretations. To some, but not all, prostitutes were, by definition, "common women," who could not withhold sexual consent.[1] Similarly, parents might interpret an event as a rape, whereas to the couple it was an elopement (Greilsammer 70; Benveniste 13–35). In the cultural domain, most manuscripts expressed certain conventional assumptions about the nature of rape, but Christine, through her manuscripts, revised this received tradition.

This essay will examine Christine's interpretation of the nature and "proper" response to rape by exploring how her work negotiates the web of social and economic contexts in which she lived as a woman who was simultaneously a widow lacking the protection of a man, a resistant female reader of misogynist texts, a participant in the cultural production of the Valois courts, and a worker in the Parisian book trade. By analyzing the images executed for Christine's *Epistre Othea* or influenced by her *Cité des dames*, we can explore how Christine, working within the discourse of classical myth and legend, challenged its misogynist constructions. While recognizing the complexity of her ideas and the ingenuity of her strategies for rewriting rape, this essay will also suggest that she was not alone in her condemnation of sexual violence or in her vision of a response to rape that entailed forceful action against the assailant.

Christine lived in a world in which rape was prevalent. Historians of medieval crime have documented that sexual violation was a severe problem in France and Burgundy during the fourteenth and fifteenth centuries.[2] Indeed, Walter Prevenier has concluded that "the everyday climate [was] one of danger for single women in a medieval metropolis" (276). Furthermore, an analysis of published cases reveals why rape may have been of particular concern to Christine: unmarried women, including widows such as herself, were especially vulnerable to attack. Prevenier has convincingly demonstrated that widows were considered "an ideal prey for men who were eager for sexual adventures" (269).

The case of the rape of Ysablet des Champions, a Parisian widow, is particularly relevant. Christine may well have known about the crime, since it was perpetrated by servants of the duke of Burgundy during their visit to Paris in 1393. Moreover, Ysablet's actions suggest that Christine's forceful response to rape was not unique. First Ysablet tried to deter two rapists by falsely claiming to be married. When this failed, the spunky Ysablet made sure to raise the "hue and cry" required by law codes to convict rapists (Wolfthal 43). Her screams were designed to attract the attention of a series of witnesses throughout the night of the attack, and her court testimony was composed so as to convince the judges that she had been raped, not seduced. She testified, for example, that while being violated, she had cried out: "I am not mistress of my own body at present.... all that you have done, are doing, and will do is contrary to my desire and will" (264). Furthermore, when one set of judges failed to convict her assailants, Ysablet appealed to the Parliament of Paris. Apparently, she devised a two-part strategy. On the night of the attack, she attempted to resist her rapists, an effort that failed, but concurrently, she began to build the legal case against them and succeeded in this endeavor.

Whereas the everyday reality of such rapes may well have contributed to Christine's interest in the issue, it was her literary studies that offered her a framework for exploring the cultural contexts of sexual violence. Christine had access to some of the finest libraries, and, since she worked as a scribe and hired illuminators, she had an intimate knowledge of the Parisian book trade.[3] In fact, rape was a popular subject in manuscripts of the time and was treated in a broad range of texts, from moralized Ovids to moralized Bibles. Images reveal a variety of approaches. Some sanitized sexual violence, such as a *Rape of the Sabines* from Saint Augustine's *City of God* (Wolfthal fig. 1), which shows a Sabine woman strolling off happily arm-in-arm with her assailant; others condemn it, explicitly exposing its violent and sexual aspects, such as a *Rape of Dinah* from a *Bible moralisée* that belonged to Duke Philip the Bold of Burgundy, which shows the victim forcefully resisting Shechem's brutal attack (Wolfthal fig. 25). Terence's *The Eunuch*, created for Jean, duke of Berry in 1408, is comedic in tone. The humour hinges on the fact that the rapist has disguised himself as a eunuch in order to gain entry into his victim's home.[4]

Especially popular were themes that depicted women framing innocent men for rape, such as a miniature of *Joseph and Potiphar's Wife* from the duke of Burgundy's *Bible moralisée* (Meiss, *Limbourgs* 2: fig. 303). A few miniatures even explore women's sexual assault of men, such as the *Temptation of a Christian* from the *Belles Heures* of the duke of Berry (Meiss and Beatson, *Belles Heures* fol. 191; Meiss, *Limbourgs* 1:349), or same-sex rape, such as *Jupiter and Ganymede* from Saint Augustine's *City of God* (Philadelphia Museum of Art, MS 45–65–1, fol. 33r). Critical for Christine were the allegorical rape images in the *Roman de la Rose*, such as those in a manuscript of 1403, once in the collection of the duke of Burgundy, which depict the storming of the castle or the lover inserting his staff within the vaginal opening of a statue whose raised hand indicates her resistance.[5]

The *Epistre Othea*

Christine explores a series of mythological narratives of rape in the *Epistre Othea*, written in 1399–1400. Her most popular work, the *Othea* was composed for a young prince (Hindman, *Christine* xix–xx, 34; Meiss, *Limbourgs* 1:23). Christine supervised the production of several surviving versions of the *Othea*, but I will consider only the last two, which were lavishly illuminated. I will not discuss the earliest manuscript, BNF, MS fr. 848, which was executed around 1400–1401 (Laidlaw, "Author's" 544). Dedicated to Louis, duke of Orléans, it was decorated with only a small cycle of six miniatures (Hindman, *Christine* xix, 42–44, 53–54, 100–142). Two later manuscripts are remarkable for their extensive cycle of illuminations. The manuscript in Paris, BNF, MS fr. 606, was executed over the years 1407 to 1408 and forms part of a volume of Christine's collected works that was presented to Jean, duke of Berry (Laidlaw, "Author's"). The version in London, BL, Harley 4431, which was presented to Queen Isabelle of France and most probably dates from 1410–11, is often cited as the definitive version because it was the final edition supervised under Christine's direction, was written entirely by her hand, and has been judged more refined in its arrangement of text and image.[6] Scholars have convincingly demonstrated that Christine closely supervised the illuminators, formulating their iconography, and even furnishing them with visual models, so that the miniatures would conform to her ideas (Hindman, *Christine* 63–77, 92, 98; Meiss, *Limbourgs* 1:8–15).

Each chapter consists of four parts—the miniature, verse, gloss, and allegory—that independently interpret a single subject. Rosemond Tuve has justly characterized the text as "Christine's deliberate action of directing us towards multiple readings of a classical story"(38 n). In some respects, however, the images are the most important variation on the theme, since, as Marilynn Desmond and Pamela Sheingorn recently demonstrated, readers would more easily remember the brightly colored, strikingly inventive compositions that serve to introduce the textual material in each chapter. The *Othea* is an anthology of classical myths, a category of literature that was highly esteemed at the Valois courts (Meiss, *Limbourgs* 1:19–22). Rape is rampant in this tradition (Keuls 34, 37, 39; Zeitlin 122), and for this reason when Christine decided to focus on Roman mythology, she of necessity agreed to negotiate a series of rape narratives. But her interpretations are strikingly different from earlier versions in several ways. First, in the *Othea*, Christine chose to avoid the explicit depiction of sexual violence. She omitted several myths that had in earlier manuscripts suggested the sexual or violent aspects of rape. For example, two versions of her primary source, the *Ovide moralisé*, include an extensive cycle of illuminations that relate the story of Tereus's rape of Philomela. Miniatures showing Tereus cutting out his victim's tongue in order to ensure her silence make clear the violent nature of his crime (Figure 4).[7] The sexual aspect of rape is revealed in miniatures of Boreas and Orethia, also found in the *Ovide moralisé* (Figure 5). The god of the north wind fondles his victim's hair, places his hand on her shoulder, and brings his face and body close to

Figure 4. Tereus and Philomela. From the *Ovide moralisé.* Paris, Bibliothèque de l'Arsenal, MS 5069, fol. 88v.

Figure 5. Rape of Orethia. From the *Ovide moralisé.* Paris, Bibliothèque de l'Arsenal, MS 5069, fol. 92r.

hers. Orethia tries to resist by turning her body away from her assailant: her outstretched arms and left leg suggest her futile attempt to escape his embrace. Christine certainly knew these or similar images; a major source for the *Othea* was the *Ovide moralisé* (Hindman, *Christine* 93), which included relentless depictions of sexual violence. But Christine chose to exclude such visualizations from the *Othea*.

Not only does Christine omit several rape narratives, but even the few she includes are stripped of any reference to sexual violence. For example, illuminations dating prior to Christine's *Othea* at times show Paris seizing Helen's wrist, a sign of force (Hedeman figs. 1–2; Wolfthal), or placing his hand on her chest, a sign of possession (Buchthal pls. 4a and 13b; Garnier 191). In an *Ovide moralisé,* Paris wears armor and is accompanied by soldiers (Figure 6). He comes from behind to seize He-

Figure 6. Paris and Helen. From the *Ovide moralisé.* Paris, Bibliothèque de l'Arsenal, MS 5069, fol. 162v.

len, an act that implies a sneak attack in a poem by Eustaches Deschamps (Deschamps 3:231–32). Helen pulls away from Paris, her arms again outstretched before her, as in the *Rape of Orethia* in the same manuscript (Figure 5). But in the miniature in Christine's *Othea*, Helen is constructed as a willing lover, who places her arm around Paris's waist (Figure 7). Although in the *Othea* manuscripts under discussion Helen is subsumed within Paris's massive form, he employs no physical coercion against

Figure 7. Paris and Helen. From the *Epistre Othea*. Paris, Bibliothèque Nationale de France, MS fr. 606, fol. 35r.

her. Furthermore, Christine uses the verb *ravir* to describe Paris's action.[8] At this time, the word *ravir* had a range of meanings, most often "to abduct," but at times "to exalt"; it was certainly not synonymous with our word "rape."[9] Christine chose in both text and image to avoid the explicit depiction of sexual violence in her miniature of Helen and Paris.

Christine also explores the issue of sexual violence in her interpretation of the story of Bellerophon, which involves a classic misogynist stereotyping of woman as sexual aggressor:

> Sa marrastre fu si esprise de s'amour que elle le requist et, pour ce que il ne se voit consentir a sa voulente, elle fist tant que il fu condampnez a estre devourez des fieres bestes. (Loukopoulos 35:203)

> [(Bellerophon's) stepmother was so taken with love for him that she desired him, and because he would not consent to her wish, she arranged for him to be devoured by beasts.]
>
> (My translation)

Although in her text Christine maintains many elements of her source, the *Ovide moralisé,* she also rewrites it in several ways (Campbell, "L'Epître Othéa" 113; *Ovide moralisé* 4:33–37). First, she downplays aspects of the story that cast the queen in a negative light. She only briefly mentions the queen's misconduct, omits numerous criticisms of her, and eliminates a lengthy episode in which she frames Bellerophon for rape. She also excludes any reference to the king, a major figure in the *Ovide moralisé:* he serves as judge when the queen falsely accuses Bellerophon, his feelings are explored at length, and it is he who sentences his son to death. Christine, in contrast, has the queen arrange the youth's demise; her version grants the stepmother greater agency and authority. Christine further modifies her source by focusing on Bellerophon's virtuous resistance. She constructs him as an ideal model for the young prince for whom she wrote the *Othea.*

Like the text, the image of Bellerophon subtly transforms its model (Figures 8 and 9). First, it illustrates a different episode. Whereas the miniature in the *Ovide moralisé* shows the queen accusing her stepson, that in the *Othea* substitutes an earlier moment in the narrative. In the London version, the gestures of Bellerophon and his stepmother indicate that they are speaking; presumably she is requesting his sexual favors, while he is declining. Bellerophon gently sways away from her; both his pose and the gesture of his right hand resemble those in images of Joseph resisting Potiphar's wife (Haussherr 2: pl. 17). The stepmother, elegantly dressed in necklace, crown, and ermine-trimmed gown, stands in profile, facing Bellerophon; her low-cut neckline and direct glance suggest that she is attempting to seduce him. Eustache Deschamps, for example, in a poem of 1406, wrote that married women wore dresses with wide necklines in order to make other men desire them (9:40). Fur-

Figure 8. Bellerophon and his stepmother. From the *Ovide moralisé*. Paris, Bibliothèque de l'Arsenal, MS 5069, fol. 60r.

thermore, unlike the stepmother, proper women lower their eyes when facing a man (Wolfthal 62).

In the image, as in the text, the king makes no appearance. Unlike the illuminations in the *Ovide moralisé* (Figure 8), the scene in the *Othea* focuses solely on the actions of Bellerophon and his stepmother. Furthermore, in the *Ovide moralisé* in Rouen, the queen has loosened and disheveled her hair and removed her crown, so as to look the part of a rape victim (Wolfthal 44–45). In the *Othea*, by contrast, her hair is neatly pinned up and topped by a crown. By eliminating the accusation scene, Christine avoids depicting the stepmother as rape victim.

Furthermore, compared with other images that construct woman as a sexual menace, the miniature in the *Othea* downplays the queen's aggression. Unlike a representation of Potiphar's wife from the duke of Burgundy's *Bible moralisée* (Meiss, *Limbourgs* 2: fig. 303), the queen does not tower threateningly over her victim, lunge at him, or grab his clothes. Nevertheless, the lion, fox, camel, and dragon, shown eagerly awaiting the youth in their barren, mountainous wilderness, serve to remind the viewer that the queen caused Bellerophon's demise. Although Christine succeeds in excluding an image of woman as rape victim, she helped keep alive in the viewer's mind the traditional misogynist stereotype of woman as sexual aggressor. Of all the medieval conceptions of the sexual aggressor, that of the older woman pursuing a youth was by far the most popular, depicted by the theme of Potiphar's wife and its variants.

49

Figure 9. Bellerophon and his stepmother. From the *Epistre Othea*. London, British Library, Harley 4431, fol. 111v.

Christine's illumination of *Apollo and Daphne* is typical of those in the *Othea*, since, like the miniatures of Helen and Bellerophon, it avoids representing women as victims of sexual violence (Figure 10). But the image of Daphne differs from the others in its originality, complexity, and haunting mood. The *Ovide moralisé*, one of Christine's sources, unequivocally constructs this story as an attempted rape:

Figure 10. Apollo and Daphne. From the *Epistre Othea*. London, British Library, Harley 4431, fol. 124v.

Dané fu une damoisele,
... qui vault vivre en virginité,
... [Phebus] la cuida forçier
Et folir li son pucelage.
      (1:3077, 3080, 3092–93)

[Daphne was a maiden ... who wanted to keep her virginity ... [but Apollo] intended to force her and take [it] away.]

                                  (My translation)

To avoid this fate, Daphne was transformed into a laurel tree. Neither Christine's text nor the accompanying image makes any reference to the attempted rape that is related in the *Ovide moralisé* (Loukopoulos 272–73; Scrope 109–10). Although North Italian miniatures of the fourteenth century show Apollo seizing Daphne (Stechow Taf. IV, Abb. 10–11), the illumination in the *Othea* does not. Rather, in the *Othea*, Apollo stands away from the nymph and is careful not to touch the human part of her body. Instead, he plucks a leaf from her branches to add to the wreath that he holds in his left hand. This avoidance of the explicit depiction of sexual violence is characteristic of the *Othea*, as we have seen.

    The motif of Apollo's pursuit of Daphne is a standard element in narratives of the myth and, indeed, Christine's text mentions this action several times. But in the accompanying illumination Apollo stands still. This is particularly striking since images in the *Ovide moralisé* (Figure 11), Christine's primary source, portray Apollo chasing Daphne (Lord 165 fig. 1; Stechow Abb. 3, 120). Perhaps Christine wished to avoid the Ovidian paradigm of sexual relations as a predatory hunt (Curran 280).

    Another striking difference between the illumination of Daphne in the *Othea* and those in earlier manuscripts is the way the nymph's body is depicted. Although some scholars have constructed Christine as a prude,[10] the illuminations in the *Othea* suggest just the reverse, since they include an unusual number of representations of naked bodies. Although Christine's text does not specify whether Daphne is clothed (Loukopoulos 272–73; Scrope 109–10), Millard Meiss and Charles Sterling have termed the miniature of Daphne the first nude representation of the nymph in postclassical art (Meiss, *Limbourgs* 1:29; Sterling 314). Indeed, earlier images show Daphne either clothed, or as a tree, or as a tree with a human head; none show her with a nude human body (Barnard fig. 5). Daphne is not the only nude or partially nude figure in the *Othea*. Argus is dressed only in his eyes, unlike his clothed predecessors in the *Ovide moralisé*, and Diana, Hermaphrodite, and Salmacis emerge partially nude from their baths. The drowned Leander floats only in his bathing trunks, while the male prisoners before King Minos are similarly attired. The four men that Latona will transform into frogs omit even this minimal covering.[11] In short, Christine includes a series of nudes or seminudes, mostly

Figure 11. Apollo and Daphne. From the *Ovide moralisé*. Paris, Bibliothèque de l'Arsenal, MS 5069, fol. 4r.

of the male gender, and often without precedent. These images refute Christine's reputation for prudishness and suggest that she had other reasons for avoiding scenes of sexual violence.

Christine's unprecedented manner of representing Daphne's body is a key to understanding her interpretation of this myth of attempted rape. Why did Christine break with tradition to show Daphne's body without clothes? Nudity at this time had a range of associations.[12] It was often employed as a sign for exotic and fantastic peoples, and Christine may have introduced it here for this reason (Buettner, "Profane Illuminations" 86). Since clothing served as a "metaphor for the social body" and "nudity signified withdrawal from social intercourse," nudity would have been particularly appropriate for Daphne, a nymph who was transformed into a tree (Régnier-Bohler 370; Braunstein 581).

Because Meiss privileged classical form, he termed Daphne a nude when he saw her bare legs and torso and her lack of clothing. But her body as represented in the *Othea* is far from normative. Unlike images of Eve, Daphne lacks arms and breasts and is part tree. Christine's conception of this unusual illumination must have been the result of a very complex process. It probably began with an image from the *Ovide moralisé*, but Apollo's action was modified so that he stood still and did not touch Daphne's body. As Wolfgang Stechow proposed, Daphne's form was probably influenced by an image of a mandrake depicted as a nude body topped by a fan of foliage. Stechow suggested that Christine's model was a North Italian illumination, dated circa 1400, that shows a human body from the shoulders down topped by a fan of leaves (14–15). Other images, however, show the mandrake as female, such as an illustration in a volume of Guillaume le Clerc's *Bestiaire divin*, executed at Saint Albans circa 1270 (BNF, MS fr. 14969 [pl. 7]). Two mandrakes, one male, the other female, grow head-down in the ground. The woman's hair and arms form the roots of the female mandrake; her torso and legs comprise the rest of the plant. When this image is viewed upside-down, it is quite close to the Daphne in the *Othea*, especially the raised position of the arms. Since the *Bestiaire* belonged in 1405 to the collection of Marguerite of Flanders, duchess of Burgundy (Winter, *Bibliothèque* 47, 71–73, 142, 156, 240–42), Christine may well have known it.

But neither Christine's text nor any earlier image (Blunt) explains one aspect of the miniatures. The version in Paris (Figure 12) differs from both its models and its variant in London in one key respect: it shows bark growing over Daphne's chest. This motif probably derives from the text of the *Ovide moralisé*, which describes how Daphne's sides became

> ... tous de tenvre escorce çains;
> Ses crins dorez et flamboians
> Devindrent fueilles verdoians;
> Ses bras sont en lons rains muez.
>   (*Ovide moralisé* 1:3028–31)

> [encircled with tender bark; / Her gold and flaming hair / Became green leaves; / Her arms were changed into long branches.]
>   (Barnard 59)

Although none of these elements appears in fourteenth-century illuminations of the *Ovide moralisé*, all are depicted in the Paris version of the *Othea*. Christine probably selected as sources for Daphne an image of a mandrake and the text from the *Ovide moralisé* because together they helped suggest the process of the nymph's transformation from woman to tree.

But this unusual conception of Daphne would have pleased Christine for other reasons as well. For the male heterosexual viewer of the time, the usual erotic focus was the upper part of the female body, particularly the breasts (Buettner, "Dressing" 385–86; Easton 83–118). Perhaps Christine eliminated Daphne's breasts in part because she wished to avoid portraying the nymph as a sex object. As Sylvia Huot has observed, Christine opposed seeing a woman as an "opaque ... surface on which to project [men's] fantasies [and] desires" ("Seduction" 370).

But Daphne's lack of breasts not only suggests the idea of metamorphosis and prevents her from being viewed as a sex object; it also constructs her as sexually ambiguous, particularly since, consistent with the usual practice of the first decade of the fifteenth century, she also lacks

Figure 12. Apollo and Daphne. From the *Epistre Othea*. Paris, Bibliothèque Nationale de France, MS fr. 606, fol. 40v.

genitals. (Daphne's genitals seem to be present today in the Paris version only because damage has erased the upper part of the outline of her thighs.) In fact, none of the nudes in the *Othea* show genitals, which first appear in Parisian manuscripts circa 1410 (Meiss, *Limbourgs* 2: fig. 169). I will explore the idea of sexual ambiguity more later, but for now it is important to remember that although Christine defends herself as a female author in her biography of Charles V (Laird), she often constructs herself as male. In the *Livre de la mutacion de Fortune,* dated between 1400 and 1403, she envisions herself as a woman who has been transformed into a man (Huffer 61–63). Later, in the *Avision,* she repeats this formulation, and in the *Livre des trois Vertus,* she cautions that the widow "prengne cuer d'omne" (will have to take the heart of a man) (Desmond, *Dido* 185–196; Dulac, "Mystical Inspiration" 243). Finally, in the *Cité des dames,* she again reveals her uncertainty concerning her own gender identity. Reason tells Christine:

> Tu ressembles le fol dont la truffle parle, qui en dormant au moulin, fu revestu de la robe d'une femme, et au resveiller, pource que ceulx qui le mouquoyent luy tesmoingnoyent que femme estoit, crut myeulx leurs faulx diz que las certainete de son estre. (Curnow, "*Cité*" 622–23)

> [You resemble the fool in the prank who was dressed in women's clothes while he slept; because those who were making fun of him repeatedly told him he was a woman, he believed their false testimony more readily than the certainty of his own identity.]
> (Christine, *City* 6)

Others also viewed Christine this way; Jean Gerson described her more than once as a "virile woman" ("virilis illa femina," "illa...virago"; Hicks, *Débat* 168).

Medieval society often termed women virile if they forcefully defended their chastity. Women were praised as "male" or "virile" if they cut off their breasts or otherwise denied their female form (Schulenburg, "Heroics" 29–72; Miles 53–77). Boccaccio, among others, expressed the dominant way of thinking. A few exceptional women could become heroes, he felt, but there was only one route; they must "put aside the characteristics of a woman for those of a man" (Wayne). Such thinking, as Valerie Wayne has observed, valorized masculinity, yet also permitted women, at least on a theoretical plane, to step outside their gender roles (52). Feminist scholars have demonstrated that in order to convincingly portray a woman's heroism, it was at times necessary to alter her body so that it appeared more masculine; a female form was deemed inadequate to express heroism.[13] This may well be another meaning for Daphne: because she heroically resists sexual violation, Christine imagines her without breasts.

So far I have constructed Christine as the sole creator of the images in the *Othea,* but artists and patrons affected their conception as well. The two illuminators had distinct styles. The Paris miniatures exhibit muted, pastel tones and soft, loose brushwork; they often include a blue sky that extends the pictorial space. The London illuminations, in contrast, display bold, bright colors, sharp lines, and flat, diapered backgrounds. The Paris master's abilities are nowhere so striking as in the illumination of Daphne (Figure 12). The colors are exquisite: the red of Apollo's face and hands, the sizzling rays of his halo, the clear blue of the endless sky. The quality of light is magical, and, compared with the London version (Figure 10), the process of metamorphosis is more convincingly rendered. Daphne's personality is stronger as well. Her branches inscribe a wider arc and her more luxuriant growth of foliage seems to dwarf Apollo, almost overpowering him. The lowest limb on the right seems to threaten the god, pointing directly at his eye. The illuminator of the Paris *Othea* is better able to visualize Daphne's agency, while at the same time creating a magical, haunting, dreamlike mood.

Daphne's form may also be explored from the collective point of view of the Valois court. Brigitte Buettner has argued with reason that the royal and ducal courts promoted images of the nude body ("Dressing"). They were also fascinated by representations that blur the distinction between the genders. For example, in an image of Chaldea, from a *Livre des merveilles,* men and women cross-dress, and their bodies are visualized as having aspects of both sexes. Especially relevant is the way that the women's bodies are constructed with the flat chest and erect stance normally assigned to men (Scott, *History of Dress* fig. 17). Perhaps the clearest example of sexual ambiguity is an illumination of the *Land of the Hermaphrodites,* also from the *Livre des merveilles* (Paris, BNF, fr. 2810, fol. 195v).[14] Here bodies are defined as either male or female, except that each sports both a penis and a vagina. Even less exotic subjects are androgynized. In a volume of the collected works of Virgil, Bacchus wears a gown that emphasizes his breasts (Meiss, *Limbourgs* 2: fig. 247), and a tonsured, bearded Saint Jerome is depicted in the *Belles Heures* dressed in women's clothes (Meiss, *Belles Heures* fol. 184v). The androgynous image of Daphne, which lacks both breasts and genitals, would have suited the Valois taste perfectly.

Despite the incredible complexity of ideas that may have been associated with the miniature of Apollo and Daphne, for Christine a key issue in the *Othea* seems to have been the avoidance of the explicit representation of sexual violence. Why was this so? In the *Querelle de la Rose,* she objected to Jean de Meun's construction of love as sexual conquest and his approval of force as a means to win sexual favors. She feared, furthermore, that readers would applaud such ideas (Huot, *Rose* 22). Indeed, Huot's analysis of glosses in manuscripts of the *Rose* confirms that Christine's fears were justified. In 1402, Michel Arès, a cleric, felt compelled to comment on the passage in which Ami recommends that the lover use force to get his way with the Rose. Arès noted "when the opportunity presents itself, I pray you, be a man" (Huot, *Rose* 44). A university-educated reader of the mid–fourteenth century commented, "She thinks it better to lose her virginity by force than to say 'Now do as you will with me'" (Huot, *Rose* 48–50). And a late-thirteenth-century reader wrote, "Note that a woman wants to be conquered" (Huot, *Rose* 62). Perhaps as a corrective to such attitudes, Christine wished to avoid representations of rape. In the *Othea*, Christine shows great interest in other issues, such as granting female characters agency or constructing them as contributors to culture.[15] Certainly images of women as victims of sexual violence would undermine these goals. Furthermore, the *Othea* is ostensibly an epistle addressed to a young man. Perhaps this also contributed to Christine's refusal to indulge in the Valois appetite for images of sexual violence.

Sharon Marcus has recently suggested a series of strategies that would enable women to rewrite the dominant rape script in which man is the powerful rapist and woman his defenseless victim. With Bal, she stresses that "rape is a question of language, interpretation, and subjectivity." One strategy that Marcus proposes is "to imagine women as neither already raped nor inherently rapable" (387). This is precisely what Christine has done by avoiding certain rape themes and revising others, such as Helen, Bellerophon, and Daphne. The imagery of the *Othea* never portrays women as rape victims. Furthermore, some women, such as Venus and Bellerophon's stepmother, become powerful figures on whom men are dependent. Christine, like Marcus, refuses to accept the idea that women are "inherently rapable" (Marcus 387). Instead, through her manuscripts, Christine disrupts the Ovidian rape model, thereby transforming a dominant cultural script. Marcus criticizes "the grammar of violence in which the male body can wield weapons, can make itself into a weapon" (395). But with Christine, Paris never takes possession of Helen. Marcus concludes, "We can begin to develop a feminist discourse on rape by displacing the emphasis on what the rape script promotes — male violence against women — and putting into place what the rape script stultifies and excludes — women's will, agency, and capacity for violence." While at first glance the *Othea* may seem to be simply avoiding the unpleasant subject of sexual violence, Marcus's formulations help us to see an alternative interpretation, that Christine may be adopting strategies in an effort to disrupt and revise traditional thinking about rape.

The *Livre de la cité des dames*

Six years after she wrote the *Othea*, Christine explored the issue of sexual violence in the *Livre de la cité des dames*. Unlike the lavishly illuminated versions of the *Othea*, those of the *Cité des dames* made under

Christine's supervision do not include any depictions of mythological subjects. The text is critical, however, not only because it enriches our understanding of Christine's interpretation of rape, but also because it influenced later rape imagery. I will therefore examine the text of the *Cité des dames* first and then discuss its subsequent influence on manuscript production.

Compared with her treatment of rape in the *Othea*, Christine adopts a strikingly different approach in her later text. Unlike her organization in the *Othea*, Christine does not disperse themes of sexual violence throughout the *Cité des dames*, but rather groups all but one together in three consecutive chapters (Christine, *City* 160–64, 147–50). Similarly, rather than offering multiple interpretations of each myth, Christine unites a series of narratives under a single idea, the unambiguous condemnation of rape (Curnow, *"Cité"* 885, 887–88). Christine transforms her language, shifting from the more ambiguous "ravir" of the *Othea* to the unequivocal "efforcer," to force or rape, of the *Cité des dames*.[16] The passages that concern rape in the *Cité des dames* also differ from those in the *Othea* in their consistent tone of moral outrage; Christine paints a vivid picture of the brutal nature of rape, even when treating narratives that traditionally whitewash it. Unlike the *Othea*, the *Cité* avoids perpetuating the stereotype of woman as sexual aggressor and instead constructs all sexual aggressors as male. Furthermore, she broadens her condemnation by including medieval as well as classical examples. Perhaps most important, in the *Cité des dames* Christine revises her view of women's proper response to rape, so that it entails forceful action against the aggressor.

In the two texts Christine offers a similar explanation for rape, one based on classical sources, but whereas in the *Othea* Christine only briefly discusses this, in the *Cité des dames* she develops the notion at greater length. Although Jean Froissart in his late-fourteenth-century *Chroniques* had presumed that the devil made men do it (Froissart, *Chronicles* 309–15; Pistono), Christine does not invoke a Christian causality. Rather, in the *Othea*, she writes that Bellerophon's stepmother was "seized by love." This conception of sexual passion as an irresistible force may be traced back to antiquity. For example, a Greek vase shows Eros forcibly prodding Zeus to rape Ganymede (Kaempf-Dimitriadou Abb. 1). In the *Cité des dames*, Christine develops this narrative script further. She expresses the view, voiced not only by Ovid but also by accused rapists in quattrocento courts, that once men are aroused, they resort to force (Ruggiero 156). For example, Christine writes that the Galatian queen "plus moult" (greatly pleased) the officer who kept her captive:

Si la pria moult et requist par grans offres; mais quant il vid que prieres riens n'y valloit, it l'afforça de fair. (Curnow, *"Cité"* 887–88)

[He entreated her and coaxed her with fine presents, but after he saw that pleading would not work, he violently raped her.]

(Christine, *City* 162)

Similarly, Tarquin first coaxed Lucretia with promises and gifts before raping her (Curnow, *"Cité"* 886; Christine, *City* 161).

The distinction between rape and seduction was a critical issue in the Middle Ages (Brundage, "Rape" 141–48). Medieval society had great difficulty deciding where seduction ended and rape began, but Christine, in the *Cité des dames*, makes clear the one element that separates the two, the use of violence. Furthermore, she suggests a change in the evidence that was necessary to prove rape in a court of law; rather than requiring that women cry out during rape, as contemporary legal treatises did, she felt that a simple *"escondissent de bouche"* (verbal protest) was sufficient (Curnow, *"Cité"* 885; Christine, *City* 161).

Christine also challenges the myth that rape is heroic by rewriting several narratives. With the exception of Saint Augustine, medieval writers and artists had generally accepted the Roman view of the rape of the Sabines, constructing it as a heroic act that was necessary for the founding of Rome. Both words and images traditionally sanitize the event and depict its happy ending (Wolfthal fig. 1). Christine, however, imagines the incident from the Sabine point of view. She notes that they were not favorably impressed by the Romans, whom she terms *"trop ... voulages"* (extremely unstable) and *"fier et divers"* (haughty and strange) (Curnow, *"Cité"* 864; Christine, *City* 147). She also makes clear the violence of their actions. They

tous coururent vers les dames ... a force les leverent sur leurs chevaulx, et a tout s'en alerent fuyant vers la cité. (Curnow, *"Cité"* 865)

[rushed at the ladies ... forcibly lifted them onto their horses and fled to the city.]

(Christine, *City* 148)

Finally, she notes the tragic outcome: *"la criee et le dueil ... des dames"* (the outcry and sorrow of the ladies) (Curnow, *"Cité"* 865; Christine, *City* 148).

Christine suggests three possible responses for the rape victim: to grieve, to commit suicide, or to seek justice. She terms rape the *"douleur sur toutes autres"* (the greatest possible sorrow) and *"importable"* (unbearable) (Curnow, *"Cité"* 885, 888; Christine, *City* 161, 163). She notes that not only the Sabine women, but also the Galatian queen *"ot moult dueil"* (suffered terrible sorrow) and describes Lucretia as *"oultrec de grant douleur"* (overwhelmed with grief) (Curnow, *"Cité"* 886–87; Christine, *City* 162). The view that the rape victim grieved, as if she were in mourning, was a common one, which had been visualized in earlier illuminations, for example that of *Tamar* in the Morgan Picture Bible (Cockerell fig. 262).

Christine constructs suicide as a second possible response to rape. She includes the legend of Lucretia, who killed herself after being violated. Indeed, contemporary texts and images present suicide as the ideal response to rape. Lucretia became a popular subject in Europe at the end of the fourteenth century with the translation into French of Boccaccio's *De casibus* and *De mulieribus claris,* Christine's primary source for the *Cité des dames.*[17] In order to understand the significance of Christine's revisionist reading of Lucretia, I will take a moment to explore traditional images of this subject.

At this time French and Flemish workshops began producing luxury manuscripts that included depictions of Lucretia, such as those for the dukes of Berry and Burgundy (Figure 13). Boccaccio's narrative of Lucretia involves numerous episodes, but most early representations portray only the suicide, omitting the events leading up to the rape, the rape itself, and the aftermath of the suicide. Lucretia does not seem to suffer great harm, either emotionally or physically; her dagger seems only to prick her, and her demeanor remains calm. None of the male witnesses tries to prevent her suicide; nor do they show any signs of disapproval or anguish. Linda Hults has justly concluded that the dominant message of such renderings is that "female chastity is a supreme value well worth the cost of a woman's life"(Hults 211).

Despite church teachings to the contrary, Christian authors at times supported the classical view that the proper response to rape was suicide. In the *Livre des bonnes moeurs,* presented to the duke of Berry in 1410, Jacques Legrand praises Lucretia for killing herself following her "dishonor" in a chapter entitled "Comment on doit mépriser la vie présente" (How one must value very little one's present life). Legrand also cites Sedaza's daughters, who were violated by men who pretended to be pilgrims in order to gain entry into their victims' home. Legrand praises their subsequent suicides under the title "Comment se doit maintenir virginité et pucellage" (How one must maintain one's virginity and maidenhood) (Buettner, "Profane Illuminations" 79; Garnier 2:412). In short, narratives of Lucretia and Sedaza's daughters reinforced the view that virtuous women will kill themselves rather than continue to live after being raped. Such suicides serve to preserve not only the women's honor, but also that of her male relatives, so often portrayed silently witnessing the woman's sacrifice.

Although most medieval representations construct a bleak aftermath to rape, a small group suggests quite a different scenario. In his examination of the theme of Lucretia, Ian Donaldson concludes: "Revenge, retaliation, hitting back at the enemy—all these are tasks for men, not for

Figure 13. Lucretia. From Boccaccio, *Des cleres femmes.* Paris, Bibliothèque Nationale de France, MS fr. 598, fol. 71v.

the injured woman"(Donaldson 11). In accordance with this paradigm, male relatives avenge the rape of Lucretia. But there is a different model: it is the victim who takes justice into her own hands in the legend of the Galatian queen.

Boccaccio relates that Roman soldiers captured the queen, along with several of her subjects. She was guarded by a centurion, who raped her "sed deffendent de toutes ses forces tant comme elle pouoit" (although she struggled against him as much as she could) (Baroin and Haffen 69; Boccaccio, *Women* 161). The queen plotted revenge. When her assailant was preoccupied with weighing her ransom money, "la ditte dame en son langage, que les Rommains pas n'entendoient, commenda a ses sergens que eux ferissent Centurion et que la teste lui coupassent sans arrester" (she ordered her servants in her own tongue, which was unknown to the Romans, to kill [him] and cut off his head) (Baroin and Haffen 69; Boccaccio, *Women* 161). On her release, she presented the head to her husband.

Early-fifteenth-century images, such as one from the duke of Burgundy's version of Boccaccio's *Des cleres femmes*, generally indicate only the moment when the queen presents the head to her husband (Figure 14). The queen, elegantly dressed in liripipes and a crown, genuflects before

Figure 14. Galatian queen. From Boccaccio, *Des cleres femmes*. Paris, Bibliothèque Nationale de France, MS fr. 12420, fol. 111r.

her husband and gazes up at him as she offers him her rapist's head. To the far left are two subjects; one holds an ax to indicate that it was he who decapitated the centurion. Although some viewers, especially men, might have focused on the restoration of the king's honor and the beauty and submissiveness of his queen, others, especially women and perhaps even Christine herself, might have seen instead a triumphant rape victim, presenting her booty, the gruesome head of her attacker, while standing beside his headless corpse, whose bloody neck and bound wrists are displayed for the viewer. Unlike Lucretia, the Galatian queen acknowledges no guilt concerning the rape, but rather demonstrates by her actions that the rapist is solely at fault. Furthermore, she does not harm herself, but rather, after killing her rapist, remains not only alive, but triumphant.

The connection between Lucretia and the Galatian queen is not arbitrary. Boccaccio himself explicitly links the two, arguing that they were "de la compaigne Lucresse" (of the same breed) because they both preserved their "l'onneur de femme mariee" (womanly honor). The queen, like Lucretia, had proved with "osemans et grant peril de mort n'eust peu prouver, le corps violé, le pensee avoir esté sans violer" (great daring and great danger that in her defiled body the mind had been chaste). Boccaccio further argues that the queen presents the head of the rapist "c'estoit le pris et la venjance de la deshonneur qui l'avoit peu purgement, avoit avecques elles apporté" (as if it were the price of her dishonor and womanly shame) (Baroin and Haffen 70; Boccaccio, *Women* 161).

Not surprisingly, when Christine included the legends of Lucretia and the Galatian queen in her *Cité des dames,* she modified her source in several ways (Quilligan 156–61). Boccaccio organized his stories chronologically, but Christine grouped them thematically. She linked the two legends under the title "Contre ceulx qui dient que femmes veullent estre efforciees" (Refuting those men who claim women want to be raped) (Curnow, *"Cité"* 885; Christine, *City* 160). She also rewrote the narrative of the Galatian queen so that it is the queen herself, not a male subordinate, who kills the rapist. Christine transformed the Lucretia story as well, so that the motivation for the suicide is not to maintain honor, but to show the horror of rape. Christine ends her story by calling for the enactment of a law that requires the execution of rapists, a law that would be "couvenable, juste et sainte" (fitting, just, and holy) (Curnow, *"Cité"* 887; Christine, *City* 160–63).

In the *Cité des dames,* Christine adopts a different strategy than in the *Othea.* In both manuscripts, she revises the traditional rape script, but whereas in the *Othea* she refuses to portray women as rape victims, in the *Cité des dames,* she envisions them as able to inflict violence against rapists. This is precisely what Sharon Marcus advises:

Another way to refuse to recognize rape as a real fact of our lives is to treat it as a *linguistic* fact: to ask how the violence of rape is enabled by narratives...which derive their strength not from outright, immutable, unbeatable force but rather from their power to structure our lives by imposing cultural scripts. To understand rape in this way is to understand it as subject to change. (387)

In particular, as Marcus observes, "many current theories of rape present rape as an inevitable material fact of life and assume that a rapist's ability to physically overcome his target is the foundation of rape" (387). Marcus suggests an alternative, that we "begin to imagine the female body as subject to change, as a potential object of fear and agent of violence" (400). This is precisely what Christine does. She subverts the narrative tradition by constructing a new scenario in which a woman kills her rapist.

Manuscripts of the *Cité des dames* made directly under Christine's supervision do not illustrate the mythological subjects. But at least one manuscript suggests her influence, Spencer 33, a volume of Boccaccio's *Des cleres femmes* produced in Paris around 1470 (Belin; Friedman 3–17). This suggests a complex relationship: Christine's response to Boccaccio manuscripts in turn influenced later Boccaccio imagery. In contrast to the earlier Boccaccio illumination of the Galatian queen (Figure 14), the miniature in Spencer 33 constructs the queen as the dominant figure; she appears three times, more than any other character (Figure 15). The image shows several episodes depicted within a single landscape setting: in the left middle ground, the invasion of the Roman army; to the right, the centurion raping the queen within a tent; in the left foreground, a soldier weighing the ransom; and, at the right, the queen carrying her rapist's head. Although in the earlier Boccaccio illumination the queen carries the severed head on a platter, the way the evil Salome displays the head of Saint John the Baptist, in Spencer 33 the queen wraps the head in her skirt, an action visually recalling the heroine Judith. Furthermore, the scene takes place on a battlefield, which suggests the military idea of the decapitated head of the slain enemy as a victory trophy (Allaire 348–49).

But it is in the center foreground, the place of honor, that Christine's influence is most clearly revealed: now the *queen* is shown as the avenger. She comes from behind to forcefully decapitate the centurion. She jerks his head back and steadies it against her shoulder, as she slices his throat. In striking contrast to so many rape scenes, it is now the woman who is in control: it is *she* who forces *his* unwilling body close to hers. Such an image visualizes Christine's belief that women do not enjoy rape, and, following Christine's text, not Boccaccio's, it is the queen herself, not her servant, who acts as executioner. In the *Cité des dames* Chris-

Figure 15. Galatian queen. From Giovanni Boccaccio, *Des cleres femmes*. Paris, ca. 1470. New York, New York Public Library, Spencer 33.

tine rewrites Boccaccio; Spencer 33 demonstrates that her revisions were successful: at least one later artist visualized her version of the story, not Boccaccio's, even when illustrating a Boccaccio text.

The *Cité des dames* is often said to be Christine's most feminist work, and some scholars assume that her feminism gradually grew stronger as the *Querelle des femmes* radicalized her and her growing success lent her voice greater confidence and authority.[18] But Christine's development was not linear. In a letter dated 1400–1401, she argues that women never pursue or rape men:

Sans parler a volenté, de quelz grans crimes les peut on accuser? Et mesmes les pires et qui deçoivent, que peuent elles fere? . . . Te vont elles en ton hostel querir, prier ou prandre a force? (Hicks, *Débat* 54).

[Let us speak of the great crimes that one can attribute to even the worst and most deceitful of women. What do they do? . . . Do they go into your house to woo, pursue or rape you?]
(Baird and Kane 52).

Yet six years later, in the *Othea*, she constructs Bellerophon's stepmother as a sexual aggressor. Similarly, the clear condemnation of rape found in the *Cité des dames* is missing from the *Othea* illuminations, which were produced a few years later.

Bal has noted that the conception of rape changes from culture to culture, and Christine's ideas about rape in the *Cité des dames* must be viewed in the context of the time and place in which she lived. Unlike many of her contemporaries, Christine recognized that rape has both violent and sexual aspects, termed it an outrage, refused to distinguish between virginal and married victims (as medieval law codes often did), and called for the severe punishment of the rapist. Yet she also accepted the commonly expressed medieval belief that it is the loss of chastity that makes rape so abhorrent to women. She invokes the word "chastity" or its variants no less than four times in the Lucretia narrative alone. Furthermore, in the last chapter of the section devoted to rape, she praises a series of women—Hyppo, the Sicambrians, and Virginia—because they thought it better to die than to be raped.

Christine was not the only medieval writer to critically rewrite ancient rape narratives. Sheila Delany notes that John Gower's *Confessio Amantis*, dated 1390, includes antirape revisions of classical myths (Gower; Delany, "History" 198). Augustine, who is known to have been a source for the *Cité des dames* (Desmond, *Dido* 202), had long before condemned the Romans' rape of the Sabines (1.197).[19] Illuminations also criticized rape, such as a depiction of Dinah in a *Bible moralisée* that Christine may well have known (Wolfthal fig. 25). Nor were writers and artists the only ones to condemn rape. Ysablet des Champions forcefully denounced the men who had violated her. Nor was the story of the

Galatian queen totally divorced from actuality. In late-fourteenth-century Ghent, Callekin Van Laerne defended herself against a sexual assault by stabbing her assailant with a knife "immorally above and below." When her assailant sued for recompense, the judges showed him no sympathy, ruling that "he got what he deserved" (Nicholas 64).

Maureen Cheney Curnow has demonstrated that the *Cité des dames,* unlike the *Othea,* is pervaded by legal language ("'La Pioche'" 157–72). In fact, both Ysablet and Christine had close contacts with the legal profession; Ysablet's first and second husbands were lawyers and Christine's husband prepared legal acts (Prevenier 274; Curnow, "'La Pioche'" 157–72). Ysablet's knowledge of the law enabled her to establish a convincing case against her rapists; Christine, in the *Cité des dames,* interpreted the issue of rape much more in terms of law than she had in the earlier *Othea.* In the Lucretia narrative, Christine imagined a law that would require the execution of convicted rapists. But what actually happened to rapists in the fifteenth century? Ysablet's assailants, though convicted, served only two years and two months; they were released because her new husband granted permission in her name. Callekin Van Laerne's assailant wasn't even convicted. But Christine's response to society's leniency toward rapists was not one of pessimism. Rather than constructing the rape victim as futilely resisting her assailant with outstretched arms, like the Orethia or Helen of the *Ovide moralisé* (Figures 5 and 6)—and we might add other images, such as a Trojan woman raped by a Greek soldier (Meiss, *Limbourgs* 1: fig. 274) or an unpublished miniature of Europa in Spencer 33 or a Sabine attacked by a Roman (Figure 16)—Christine instead envisioned Daphne poking Apollo in the eye and the Galatian queen slitting her rapist's throat. Such representations reverse the usual power dynamics of gender relations, at least in the viewer's imagination. Women like Christine de Pizan, Callekin Van Laerne, and Ysablet des Champions helped keep alive the idea that there was a third possible response to rape: not to mourn, not to kill oneself, but to take justice into one's own hands; these women envisioned the possibility that women need not be helpless victims, but could ensure that justice prevailed. Christine in her manuscripts, Callekin on the street, and Ysablet in the courts made clear their opposition to rape. Their disruptions of the dominant discourse may have had little long-term effect. But Christine's complex and original voice served, at least for a brief moment, to disrupt the script that constructed women as powerless victims of male sexual aggression.

Notes

I am grateful to Pamela Sheingorn, Corine Schleif, and members of the National Endowment for the Humanities Institute for Sex and Gender in the Middle Ages for their many perceptive comments on previous drafts of this essay. I would also like to thank

Figure 16. Rape of the Sabines. From Augustine, *City of God.* Philadelphia, Museum of Art, MS 45-65-1, fol. 45r.

Brigitte Buettner and Eric Hicks for their suggestions. For the phrase quoted in the title ("the greatest possible sorrow"), see Christine, *City* 161; Curnow, *"Cité"* 885.

1. Brundage, *Law* 394, 529; Otis 22, 42, 68–69, 112.

2. Brondy, Demotz, and Leguay 364; Chiffoleau 182–83; Gauvard, *"Grace"* 813–17; Gauvard, "Violence" 1113–26; Nicholas 54, 62–67; Prevenier 263–84.

3. Hindman, *Christine* xix–xx, 13, 15–16; Willard, "View" 94–95; Ouy and Reno 227, 230.

4. Paris BNF, lat. 7907A, fols. 40, 40v, 44; Martin, *Térence* 10–11; Sterling 323; Meiss, *Limbourgs* 1:41–50.

5. Camille 321–24; Fleming 238–39, figs. 41–42; Wolfthal; Calin 123.

6. Hindman, *Christine*; Laidlaw, "Author's"; Ouy and Reno.

7. Meiss, *Limbourgs* 1:27; Hindman, *Christine* 82; Loukopoulos 76.

8. Reno, "Feminist" 2, 275; Campbell, *"L'Epître Othéa"* 52, 81; Loukopoulos 213, 245, 258, 262.

9. Gravdal 5; La Curne de Sainte-Palaye 9:53; Greimas, 537.

10. Huot, "Seduction" 363, 370; Reno, "Christine" 184; F. D. Kelly 69; Delany, "History" 203.

Diane Wolfthal

11. Hindman, *Christine* figs. 9, 26; Buettner, "Dressing" fig. 9; Lord 156, figs. 5–6.

12. Buettner, "Profane Illuminations" 86–88; Mellinkoff 1:203–4; Garnier 2:260–71; Régnier-Bohler 367–70.

13. Keuls 248, 251, fig. 228; Garrard 141–79; Even, "Castagno's" 37–42; Even, "Mantegna's" 8–20; Even, "Michelangelo's" 29–33.

14. Lucie-Smith 40; Sterling 375, 371; Meiss, *Boucicaut* fig. 97.

15. Reno, "Feminist" 271–76; Hindman, *Christine* 91, 99; Kellogg, "Christine" 115–16; Desmond, *Dido* 195–224.

16. Curnow, "*Cité*" 885, 887–88; Reno, "Feminist" 275; Campbell *L'Epître Othéa* 52, 81; La Curne de Sainte-Palaye 5:288; Greimas 252.

17. Quilligan 70; Boccaccio, *Women* 101–3; Baroin and Haffen.

18. Quilligan 37; Huot, "Seduction" 373; Schibanoff 91–97.

19. He did, however, initiate the debate about whether Lucretia had enjoyed being raped.

CHAPTER 4

Christine de Pizan and the Authority of Experience

Mary Anne C. Case

Christine de Pizan and the *Querelle des femmes* tradition of which she forms a part have much to contribute to ongoing debates in feminist jurisprudence. Her condemnation of the *Roman de la Rose*, for example, is an important precursor of the MacKinnon-Dworkin view of pornography. In responding to those who value the poem's literary merits over the adverse effects its message may have on the lives of women, Christine comes very close to asking, with Catharine MacKinnon, "If a woman is subjected, why should it matter that the work has other value?" (MacKinnon, *Feminist Theory* 202). More generally, Christine presages the "sameness" feminism of the legal academy by arguing on behalf of the exceptional woman who succeeds in traditionally male fields of endeavor and by insisting that differences between the sexes, apart from those directly connected to reproductive physiology, are the product of education and custom, not of nature. If women were given the education and opportunities available to men, Christine contends, they would achieve as men have. As Reason explains, "[S]e coustume estoit de mettre les petites filles a l'escolle et que suyvantment on les faist aprendre les sciences, comme on fait au filz, qu'elles appren / droyent aussi parfaittement et entendroyent les soubtilletez de toutes les ars et sciences comme ilz font" (If it were customary to send little girls to school like boys, and if they were then taught the sciences, they would learn as thoroughly and understand the subtleties of all the arts and sciences as well as boys) (Curnow, "*Cité*" 1.27.1).

Finally, in her use of narrative and personal experience to give voice to oppressed women, Christine may be one of the earliest proponents of what has come to be called outsider jurisprudence. Christine realized that what critical race theorist Mari Matsuda has called an "outsider" perspective is just as importantly an "insider" perspective—a characteristic of subordinated groups is that they are spoken about, described, and defined by "outside experts" from the dominant group; the "inside story" from a member of the group discussed can thus be a powerful corrective to the authority of these experts: as Christine pointed out, "tant comme voirement suis femme, plus puis tesmoignier en ceste partie que cellui qui n'en a l'experience, ains parle par devinailles et d'aventure" (as a woman...I can bear better witness than those who have no experience of the state but speak only in suppositions or in general terms) (Hicks, *Débat* 19). As modern-day jurisprudence struggles with the limits of the uses of narrative, it may be well to remember the uses to which our predecessors put women's stories. To this end, this essay will consider the various ways in which Christine claims authority for women's experience.

Does experience grant or rob one of authority? This is an old problem, both for the law and for feminism. The institution of the jury, for example, began with a perceived need to select persons with experience of both the local customs and the parties to whom they would be applied, but it has evolved to a point in which any prior experience at all with matters at issue is equated with bias or prejudice.[1] As experience has been devalued, it has also been associated with women. Thus, in a replay of the early modern battle between "experienced" midwives and "knowledgeable" physicians, cross-examining lawyers today ask physicians about their "knowledge," but ask nurses only about their "experience." "Experience in our society is considered second-class compared to knowledge" (Code 222). Yet, in recent years, feminists and critical race theorists in the legal academy have sought to recoup authority for experience. They remind us that experience is both logically and etymologically the root of expertise as they weigh in on the difficult epistemological problem of the extent to which one should privilege testimony by a speaker about that speaker personally or the group to which [s]he belongs.

Christine de Pizan lines up very clearly on one side of this debate: "[V]raiement je ne pouroie d'aucune chose repondre si proprement comme de mon propre fait: si puis en ceste partie tesmoignier verité de certainne science" (Nothing gives one so much authority as one's own experience. Hence, in this case I can speak the truth from certain knowledge), she writes to Pierre Col (Hicks, *Débat* 148). Like many other female participants in the *Querelle,* Christine seems to have been radicalized by her femaleness into doubting the established order as she realized that male authority was contradicted by her experiences as a woman. Certainly this is the path she charts for her fictional persona in the *Livre de la cité des dames.* At the beginning of that book, Christine the narrator is thrown into a deep depression by her realization that all authorities "concur in one conclusion: that women are inclined to and full of every vice" ("tous accordent une semblable conclusion, determinant les meurs femenins enclins et plains de tous les vices") (Curnow, "*Cité*" 1.1.1). The authority of men causes her to "detest [her]self and the entire feminine sex" ("deprisant soi meismes et tout le sexe feminin") (Curnow, "*Cité*" 1.1.1), until the personification of Justice reprimands her for putting less faith in "la certaineté de son estre" (the certainty of your own being) than in "ce que tu ne scez, ne vois, ne congnois autrement fors par pluralité d'oppinion estranges" (what you do not know or see or recognize except by virtue of a plurality of strange opinions) (Curnow, *"Cité"* 1.2.2). Throughout the book, Christine follows Justice's advice by repeatedly contrasting the negative pronouncements of male authorities with the positive female behavior she has personally experienced. She responds elsewhere to male critics of her partisanship and prejudice in favor of her own sex: "[M]on motif n'est simplement fors soustenir pure verité... et de tant comme voirement suis femme, plus tesmoingnier en ceste partie que cellui qui n'en a l'experience, ains parle par devinailles et d'aventure" (My motive is merely to uphold the truth... but as indeed I am a woman, I can bear better witness to the truth than those who have no experience of the state, but only speak through suppositions or in general terms) (Hicks, *Débat* 19; Christine, "Letter" 344). This emphasis on the authority of personal experience permeates Christine's contribution to the *Rose* debate.

There are interesting analogies between the constitution of women's voice in Christine's work and "voice" as that term has recently come to be used in the legal academy. By the emphasis she places on "when and where I enter" (Giddings), with "I" signifying the speaker both as perceiving subject and as member of a marginalized group, Christine echoes the concerns, not only of her modern counterparts, but also of critical race theorists. Compare, for example, the voice of Christine with that of Richard Delgado in "The Imperial Scholar" and "When Is a Story Just a Story?" Both are confronted with the problem of exclusion from the discourse about themselves when they eagerly turn from professional research on other subjects to face a stack of reading specifically about their group. In Christine's case, a borrowed book she picks up for relaxation after a hard day of study does not, as promised, speak well of women's worth, but rather, like the treatises of so many different learned men, accuses them of a multitude of faults and deficiencies; this is for her the last straw; she is overwhelmed by the discrepancy between her own view of women and that of the many men who purport to write authoritatively about women's nature.[2] Delgado, newly tenured, for the first time feels free to do work on civil rights; when he asks his research assistant to bring him the twenty leading articles in the field he is at first puzzled to see that they are not only all written by white men but also cite no minority scholarship.

The question that both then pose is "what difference does it make if the scholarship about the rights of group A is written by members of group B?" (Delgado, "Imperial Scholar" 566). As Christine puts it in her *Epistre au dieu d'Amours*, "[L]es livres ne firent / Pas les femmes, ne les choses n'i mirent / Que l'en y list contre elles et leurs meurs. /... Mais se femmes eussent li livre fait, / je sçay de vray qu'aultrement fust du fait, / Car bien scevent qu'a tort sont encoulpees. / Si ne sont pas les pars a droit coppees, / Car les plus fors prennent la plus grant part, / Et le meilleur pour soy qui pieces part" (The books were not composed by women nor did they record the things one may read against them.... Yet men write on, ... the ones who plead their cause without debate.... If women, though, had written all those books, I know that they would read quite differently for well do women know the blame is wrong. The parts are not apportioned equally, because the strongest take the largest cut and he who slices can keep the best) (Fenster and Erler 54, 55). For both race and sex, there is no neutral, disinterested standpoint; a double distortion results when one side simultaneously dominates the discourse and obscures its own partiality. As a corrective, both Delgado and Christine seek to give authority to the experience of the marginalized.[3] Like Delgado's marginalized scholars, Christine is able to tell stories different from the ones legal scholars normally hear. With her privileged access to the experience of being a woman and to the voices of other women, she can provide useful, concrete correctives to the misogynists' overgeneralizations. Not only does she discuss the problems elite women have in gaining access and respect in the public sphere, she also includes the voices of poor women whose abusive husbands spend the meager family income on drink, and those of battered women (Curnow, *"Cité"* 2.23.2) and women subject to rape (2.44.1) and sexual harassment (2.65.2). In each case, she uses the women's voices to contradict what male authorities have said about women in their situation (e.g., that women enjoy being raped); she urges changes, not only in public opinion, but in the law.

The corrective technique she endorses comes close to that of consciousness raising as practiced in the 1970s and as theorized by Catharine MacKinnon. That is, she begins by comparing the male experts' view of women with "moy meismes et mes meurs comme femme naturelle et semblablement discutoye des autres femmes que j'ay hantees: tant princepces, grandes dames, moyennes et petites a grant foison, qui de leurs graces m'ont dit de leurs privetés et estroittes penssees" (myself and my character and conduct as a natural woman and, similarly, I considered other women I spent time with, princesses, great ladies, women of the middle and lower classes, who had graciously told me of their most private and intimate thoughts) (Curnow, *"Cité"* 1.1.1). Although "pushed to see reality in [male] terms," she, too, becomes aware that "this denies their vantage point as women in that it contradicts at least some of their lived experience" (MacKinnon, *Feminist Theory* 114).

The contemporary question of false consciousness may also have its parallel in Christine. As Monica Green points out in chapter 8 of this volume, misogynists also tried to mobilize the authority of women's experience on their side of the *Querelle*. Thus, it is said of Trotula, teller of "women's secrets," that her "authoritative knowledge" of the "nature of women" has two sources, her personal experience of being a woman and her ability as a woman to induce other women to "disclos[e] their thoughts to her more readily than to any man." But, unlike Christine, whose experience conflicts with what the male authors she reads have said of women, Trotula "looked in her books and found there concordance with that which her nature revealed to her."[4] As Christine seeks knowledge as to women's nature from the same sources with a different result, it is not surprising that, as Green convincingly argues, Christine must de-authorize Trotula.

The epistemological progress to an authoritive position charted by Christine's narrator closely parallels what a group of psychologists have called "women's ways of knowing" (Code 252). She begins at the stage of "'received knowledge' where [she] believe[s] that truth comes from experts"; becoming aware that the experts contradict her own experience of being female, she progresses to the stage of "'subjective knowledge,' where [she] learn[s] to trust [her] inner sense."[5] But she does not stop there. As the figure of Reason leads her to apply the misogynists' own methodology to debunk them, she enters the stage of "procedural knowledge denominated 'the voice of Reason.'" Both in seeking contextual explanations for the misogynists' views and in listening to the voices and experiences of other women, she engages in the "separate and connected knowing," which is the second stage of "procedural knowledge." Finally, as her city is built and she can usher women into its shelter, Christine achieves "constructed knowledge" by "integrating the voices" of "personal experience . . . with a newfound capacity to evaluate and discriminate" (Code 252).

Once she has learned to evaluate its lessons, what does lived experience teach Christine? First, as noted above, that in debates between the sexes there can be no neutral, disinterested perspective. All perspectives, male as well as female, are situated. Although her culture insisted that women were defined and limited by their bodies, embodying the physical, incarnating carnality, Christine never lets us forget that men, too, inhabit bodies and that their opinions of women are similarly embodied and partial. For example, she used biographical data to explain the particular biases of certain male authors. Ovid, she noted, was castrated for his amorous indiscretions, Aristotle was deformed; of medieval misogynists, Cecco d'Ascoli was a homosexual and Matheolus impotent. No wonder these authors sought to malign the female sex—since they could not enjoy healthy relationships with women, they sought to spoil the fun for others (Curnow, "*Cité*" 1.9.2). The lesson Christine teaches about the partiality of all perspectives is one that lawyers are still only slowly learning. Thus, the prestigious law firm of Sullivan and Cromwell all too recently asked federal judge Constance Baker Motley to recuse herself from judging a sex discrimination lawsuit because as a woman she might be biased. Of course, as Motley acidly pointed out, males no less than females have a sex, and therefore a potential bias (*Blank v. Sullivan and Cromwell*, 418 F. Supp. 1 [S.D.N.Y. 1975]). As legal theorist Martha Minow reminds us, to remember that all "claims to knowledge bear the imprint of those making the claims" and all judging is done by "people who have genders, ... people who are themselves situated in relation to the differences they discuss," remains "a difficult commitment" (Minow 13).

Although Christine may take "experience as the origin of all knowledge," as Joan Wallach Scott criticizes historians for doing, she does not quite leave aside "questions about the constructed nature of experience, about how subjects are constituted as different in the first place, about how one's vision is structured" ("Experience" 22–40). Like many postmodern or deconstructionist scholars, Scott might criticize Christine's as an overly simple, comfortable and limiting view of difference. After all, her narrator comes perilously close to internalizing the male authorities' vision of woman as "ville chose ... tant abominable ouvrage ... monstre en nature" (vile creature, ... an abominable work ..., monstrosity in nature) (Curnow, "*Cité*" 1.1.1).[6]

But, as Reason reminds her, the second lesson of experience is even more important than the first. It is that one's situation never completely defines or confines one. Paradoxically, Christine uses a potentially multivalent parable to make this point: in counseling the narrator to cease privileging male authority over the authority of her own intellect and experience, Reason tells her, "Tu ressembles le fol dont la truffe parle, qui en dormant au moulin, fu revestu de la robe d'une femme, et au reveiller, pource que ceulx qui le mouquoyent luy tesmoignoyent que femme estoiet, crut myeulx leurs faulx diz que la certaineté de son estre" (You resemble the fool in the prank, who was dressed in women's clothes while he slept at the mill; because those who were making fun of him repeatedly told him he was a woman, he believed their false testimony more than the certainty of his own being) (Curnow, "*Cité*" 1.2.2). A postmodern would read the fool's story quite differently — as evidence above all for the constructed nature of gender. But, for Christine, clothes do not make the man, or the woman; neither does the cultural conditioning that goes with them. There is an essential nature, a "certainty" to one's own being, that may be occluded, but can never quite vanish. Yet a woman's authentic identity need have no resemblance to that which has been constructed for her — the voices of authority can no more transform a man into a woman than they can transform a woman into their negative image of her.

At first glance, Christine, like the critical race theorists, may have what to postmodern sensibilities may seem an overly simplistic view of the emergence of the marginalized voice. There seems to be for her, as there may not be for theorists such as MacKinnon, an "authentic" female voice, which can be heard clear as a bell once women learn to tune out the static of male discourse about them.[7] But Christine is no vulgar essentialist defender of "the eternal feminine."[8] Rather, for her, woman's essence is defined by potentiality. This should hardly be surprising, because, for Christine, women are, above all, human.[9] She asks men who would deceive women, "Qui sont fames? Qui sont elles? Sont ce serpens, loups, lyons, dragons, guievres ou bestes ravissables devourans et ennemies a nature humainne...?...Et par Dieu, si sont elles vos meres, vos suers, vos filles, vos fammes, et vos amies; elles sont vous mesmes et vous mesmes elles" (Who are women? Who are they? Are they serpents, wolves, lions, dragons, vipers, or raging devouring beasts, and enemies of human nature...?...And by God, if they are your mothers, your sisters, your daughters, your wives and your girlfriends, they are yourselves and you yourselves are they) (Hicks, *Débat* 139). Her own answer to the question is clear: "Et n'est mie doubte que les femmes sont aussi bien au nombre du peuple de Dieu et de creature humaine que sont les hommes, et non mie d'une autre espece" (There is not the slightest doubt that women belong to the people of God and to the human race as much as men, and are not another species) (Curnow, *"Cité"* 2.54.1). For Christine, women's humanity is essential; sex and gender are, to use philosophical parlance, accidents. She uses every opportunity to highlight this point, even through her choice of words. For example, in reproaching God for bringing her into the world in a feminine body, she notes that, had she been of the masculine sex, she might have been "de si gran parfeccion comme homme masle ce dit estre" (as perfect as a male human being is said to be) (Curnow, *"Cité"* 1.1.2).

Because women are human, no human activity is out of their reach. The gravamen of the *Cité des dames* is to "donne manifeste experience que femme qui a entendement est couvenable en toutes choses" (provide obvious demonstration that a woman with a mind is fit for all tasks) (1.11.1). Of all the lessons of experience Christine teaches, this emphasis on women's potential is one of the most important for contemporary feminist debates. Unfortunately, although Christine repeatedly endorses women's potential on a theoretical level, she stops well short of urging them to exercise it under ordinary circumstances. Thus, for example, although she insists that "se aucuns vouloyent dire que femmes n'ayent entendement souffisant pour apprendre les loys, le contraire est magnifeste par preuve de experience" (if anyone maintained that women do not possess enough understanding to learn the laws, the opposite is obvious from the proof afforded by experience) (1.11.1), she stops well short of urging more women to practice law. On the contrary, she notes that there are already "enough men who do so" ("il y a assez [des hommes] qui le fait"). It is these practical counsels of moderation that may most limit Christine's appeal and hence her influence in today's legal academy.[10]

Nevertheless, the message that women are human has been slow to infiltrate the law and the legal academy. According to feminist legal theorist Robin West, to this day "women are not human beings" under most legal theorists' definition of human because experiences such as pregnancy, which connect women to others, do not fit the theorists' definition of human beings as essentially separate from one another (West 1). Even more troublingly, on too many of those rare occasions when connection to others is valued in law and legal theory, it is so thoroughly gendered feminine and associated with difference that it risks being relegated to women and not expected of men (Du Bois et al.). Christine's approach to women's humanity could make a contribution to the current jurisprudential debate. Christine neither limits herself to expounding women's ability to succeed in traditionally masculine endeavors, as traditional sameness feminists do, nor relegates an ethic of care to a female sphere. Rather, even as she stresses women's successes and men's failures at connection to others, she sets forth the ethic of care as something fundamentally human to be expected of both men and women. Thus, for example, in book 2 of the *Cité des dames*, she praises women who care for their aged parents, but does not see this connection to others as a peculiarly feminine obligation "qualitatively beyond the pale of male effort" (West 40). It is, for her, instead, something all, including men, "ought to do," although men in her day and in ours do it less often than women. As Droiture says, "Regardes quans filz tu trouveras qui nourrissent pere et mere en leur viellesce doulcement et humblement, si que doivent faire. Je tiens que ilz sont clersemez" (See how many sons you will find who gently and humbly care for their father and mother in their old age as they ought to do. I maintain they are few and far between) (Curnow, "*Cité*" 2.7.1).

In book 3 of the *Cité des dames*, Christine again combines the best of both sameness and difference feminism as she reinforces the point that traditionally masculine and traditionally feminine qualities are both to be valued and are both within the capacities of women. Her hagiographies begin with those, such as Catherine of Alexandria, who excelled at the masculine art of learned philosophical argument ("comme grant clergesce et aprise es sciences, prist a prouver par raisons philosophiques que il n'est qu'un seul Dieu, ... noble, belle et de grant auttorité") (Curnow, "*Cité*" 3.3.1);[11] Margaret, who slew a dragon and wrestled a devil to the ground; and various saints whose preaching, philosophizing, and skillful arguments impressed their listeners. There follow lives of female saints who passed as male, performing in male guise feminine works of charity and humility (Curnow, "*Cité*" 3.12.1ff.). Christine concludes with the stories of holy women engaged in quite traditionally feminine acts of service, such as tending to the needs of male saints and of the poor (Curnow, "*Cité*" 3.18.2–7). Firmness and strength, humility and kindness, she stresses, are all represented in and all valuable to the City of Ladies.

Stressing women's essential humanity allows Christine to steer a safe course between the Scylla of vulgar essentialism and the Charybdis of social constructionism. Her implicit vision of women's human nature marks Christine as a Renaissance woman, for Christine's woman, like Pico's man, is "a creature of indeterminate nature," capable through self-fashioning of rising to the highest or degenerating to the lowest form of life (Kristeller 224). Christine attributes the same limitless potential to men, noting, in a passage with radical egalitarian implications, that nature has provided peasants and apparently savage people with the same qualities of mind as the most learned; only lack of education accounts for differences between them, as it does for differences between the sexes (Curnow, "*Cité*" 1.27.1).

That essence is potential for Christine has several important implications. Most notably, it allows her the neat trick of simultaneously distancing herself from notoriously bad women and getting rhetorical mileage out of the deeds of women famous for their positive accomplishments. It allows her to argue, in contrast to the misogynists, that women should be judged individually rather than lumped together as a group. But it also enables her to claim that the actions of extraordinary women are exemplary, not freakish.

What Christine, in common with early feminists of both sexes, realized is something that both self-consciously exceptional women and misogynists[12] seemed to miss — the true relationship between the exception and the rule. The exception does indeed prove the rule, not in the colloquial, corrupted sense of reaffirming it, but in the original, proper sense of "prove," that is testing its limits. For feminists like Christine, there are no monstrosities in nature; the behavior of any woman is that of "a natural woman," so that if any woman can x, then women can x (with x a placeholder for any activity traditionally closed to women as beyond their capacity, from leading an army to ruling a state, to producing great literature or art or philosophy, to keeping a secret). Such a woman becomes, not an exception, but an exemplar. This may explain the tendency of many *Querelle* texts to degenerate into catalogs of famous women. For the misogynists, such catalogs were collections of the monstrous, like the "Wunderkammer" so beloved of Renaissance collectors. But for feminists, the existence of a single woman who succeeded in any activity without extraordinary divine intervention proves conclusively that such an activity was within the natural capacities of womankind. If the assertion is of the form "women don't" or "women can't" or "women are," even a single counterexample suffices to disprove the assertion. Such an example can have powerful persuasive force, both logically and rhetorically.[13] It is thus the nature of their opponents' claim, more than any presumed tendency for women to prefer narrative and the concrete to analysis and the abstract, that causes the writers of the *Querelle*, both male and female, to focus on the concrete experiences and narrative histories of individual women.

The use Christine and other *Querelle* feminists of both sexes make of women's achievements contrasts sharply with the attitude, not only of male misogynists, but also of their female contemporaries. In insisting on the exemplary rather than the exceptional character of her own achievements and those of other women, Christine marks herself as one of what I shall call "knowing and singular" feminists, a tradition of independent female intellectuals in Renaissance and early modern Europe who became feminists out of the necessity of defending their own activities. I use this term, whose source is an essay by the seventeenth-century English author Lady Damaris Masham (Goreau 29), to refer to a number of women who were singular in their achievement, but also on occasion in their eccentricity and their isolation; whose knowledge was not only the sort of learning unusual for their sex, but also the cognitive autonomy necessary to persist in unusual views and lifestyles, and the awareness both that they needed to defend their whole sex in defending themselves and that such a defense was possible.

The first of those I have called "knowing and singular" feminists may not have been Christine, but rather a denizen of her City of Ladies, Novella, daughter of the noted fourteenth-century canonist Johannes Andreae.[14] Christine describes Novella as "si avant es loys que, quant [son pere] estoit occuppez... il envoyoit sa fille en son lieu lire aux escolles en chayere" (so educated in law that when [her father] was otherwise occupied... he would send his daughter in his place to lecture to his students) (Curnow, *"Cité"* 2.36.3). Novella is today chiefly remembered for the story Christine tells of her lecturing from behind a curtain, so that law students at the University of Bologna would not be distracted by her beauty. But she also may be the first woman on record as defending the equality of the sexes. Ironically, Novella appears as a defender of her sex in Jean Le Fèvre's "Livre de Leesce," the translator's apologetic preface to the *Lamentations* of Matheolus, the very book whose overall disparagement of women sends the narrator of the *Cité des dames* into the depression from which the three ladies rescue her. According to Le Fèvre, Novella undertook to prove scientifically in a public lecture that women are equal to men, putting forth more than seventy reasons so convincing that no man could dispute them: "La fille maistre Jehan Andrieu, / Qui lisoit les lois et les drois, / Se leva matin une fois, / Pour monstrer par vraye science / Devant tous en plaine audience / Que femme est a l'omme pareille, / Et proposa mainte merveille / Pour l'onneur des femmes garder / Et pour leur blasme retarder. / Tous le jour dura sa lecture / Jusques bien près de nuit obscure. / Des raisons mist plus de soissante, / voire, ce croy, plus de septante, / Et si bien y continua / Qu'homme ne l'en redargua" (Matheolus 2:1145–54).[15]

This tradition's most notable exemplars include not only Christine, but also Laura Cereta in the fifteenth century, Marie le Jars de Gournay in the early seventeenth century, Mary Astell in the early eighteenth, and Marie Olympe de Gouges in the late eighteenth. Those I have termed "knowing and singular" feminists were a distinct minority even among those inclined toward feminism in the years before 1800. In the first place, of course, most early advocates of feminist views, among them some of the most radical, were male. For the men, feminism was often little more than a game, a chance to show off their rhetorical skill by taking a position so contrary to common sense and received opinion that only an accomplished rhetorician could begin to find arguments in its favor. At most the defense of women may have offered some of the men a chance to play with dangerous ideas such as radical egalitarianism and skepticism about received authority in a comparatively safe format.[16] Even if the revolution to be brought about is one in thought alone and not in social structures, dangerous analogies to other forms of prejudice and oppression are possible: if women need be neither subject to men nor confined to their households, then perhaps nothing need be as it is—feminist sentiments bear within them an implicit critique of the entire political and social order, of ethnocentricism, of intellectual and religious authority. If all we believe with respect to women has no support beyond custom, is our opinion on other matters, our belief in the religion of our ancestors, for example, any more solidly based? If all laws and pronouncements with respect to women are the result either of blind prejudice or of the cynical conspiracy of men seeking to keep power in their own hands, what of the laws of church or state that keep prelates and princes in power? Is the inferiority of peasant to king, or of savage to civilized European, any more "natural" than that of woman to man? What early female feminists such as Christine add to the abstract arguments of the men are the lessons of experience and an urgency about real-world effects. The progress from male to female feminists in the *Querelle*, I would argue, is much like that from the mirror of Reason to the measure of Justice, that is to say from abstract argument intended at most to produce a clearer vision of sex/gender relations to rhetoric in a voice unambiguously intended, not only to persuade, but by persuading to change the conditions of women's lives.[17]

At the opposite extreme from the sometimes arid theorizing of male participants in the *Querelle* are those women Joan Kelly has called "feminists in action," persons who "rather than elaborating their ideas in writing, . . . used them to modify or organize social forms in which women might be free of male power and authority over them" (*Women* 65, 68).[18] What separates these "feminists in action" from the "knowing and singular" feminists is not only their absence of articulated feminist theory, but also their tendency to act in or form groups of women and their corresponding insistence on a peculiarly female sphere, albeit not the one set forth by antifeminists.[19] What I have called the "knowing and singular" feminists were those who moved from practice (usually as professional intellectuals) to theory (usually at well-developed length) when they saw no other means to overcome the prejudice that caused them to be viewed as eccentric outsiders.

Although separated by centuries, these women may fruitfully be viewed as part of a common tradition because of the great similarities in the problems they faced and the solutions they proposed. For each, the main obstacle to the professional opportunities they sought lay in the minds of men, not in the law. For example, unlike Myra Bradwell, who was prevented by the courts of her state from practicing law (*Bradwell v. Illinois*, 83 U.S. 130 [1873]), and unlike the women of France in the nineteenth century, who were excluded by Napoleonic law from institutions of higher learning (Title XIII, Moniteur 79, March 19, 1808), Christine faced no formal legal barrier to her participation in debates on public policy such as the *Querelle de la Rose*. Her chief obstacle lay in persuading her interlocutors that a woman could be worth listening to. This is a problem she shares, not only with the other early modern female authors I have called "knowing and singular" feminists, but also with female intellectuals today. The formal legal barriers that impeded women's professional opportunities in nineteenth- and early-twentieth-century America have gradually been dismantled. With the Supreme Court's decision last term mandating women's admission to the Virginia Military Institute, one of the last bastions closed to women has been forced open. But true acceptance as an equal and capable participant in public life requires a different form of persuasion than is necessary to win a mere court case about formal exclusion. It is with this form of persuasion that the experience of Christine and the other "knowing and singular" feminists can be most useful.

These women authors, unlike the men, became feminists by necessity, in self-defense. What they sought, above all, was the right to be taken seriously. Each pursued a career as an intellectual and wished to express her opinion on many other topics besides the equality of the sexes: Novella is said to have taught law; Christine, justly described as a polyscribator, was particularly concerned with the traditionally male field of political science; Laura Cereta's interests parallel those of male humanists; Marie de Gournay held controversial views on the development of the French language; Mary Astell was a theologian; and Olympe de Gouges wished a role in shaping the new French state. But each found that whatever she had to say on any subject could be dismissed by the male listener as "avec un sourire seulement, ou quelque branlement de tête, son éloquence muette aura dit: C'est une femme qui parle" (with just a smile or a shake of the head he seems to say with mute eloquence... "It's a woman talking") (Gournay 129). As women they were prohibited "all action, all judgment, and all true speech, and the authority to be believed, or at least to be heard" (Gournay 129).

In matters apart from women's rights, these "knowing and singular" feminists were considered by their contemporaries to have moderate to conservative views on issues ranging from religion and politics to grammar:[20] Christine is alternately praised and condemned by modern scholars for counseling moderation to those disadvantaged by the status quo (Delany, "Mothers"), Marie de Gournay fought a rearguard action against the reforms of the French Academy and was satirized in her lifetime as a specter from a vanished age, Mary Astell was a pious Tory, and Olympe de Gouges's support of constitutional monarchy at the height of the French Revolution led to her execution. But each was prompted by her experiences as a woman to radicalism on the question of the equality of the sexes.

Like Christine, the "knowing and singular" feminists saw in themselves a natural inclination toward learning (Curnow, "*Cité*" 2.36.4) that informed their behavior from an early age. Most were eldest children (Novella, Christine, Cereta, Gournay) and were encouraged in this love of learning by a father to whom they were quite close (Novella, Christine, Cereta) or by a more distant, admired father figure (Gournay by Montaigne, Olympe de Gouges indirectly by the man she claimed was her natural father, the poet Le Franc de Perpignan). By contrast, their mothers and the women around them often attempted to prevent them from engaging in "unfeminine" pursuits, perhaps out of fear the girls would grow into misfits, perhaps out of envy or a firmly inculcated sense of female inferiority. Droiture cites as the major obstacle to Christine's being more involved in learning "the feminine opinion of [her] mother... who wished to keep [her] busy with spinning and silly girlishness following the common custom of women" ("l'oppinion feminin de ta mere, qui te vouloit occuper en fillasses selonc l'usage commun des femmes") (Curnow, "*Cité*" 2.36.4). Maternal opposition forced Gournay to teach herself Latin and Greek in secret; her mother prescribed a sedative to cure her of her enthusiasm for Montaigne's essays and only accepted Gournay's high opinion of them after it was seconded by distinguished male authors. Accused by some women of passing off her father's Latin epistles as her own, ignored by others to whom she wrote for support, Laura Cereta directed one of her bitterest invectives against "women who disparage learned women" (Cereta, "Lucilla Vernacula" 85–86). Early personal experience helped many of the women realize that men were not the only ones who needed to be convinced of woman's worth.[21]

Among the women they needed to convince were not only those who, like their mothers, shunned education and achievement, but also many of their most learned and prolific female contemporaries. These other accomplished women allowed themselves to be isolated on a pedestal from the rest of their sex. Succumbing to the dangerous flattery of men who called them "marvels," "prodigies," "extraordinary," "miraculous," "exceptional," even "freaks of nature," they often denied that other women could or should follow their example. Thus, Anna Laetitia Barbauld, an eighteenth-century English bluestocking, after recommending that women not be sent to school, but rather that they learn only what their husbands or brothers chose to teach them, observed, "You may think that having myself stepped out of the bonds of female reserve in becoming an author, it is with an ill grace I offer these sentiments, but my situation has been peculiar, and I would offer no rule for others" (Williamson 3). By contrast, Christine and other feminists insist that their own achievements, like those of all other "extraordinary" women, should be seen as exemplary, not exceptional. They saw the potential for themselves and other women inherent in the achievements of great women of the past. They also saw the danger in acknowledging themselves to be "extraordinary." "You pretend to admire me as a female prodigy," wrote Laura Cereta,

> but there lurks sugared deceit in your adulation. You wait perpetually in ambush to entrap my lovely sex...[S]howing your contempt for women, you pretend that I alone am admirable because of the good fortune of my intellect....Do you suppose, O most contemptible man on earth, that I think myself sprung from the head of Jove? I am a school girl, possessed of the sleeping embers of an ordinary mind...conscious of my obligation to defend my sex. For absolutely everything—that which is within us and that which is without—is made weak by association with my sex." (Cereta, "Bibulus Sempronius" 81–84)

By defending their sex, therefore, Christine and the other female authors in the *Querelle* were defending themselves. Their claim was that experience with even one capable woman should persuade doubters of the natural capabilities of the entire sex.

The epistemological progress of the women of the *Querelle* was, in a sense, the reverse of the men's. The more radical of the men of the *Querelle* were no less skeptical of received authority than the women. But whereas the women seemed to have learned skepticism from the discrepancy between their own experience and authoritative pronouncements on women,[22] the men generally began with a broadly based inclination toward skepticism and then applied it to received wisdom on women as to a test case.[23]

The *Querelle* authors all begin by reacting against a misogynist tradition in which male authors rely in large part on the authority conferred by their maleness and on universal consensus to prove women's inferiority. For the misogynists, male authors are presumptively to be valued, women's voices presumptively to be discounted (they lack authority, they are "only women"). But the cumulative result of the work of the male and the female defenders of women comes close to reversing all these notions of authority. The male authors, true to their skeptical roots, used reasoned argument to undermine the authority, both of other men and of general consensus; they demonstrated that the misogynists, though more likely to be believed, are not more likely to be right. Women like Christine then used the new authority of their own experience to prove their case; instead of being discounted, the women's voices thus become privileged as the male voices lose their privilege.

This process of authorizing women's experience follows the model endorsed by Richard Rorty in his Tanner lecture advising feminist legal theorists to become pragmatists. In building her city of ladies, Christine has, as Rorty suggests, used her "imagination . . . to hear [her]self as the spokesperson of a merely possible community, rather than as a lonely, and perhaps crazed outcast from an actual one" (Rorty 240). Although she began, as Rorty predicted, "torn, split, between the men's description of [herself] and whatever alternative descriptions [she has] given to [her]self" (Rorty 244), she was able to achieve "semantic authority over [her]self" through the prophetic act of "creating [women's] experience by creating a language, a tradition, and an identity" that can be shared with other women (Rorty 238). The community Christine imagined has space within it, not only for the exemplary women with which she peopled it, but for the generations of women who followed. Although it is a pity we may still need its shelter from those who yet deny women's humanity, Christine's City has, in Rorty's terms, expanded the logical space for us all.

Notes

1. Compare Constable's discussion of the medieval jury with reports of the selection of the jury in Oliver North's criminal trial in Moran and d'Errico. Because the judge in the North case excluded all those who had "heard or read" of North or the Iran-contra issue, his jury was an unrepresentatively uninformed lot whose ignorance supposedly guaranteed its impartiality.

2. The book is the 1371 French translation of the late-thirteenth-century Latin *Lamentations* of Matheolus. The progress from Matheolus to Christine can be read as a microcosm of the *Querelle des femmes* in that it is one from male misogynist author to male defender of women to female feminist. Matheolus was a cleric who blamed his marriage to a widow for all the troubles in his life and wrote a virulently misogynistic warning to other men tempted to follow his example. His *Lamentations* were translated into French in 1371 by Jean Le Fèvre, who accompanied them with his own apologetic defense of women, the "Livre de Leesce," which includes the story of Novella cited below. When Christine's source informed her Matheolus spoke well of women, [s]he doubtless had in mind Le Fèvre's accompanying text.

3. Delgado speaks favorably of social sciences in which "minority status constitutes virtually a presumption of expertise" ("Imperial Scholar" 564).

4. *Placides et Timéo,* cited by Green in this volume, chapter 8, n. 58.

5. Like Christine, the women in the modern survey claim that "the turning point often was a vividly remembered, precise moment in time" (Mary Field Belenky et al. 56). They, too, then come to experience "conflict between the absolute dictates of the authorities and the women's own subjectivism," first as "an attempt to stifle their inner voice" (Belenky et al. 88).

6. Before dismissing this negative reaction as mere false consciousness, it is important to note that it occurs after Christine has observed, in what may be deemed a consciousness-raising session with other women, the great discrepancy between the authorities' view of women and women's own experience.

7. MacKinnon has been quoted as saying she found the concept of an authentic self "unhelpful" (Colker 221). MacKinnon's image, by contrast, is that of "his foot on her throat," denying women "the power to develop what our [values] really would be." Even if the foot should be removed, the vocal cords might remain bruised, bearing the marks of oppression. MacKinnon is thus reluctant to identify women with any voice we now can hear. For her, it may be "male dominance that has created people in these images." For her, then, sexism may, for now at least, run deep and ineradicable, contaminating even the most thoroughly raised consciousness in this male-dominated society: "No interior ground and few if any aspects of life are free from male power" (DuBois et al.).

8. Earl Jeffrey Richards demonstrates this eloquently and at length in "Rejecting Essentialism."

9. This was not an entirely obvious and uncontroverted point in Christine's day, when participants on both sides of the *Querelle* made much of the Council of Mâcon's alleged debate on women's humanity. The debate remained salient through the French Revolution, when otherwise anticlerical legislators invoked the Council of Mâcon to justify denying women the vote.

10. The injunction in *Cité des dames* 2.19.2 that wives be submissive to their husbands is similarly off-putting to the modern feminist reader. It, too, marks Christine as uncomfortably willing to come to terms with the practical realities of the status quo, notwithstanding the radical implications of her theoretical stance.

11. The literal translation of the passage is "Of great scholarly attainment and learned in the sciences, [she] proceeded to prove on the basis of philosophical arguments that there is only one God.... [She was] noble, beautiful, and authoritative."

12. And the occasional Supreme Court Justice; see *Bradwell v. Illinois*, 83 U.S. 130, 141 (1872), (Bradley, J., concurring) (denying a woman license to practice law on grounds that "the rules of civil society must be adapted to the general constitution of things, and cannot be based on exceptional cases").

13. Even the appellate court in *E.E.O.C. v. Sears, Roebuck*, 839 F.2d 302, 311 (7th Cir. 1988) acknowledged the power of individual anecdotal counterexamples. In that notorious case, the defendant successfully argued that women generally lacked interest in commission sales jobs. Testimony was confined to experts (albeit themselves female) talking about women; no woman who had been kept from the disputed job was called to testify as to her interest in it. "We do not agree that examples of individual instances of discrimination must be numerous to be meaningful," said the appeals court. "Even a few examples would have helped to bring 'cold numbers' convincingly to life."

14. While I concede that the stories told of Novella may well be apocryphal, I nevertheless find it intriguing to see them accepted by contemporaries and near contemporaries. To Novella herself, I am, however, unwilling to concede mere apocryphal status, despite the remarkable coincidence of her name with that of her father's most famous work, the *Novella super decretalium.*

15. A literal translation might read, "The daughter of Master Johannes Andreae, who read law, got up one morning to demonstrate by true learning before all in a public lecture that woman is equal to man, and she presented many marvels to preserve the honor of women and to diminish their blame. Her lecture lasted all day until almost nightfall. She put forth more than sixty reasons, indeed, I believe, more than seventy, and went on so well that man could not dispute them."

16. There is a radical undercurrent in the defense of women. Serious commitment to the notion that the sexes are equal might lead to a total restructuring of society; women might indeed, despite Poulain de la Barre's reassurance, rise up against men who do not treat them as their equals or partners (Poulain de La Barre). Although he stops short of demanding a change in the laws, Agrippa of Nettesheim fulminates against "the tyranny and ambition of men [who] have seized the upper hand, contrary to divine and natural law; ... women's original liberty has today been forbidden them by unjust laws, suppressed by custom and usage, extinguished by education" (Agrippa von Nettesheim 534).

17. I do not by any means intend to suggest that reason is a peculiarly male attribute nor (*pace* Carol Gilligan) that women embody an ethic of justice. Rather, the contrast I wish to draw is less between reason and justice than between a mirror and a measure, that is between a tool for reflection and one for action.

18. Joan Kelly, who sees in these women the precursors of "the women of the French and nineteenth century revolutionary movements," specifically mentions the Beguines and the seventeenth-century English and American female preachers, such as Anne Hutchison and Margaret Fell Fox (J. Kelly, *Women*). To these I would add, in the religious sphere, among others, the thirteenth-century Guiglielmites and other heretical groups favoring admission of women to the hierarchy or the advent of a female messiah, the women of the more radical Continental Protestant sects, and mystics such as Jacqueline-Aimée Brohan, who thought eighteenth-century France could only be saved by faith in women. In the secular sphere, I would add, for example, the Précieuses, who set up an elaborate female language as a counterpoint to the spare purity of the all-male French Academy's contemporaneous attempt at language reform and whose equally elaborate drawing-room rules of conduct for the "accomplished woman" were designed as a counter to "those tiresome maxims of our forefathers who approve of women only in the home and . . . who prefer the rags of the housekeeper to the ornaments and proprieties of a coquette" (de Pure, *La Prétieuse*). Across the Channel, the Précieuses had their counterparts in the the "matchless Orinda's" "Society of Friendship" and the Bluestockings.

19. Nor would I group together all those women who did write on feminist issues. I would exclude, for example, all those whose depiction of women's oppression is expressed only obliquely, through fiction (for example Marguerite de Navarre, Mme Riccoboni); those whose demands extended no further than improved education for their sex (for example, Anna Maria van Schurman, Amalia von Justi Holt); and those who wrote forcefully in opposition to male denigration, in particular in love relationships, but appear to have expressed little active interest in challenging the boundaries of the feminine sphere (for example, Jane Anger and the respondents to Swetnam).

20. This was not true of the men. Many of the most radical of the early male advocates of women tended to hold other views deemed by their contemporaries to be more than mildly subversive—Agrippa of Nettesheim, for example, was accused of heresy; Poulain de la Barre, a French Catholic priest in a time of official persecution of Protestants, converted to Calvinism and fled to Geneva; heretics such as the Lollard Walter Brut defended women's authority to preach, teach, and administer the sacraments. On the latter, see Blamires et al. 250.

21. Similarly, some critical race theorists find themselves in bitter opposition, not only to the white power structure, but also to blacks "willing to minimize the effects of racism" and disparage other blacks (Derrick Bell 114).

22. The exception may be Gournay, who applies the established skeptical methods of her covenant father Montaigne.

23. Agrippa of Nettesheim's's most famous and controversial work *De Vanitate* (*On the Vanity and Uncertainty of the Sciences*) was condemned by several theological faculties for its skeptical attacks on established authorities and the moral order (see Nauert). Poulain, a Cartesian, explicitly chose the commonly held belief in the inequality of the two sexes as a test of his principles, "afin qu'aprés avoir démontré qu'un sentiment aussi ancien que le Monde, et aussi universel que le Genre humain, est un préjugé ou une erreur, les Sçavans puissent etre enfin convaincus de la necessité de juger des choses par soi-meme, aprés les avoir bien examineés, et de ne s'en point rapporter a l'opinion ni a la bonne foy des autres hommes si l'on veut éviter d'estre trompé (So that after demonstrating that an opinion as ancient as the world, as widespread as the earth, and as universal as the human species is a prejudice or an error, knowledgeable people will finally be convinced of the necessity of judging things (after having carefully examined them) for themselves and of not abiding by the opinions or testimonies of others if they want to avoid being deceived) (Poulain de La Barre 10).

PART II

⁜

Situated Knowledges

Je ne suis nulle fois certaine car se certainete y avoit ce ne seroye mie.

[At no time am I certain; if there were certainty, I would not be there.]
—Opinion, *Avision 2*

CHAPTER 5

✣

"Perdre son latin"
Christine de Pizan and Vernacular Humanism

Thelma Fenster

Recent criticism on Christine de Pizan has renewed an earlier query: did Christine know Latin, and if so, how well? In part, however, the question invites worn-out conclusions about men and Latin, women and the vernacular and the oral, and in the end we may wonder about its strict relevance to Christine studies. Early French humanists such as Jean de Montreuil, Gontier Col, Nicolas de Clamanges, Ambrogio Migli, Jean Muret, and others sought to achieve eloquence in Latin. Christine, on the other hand, has left a body of writing only in French. A good deal of her work participated in a rival movement, encouraged by the growing consciousness of a national language (see Ouy, "Paris" 85–93, esp. 90): the desire to install French as a language of learning. Christine began her career writing French poetry but later turned to writing in prose, which she came to prefer. She transposed into her prose works passages from the French translations of Aristotle, John of Salisbury, Valerius Maximus, and others, utilizing both the translations per se and the translator's commentary. She wrote in a prose that can be complicated and daunting, and scholars have for the most part avoided studying it.[1] Yet Christine's urge to disseminate the substance of Latin writing and her confidence that it could be transmitted in French recall the impulse that had stamped the reign of Charles V, who ruled from 1364 to 1380, while Christine was growing up. As a humanist in the vernacular, she broke ground principally by transposing parts of a formerly Latin culture, the one rendered into French by Charles V's team of translators, and creating a new one in the process, a hybrid culture that brought together the closed world of masculine, Latin letters and the more open and accessible arena of vernacular scholarship. Nowhere is this clash more sharply foregrounded than in the Debate of the *Rose,* conducted alternately in French and Latin letters.

In that discussion of Jean de Meun's *Roman de la Rose,* Christine de Pizan and Jean Gerson, on one side, and the three Latinists and humanists, Jean de Montreuil and the brothers Gontier and Pierre Col, on the other, engaged in several simultaneous confrontations, not all of them explicit: literary, social, political, ethical, and, not least, gender and linguistic. Given that Christine's opponents wrote both in French and in

Latin while she herself wrote only in French, it is tacitly assumed in some modern scholarship that Christine did so only because she lacked sufficient training in Latin. In that reading, her use of French could have earned validation only with the putative victory that came of having made the letters public. Early modern scholars such as Gaston Paris and P. G. C. Campbell (*"L'Epître Othéa"* 132 n. 1) in fact doubted that she knew any Latin but provided no evidence. The discussion has been inadequate, however, because it has invoked only one, somewhat imperious, yardstick to measure what it meant to "know" Latin at the turn of the fifteenth century, namely, clerical capacity to read and comment upon learned Latin texts. In view of the erosion in Latin preparation and the rise of the vernacular that occurred over the fourteenth century, there must have existed in late medieval France something of a hierarchy in Latin knowledge, perhaps resembling the one that Paul Gehl has described for medieval Florence (204–5). If so, it is questionable whether Christine and her contemporaries would have held quite the same idea of Latin competency as the one some of her modern interpreters have put forward.

Christine herself may have encouraged hasty, negative conclusions by explaining as she did in the *Livre de la cité des dames* (1405) that her mother had prevented her from obtaining the education she had hoped for: "Mais l'oppinion femenine de ta mere, qui te vouloit occupper en fillasses selon l'usage commun des femmes, fu cause de l'empeschement que ne fus en ton enfance plus avant boutee es sciences et plus en parfont" (But the feminine opinion of your mother, who wanted to keep you busy with girlish pursuits, according to a woman's usual occupations, was the reason that in your childhood you weren't set to acquiring greater and deeper knowledge) (British Library, Harley 4431, fol. 340v; Curnow, *Cité* 2.36.4). Later, in her *Avision,* Christine says that while her husband and father lived, "les ruminacions du latin et des parleures des belles sciences et diverses sentences et polie rethorique" (sounds of Latin and the discourses of fine learning, and various sayings and polished rhetoric) reached her ears, but she claims to have retained little of it. Although inclined from birth toward such subjects, the responsibilities of a young wife, including childbearing, and the natural flightiness of youth were to blame (161). Nonetheless, several scholars have conjectured plausibly that Christine had a reading knowledge of Latin, at least: her use of *florilegia* such as the *Manipulus florum* by Thomas Hibernicus, available to her only in Latin,[2] and the need for knowledge of Latin to read the letters in the Debate are two examples (*City* xxvii). More recently, however, the evidence has become concrete: Liliane Dulac and Christine Reno have shown that in her *Avision* Christine translated about twenty paragraphs from the first book of Thomas Aquinas's *Commentary on Aristotle's Metaphysics* ("L'Humanisme").[3] In a later article, they add that Christine translates faithfully and in the order of the Latin text ("Traduction et adaptation").[4] Liliane Dulac's further work on Christine's *Heures de Contemplation* has revealed Christine's own claim to have herself translated that work from Latin into French.[5]

In spite of that evidence, whether Christine could write in Latin is not known. She would not have been the only female Latinist among her contemporaries, had training in composition been given to her. Several generations of Italian humanist women, from the late fourteenth century on, wrote a highly accomplished Latin and left a body of work (see King and Rabil). In particular, Maddalena Scrovegni, who lived from 1356 to 1429, and was therefore as contemporary with Christine as a modern scholar might hope, wrote Latin letters. We are left to wonder whether Tommaso da Pizzano, the well-placed Italian-born astrologer who gave his sons a Latin education (and we know that girls were often educated with their brothers), failed to provide a Latin tutor for his clever daughter, even though he took great pleasure in her inclination to learn (*Cité*). Did Christine's mother really prevail to such an extent? Or was Christine's participation in a vernacular learned culture as much a matter of choice as of anything else? Sooner or later, we must ask what she would have gained had she written in Latin.

The improving fortunes of the French language during Christine's childhood in France certainly made writing on serious subjects in the vernacular less of a demerit than it would have been earlier. The diglossia of the French Middle Ages had of course privileged Latin. If French was the vehicle of everyday spoken exchange, poetic expression, preaching, historiography, civil administration, and customary law, Latin was the language of religious and institutional ritual, learning, and school instruction (Lusignan, *Parler vulgairement* 35), and it served as a lingua franca among nations (Lusignan, "Le Latin" 265). *Grammar* was the study — the theory[6] — of Latin, an immutable language in comparison with French or any other vernacular. Medieval scholars thought Latin was endowed with sapiential and sacred qualities, like Hebrew and Greek (Copeland 105; Lusignan, "Autorité et notoriété" 185). But increasingly, intellectual court circles had begun to laicize. Philippe le Bel was the first French king to alter the exclusively ecclesiastical quality of the chancellery when he appointed Pierre Flotte, knight and lord of Revel, as chancellor (Morel 8); he also began to admit laymen into the corps of notaries (Morel 55). Jacques Monfrin[7] and Serge Lusignan[8] have raised salubrious doubts about how well king Charles V and others, including even clerics, knew classical Latin. In two instances Christine herself praised Charles's Latin. In the *Livre du chemin de long estude* she says that

Combien que le latin tout emple
Entendist, les voult il avoir
Afin de ses hoirs esmouvoir

A vertu qui pas n'entendroient
Le latin, si s'y entendroient.
                    (Lines 5022–26)

[Although he understood Latin well, he wanted to have them [the translations] so that his heirs might be moved to virtue, [so that] those who did not understand Latin would become knowledgeable.]

Again in the *Livre des fais et bonnes meurs du sage roy Charles V,* she says that "la sage administracion du pere le fist introduire en lettres moult souffisement, et tant que competemment entendoit son latin et souffisamment sçavoit les rigles de gramaire" (the wise upbringing of his father [Jean le Bon] introduced him very amply to letters, and such that he understood his Latin competently and knew the grammar rules sufficiently well) (16). But then, in that same biography of Charles V, she explains: "[E]t, pour ce que peut-estre n'avoit le latin, pour la force des termes soubtilz, si en usage comme la lengue françoise, fist de theologie translater plusieurs livres de saint Augustin" (And perhaps because, by virtue of the learned vocabulary, he did not know Latin as well as French, he had several books of Saint Augustine's theology translated) (13). As against that observation, Christine herself, as we recall, actually translated paragraphs from Thomas Aquinas's *Commentary on Aristotle's Metaphysics,* which no doubt contained many *termes soubtilz* for the translator.

Under Charles V, in fact, French had succeeded in encroaching upon the hegemony of Latin.[9] During his reign, French became premier in the practice of power, according to Françoise Autrand. In law, although certain bilingual practices remained in place, actual legislative texts in Latin became rare. Most of the king's statutes, mandates, and letters were in French, as was his will. He practiced a veritable "politique délibérée de diffusion de la culture et de promotion de la langue française" (intentional politics of cultural diffusion and promotion of the French language), for his aim, and that of his learned friends, was "la promotion de la langue française dans l'activité intellectuelle et dans la réalité politique. Parler, faire parler français, même pour la science, la philosophie, le pouvoir, telle est leur volonté" (the promotion of the French language in the intellectual sphere and in political exchange. To speak French, to have French spoken, even for learning, for philosophy, for the exercise of power— such was their desire) (Autrand, "Culture" 103, 105).[10]

Chief among Charles V's endeavors to use the French language toward strengthening the monarchy was the translation project he authorized, a continuation, but on a far greater scale, of his father's policy and of even earlier trends. Thanks to Charles V, canonical medieval philosophical, theological, scientific, and political works made their way into French from Latin. These included Aristotle's *Politics* and *Ethics,* Augustine's

City of God, the Bible, and John of Salisbury's *Policraticus.*[11] Charles was fortunate to have among his translators the learned and astute Nicole Oresme. Early in his association with Charles, Oresme, who had been educated at the College of Navarre, where Latin was the unique recognized language of learning, saw the royal predilection for French and understood its political implications. As of 1360, when he rallied to Charles's side, Oresme wrote only in French (Autrand, "Culture" 105).[12] Of all the king's translators, he alone discussed the political value of putting knowledge into French, and in his commentary to Aristotle's *Politics* he interpreted Aristotle in ways that could further French monarchic interests. Because translation into French generally obviated the need for explication that the Latin text required, Oresme had greater opportunity to make the *Politics* "relevant." This he did, according to Jean Dunbabin, by arguing for restrictions on the power of the papacy and on the way ecclesiastical benefices were distributed and by writing against the election of kings and in favor of hereditary succession; finally, he preferred consent by a group composed of qualified aristocratic men (730–32).

Oresme provided Charles V with the theoretical underpinning for the use of French over against Latin. In the *Excusacion et commendacion de ceste oeuvre* (Apologia and justification for this work) that accompanies his translation of Aristotle's *Ethics* and *Politics,* both completed in the early 1370s,[13] Oresme said it was good to translate such works for *le bien public* (the public good) and because their study creates *affeccion et amour au bien publique* (love for the public good). Unlike a number of other translators who thought French impoverished compared with Latin, he argued that French was "the richest and most precise language of the age," that it was "well equipped to render even the most complex thoughts," and that it could "play a role equivalent to the one that Latin had played in antiquity." As once "les sciences" had been translated from Greek into Latin, so now they would be translated from Latin into French; as Greek had been to Latin, Latin would now be to French.[14]

While Charles V lived, the program flourished. But by the time of the Debate of the *Rose,* Charles VI was king of France. Charles VI took far less interest in scholarship than his father had, and his unfortunate bouts of insanity increasingly made him an unfit ruler. Even so, the translation program had not been entirely forgotten: in 1404, for example, Nicolas de Gonesse completed the translation of Valerius Maximus's nine-book *Dicta et facta memorabilia,* of which the first volume, containing books 1–4, had been offered to Charles V in 1375 by Simon de Hesdin, who had stopped working at book 7. But under the influence of Italian humanism, which had begun to take hold in France as a result of Petrarch's great prestige there, Latin once again prevailed among intellectuals, especially among the group of royal secretaries. Jean de Montreuil and Gontier and Pierre Col counted themselves among the humanists. But indeed, humanism's preoccupation with Latin style, ever increasing, would later lead to a debate between *forme* and *fond.* For the humanists, as Jacques Le Goff has observed (179), form was all, while for the earlier scholastics it was the servant of thought. Le Goff states that if scholastic Latin was already moribund, humanist Latin would deal it a death blow, relegating it to the status of an elite treasure (180; see also Hicks, Introduction xxxiv).

The Debate of the *Rose*

The Debate thus occurred at a watershed moment in the social history of the French language, when French intellectuals were closing the window that Charles V had opened to the vernacular as a language of learning. Jean de Montreuil was already forty-five years old in 1401, when, at the instance of his friend, Gontier Col, he read the *Roman de la Rose* for the first time. Montreuil wrote an enthusiastic *Rose* treatise, exceptionally, in the French language (*gallica scriptione;* he composed his other letters in the Debate in Latin), which he then sent to someone identified only as a *notable clerc* (worthy cleric) and to Christine de Pizan. Eric Hicks has pointed out that by offering his treatise in French to both, Montreuil willed it a "double destiny," the private one of Latin correspondence and the public one of the French language (Introduction xxxiii). Modern Debate scholars such as Hicks, Pierre-Yves Badel (413), and Helen Solterer emphasize that Latin letters constituted a private, literate exchange, while French ones, by their very accessibility to a larger audience, were public vehicles. But Montreuil, although he wrote in French, came to worry that others might accuse him of lack of seriousness or even of buffoonery for having done so (Montreuil's letter 119 [*Ex quo nugis*], in Hicks, *Débat* 30). No doubt he did not expect the distribution of his treatise to become as wide as it did when Christine presented a dossier of Debate letters to Queen Isabeau. His treatise later disappeared; was that due in part to the status of the French language in humanist bilingualism, as Hicks suggests (Introduction xxxiii)?

The debate of course centered upon questions of language and social responsibility, on what an author allegedly intended and what various audiences heard. To add to that, both Christine and Jean de Montreuil betray a self-consciousness about their own language choices and abilities, and they do so in at least equal measure, albeit for different reasons. Christine's writing up to that point had consisted in lyric and narrative poetry; the debate format invited her to write in prose. She had often expressed views in her poems that she would take up later in prose, but this was the first opportunity, and possibly the first time, that she wrote and "published" in French prose.[15] Her opponents were more experienced at such literary debate, but in Latin rather than in French. Now she, too, would participate in a literary debate, obliging her interlocutors to do in the vernacular what they considered most appropriate in Latin; this would become the first recorded literary debate in French. As for Montreuil, Badel has observed that he had never before written an original work in French: the *Roman de la Rose* was a "revelation" as a French work (434), and he undertook to write a letter about it in French.

The novelty of her venture is one Christine herself records. She writes:

> Ne vous soit a merveille, pour ce que mes autres dictiez ay acoustumez a rimoyer, cestui estre en prose. Car comme la matiere ne le requiere autressy, est droit que je suive le stille de mes assaillans, combien que mon petit sçavoir soit pou respondant a leur belle eloquence.

> [Don't be surprised, since I've been accustomed to rhyme my other writings, if this one is in prose. For as the matter does not demand otherwise, it's right that I follow the style of my assailants, even though my small learning may be unequal to their fine eloquence.]
> (Letter to Guillaume de Tignonville, in Hicks, *Débat* 8)

Eloquence as a concept figured prominently among desirable humanist characteristics, along with such other attributes as fortitude, prudence, love of honor, and the like. Eloquence belonged to the sphere of the active, participating citizen, not to the contemplative soul. More than an aesthetic ideal, it could move others to action. The humanists cultivated eloquence to move men to their idea of virtue; in some hands it became a powerful tool.

But eloquence could also serve a less serious purpose. As practiced in many a literary exchange of Christine's day, it amounted to rhetorical jousting (Ouy, "Paris" 85–86).[16] It was thus a weapon that Christine's *assaillans* could use against her. In choosing to call her opponents *assaillans*, therefore, Christine recognized the ludic aspect of the Debate.[17] Further, the contrast between *sçavoir* and *eloquence,* with its hint at a difference between *fond* and *forme,* already foreshadows Renaissance debates. Christine becomes a champion of a plain style; she will continue to write despite the infelicities of her composition, feeling sure that the quality of her thought will carry. Her opponents, by comparison, will be eloquent, but will their eloquence guarantee right thinking? Indeed, the passage already echoes the accusation she will make against Meun himself—that he obscures with language (Huot, "Seduction").[18]

In the end, Christine's demurral suggests that more real to her perhaps than the distinction between Latin and French was the divide between prose and poetry. Success as a lyric poet had already established a worldly audience for her work. Christine's passage into prose, however, would bring with it a change from courtly composition to learned material. Her letters in the *Rose* debate thus presage the later emphasis. Although Christine had advanced her moral program even in her lyric and narrative poetry, poetry itself as a genre took its source in the oral, which, as Jeffrey Kittay and Wlad Godzich have argued, lost prestige during the Middle Ages with the move toward prose. Verse, which had of course been written as well, continued to be written, but prose emerged "untainted by any previous oral life" and "as the very embodiment of writing" (195). The freedom and responsibility that Christine felt to individualize her prose, even as she, like the Latin humanists, turned to classical sources, came from her sense that as a female writer of learned, vernacular prose she could claim novelty on two fronts.

Christine's writing, especially in prose, could capture both the letter and the spirit of the translations produced under Charles V. The chancellery influence on her style has often been noted, but rarely the link between her style and that of the translators,[19] whose prestige no doubt encouraged emulation. The translators' approaches to their tasks varied. In one instance, the translator was instructed to clarify the matter by getting at the sense without following the words of the text exactly. But in other instances, translators say that they have been faithful to the text, rendering it "word for word." Christine herself made generous use of the French rendering of Valerius Maximus's *Facta et dicta memorabilia,* among other translated Latin works. Valerius's version of Roman history in the form of collected anecdotes enjoyed tremendous popularity in the Middle Ages, and in France became especially beloved through the Hesdin-Gonesse translation; in the mode current at the time, the translators took great liberties with their source, adding lengthy commentary to small amounts of translated material. Evidence that Christine worked from their French translation can be found in several of her books, including the *Livre du corps de policie,* the *Fais et bonnes meurs du sage roy Charles V,* and the *Livre de la paix.* In the *Corps de policie,* Christine explains that she often uses material from Valerius Maximus because she wants to move people to virtue and right living; Valerius shows by example more than by simple words how that can be done. Tellingly, she says that she is following the "style of that noble author Valerius" (41) and that she has "gathered the words of his book word for word" (44). While the language of this last statement seems an uncomplicated reference to the flower imagery of the *florilegium,* it also recalls the language of some translators. Her project, in fact, might qualify as intralingual translation, as she "carried over" scholarly material by moving it from its academic framework into her own diverse discourses. Nonetheless, her claim to have worked "word for word" needs some qualification. Here, for example, is Hesdin's rendering of Valerius Maximus:

Age etc En ceste partie Valerius commence a mettre exemples d'aucunes parolles saiges [de Solon] selon qu'il bailla aux Atheniens leurs loys. Et de lui est parlé ou quart livre ou premier chappitre es estranges en la lettre piscatoribus ou il est parlé des sept saiges et en sera aussi parlé ou .viij. livre ou chappitre de industrie. Si viens doncques a la parolle de Solon, laquelle est contre ceulx qui en ce monde se cuident estre et reputent bons et eureux pour leur richesses, honneurs et delices. Moult parloit Solon prudentement, qui disoit qu'on ne devoit point tenir pour eureux homme tant qu'il vesquist en cest monde. Car nous estions et sommes jusques au jour de notre fin subget a doubteuse et muable fortune, la muableté de laquelle consume et oste le nom de humaine felicité en ceste vie mortelle. (Bibliothèque Nationale de France, MS fr. 282, book 7, ch. 1)

[*Age etc.* In this part Valerius begins to give examples of some [of Solon's] wise words, according as he gave the Athenians their laws. He is spoken about in the fourth book in the first chapter on foreigners in the section on fishermen, where the seven sages are also spoken about, and he will be spoken about again in the eighth book in the chapter on industriousness. So I come, then, to the word of Solon, which is against those who in this world count themselves good and happy because of their riches, honors, and pleasures. Solon spoke very prudently, who said that one must never hold a man happy as long as he lives in this world; for we were and are to our death subject to fearsome and unstable fortune, whose changeability takes away and consumes the name of human happiness in this mortal life.]

As can readily be seen, the "translation," as we understand the idea, is but a small part of what Hesdin has produced, for the passage contains a good deal of his own commentary, and is introduced by an indexing device.

Christine employs the same comment in her *Corps de policie*, sometimes using the same words, but more often introducing slight variations:

a nostre propos est bien averié la parole que dit Solon qui fu ung des sept sages contre ceulx qui cuident en ce monde avoir et trouver eur et felicité par richesses, honneurs et delices. Dit icellui qu'on ne doit point tenir pour heureux homme tant qu'il vit en ce monde, car nous sommes jusques a nostre darrain jour subgés a fortune qui est doubteuse et muable, pour laquele muableté est souvent osté le nom de felicité a creature humaine. (60)

[fitting to our subject is the dictum uttered by Solon, who was one of the seven wise men, against those who believe they have found fortune and happiness in this world through riches, honors, and pleasures. He says that one must not hold a man to be fortunate as long as he lives in this world, for we are subject until death to fortune, who is fearsome and changeable, and through whose fickleness the name of happiness is often lost to humans.]

Christine's rendering is rather close to Hesdin's, but it is not as faithful as some of Antoine de la Sale's borrowings, in *Le Petit Jehan de Saintré*, from Hesdin-Gonesse. Here is a small section of the French Valerius, followed by Antoine de la Sale's reinscription of it:

> En ceste partie commence Valerius a mettre exemples de ceste matiere; est assavoir que a Romme ou mont Adventin assez près de la porte par ou on va maintenant à St Pol et assez près d'une masse de pierre qu'on dist la tumbe Romulus fu jadis un noble temple de Diane *la ou est maintenant la maison de nostre religion et une chappelle en laquelle est une ymaige, laquelle on dit que Saint Pol tailla de sa main.* (Lecourt 45)

> [In this part Valerius begins to enter examples of this material; that is to say that at Rome at the Aventine hill near the gate through which one passes now on the way to Saint Paul's and fairly near a mound of stone that is called Romulus's tomb there once was a temple of Diana, where now stands the house of our religion and a chapel in which is a statue, which they say Saint Paul carved himself.

Antoine de la Sale's reappropriation:

> En ceste partie commence Vallerius à mettre exemples de ceste matiere; est assavoir que a Romme, ou mont Aventin, assez près de la porte par ou l'en va maintenant a Saint Pol et assez près d'une grant masse de pierre que on dist la tombe Romulus, ou fut jadiz ung noble temple de la deesse Dyane, *la ou est maintenant la maison du temple de Saint Jehan et une chappelle en laqualle a une ymaige de Nostre Dame, laquelle on dit que Saint Luc entailla de sa main.* (Lecourt 45)

> [In this part Valerius begins to enter examples of this material; that is to say that at Rome at the Aventine hill near the gate through which one passes now on the way to Saint Paul's and fairly near a mound of stone that is called Romulus's tomb, where once there was a noble temple of Diana, where now stands the house of the temple of Saint John and a chapel that has a statue of Our Lady, which they say Saint Luke carved himself.]

Where Christine tends to weave the borrowed material into her own, de la Sale leaves it almost entirely intact, except when he makes precise the name of the church and changes Saint Paul to Saint Luke. The folding-in of male voices, as in that example from Valerius Maximus, is structurally foregrounded in at least two other works by Christine. In her very first narrative poem, the *Epistre au dieu d'Amours* (1399), Christine receives dictation from Cupid. The god's voice passes through her own, as she assumes the position of royal secretary; a secretary, more important than a notary, took dictation directly from the king (Morel 67), as Christine's narrating alter ego does from the God of Love (see Fenster and Erler). In the *Livre du duc des vrais amans*, written several years later, the Duke of True Lovers' voice is captured by that of Christine's female narrator, but in a manner once more that turns the narrator into a recording agent. The Duke, however, who imparts no book learning, is a far cry from the learned men whose voices harmonize in Christine's prose.

Masculine French, Feminine Latin

To help shift the balance in favor of French, Charles V and Oresme had each described the new linguistic hierarchy in gendered terms. The ancient Romans, who had regarded their language as part of the patrimony, called it *sermo patrius* (Batany 95). Its use principally by men in the Middle Ages allowed it to take on the perceived characteristics of those who used it. But as early as 1358, Charles V became the first to label the University of Paris *sa fille aimée*. Several decades later Jean Gerson, in his speech *Vivat Rex*, sounded the same note, and "du coup clergie acquiert des caractères nettement féminins" (Lusignan, "La Topique" 315).[20] A further blow was struck when Oresme, alone among Charles's translators, designated Latin the "mother tongue" of the Romans (Lusignan, "La Topique" 312). This meant that the Romans had mastered Latin without rules and by imitation, whereas to medieval scholars a learned language like Latin could be acquired only through the study of grammar.[21] They balked at the notion of Latin as common (Batany 103), for such an idea had to damage its transcendance and atemporality. But Oresme aimed at demonstrating that Latin, like French, had served both everyday and literary purposes. Lusignan maintains that Oresme took this argument further than Dante did, because Dante believed that Latin was fixed in both time and space, and was thus an international scientific language; Oresme, however, gave to Latin an "irrémédiable caractère historique" (Lusignan, *Parler vulgairement* 163). His formulation had political value as well: his "feminization" of Latin, designed to weaken Latin's hold upon learning, lent to French the "masculine" strength that had formerly belonged exclusively to Latin.

Christine reacted self-consciously (and necessarily so) to her culture's linking of gender and language, and therefore of gender and writing. She felt that she had become a man in order to write. In the *Mutacion de Fortune*, she states that she "de femelle devins masle" (from a female became a male) (line 142), because Fortune, who desired it, "me mua et corps et voult / En homme naturel parfaict" (changed me, body and face, into a natural man) (lines 144–45). Much more than a mere trope, this claim reflected a social and cognitive reality. Thus the learned Italian women trained in Latin by students of famous humanist teachers like

Guarino of Verona were advised to become men if they wished to write. Such notions would continue into the sixteenth century and well beyond. Christine was not alone, therefore, in expressing a social perception. In part, the explanation for the Italian women's "masculinization" lay in the purposes of education, which focused on preparing men for a career in the public arena, a place where women were not expected to go (Jardine). Rhetoric, therefore, did not suit a woman's program of study. About Christine, however, Dulac has commented astutely that she was "une femme auteur qui s'affirme en fait comme un homme public" ("Figure" 123). Christine's writing, with its strong vein of advocacy, was public and active. In prose works like the *Corps de policie,* the biography of Charles V, the *Livre de la paix,* and even in the *Cité des dames* and the *Livre des trois Vertus,* Christine enters into matters of government. Her outlook may be said to lie at a point of confluence between the thinly disguised *translatio imperii* impulse of Oresme's *bien public* and Dante's relationship with the vernacular. Dante shared his culture's view of Latin as immutable, but he nonetheless believed strongly in "public communication for the public good," which necessarily had to occur in the vernacular (Copeland 182). Dante's *De vulgari eloquentia* "sets forth a rhetorical program for the vernacular," and the *Convivio* in particular "strives after public benefit, to move men to wisdom and virtue" (Copeland 181). Had Christine written in Latin—especially had she done so exclusively—she could well have locked herself into a masculine world of *litterati* where the idea of writing as a form of moral, public activism was of little interest.

The reasons for which Christine took up prose, and the variegated texture of that prose as it incorporates masculine sources, make it an object for exploration and description. Yet earlier students of late medieval prose, such as Jens Rasmussen, who was surveying Middle French prose in general, cited Christine's prose as an example of what was bad in the fifteenth century—principally because she larded her sentences with as much learned vocabulary and as many clauses as she could. He gave this example from the biography of Charles V:

Les choses expedientes et comme neccessaires à l'edifficacion de meurs vertueux et louables de commun cours, veons par les sapiens en leurs escrips amenteus et ramenez à memoire pour nostre instruction en ordre de bien vivre, si est digne chose que, avec les vehementes raisons prouvées et solues, d'eulz bailliées, exemples vrais et notoires soient certificacions des choses conduittes en ordre de parleure; pour ce, moy Cristine de Pizan, femme soubz les tenebres d'ignorance au regart de cler entendement, mais douée de don de Dieu et nature en tant comme desir se peut estendre en amour d'estude, suivant le stille des premierains et devanciers, noz ediffieurs en meurs redevables, à present, par grace de Dieu et solicitude de pensée, emprens nouvelle compilacion menée en stille prosal et hors le commun ordre de mes autres choses passées,... (Rasmussen 30–31)

[We see among learned men the things that are profitable and necessary to the teaching of virtuous and praiseworthy practices, set down in their writings and recalled for our instruction, in order that we may live properly; so it is a worthy thing that, with cogent arguments demonstrated and offered by them, the true and notable *exempla* may show the certitude of the matters presented here in order of discussion; for this reason, I, Christine de Pizan, a woman in the shadow of ignorance where clear understanding is concerned, but gifted with the gift of God and of nature insofar as desire may imbue a love of study, following the style of our predecessors and first writers, our teachers in matters of exemplary customs, at present, by the grace of God and with care for thought, undertake a new compilation in the prose style and outside the common course of my other, past things...]

Janet Ferrier, too, found Christine's prose wordy, unoriginal, pedantic, and confused, although she regretted having to say so (100).[22] Yet Christine's attempt to imitate Latin periodic construction, the learned vocabulary (the influence of the translators, who were responsible for numerous neologisms and *calques*, appears in *expedientes*, for example, first attested in the Latin-French translations of Nicolas Oresme, who patterned it after the Latin *expediens*, from *expedire* [*Dictionnaire du moyen français* 273]), and the way in which doublets are used demand that we situate Christine's prose historically, then examine its peculiar traits. Her style betrays a complicated relationship with its learned sources, suggesting that her desire to communicate did not always proceed in the most straightforward manner. That is, both Christine and Jean Gerson, for example, had a utilitarian approach to the use of French (Gerson favored French to persuade, to reform, and to guide). But the kinds of prose each wrote differed widely: Gerson produced "simple sermons" in the vernacular, reserving Latin composition for the loftier subjects he discussed with the educated; Christine, whose compositions are unilingual, sought a relatively more elevated vernacular register. She must have hoped to legitimize her prose by Latinizing her syntax, vocabulary, and orthography, and by redeploying Latin sources rendered into French by the best translators of her time.

Rasmussen's repugnance at Christine's prose is perhaps understandable from an early researcher in the field of Middle French style. In the end, however, it sounds a bit like modern descriptions of the *excess* associated famously with women in the Middle Ages (Bloch). Christine's inelegant, sprawling prose, like the "fat lady's" escaping flesh (see Parker), defies containment. It spills out in several directions and reaches closure only when all the ripples have died away. Paradoxically, the very same Latinate constructions that Christine sought out for authority's sake weigh down meaning, crushing it under the torpor of being de trop. In fact, the obstacles placed in the way of a "quick read," or even sometimes of grasping meaning upon a first reading, conjure the modern, antilinear constructions of a Luce Irigaray, Catherine Clément, or Julia Kristeva. Such experimenting with rupture, with a static "thickening" that works vertically to interrupt forward flow, figures as part of Christine's stylistic approach, whether in the manner of her subordinate clauses in prose or in the way she handles rhyme and enjambement in her poetry. And while much fifteenth-century writing in prose shares a love for long sentences, embedded clauses, lexical doublets, and the like, Christine's practice is at once more exaggerated and less patient, cutting across received masculine rhythms to register her own style, which bears the marks both of established masculine discipline and of personal, idiosyncratic laissez-faire.

We may perhaps return to Christine's statement in the *Rose* debate concerning her adoption of a style she claims belongs to her opponents, not to her. The paradox in saying that she will write in the style of her assailants is that she does, and she doesn't. After all, when Montreuil and especially the Col brothers write in French on a literary subject, are they writing in their own style — or in hers? To all appearances, they have been drawn into writing in "her" style. And why did Montreuil fear that he seemed a buffoon in his French treatise? If Dante himself construed the vernacular as a language in which "even little women comunicate" (Ahern 3), Montreuil, who did not share Dante's eagerness to communicate with hoi polloi, could not have thought otherwise.

Montreuil's opinion of the vernacular notwithstanding, Christine's writing marks an important evolutionary step in the social history of the French language. Although she surely owed a large debt to Charles V's translators for having cleared the way, her own efforts, far from debasing vernacular composition, must have lent to learned writing in French a freshness, even a note of surprise, that masculine vernacular writing could not have hoped to achieve. That is, Christine's coming to learned writing as a *woman* was an act without a history, just as prose writing itself arose "untainted" by any oral history. In this light, the lack of precedent that Christine herself so often mentions, generally considered a handicap by modern criticism, should rather be read here as an advantage. It would have been a privilege not available to male writers — not to Montreuil, for one, whose personal history as a Latinist brought him only timorously to literary writing in French. The Debate of the *Rose* thus foreshadows Christine's later project by offering the spectacle of a confrontation of cultures, one learned and exclusivizing, the other in the language of the majority, but learned, too.

Given Christine's keen awareness of language and her evident interest in enhancing her own French prose, and thus French prose itself, the persistence of doubt about her grasp of Latin emerges as an enduring, twentieth-century preoccupation with the elite value of Latin, one that continues to pose an obstacle to appreciating women's writing for what it is. It would be more useful to embrace Christine's contribution to vernacular humanism without dwelling upon whether she could do what she herself never put forward as her central accomplishment.

Notes

1. A notable and useful exception is Gaston Zink's article on Christine's sentence structure in the *Livre du corps de policie.*

2. In reviewing this observation during a session at the 1995 Christine de Pizan conference at Binghamton, New York, Lori Walters concluded that although Christine may well have had a reading knowledge of Latin, she had "ideological reasons for supporting a vernacular tradition....Christine tries to increase women's importance by removing them from a love situation [as in the romance, where women characters are prominent]... and establish them in a system based on a female rather than a male norm." (I thank Professor Walters for letting me see the text of her comments.)

3. See 162–63 of Dulac and Reno, "L'Humanisme," text and notes, for a summary, with bibliographic citation, of modern scholarly attitudes on this question.

4. I thank Professors Dulac and Reno for allowing me to read their essay in its unpublished form. Joël Blanchard has objected to their findings, first presented as a paper. He states that they do not show more than minimal competence in Latin *as compared with clerical knowledge* ("Tradition" 206 n. 14; emphasis added).

5. "...ainsi comme je l'ay, par pitié et faveur de vous, translatee de latin en françois et mis en forme de service de Heures, aprés le texte de la sacree Ystoire et lez dis de pluseurs sains docteurs, et meismement si comme devotement se peut dessus mediter" (So I have, through pity and concern for you, translated it from Latin into French, and put it into the form of the reading of the Hours, according to the texts of Sacred History and the words of several holy doctors, principally so that it can be meditated upon") (BNF, fr. nouv. acq. 10059, fol. 114b, transcribed and edited by Liliane Dulac; made available to me by Charity Cannon Willard, with permission of Mme Dulac).

6. These questions are treated fully by Lusignan in *Parler vulgairement* and in several of his articles, and by Rita Copeland. See also Poirion, "L'Epanouissement" 32. Concerning grammars of French, see Lusignan, "Le Français."

7. Over thirty years ago Monfrin suggested that in the fourteenth century people— even clerics—read classical Latin poorly and that the translations may have been destined not only for the lay reader ("Les Traducteurs" 5–20).

8. "Jean de Meun traduit en français l'ouvrage de Boèce pour faciliter au roi l'acces du texte. Bien sûr, il laisse entendre que le roi connaît bien le latin. N'avons-nous pas vu Christine de Pizan affirmer la même chose à propos de Charles V?" (Jean de Meun translates Boethius's work into French to facilitate the king's access to the text. He of course lets it be understood that the king knows Latin well. Haven't we seen Christine de Pizan assert the same idea regarding Charles V?) (Lusignan, *Parler vulgairement* 149).

9. In fact, French had enjoyed greater prestige abroad, in England and elsewhere, than in France generally. The Crusades had made French the language of the Latin states in the eastern Mediterranean and of the Latin empire of Constantinople. Italians such as Brunetto Latini, Martino da Canale, Marco Polo, and Philippe de Novare had already written their most important works in French. The aristocracies of England, Germany, and Flanders spoke French. Primary schools in England taught in French, even though university instruc-

tion was in Latin (see Colette Beaune 271 [trans. Susan Huston]). Interestingly, Charles's move to render legal documents in French coincides in date with the enactment of a statute in England that banned the use of French for pleas in the law court (David N. Bell 57–58).

10. Autrand reports further that for the visit of the emperor Charles IV to Paris, Charles V had a *Recueil des alliances* drawn up, in which each act written in Latin was translated into French ("Les Livres des hommes").

11. A thorough introduction to the translations is that of Bérier. Indispensable earlier studies include the two by Monfrin.

12. Oresme's intellectual breadth and his influence emerge clearly from Sherman's recent study of his supervision of the manuscript illustrations to his translations.

13. See the editions: *Maistre Nicole Oresme: Le Livre de Ethiques d'Aristote,* ed. Albert Douglas Menut (New York; Stechert, 1940), and *Maistre Nicole Oresme: Le Livre de Politiques d'Aristote,* ed. Albert Douglas Menut, Transactions of the American Philosophical Society, n.s., vol. 60, pt. 6 (Philadelphia: American Philosophical Society, 1970), and the discussion by Lusignan, *Parler vulgairement* 154–66.

14. Beaune 270; in the prologue to the translation of Aristotle's *Ethics* as cited by Bérier 228 n. 39.

15. Christine's *Epistre Othea,* which is a mixture of prose and verse, has been dated at ca. 1400 and thus may precede the Debate letters.

16. Ouy has observed that eloquence and fine style were redoubtable weapons to men of that time. It was no mere witticism, therefore, when the duke of Milan stated that a single one of Coluccio Salutati's letters was worth a thousand armed men ("Paris" 83).

17. Interestingly, the word *assaillans* also described the besiegers of that symbolic castle-stronghold that was woman—the "assailants" of the Rose in the *Roman de la Rose.*

18. Eloquence not in the service of utilitarian goals surely seemed suspect to Christine and to her ally Jean Gerson, whose judicial advocate in his *Treatise against the Romance of the Rose,* a qualified Eloquence Theologienne, is a character of high seriousness. Grammatical gender notwithstanding, Eloquence Theologienne is a man; he speaks *par grande auctorité* and *digne gravité;* he is *saige* and *bien apris,* holding his head thoughtfully lowered (*en guise d'ung home aucunement pansif*), then he gets up *meurement* and *seriement,* then opens his mouth, from which issues his voice *raisonnant, doulce,* and *moyenne* (Hicks, *Débat* 66).

19. Joël Blanchard discusses the influence of the translators from a somewhat different perspective, arguing that the unstable political climate in France around 1400, combined with Christine's foray into learned terrain as (in his view) a non-Latinist, left her always anxious about patronage and thus seeking both *auctoritas* and *légimité.* The translators, on the other hand, formed an elite corps that enjoyed privilege and prestige. In a pair of articles (one revises the other), Blanchard advances a number of exciting observations, but his conclusion disappoints. He says that Christine creates her own space "qui révèle une sensibilité personnelle et, bien sûr, féminine" ("Une laïque" 225; "Tradition" 231), where (in the absence of any other explanation) what is feminine is defined as what is personal. Further, although he wishes to bring out Christine's novelty in saying that she took up a "personal" portrait of King Charles V in the *Fais et bonnes meurs du sage roy Charles V,* in the end he places her in a default position, since she did so, in his implicit view, because she was incapable of Latinizing like a cleric. (See "Tradition" 206 n. 14 for Blanchard's opinion of Christine's Latin.)

20. The complete citation may be found in Lusignan 315 n.1. In it Gerson refers to the king as the "true father" of the University.

21. Oresme thus anticipated the argument that, more than half a century later, Flavio Biondo would advance against Leonardo Bruni. Around 1435 Bruni said he could not imagine that women in ancient Rome spoke Latin "just as Cicero and others wrote it." He concluded that Rome must have had two languages, Latin and the vernacular, just as in his day (Grayson 11; but see also Tavoni).

22. Ferrier cites the passage in the *Avision* where Christine notes that even her contemporaries have taken her to task for her prose style: "Les autres dient ton stille estre trop obscur et que on ne l'entent, si n'est si delictable. ... Les uns sur le langage donront leur sentence en plusieurs manieres: diront qu'il n'est pas bien elegant; les autres que la composition des materes est estrange" (Others say that your style is too obscure and incomprehensible, thus not enjoyable. People will pronounce on my language in several ways: some will say it isn't elegant, others that the ordering of material is odd).

In the *Fais et bonnes meurs*, she says: "Ceste femme ne dit mie de soy ce qu'elle explique en son livre, ains fait son traictié par proces de ce que autres acteurs ont dit à la lettre" (This woman doesn't herself write what she says in her books, but rather she composes her treatise according to what other authors have said on the subject). Christine retorts by saying that a mason does not make the stones or an embroiderer the thread with which they work: "il me souffit seulement que les sache appliquer à propoz, si que bien puissent servir à la fin de l'ymaginacion à laquelle je tiens à perfaire" (it suffices that I know how to apply them properly, so that they may serve the ends of the picturing I intend to complete) (Ferrier 100–101).

107

⁂

CHAPTER 6

The Critique of Knowledge as Power
The Limits of Philosophy and Theology in Christine de Pizan

Benjamin M. Semple

A s a late medieval woman author composing her works in the vernacular, Christine de Pizan is not necessarily a writer we would expect to have taken part in philosophical or theological speculation. In several significant ways, she lacked the requisite "qualifications" for the study of these disciplines. Their traditional language was Latin, yet she wrote in French; the usual participants in these branches of inquiry were men; and authority in either discipline generally required a university education and an institutional rank (such as doctor of theology or clerk).

However, if we examine the evidence provided by her works, particularly in the wake of the debate on the *Roman de la Rose,* allusions to philosophy and theology, to their terminology and methodology, or to historical figures who practiced these disciplines, abound. For example, her *Livre du chemin de long estude* contains a number of portraits of philosophers of antiquity, such as Democritus (lines 4813–24), Antisthenes (4701–26), and Diogenes (4749–4800), to name only a few. In her *Avision-Christine,* she presents a history of the development of philosophy, recounted at the beginning of Opinion's speech in the second part of the work. In the third part of the *Avision,* she declares that she has received the teaching of "Holy Theology" (79b; ed. Towner, 191) from the mouth of Philosophie.[1] In the *Livre de la cité des dames,* she depicts herself as debating against philosophers who have expressed invalid opinions about women.

In each of these works, she investigates the relation between philosophy and theology. The Middle Ages viewed these branches of study as associated disciplines. Many philosophers were, first and foremost, theologians (Maurer 176–77). From the thirteenth century onward, medieval theologians such as Aquinas and Bonaventure (Copleston 183) spoke of philosophy and theology in relation—or in opposition—to each other, philosophy being the search for truth using natural reason alone, while theology is the investigation of revealed truths (Tranøy 101–2; Copleston 181–82). Philosophy uses human means without divine illumination, while theology uses reason to attempt to clarify superrational truths. The two disciplines enjoined different dispositions on the thinker. Since revelation does not guarantee the conclusions of philosophy, these conclusions are uncertain and doubt is permitted; on the other hand, theology attempts to elucidate the tenets of Christian belief, which must be held by faith. Thus, philosophy and theology differed in three key ways: in terms of the truth value of the object of knowledge (humanly obtained truth versus revealed truth); in terms of the quality of the knowledge obtained (uncertain versus certain); and in terms of the prescribed mental attitude of the knower (doubt, or at best provisional assent, versus faith). In spite of these distinctions between methods, however, theologians also held that philosophy, in its proper subordinate relationship to theology, could be useful as an *ancilla theologiae,* a servant of theology (De Rijk 73; Copleston 13).

In Christine de Pizan's treatment of philosophy and theology, she reflects on the use of the philosophical or, conversely, the theological method, and on the types of outcomes to be expected from each. She shows how these speculative tools embody risks when they are employed without an awareness of their sphere of application and their limitations. Without vigilance on the part of those who practice these studies, they may become instruments to wield power rather than ways to seek truth. Her critique of philosophy and theology also includes a new, broader definition of both disciplines, suggesting that philosophy and theology are not confined to an academic setting. They are open to nonspecialists of sufficient understanding, not only to those who officially bear the title of philosopher or theologian.

The *Cité des dames:* The Limits of Philosophy

Let us briefly consider the opening scene of Christine de Pizan's best-known work, the *Cité des dames.* This initial episode dramatizes the confusion that results from the misapplication of philosophical methodology; consequently, the episode clarifies the limits of philosophy. The narrator's experience in this first episode of the work subtly recalls the plight of Dante as he sets out at the beginning of the *Commedia,* unaccompanied, as yet, by Virgil. Like Dante, Christine will descend into a spiritual abyss necessitating the intervention of guide figures, three "daughters" (Curnow, "*Cité*" 627) of God, Reason, Droiture, and Justice. Dante sinks into despair after having attempted to climb a mountain, only to be thwarted by three mysterious animal adversaries. For Christine, the moment of hopelessness arrives after she has glanced at the *Lamentations* of Matheolus. This brief reading of a book leads her to encounter her own internalized psychological obstacle, an invasion of male voices derived from her reading experiences. Christine's reaction is remarkable for what she does *not* do: she fails to debate with, or respond to, her clerkly opponents.

This absence of a reply is all the more striking in light of Helen Solterer's recent discussion of the ways in which medieval literature imputes to women the capacity to respond. Courtly writers, for example, cast male-female dialogue in adversarial or agonistic terms: the lady refutes or contradicts the suitor's declarations in a verbal sparring match. As Solterer shows in an analysis of the *Rose* debate (151–55), Christine de Pizan was particularly adept at countering male misogyny through the format of the *disputatio,* which she also altered by removing disputation from its narrow academic or literary setting into the sphere of civic virtue, treating clerical opinions on women as a criminal defamation, an assault on the public good.

Christine de Pizan's talent for debate makes her initial failure to rebut clerkly opinion all the more puzzling. She even replicates the male voice and sides with the authorities against women: "j'arguoye fort contre les femmes" (I argued strongly against women) (Curnow, "*Cité*" 619). Given her poetic record of refutation and disputation, this incapacity to respond is a calculated anomaly. Her narrator's silence sets up a dialectic between two attitudes, one that bows to human authority and accepts received wisdom, and a second attitude that is grounded on revelation and grants such allegiance only to divine authority. The various male figures whom she mentions—"philosophers," "clerks," "poets," "orators," "reputable men" (618)—represent the collective human search for truth on the nature of women. As a conclusion reached through human reason, however, the male unanimity on woman's essence is a philosophical conclusion. Christine nowhere attributes to it any divine authority. Against these philosophical conclusions, she juxtaposes her own revelation, which begins when the three allegorical ladies descend to her.

In setting up an opposition between philosophical thought and revealed truth, Christine implies that the origin of the narrator's predicament lies in an a priori acceptance of a human opinion as if it were an object of faith. The passage containing the evocation of her initial misguided use of a philosophical stance alludes, intertextually, to the work of Aristotle, known to his medieval readers as *the* Philosopher. As Christine reflects on the *Lamentations,* she begins to recall all the clerks who have committed slander against women:

> [L]a veue d'icelluy dit livre, tout soit il de nulle auttorité, ot engendré en moy nouvelle penssee qui fist naistre en mon couraige grant admiracion, penssant quelle puet estre la cause, ne dont ce puet venir, que tant de divers hommes, clercs et autres, ont esté, et sont, sy enclins a dire de bouche et en leur traittiez et escrips tant de diableries et de vituperes de femmes. (Curnow, "*Cité*" 617–18)

> [The sight of this book, although it was of no authority whatsoever, engendered in me a new thought, which gave birth in my mind to a great wonder, as I asked what could be the cause, and what could

be the origin, that so many different men, clerks and others, have been, and are, so inclined to say orally and in their treatises so many vituperative remarks about women.]

A medieval clerk versed in Aristotle would not have failed to see in terms such as "admiracion" (wonder) and "cause" key words from the *Metaphysics*, where Aristotle states that philosophy originated in the sense of wonder (1:13.982b) experienced by human beings faced with unknown or inexplicable phenomena and their subsequent attempts to find the causes of these phenomena (1:17.983b). Rather than present herself here as a "professional" philosopher, educated in the schools, Christine, situated in the private, noninstitutional space of the home, spontaneously engages in philosophical speculation, which in this context requires no university study, no official title, and no specialized discourse.

The narrator's experience in the *Cité des dames* suggests that there are, however, limits to philosophy that any medieval philosopher needed to properly comprehend. Initially, the use of philosophy leads Christine to an untrue conclusion, namely, that her nature as a woman is fundamentally defective, her own experience notwithstanding. She says, "[J]e determinoye que ville chose fist Dieux quant il fourma femme" (I determined that God made a vile thing when he formed woman) (Curnow, "*Cité*" 620). "Determination" — reflected here in the verb "determiner" — is a learned term that suggests a definitive and closed conclusion, as opposed to one that is merely probable or open-ended; it is "that concluding stage in scholastic disputation where every question is finally resolved and every interlocutor falls into line behind the *magister*" (Solterer 91; see also 163). But Christine's "determination" is premature. Only the arrival of three allegorical ladies, Reason, Droiture, and Justice, will cure the narrator of her ignorance, removing the risk of a heretical untruth. But then, to what are we to attribute the narrator's momentary lapse into false belief? One answer comes early on in Reason's speech, when it becomes apparent, through Reason's admonishments, that the narrator has confused the mental dispositions of the philosopher and the theologian: "Et il semble que tu cuydes que toutes les parolles des phillosophes soyent article de foy et qu'ilz ne puissent errer" (And you seem to think that all the words of philosophers are articles of faith and that they cannot err) (Curnow, "*Cité*" 624). Reason goes on to remind Christine that even Aristotle, the greatest of philosophers, is not exempt from error. Reason's use of the term "article de foy" (article of faith) implies that Christine has misguidedly placed in the speculations of philosophers a trust reserved only for tenets of faith. She has adopted a theological method and attitude in a philosophical context, treating the opinions of philosophers as if they were revealed truths to be believed unwaveringly. However, the judgments of philosophy, as products of human rea-

111

son (philosophy being by definition the search for truth using only the human intellect) are never of a type to deserve faith. Christine could assent to them, but her conviction should always be provisional, and open to reevaluation. For if there has been no revelation on a given topic, but only a human investigation about what to believe, then faith is not possible: in the absence of revelation, it would not only be misplaced but idolatrous, for it would attribute to the intellectual constructions of human beings an adherence reserved for God-given insights.

Philosophy, Theology, and the Liberty of Thought in the *Avision-Christine*

This short episode from the prologue of the *Cité des dames* illustrates a problem that occurs frequently in Christine de Pizan's works from this period, the problem of clarifying the relation between philosophy and theology and their respective uses. The theme itself is not surprising or novel. The distinction between philosophy and theology had preoccupied university philosophers and theologians since well before Christine de Pizan's time. Discussions of the nature of philosophy, both as a practice of the ancients and as a medieval discipline, were prevalent in theological texts. The relation between the two disciplines was a recurring topic in academic circles. However, Christine de Pizan was not a professional philosopher. Written as vernacular narratives, her works are not treatises addressed exclusively to a narrow group of specialists. Thus her treatment of this topic does not indicate her desire to enter into dialogue with academicians.

We move closer to the reason for Christine de Pizan's interest in this issue when we consider philosophy and theology not simply as branches of study at the university but as modes of thought, each with its own distinct character, existing not only in the scholastic milieu but in many other domains as well. More than university disciplines, philosophy and theology were the intellectual working out of the relation between a rationalistic and a mystical sensibility, and an attempt to reconcile the two, or at least to define how faith and reason might work in conjunction with each other, and what were the proper objects of each. These disciplines were also epistemologies with a wide diffusion through all levels of the culture. Looking at philosophy and theology from this broad perspective, we could say that any medieval person could think *philosophically* when he or she used natural reason to seek truth, just as he or she could think *theologically* when he or she held a belief by faith, but then investigated it using reason. Obviously, the theological method, which posed an unquestionable or irrefutable truth and compelled the believer to adhere to it by faith, was subject to manipulation. For this reason, the mystical worldview constrained the liberty to doubt and investigate. On the other hand, the rationalistic approach of philosophy held procedural disadvantages, as we see at the beginning of the *Cité des dames,* where the narrator is led astray by the arguments of philosophers. Philosophy might confine reason to a specific group that would claim for itself superiority in the use of human intelligence, thus establishing a hegemony over rationality. In treating philosophy and theology, Christine de Pizan was formulating a series of questions for her society. What is the proper object of faith and in what contexts is submissive belief—as opposed to dispute, dissent, or additional rational investigation—required? What precisely is revelation? How does one distinguish between revelation and the process of interpreting it (which usually falls to theology)? Does faith have to extend to authoritative interpretations of revelation, or do the believer's personal interpretations have their own validity? Alternatively, what are the other areas in which faith is not only unnecessary but definitionally impossible? What kind of truth can people expect to find in these areas? Is there only one human reason, or is reason plural and diverse? Do some have more reason than others? If so, how much trust should one place in their superior rationality?

In the *Cité des dames,* Christine de Pizan exposes the tendency of human thought, with whatever apparent logic or authority an opinion may have been formulated, to fall into falsehood. Even the philosophers, who possess the highest of human intellectual powers—along with many clerks and poets—have been wrong in their pronouncements about women. The revelation delivered to the narrator, which comes directly from God's emissaries, confirms their error. But does this mean that Christine de Pizan consistently offers the certainty of her own revelations as a retort to the uncertain outcomes of philosophical inquiry? In this case, revelation would be reduced merely to an additional arm in her rhetorical arsenal. In fact, there are two ways in which she limits revelation in her writings. First, she acknowledges the value of uncertainty by showing that in most realms of debate, uncertainty is all that human beings can expect. Second, she shows that human access to revelation is never absolute but is dependent on means of transmission: schooling, literacy, the book, language. A society develops ways of speaking of the divine, yet these discourses are not the divine itself. Revealed truth is filtered into human existence through processes of interpretation and mediation, and there is always the risk of mistaking these hermeneutical procedures and their product for the revelation itself.

Christine de Pizan perceived a need to reaffirm the transcendent nature of the divine and the inadequacy of human thought or representation to claim complete knowledge of it. We can see this from a work contemporaneous to the *Cité des dames,* her *Avision-Christine,* composed in 1405. Like the *Cité des dames,* the *Avision-Christine* portrays the narrator's gradual intellectual and spiritual illumination. However, the part Christine de Pizan assigns to the uncertain conclusions of philosophy is greater, while the objects of her revelation—the Incarnation and the Trinity—are more traditional than in the *Cité des dames.* Since she reserves the experience of revelation only for those truths theologians habitually regarded as, of necessity, revealed (since human natural reason is not adequate to discover them), she effectively places limits on revelation as a means of knowing. If revelation is confined to specific matters, and occurs only with respect to certain objects, then participants in all other types of inquiries cannot claim the authority of revelation, but must acknowledge that they are using only their own human reason, with all its deficiencies. Although this appears to be a constraint, we may also think of it as a salutary means of equalizing the status of disputants normally separated by hierarchical categories (for example, the clerk as opposed to the layperson): in spite of differences in the ability to command language or to employ logic, human beings all use essentially the same faculty of reason, a capacity that, as Christine de Pizan will show, is highly subject to error.

Christine's categories for philosophy and theology in the *Avision* arise because she simultaneously elaborates a critique of the prevailing use of these disciplines in her time even as she portrays what they could be if they were reformed. In particular, she examines the way in which these disciplines consolidate intellectual power in the hands of a few. The development of philosophy and theology created "insiders"—those practiced in these studies and possessing the education to engage in such inquiry. They posited their methods and techniques as authoritative. The *Avision* responds to this intellectual hierarchy by restating the uncertainty of philosophy in emphatic terms, and by outlining a renewal of the field of theology based upon God's revelation as addressed to people of simple faith, and not only to erudite clerks. The *Avision* repeatedly asks how human beings come to know God and whether certain persons, because of their intellectual powers or their institutional rank, can claim to have an access to God that others do not. We find the author constantly subverting the established hierarchies of education and privilege, not only in the reception of revealed truth, but even in the claim to natural intelligence.

In proposing a theology that was as accessible to those of untutored faith as to clerks, Christine de Pizan was calling for a renewal of theology. It is important to remember how much theology had distanced itself from the concerns and intellectual universe of laypeople in Christine's time by its abstract philosophical vocabulary, methodology, and use of the Latin language. Late medieval theology illustrates the "division of religious labor" to which, for Pierre Bourdieu, the evolution of religion tends:

The history of the transformation of myth into religion (ideology) cannot be separated from the history of a constitution of a body of specialized producers of religious rites and discourse, i.e. from the development of the *division of religious labor*.... This religious division of labor leads, among other consequences, to members of the laity being dispossessed of the instruments of symbolic production. (168–69)

We can observe the traces of this separation of laypeople from "specialized producers of religious discourse" in the allusions to the "religious other" found in theological texts. When laypeople are discussed, they are frequently designated as *"simplices,"* the simple people. The references to the *simplices* testify to the gap, perceptible to theologians, between their understanding and that of nontheologians. Among the many meanings of the term, *simplices* connotes people uneducated in the niceties of erudite speculation, that is, nonspecialists. However, by the early fifteenth century, circumstances had become favorable to a recuperation and a new validation of the simple person's faith. In fact, for some, like Christine de Pizan, the simple person had become a symbol of the piety that many clerks had lost through their overreliance on their own intellectual powers. One of Christine de Pizan's maneuvers to criticize theology and philosophy, and to outline a new path for these disciplines, will be to identify herself with the simple person.

To recapitulate, then, in the *Avision* we will find Christine de Pizan offering a three-part reevaluation of the disciplines of philosophy and theology. First, she reaffirms the radical uncertainty of all that is known through human reason. There is always the possibility of new insight since philosophy, as Christine de Pizan portrays it, is prone to error. In addition, this uncertainty leads to a constant shifting of the locus from which insights will emerge, as well as a fluidity in the types of knowledge to which authority is to be assigned. Second, she reminds her readers that revelation, while it compels the obedience of faith, is also brought into the human community through processes of interpretation that are not identical to revelation but in fact are subject to the same uncertainties as all human knowledge. Revealed truth is not a static object but changes because of the limits of the human point of view as human beings attempt to understand it. Furthermore, access to revelation and ability to interpret it are not the exclusive prerogatives of theologians. These first two parts of her presentation of philosophy and theology have the force of logic, for philosophers and theologians would have conceded both. She evokes premises of these disciplines that are not hers but those of the disciplines themselves, and that their practioners cannot refute without entering into contradiction with their own avowals. Christine's goal is not to redefine the disciplines but to highlight in public fashion, using the vernacular, the uncertainty that they themselves confess in their closed circles.[2] Third, there is a promotion of the simple person. This theme destabilizes these disciplines and suggests that the outsider— the nonphilosopher, the nontheologian—may yet discover truths that have escaped the experts. This valorization of the simple person is hardly surprising in a writer whose lack of "qualifications" to treat philosophical and theological topics I evoked at the outset of this study. The simple person is an appropriate figure for Christine de Pizan, given her lack of official institutional status, her use of the vernacular, and her identity as a woman.

The Revelation of the Simple Person

The *Avision-Christine* recounts a vision that came to the narrator in her sleep. The vision is divided into three parts, and a different allegorical figure speaks with the narrator in each successive part of the work: France is her interlocutor in part 1, Opinion presides over part 2, and finally, in part 3, Philosophie, the ultimate goal of the narrator, appears. The topic of philosophy and theology frequently recurs in this text, especially in the second and third parts, which, in the evolution they trace, thematize the search for knowledge through purely human means (part 2) and the acquisition of knowledge through revelation (part 3).

As part 1 of this work opens, Christine de Pizan broaches the question of which persons are capable of receiving divine truth through revelation. Her response testifies to her willingness to identify herself with the simple person and, in doing so, to imply that the hierarchy of intellectual initiates over the uninstructed outsider can undergo sudden, unexpected reversals. The first lines of the *Avision* evoke the figure of Dante at the beginning of the *Commedia*. There, the narrator proclaimed, "Midway in the journey of our life I found myself in a dark wood" (*Inferno*, trans. Singleton, canto 1, lines 1–2). In Christine's first sentence, the narrator declares, "Ja passé avoye la moitié du chemin de mon pelerinage" (I had completed the first half of my pilgrimage) (7a; ed. Towner, 73). The allusion to Dante is a sign of generic and intertextual affiliation: the *Avision* as a dream vision belongs to a class of works—the *Commedia*, the *Roman de la Rose*—in which the protagonist claims to have experienced revelation and therefore to be a prophet. But how can the poet declare himself a prophet without incurring charges of hubris, or even insanity? In the *Commedia*, the problem of the prophet's election is tempered by the hero's humble declaration: "I am not Aeneas, I am not Paul; of this neither I nor others think me worthy" (*Inferno*, trans. Singleton, 2.32–33). In the *Avision*, Christine de Pizan echoes this phrase of Dante in order to legitimize her status to receive prophetic dreams, but in a way that introduces into the work the theme of the simple person: "Tout ne soie mie Nabugodonozor, Scipion, ne Joseph, ne sont point veez les secrez du Tres Hault aux bien *simples*" (Although I am not Nebuchadnezzar or Scipio or Joseph, nevertheless the secrets of the High One are not denied to the very simple people) (7b; ed. Towner, 73; my emphasis). Unlike Dante, Christine de Pizan links her prophetic capacity to a specific category of religious outsider discussed in theological texts. Dante's phrase evokes his political and spiritual shortcomings: he is neither the destined founder of a new race, as Aeneas was, nor the "Chosen Vessel" of God (*Inferno* 2.28), as Paul was. He does not, however, call into question his genius or his learning. Christine de Pizan's choice to portray herself as a simple person, although it resonates intertextually with Dante's use of the humility topos, has a very different result: it evokes the opposition between the learned and the unlearned and proposes a system of values alternative to those of the clerk, since the simple person uses the vernacular instead of Latin, is frequently a woman, and possesses a humility giving her an intimacy with God often denied to the learned.

As we have noted, the fifteenth century was a propitious era in which to reevaluate the purposes of intellectual speculation. Others besides Christine perceived that philosophy and especially theology were no longer playing a role in fostering spiritual life, but had become areas of barren, idle curiosity. This recognition led to a call for reform and for a return to a piety and religious devotion that had characterized early Christianity. The most important French figure to emphasize theology's need for a new spiritual purpose was Jean Gerson. Gerson saw the theology of his day as a discipline too open to the new and the unexplored, contemptuous of clarity, preoccupied with sterile debates. Furthermore, he saw theology as potentially harmful to spiritual life insofar as it privileged the intellectual over the affective powers of the soul. For Gerson, the emotional life of the soul brings one more surely to God than the cognitive faculties, which are more damaged by original sin and more susceptible, therefore, to error (Ozment 115). Gerson sought, in his promotion of a new spiritual path, to "counteract the unwholesome speculation of the overly curious with simple, penitential affection" (Ozment 113–14). He also attempted to stress the exegetical duties of the theologians, reminding his audience that the goal of theology was to interpret Scripture (Pascoe 389). Gerson's proposed theology, then, would have been more affective, less given to intellectualization, and more closely bound to revelation as transmitted by biblical texts.

Gerson's call for a renewal of theology seems particularly relevant to Christine de Pizan's writings. Since she knew Gerson through their mutual participation in the debate on the *Roman de la Rose*, it certainly is plausible that she was familiar with his writings or at least with his proposals for an amended theology. Gerson had composed some of his texts on the topic, such as his two *Lectiones contra curiositatem studentium*, shortly before the *Avision-Christine*. He intended this work to bring about nothing less than the "conversion" (Combes 1:39) of the theologians of the university faculty, urging them, in the words of the Gospel of Mark, to "repent, and believe in the Gospel" (Mark 1:15). In doing this, they would expiate their sin of pride, their inflation in their own learning.

No less revealing of Gerson's view of the dangers of intellectual pride are his vernacular texts, devoted to the religious experience of laypeople; they may provide, if not actual sources, then at least intriguing contemporary parallels with Christine de Pizan's theme of the limits of the intellect, with her emphasis on the affects, desire, and the will in spiritual life, and with her attitudes toward philosophy and theology. One of Gerson's vernacular texts, the *Montaigne de Contemplation*, testifies to the new value he assigned to the simple people and their faith, and informs us about the precise associations of the term *simple* for Christine de Pizan. This work, written in 1397 and addressed to an audience of women, Gerson's sisters (Pinet, *Montaigne* 23–25), defines wisdom and contemplation of God in ways that question the adequacy of a spirituality overreliant on purely rational inquiry. For L. D. Snyder, the *Montaigne's* message is that "true wisdom means love, not knowledge; it can belong to the simple, not philosophers" (Snyder 166).

In the opening of the *Montaigne,* Gerson writes that an excessive desire for knowledge may actually be a barrier to reunion with God, for knowledge engenders pride. Learning can spiritually deplete the clerk, because of "l'orgueil et l'enfleure que la personne lettrée en prent" (the arrogance and inflation that a learned person acquires from it) (*Montaigne* 16). Pursuing this thought, Gerson maintains that the learned person will not be admitted to true intimacy with God if he "ne se veult encliner en guise d'ung petit enfant ou d'une simple femelette" (does not want to bend low in the manner of a small child or a simple little woman) (*Montaigne* 17). Here he uses the word "simple" to qualify the noun "femelette." He continues with yet another reference to the simple person, although this time he uses the substantive "simplece": "De quoy est advenu que plusieurs grans clers ont souhaitié aucune fois qu'ilz fussent demourer en leur simplece comme leur mere sans scavoir lettres" (as a consequence, many great clerks have on occasion wished that they had remained in simplicity, like their mothers, without learning to read) (*Montaigne* 17). Once again, the term is associated with women, this time with the clerk's mother. Gerson's remarks give us an indication of particular nuances that could attach themselves to the term *simple* and that make it a positive category in opposition to the clerk or the learned person. Simplicity is a quality of women and children; it is associated with a lack of study that spares the simple person from glorification in the power brought by learning. The word *simple* creates the possibility of a critique of learning when it does not serve spiritual growth but leads to the pursuit of hierarchical domination of others. Whereas many theologians of previous eras probably viewed the simple person as the one in need of instruction, Gerson affirms that, although the clerk may have an advantage in academic learning, there is a type of spiritual knowledge, rich in qualities of humility and affection, in which the simple person could have the upper hand. Gerson replaces one kind of knowledge with another. He creates a category of moral knowledge, principally experiential and practical, while he shows how in an overly intellectualized theology, the clerk's own desire for power through learning may be the principal threat to his relation with God.

This critique of intellectual speculation would not have held much hope for success were it not for the fact that it echoes aspects of Christian belief. In the Genesis narrative, a quest to gain a prohibited measure of knowledge, by eating of the tree of knowledge of good and evil, had provoked the initial rupture between human beings and God. Gerson perhaps saw the vain curiosity of the theological schools as a replication of this originary separation. His notion of reform did not necessarily imply the creation of something new, but a return to the earlier, more pristine state of the "primitive church" (Pascoe). Gerson's view of a simple, humble faith arose from his perception that it was to such simple people that the Christian message had initially been delivered. The replacement of the powerful — the religious elite — by spiritual outsiders was a process for which the Gospel narratives had provided a model.

I do not wish to suggest that Christine de Pizan wholeheartedly integrates a Gersonian view of the simple person into the *Avision-Christine.* For one thing, Gerson's *Montaigne* exalts a blissful ignorance in which the power of learning erects no barrier to the desire for reunion with God. As a woman of letters and a proponent of women's learning, Christine de Pizan could not and did not idealize the situation of the simple person in regard to this individual's untutored innocence. Rather, she emphasizes new categories of knowledge — such as experience — which she evokes as alternatives to theoretical speculation. She also shows how intellectual inquiry retains its spiritual validity only when there is a constant reflection on the potential limits of human knowledge and on the possible subversion of the quest for God into sterile self-glorification. The *Avision,* although it begins under the sign of the simple person, is characterized by a hybridization of the qualities of the simple person, linked to femininity, lack of learning, the vernacular and humble piety, and the qualities of the clerk, associated with masculinity, learning, and Latin, but also with the danger of pride.

The Limits of Philosophy in the *Avision:*
Uncertainty, Experience, and the Simple Person

The second part of the *Avision-Christine* introduces the allegorical character Opinion. As this second part begins, the narrator finds herself in a specific intellectual milieu, Paris, which she elliptically evokes when she says that she had arrived at the "cité d'Athenes" (29c; ed. Towner, 109). In the late medieval period, Paris had earned the epithet "the second Athens" in order to honor the city as a center of learning. But here, the characterization of Paris as Athens also serves to suggest Paris's link to philosophy, a discipline whose roots lie in Greece.

The chief attribute of Opinion—who rules over all human thought but expresses a special predilection for philosphers—is her uncertainty. As Opinion states in definitive terms: "Je ne suis nulle fois certaine car se certaineté y avoit ce ne seroi je mie" (I am never certain, for where there is certainty, I am not to be found) (32d; ed. Towner, 114). It becomes clear, as the second part of the work progresses, that Opinion is found everywhere in the world, not only in philosophical circles. She permeates all social classes and professions: clerks, nobles, knights, manual workers, alchemists. She has even appeared frequently in the life of Christine de Pizan herself. Here the author emphasizes the continuity of a university discipline—philosophy—with the rest of human society. Philosophy is simply a refinement of a process found whenever human beings use their own natural reason to search for truth, accepting the insecurity of this venture. Stressing the uncertainty of philosophy, Christine de Pizan evokes the theme of the *errores philosophorum* (Maurer 177) in order to attenuate the type of allegiance philosophy's propositions deserve. She evaluates the kind of authority that can be given to a philosophical argument: one can lend credence to the assertions that possess logic or are true to experience, but must always keep in mind that as a question to which philosophy, not revelation, has provided an answer, there is always the possibility of reevaluation and of renewed debate.

The scene that Christine views at the opening of the second part of the *Avision* also points out the continuity between philosophy and the rest of human thought in another way, in terms of the conflict generated when disputants fail to concede—or even lose consciousness of the fact— that their opinions are uncertain. As the narrator arrives at this "cité d'Athenes," she sees a domain of intellectual speculation in which the participants are no less antagonistic toward each other than the feuding lords of the French kingdom, whom she had graphically depicted as rending the body of France in the first part of the *Avision*. This is an implicit reprimand of clerks, far removed from the characterizations they might have chosen for themselves. Clerks would undoubtedly have preferred to see themselves pursuing the truth in humility and selflessness, acknowledging their errors when they commit them. But here the class of clerks does not transcend the rest of society, engaging in contemplative pursuits while others make their way through a fallen world. As if to stress the struggle for power and the link between verbal and physical combat, Christine observes the explosive anger that leads the clerks "from words to blows," "de verbis ad verbera" (30c; ed. Towner, 110–11). The equivalence between linguistic and corporeal violence is underscored by the play on words "verbis" and "verbera" (see Solterer 11). A further suggested pun resides in the way the phrase "chaude cole" (30c; ed. Towner, 110) evokes the word "escole," school.[3] "Chaude cole," or "hot choler," shows how a presumably collective search for truth dissolves into a divisive situation in which each philosopher or clerk is entrenched in his own opinion.[4] Significantly, these two jokes are conveyed in two different languages — French and Latin — and thus point to the different registers of the simple person and the clerk.

Christine reasserts the uncertainty of all philosophical speculation, which falls under the domain of Opinion, like the remainder of human thought dependent on natural reason; although this view is consistent with the description of philosophy found in medieval writings, it does not represent Christine de Pizan's tacit ratification of the authority of philosophy. She is pointing to the disparity between the discipline's own idealized self-depiction and the reality of its practices, to the fact that the philosophers and clerks portrayed are more willing to reveal their faults internally, to other members of the institution, than to reveal them publicly, to outsiders. Here, however, in the more public forum of a vernacular work (Fenster, chapter 5 in this volume), Christine de Pizan underscores the limits and recurring failures of philosophy. With an undoubtedly calculated irony, she also shows clerks who, in heated philosophical debate, hardly appear to be humbly acknowledging the limits of their own human reason.

Christine de Pizan destabilizes philosophy in two additional ways. First, while philosophers accepted the uncertainty of their own conclusions, they still, implicitly, viewed them as more certain than conclusions reached by other means. The philosophical methodology is thus privileged as a guarantee of the greatest relative certainty, in the absence of revelation. Against this pretension of philosophy, Christine de Pizan maintains the value of experiential knowledge. Even early in Opinion's speech, we find her alluding to the greater certainty of knowledge to which life experience can lead: "Es sages hommes suis plus certaine et plus vraie et *es anciens de longue experience*" (I am more certain and true among wise men and in the old who have much experience) (32c–d; ed. Towner, 114; my emphasis). She dramatically foregrounds this power of experience to bring insight when, at the conclusion of Opinion's speech, it is the evocation of the narrator's own life experience of opinion that provokes her final recognition of the allegorical character and her ability to name her. Opinion reminds Christine that she was the instigator of the debate on the *Roman de la Rose:*

Ne fus je celle qui mist le debat entre les clers, disciples de Maistre Jehan de Meun — comme il s'i appellent —, et toy sur la compillacion du *Romant de la Rose,* duquel entre vous contradictoirement escripsistes l'un a l'autre, chascune partie soustenant ses raisons, si comme il appert par le livret qui en fut fait? (50c; ed. Towner, 142–43)

121

Is it not I who instigated the debate between the clerks, who were "disciples of Jean de Meun" — as they call themselves — and you, concerning the compilation of the *Roman de la Rose*? Each of you wrote your contradictory opinions about it, with each party arguing for its own position, as can be seen from the book that was made from it.

Christine de Pizan cleverly alludes to the *Rose* debate and reintegrates it into the *Avision*. The debate functions as an illustration of how, on matters that revelation has not clarified, a difference of opinion is not only possible, but to be expected. Christine learns that, when she and her opponents took their respective positions, she participated in a difference of opinion like those of the philosophers. The fact that Christine recognizes Opinion directly after an appeal to her own experience suggests the value of this particular form of acquired knowledge, not to be found in clerkly writings, but in her own life.[5]

The second way in which Christine de Pizan subverts the authority of philosophy is through a depiction of the constant restructuring of intellectual hierarchies to which the uncertainty of all human knowledge leads. She achieves this disruption of the status quo through recourse to the figure of the simple person. In one particularly striking chiastic construction, Opinion explains how, because of her power, the normal categories of those who possess knowledge, and those who do not, are reversed:

> Et fais souvent des bons mauvais et des mauvais bons, les sçavens errer et dire faulz en divers cas, et les simples aler droite voie et dire voir. (32b–c; ed. Towner, 113)

> And I often turn good people into bad, and bad people into good; I make learned people stray from the right path and speak falsehoods in various cases, while I make the simple people keep to the straight path and speak the truth.

Each element in this construction is balanced by another element, to which it is correlated and contrasted. The "bons" become the "mauvais," while the "mauvais" become the "bons." The "savans" are contrasted with the "simples" and replaced by them as those who hold formal learning can suddenly be taught by those who do not. Significantly, Christine uses the word "savans" (learned) here rather than "sage" (wise). The latter term implies a person who possesses the self-mastery and humility that do not preclude error but tend to diminish one's blindness to it. "Sçavens," on the other hand, suggests a level of institutionally sanctioned learning that may result in pride, an obstacle to growth and insight. The verbal constructions "errer" and "dire faulz," both complementing the "savans," are placed in opposition to the expressions "aler droite voie" and "dire voir," actions attributed to the "simples." This contrast brings out the concrete dimension of the verb "errer," which means not only "to be in error," but also "to wander," "to stray." In contradistinction, the simple people "go in a straight line," "keep to the straight path." These expressions employ a metaphorical rather than a discursive register of language. Christine de Pizan may be exploiting this humble, unspecialized register deliberately, in order to call into question the authority of mystifying technical terminologies. In the succeeding portion of Opinion's speech, the pretension of abstract philosophical terms to grant access to a higher truth is undermined by a brief history of philosophy that would undoubtedly have been opaque to many of Christine's readers in its details but of which the main point is clear enough: in spite of philosophy's obscure vocabulary and complex rules for logical construction of arguments, some philosophers have arrived at false (though impressively stated) conclusions. Their errors illustrate how wide of the target philosophy may stray.

Recovering Theology for the Simple Person

The third and final part of the *Avision* functions as an examination and redefinition of theology, much as the second part focused on a restatement of the procedural methods of philosophy. The theology that emerges from the concluding portion is closely linked to Scripture,[6] and the entire section is framed by allusions to the principal mysteries of Christianity, first the Incarnation—at the beginning of the dialogue between Christine and Philosophie—and then the Trinity, upon which Philosophie invites her pupil to meditate at the very end of the work.[7] The initiation into these mysteries constitutes a boundary between the narrator's natural reason and revelation: medieval theologians considered these tenets of faith to be beyond the capacities of the human intellect.

Christine de Pizan concedes that knowledge helps bring the narrator closer to God, for an allegory of the disciplines of study immediately precedes the onset of revelation. The beautiful room in which she finds the door leading to Philosophie is

> tres richement peinte, ou furent pourtraictes toutes sciences et leurs dependences autour des parois. Et tout parmi ladicte sale avoit fourmes arrengees pour seoir les escoliers escoutans les leçcons des maistres la endroit lisans en chaiere. (52d; ed. Towner, 147)

> very richly painted, where all the sciences and their dependencies were portrayed all around the walls, and in the middle of the room were arranged benches so that the pupils listening to the lessons of the masters, who read from their chair facing them, could be seated.

Still, education does not guarantee revelation. Only when Christine passes beyond this room will she reach that which is divinely revealed. Nevertheless, the fact that she wends her way through these realms of formal learning before coming to God suggests that study does not necessarily prevent reunion with God, and may facilitate it, under the right conditions. The barrier of the door between the domain of human studies and the divine mysteries symbolizes how the human intellect strives to bring God into the world through study, but also how God is always beyond the efforts of language, or of study, to transmit knowledge of God. This presentation of revelation, with an opaque ivory door[8] standing between the narrator and the light of Philosophie (whom she will compare to the sun) suggests a poetic and narrative response to one of the questions I attributed to Christine de Pizan at the beginning of this essay, namely, how does one distinguish between revelation and the processes of interpretation by which human beings filter that revelation into their society? She does not diminish the value of education in coming to God quite so emphatically as Gerson does when he romantically portrays the innocent humility of the simple person in the *Montaigne de Contemplation*. Her ascent through these halls of study suggests that learning may participate in effecting this reunion. However, she does not privilege the intellect as the only or even as the primary way to acquire knowledge of God, for, among the earliest words of Philosophie, we find a phrase that makes it clear that the narrator's desire is a greater qualification than her learning or intellect; she explains to Christine that "l'amour que as a moy et le desir qui te maine en suppleant ton ignorance te sera valable" (the love you have for me and the desire that brings you here and compensates for your ignorance will be of use to you) (53b; ed. Towner, 147). Here Philosophie makes it clear that the qualities of love and desire can transcend a deficiency of knowledge. It is partly study that brings Christine to Philosophie, but it is even more importantly her own desire that focuses that study and gives it its raison d'être. The importance of the affective component in Christine's revelation finds a parallel in Gerson's insistence on love of God as opposed to knowledge of God, on "repentant affection" rather than "penetrating intellect."[9]

Let's briefly examine, from the very end of the *Avision,* one final consideration about the nature of theology. In her concluding words to Philosophie, the narrator states that Philosophie has appeared to her "en fourme de Sainte Theologie" (in the form of Holy Theology) (79b; ed. Towner, 191) and then goes on to use an analogy to describe that branch of study:

> Car tu [theology] es ainsi comme ung fleuve qui si pou parfont semble estre que ung aignel y prent pié et si parfont que un oliphant y puet nagier. Merveilleux est ton fleuve, Sainte Theologie, qui si pou semble estre parfont a un aignel — c'est a entendre a un bon simple qui y prent pié — et si est si parfont a un oliphant orgueilleux — c'est

aux plus haulz entendemens qui a peine te scevent, et non toute, comprendre. (79d; ed. Towner, 191–92)

You (theology) are like a river that seems so shallow that a lamb may walk in it and yet is so deep that an elephant can swim in it. How marvelous is your river, Holy Theology, which seems so shallow to a lamb, that is, to a good simple person, who steps into it, but which is so deep to a proud elephant, that is, those of the highest understanding, who only are able to fathom you partially, not entirely.

This image, which contains its own gloss, once again mentions the simple person, for the last time in the text. Here the simple person sees only the surface of the river, never guessing at its depths. But the simple person is likened to a lamb, a creature known for its humility and innocence, and associated with Christ. The initiates, on the other hand, plunge into the depths of the river, but they run the risk of elevating their knowledge into a pridefulness in their own power suggested by the allusion to the proud elephant. It is not clear from this image that those who plumb the depths of the river of theology gain a superior spiritual knowledge. For the message of revelation, as Christine de Pizan describes it, is not known by theory alone: it is also a practice in which one continually reflects on the way the search for knowledge can be subverted into a quest for power.

This analogy formulates the relation between learning and spirituality differently from Gerson's portrayal of the simple person in the *Montaigne de Contemplation*. Gerson set up an opposition between the intellectual knowledge of the clerk and the spiritual knowledge of the simple person. Here, the relationship between the "bon simple" and the "plus haulz entendemens" does not imply a complete opposition (although there is the contrast between the "surface" and the "depths") but also a species of continuity: the innocent faith of the unlearned is the ground upon which theology exercises its investigations. They both speculate upon the same river, although the "bon simple" is unaware of its depth. While some precedence of theology seems implicit in the notion of passing beyond the surface to the depths, at the same time, the theologian constantly runs the risk of pride, as suggested by the image of the proud elephant. There is, therefore, an equilibrium between the theological initiate and the noninitiate: the simple person always remains a point of reference for the theologian in the areas of humility and piety. Furthermore, even the specialist who possesses knowledge of theology only investigates the depths slightly, for, as the analogy concludes, we learn that "those of higher understanding" know theology only in an incomplete manner (a peine te scevent . . . comprendre). Here, revelation is reconstituted in its relation to the entire society, not only to the simple people, as a study of transcendent truth that no human being or group can claim to master or even begin to fathom.

In the final analysis, the *Avision-Christine* treats the unrestrained pursuit of knowledge and the claim to control truth. The medieval Christian ethos was preoccupied with abstinence from worldly power and possessions, embodied in wealth, social class, political might, or even in spiritual accomplishments. By the early fifteenth century, Christine de Pizan's *Avision-Christine* testifies to her acute awareness of another object of power — knowledge — and of the emerging institutions and disciplines claiming a hegemony over it. If she acknowledges the intellectual prowess of the clerks, she also suggests, by her own experience of revelation and by her identification with the simple person, that the ethical qualities of humility and simplicity are more primary to a spiritual life than are the intricate intellectual constructions of the theologians, which may appear to bring increased intellectual knowledge of the sacred but which actually lead away from God. Drawing upon the ethical tradition of Christianity, she wrote against the presumptuousness of the human intellect. Her goal was to level the hierarchization of rationality by evoking a mystery before which all human reason must confess its limits.

Notes

1. My text of the *Avision-Christine* is from the forthcoming edition of Liliane Dulac and Christine Reno. References are to folios and columns of the base manuscript for their edition, ex-Phillips 128. I would like to thank them for allowing me to use their text. However, since it is not yet available, I have also included references to the corresponding passage in Mary Louis Towner's version of the text.

2. That Christine de Pizan shows the failures of the clerks in a vernacular work highlights them in a *public* fashion, French being a language accessible to a much larger audience than Latin. On the relationship between the vernacular and Christine's public activism, see Thelma Fenster, *"Perdre son latin,"* chapter 5 in this volume.

3. This pun may seem farfetched, but the dictionary of Godefroy (s.v. "cole") supplies several examples of the rhyme "cole"-"escole," illustrating that the association between the two words was not without precedent.

4. Gerson cites one of the shortcomings of arrogant theologians as "immansio in opinionibus vel suis vel suorum" (clinging to their own opinions or to those of their group) and "pertinacia" (obstinacy) (*Lectiones* 230). The portrayal of disputatious clerks at the beginning of the second part of the *Avision* is quite similar to the situation Gerson deplored in the faculty of theology. Interestingly, however, Christine de Pizan links these clerks more to philosophy than to theology, suggesting, perhaps, that by their willfulness they have severed themselves from revealed truth.

5. In her presentation of the value of experience, Christine was probably drawing upon Aristotle (*Metaphysics* 980b–981a).

6. Philosophie announces the link between her teaching and Scripture when she proposes to heal the narrator by leading her to knowledge of her error "sus fondement de sainte Escriture" (on the foundation of Holy Scripture) (67a; ed. Towner, 170). The connection between theology and Scripture in the *Avision* recalls one of Gerson's prescriptions for theological reform (Pascoe 389).

7. Christine de Pizan places the Incarnation at the beginning of her encounter with Philosophie through a biblical allusion: we find an evocation of the meeting of John the

Baptist with Christ when, addressing Philosophie, the heroine speaks of herself as a "femme ignorant non digne de descoudre les lasceures de ta chaucemente" (an ignorant woman not worthy of undoing the laces of your shoes) (53d; ed. Towner, 148) (cf. Mark 1:7; Luke 3:16; John 1:27). Christian exegetes—such as Gregory the Great or, much later, Jean Gerson—interpreted this image of the shoes whose laces cannot be undone as a reference to the inexplicable mystery of the Incarnation.

8. Christine perhaps knew Macrobius's reading of the two gates of dreams (one of horn, one of ivory) at the end of *Aeneid* VI. Macrobius explains that these are two veils, the transparent veil of horn, which permits light to pass, and the opaque veil of ivory, which blocks the light (92). The ivory of the door at the beginning of part 3 of the *Avision-Christine* symbolizes the barrier interposed between the narrator and truth, while the moment when she passes through the door implies the beginning of revelation, in which the naked truth stands before her, figured by the unendurable light of Philosophie.

9. At the end of his *Lectiones contra curiositatem studentium,* Gerson, referring to his later treatise, the *Theologia mystica,* characterizes his future topic as the question of whether God is known more "per poenitentem affectum" than "per investigantem intellectum" (249).

CHAPTER 7

The Bath of the Muses and Visual Allegory in the Chemin de long estude

Mary Weitzel Gibbons

Although Christine de Pizan studies have exploded in the past twenty years, textual interpretations of her oeuvre have far exceeded attention to the visual images as they interact with the texts.[1] Recently, however, a few scholars, such as Sandra Hindman, have explored aspects of the intricate interplay of text and image.[2] My aim is to probe further into text and image relationships. In this essay I will focus on one miniature, *The Bath of the Muses* (Figure 17), found in Christine's *Livre du chemin de long estude*, in order to highlight the integral part illuminations play in her manuscripts: images are neither mere illustrations of specific text nor completely autonomous pictorial narratives, but are an amplification of the work. In this instance, the centrality of the nude female bodies affords the opportunity to enlarge on a significant aspect of Christine's thought and imagery. Her awareness of the female body not only as a site but a producer of diverse meanings is axiomatic.[3] It pervades her works; its visual manifestations make powerful statements. *The Bath of the Muses* illustrates the ways in which the miniatures intersect selective parts of the text and thereby intensify specific parts of the allegorical narrative; images invite an expanded reading otherwise not available to the reader. Considering text and illuminations as equal partners follows a medieval view expressed by Richard de Fournival (Fleming 12), namely, that there are two ways of learning, by word and by picture. But the illuminations in Christine's manuscripts, embedded in the text, should also be considered a visual allegory, a concurrent narrative, running parallel with the textual. *The Bath of the Muses*, in its paratextual position, functions as both a bridge and a breach between the narrator and the poet. It represents the autobiographical Christine at the same time that it reveals the narrator's point of view. The viewer is at once aware of this break and given the possibility to negotiate it. The viewer/reader then constitutes the third party in the narrative. As Gay Clifford remarks, "The greatest allegories are intransigent and elusive because they are concerned with a highly complex kind of truth, a matter of relationships and process rather than statement" (36).

The pictorial image of the bath invites the audience to produce alternative meanings supplementary to the text. Physically located in the

128

Figure 17. Bath of the Muses. Christine de Pizan. From the *Livre du chemin de long estude*. London, British Library, Harley 4431, fol. 183.

text but addressing vision, not hearing, visual images such as the bath induce the viewer to devise a story in an altogether different register than does the text. Christine, the narrator, may be our guide in this hermeneutic endeavor, as she herself asserts that there are many levels of interpretation to be derived from her allegories. She states in the preface to the *Avision-Christine:* "According to the style of the poets . . . under the figure of metaphor or veiled speech, are hidden much secret knowledge and many pure truths. What is put in poetic language can have several meanings, and poetry becomes beautiful and subtle when it can be understood in different ways" (Reno, "Preface" 209). And on folio 106v of the *Epistre Othea* in Harley 4431, she explains: "This fable can be explained in various ways, as can the others. It was for this reason that the poets made them, so that men's minds could be sharpened and refined in looking for various interpretations" (Reno, "Preface" 222).

Christine's penchant for inversion of categories, especially categories of gender, is manifest in the *Chemin*, as it is in many of her works. In the *Chemin* she adopts the metaphor of the road from Dante and turns it into a woman's quest for knowledge; that is, she genders the journey and repeatedly clarifies that she is empowering herself as a female in the world of the intellect, normally reserved for males (Richards, "Dante"; De Rentiis). Every illumination of the *Chemin* portrays the Sibyl and Christine and thereby fixes female agency in the realm of interpretation and authority.[4] Nonetheless, Christine's adherence to tradition in the text often masks her transformations of gender-based discourse. The visual image, however, can often clue us into a more nuanced reading than is initially apparent.

Thanks to the work of a number of scholars, we now know that Christine was deeply involved in the production of her manuscripts; she not only "wrote" some of them but she oversaw their visual programs[5] and was the only writer of her time who regularly commissioned illuminations for her works (Meiss, *Limbourgs* 8). Immersed in the visual program of her works, Christine often marvels at the artisans' great skill in painting realistic detail (Hindman, *Christine* 68–75). Sandra Hindman has already shown how the lavish program of illuminations in the *Othea* privileges the political theme of the work, thus amplifying the text beyond its traditional categorization as a courtesy book. She also treats the theme of universal monarchy in the *Chemin* as it emerges in the pictorial program. My focus, on the other hand, is to show how the miniature in the *Chemin* produces yet another discourse distinct from the text, a visual discourse that functions at once as a distillation and amplification of the text and adds another dimension to the scene by expanding Christine's voice. In another register of allegory the visual may serve as a lens through which we, the audience, can construct additional meaning to the *Bath*, through visual inversion of established hierarchies and fusion of disparate contexts.

Composed at an important transitional point in Christine's professional life, the *Chemin* was finished, so she tells us in the prologue, on May 20, 1403, and dedicated to Charles VI (see Laidlaw, "Publisher's"). It marks a redirection in her works toward political, didactic, and moral themes, rather than the poetic, courtly subjects of her previous writings, such as the *Cents Ballades*. The *Chemin*'s narrative format, an autobiographical dream vision, recounts Christine's pilgrimage in search of knowledge, on which she is guided by the Cumaean Sibyl, a crucial selection on Christine's part.[6] Projecting her internal experience onto the allegorical form of the poem, Christine, in the words of Helen Solterer, "cultivates...a prophetic mode" by making the Sibyl her mentor (165–66). Solterer's concept of disputing women makes the infamous debate over the *Roman de la Rose* central to Christine's development as a poet. According to Solterer, "Christine's ultimate response to the *Querelle de la Rose* emerges through the practice of sapiential writing in the *Chemin*" (173). And how did Christine acquire the wisdom essential to assume a role of such authority as to be the spokesperson against defamatory writing and for the exercise of ethical responsibility devoted to the good of the commonwealth? In the *Chemin* her education by the Sibyl prepares her to appropriate authorial authority traditionally possessed only by men. In this context, *The Bath of the Muses* is indispensable to Christine's preparation for civic duty. The female body, seen here in the form of the Muses bathing in the Fountain of Wisdom (Knowledge), becomes the sign for this appropriation, conveying the message that females are endowed with the capacity to exercise this virtue and its accompanying authority.

In the role of naive student, Christine-the-narrator sets out, filled with great excitement but also trepidation, on her long intellectual journey with the Sibyl as her guide. She describes her wonder at the sights she encounters, the first one of which is the Bath of the Muses, whose importance in the poem, but especially in the visual allegory, cannot be overemphasized. It functions as the threshold scene and sets the tone for the rest of the poem, and likewise works as a visual gloss on the title. Not only is it the first stop; it is the only earthly stop portrayed on Christine's whirlwind tour to all of the marvelous sights of the known world.

Of the surviving illuminated manuscripts of the *Chemin*, Harley 4431 is the most germane to our discussion, although there are three other known versions (BNF, MS 836; Brussels, MS 10982 [Figure 18]; and Brussels, MS 10983 [Figure 19]). Harley 4431 is one in the largely autograph collection of twenty-nine of Christine's manuscripts prepared for the queen, Isabeau of Bavaria (Hindman, "Composition" 93–123). By the time Christine had assembled Harley 4431 (ca. 1410–12), she was a well-established and respected writer. Furthermore, it is entirely possible that her patron, the queen, was an influential presence when Christine was overseeing the design of illuminations for this anthology (see McGrady, chapter 10 in this volume). The program of the other versions of the *Chemin* is similar to the Harley.[7] Of the eight miniatures in Harley 4431, four take place in the heavens, thus privileging the celestial portion of Christine's journey, where a lengthy debate on the political and moral situation in France occurs. The first miniature, *Christine Presenting Her Book*, is a typical dedication page illustration; the second miniature, *Christine's Dream*, establishes the frame for the poem, introducing the two principal characters, Christine and the Sibyl; the third miniature, *The Bath of the Muses* (Figure 17), the initial stop on the journey, sets

Figure 18. Bath of the Muses. Christine de Pizan. From the *Livre du chemin de long estude*. Brussels, Bibliothèque Royale Albert Ier, MS 10982, fol. 13v.

the stage and is therefore the threshold scene, as observed earlier, for the rest of the poem; the fourth miniature, *Christine and the Sibyl before the Heavenly Ladder*, is the prelude to what Christine, the narrator, fears will be a perilous ascent to an unknown world; the fifth miniature, *Christine and the Sibyl in the Firmament* (Figure 20), shows the two women engaged in a dialogue about the heavens. The last three miniatures, *Christine and the Sibyl before the Virtues, Christine and the Sibyl at the Court of Reason* (Figure 21), and *Christine Kneeling before Queen Reason*, are all set in the court of Reason, where an extended dialogue about the sorry state of the world and its remedy takes place. In a sense this colloquy is the culmination of Christine's instruction by the Sibyl, which began with the Bath of the Muses. It is the locus of her initiation to the new world of learning, which she has just entered. By the time she reaches the court of Reason, having been tutored by the Sibyl, she is prepared to take on the task of educating the French nobility in its responsibilities to set the affairs of France and Europe in order. After a substantive discussion at the court and with the recommendation of the sibyl, Queen Reason authorizes Christine to assume this duty.

erbes flourans natures delis
e chose bonne amedieme
rouffitable herbe flour racine
ez poulieul ysoppe et mante
e cuidez/ me que ie mente
ont tout le lieu ne soit seme
ui par ordre est bien assesme

mse de grant desir ardant
Alore par tout regardant
Lee tres beaulz lieux que ie beope
Et atout aussez beope
e bonnement faire el peusse
ais en nul ans compris ne leusse
t ainsi comme ie me tournay
ers de fere mabeue atournay
us le sommet dune montaingue
i haulte quil pert quelle actirngue
usques aux nues tant su thaultre
toy quelle y attaint sans faulte
a by fontaine clere et brue
ourdane dun groz dor qui saume
auon ni fist mur ne masiure

Figure 19. Bath of the Muses. Christine de Pizan. From the *Livre du chemin de long estude*. Brussels, Bibliothèque Royale Albert Ier, MS 10983, fol. 13.

Figure 20. Christine and the Sibyl in the Firmament. Christine de Pizan. From the *Livre du chemin de long estude*. London, British Library, Harley 4431, fol. 189v.

The representation of the Bath of the Muses is an unusual scene.[8] Modeled on the *Ovide moralisé*, its portrayal in Harley 4431 (Figure 17) differs in telling ways from Christine's own textual version of the tale, as well as from the *Ovide moralisé* text and illuminations.[9] As told in book 5 of Ovid's *Metamorphosis*, the basic story relates that Minerva visits the Muses in their habitat to verify the news she has heard of the birth of a miraculous horse from a droplet of blood from Medusa's head and the ensuing birth of the Hippocrene spring.[10] Christine's concentrated pictorial program as shaped in Harley 4431 highlights the Sibyl, Christine, and the Muses, and suppresses many of the narrative details found in the Ovidian pre-text. When Christine and the Sibyl come upon the Muses they see them, in a close-up view, densely packed in a rectangular stone basin. They are nude except for their stylish *bourrelets* (con-

Figure 21. Christine and the Sibyl at the Court of Reason. Christine de Pizan. From the *Livre du chemin de long estude*. London, British Library, Harley 4431, fol. 196v.

temporary headdresses); the water of the fountain modestly covers them from the waist down. Looking very much alike, the individual Muses are identified neither by attribute nor by name. In keeping with their antique origin, the Muses' basin is reminiscent of classical forms in its depiction as a pink rectangular shape with round-headed niches. The wondrous horse Pegasus, looming large, plays a major role in the picture as he hovers overhead. The whole scene is set in a verdant but rocky landscape.

This depiction is in marked contrast to the copiously illustrated *Ovide moralisé* of BNF, MS fr. 871 (Figure 22), which Christine probably knew (Willard, *Christine* 92, 230 n 7; Meiss, *Limbourgs* 1:24–38). Here the bath illumination portrays the Muses, hatless in classical coif, undifferentiated, bathing in a natural pool formed by the spring descending from the summit of Mount Helicon. As in the original Ovid text, Minerva stands by while Pegasus flies overhead, Apollo sits on Mount Helicon playing his lyre, and the cackling magpies chatter nearby in the trees.

Both texts, the *Ovide moralisé* and the *Chemin*, stress the purity and transparency of the water as well as the inspirational role of the Muses, thus forging their intimate association. The *Ovide moralisé* describes

Figure 22. Bath of the Muses. From the *Ovide moralisé*. Paris, Bibliothèque Nationale de France, MS fr. 871, fol. 116v.

the fountain as a place where only the virtuous who are pure of heart and possess subtle minds may drink:

> La fontaine est ou cuer assise,
> Dont sapience doit venir.
> Cele doit l'on nete tenir,
> Sans vilonie et sans laidure,
> Et netoier de toute ordure.
> Cil qui veult aprendre et savoir
> Doit le cuer pur et net avoir.
> (*Ovide moralisé* 5.2473–79)

[The fountain is situated in the heart from which wisdom must come. It must be kept clean (pure) without villany and without flaw, and free from all pollution. He who wishes to learn and know must have a pure and clean heart.]

Christine, as she did with Dante's "chemin de long estude," appropriates authority from the *Moralisé,* and expands and transforms the moral allegorization of the fountain to include her own autobiographical interpretation:

> La vi fontaine clere et vive,
> Sourdant d'un gros doiz qui l'avive.
> . . . .
> Si grant que toutes autres passe
> Les fontaines qui sont ou monde —
> . . . .
> La vi je neuf dames venues
> Qui se baignoient toutes nues
> En la fontaine, en verité
> Moult sembloient d'auctorité
> Et de grant valour et savoir.
> (*Chemin* lines 799–817)

[There I saw a clear and limpid fountain gushing from a large source that fed it. . . . it surpassed all other fountains in the entire world. . . . there I saw nine ladies who were bathing there completely nude in the fountain, in truth they seemed greatly endowed with authority, of great virtue and knowledge.]

The startling difference, noted above, between text and image in the *Chemin* is an example of their complementarity. The text conveys the fountain's purity and transparency in a way that the picture cannot; whereas the image effectively highlights Christine, the Sibyl, and the Muses. Moreover, the image counteracts the text. Roberta Krueger points out in chapter 2 in this volume that the text of the *Chemin* describing the fountain scene creates "a more powerful men's school" than the mythical "college de femme" mentioned earlier in the poem. She continues, "Even as Christine recasts the fountain as source of knowledge, it remains a site of exclusive male privilege." The visual image, on the other hand, disputes this message. In the text the Sibyl establishes the learned ethos of the Muses' dwelling place, pointing out that only eminent thinkers, philosophers, and poets (such as Aristotle, Socrates, Plato, Seneca, Cicero, Ptolemy, Galen, Virgil, Homer, Ovid, and Horace) came here for inspiration and tranquility when they felt the need to converse with the Muses (lines 1020–65). The Sibyl, a female prophet, and Christine's father, the male mentor, share her intellectual training.[11] Placing Christine's father in this august company, the Sibyl points out:

> Ton pere meismes y savoit
> Bien la voie, si le devoit
> Savoir, car bien l'avoit hantee,
> Dont grant science en ot portee.
> (*Chemin* lines 1045–48)

[Likewise, your father knew well the road, he had to know, because he had frequented much, where great wisdom resided.]

But the illustration gives an entirely different cast to the bath; it cogently pares the scene down, as we have seen, to the Muses, Christine, and the Sibyl, who take their places in the present, effectively collapsing Christine's historical moment and the mythical world. Aside from Pegasus, the viewer is confronted solely with females; there is no sign of any of the famous male poets or philosophers in the miniature. Furthermore, the pictorial version does not depict Christine excluded from the main source of knowledge, relegated to dipping into the subsidiary streams issuing from the fountain. On the contrary, it features her in the foreground contemplating the fountain itself with its distinguished nude female inhabitants. Both text and image link the fountain with authority, but only the picture literally embodies authority in the female nude. The visual image, well known as a potent memory aid by virtue of its reifying power, privileges this view of the bath over that of the discursive text.

In narrating her allegorical journey with the Sibyl, Christine evokes the classical ethos of the Muses' dwelling place, describing it as a pastoral arcadia:

> La veissiez sentiers couvers
> De haulz arbres fueillus et vers
> Qui chargies sont de flours et fruit,
> Ou oysillons mainent tel bruit

Que ce semble, pour voir vous dis,
Estre terrestre paradis.
>   (*Chemin* lines 757–62)

[There I saw paths lined with tall trees, green with leaves, which
were laden with flowers and fruit, where birds were making such a
great sound that it seemed, to tell you the truth, to be an earthly
paradise.]

This pastoral arcadia, the site of her encounter with the Muses, is not
just a place of pleasure but the place where Christine locates the begin-
ning of her account of her intellectual coming-of-age. Here she estab-
lishes her intellectual lineage from the philosophers and poets of antiq-
uity, a necessary point of departure for her own transformation.

The Sibyl, as Christine's teacher, explains to her what she is seeing:

La montaigne que vois lassus
Est appellee Pernasus,
Ou mons Helicon est de moult
Appellez ce tres biau hault mont.
La fontaine que lassus vois
Est celle qui a si grant vois
De noblece et de renommee,
Qui de Sapience est nommee.
. . . .
Des dames que tu vois baignier,
A quoy ententivement muses:
On les appelle les neuf muses.
Celles gouvernent la fontaine
Qui tant est belle, clere et saine;
Si tiennent la l'escole sainte
Qui de grant science est encainte.
>   (*Chemin* lines 977–84, 990–96)

[The mountain that you see above is called Parnassus, or Mount
Helicon, as many call this very beautiful high mountain. The foun-
tain you see upon it is that which has such a reputation of nobility
and fame it is called the Fountain of Wisdom (Knowledge).... About
the ladies whom you see bathing, upon whom you are attentively
musing: they are called the nine Muses. They watch over the foun-
tain, which is so beautiful, clear, and healthful; they hold there the
sacred school that is enveloped by great knowledge.]

Visually, *The Bath of the Muses* evokes other associations, both phys-
ical and spiritual, which can be seen as autobiographical subtexts. One

of these connections was the famed baths at Pozzuoli, near Naples, Italy, which were known for their medically curative powers. In use since the classical period, these extensive baths were acclaimed for their curative effects over disease (Kauffmann). In Christine's milieu they were known through written record, if not also directly through personal experience. Their miraculous powers were almost uniformly praised by Roman authors, among whom Ovid (*Ars amatoria* 1.255–60) is one, and their fame, as well as their use, survived throughout the Middle Ages and into the modern era.[12] Both Petrarch and Boccaccio, reflect their continuing repute.[13] Gervase of Tilbury, who visited Naples in about 1190 and from whose work Christine could easily have read about them, initiated a long-lived tradition attributing the construction of the baths to Virgil (*Otia imperiala* 15). The metaphorical allusions arising from the bath images are self-evident: beyond the literal therapeutic benefits of the baths lay the idea of relief for personal as well as political ills. Christine's own personal misfortune — her husband's early death — and her distress over the parlous times in which she lived figured as frequent themes in her writings.[14] Just as the Muses' Fountain of Knowledge could provide Christine with the intellectual sustenance she sought, so its pure, healthful waters could alleviate the pain of her personal loss and concern for her country. In addition there survives a poem on the baths of Pozzuoli, *De Balneis Puteolanus* (1211–20; Kauffmann 12), composed by a clerk, Peter of Eboli, and dedicated to Frederick II. Peter's poem describes thirty-five baths, each with its own specific healing properties. Of the ten surviving illuminated manuscripts of this poem, one of particular interest for Christine studies, BNF, MS 1313, includes a 1392 French translation.[15] The miniatures depicting the baths show many figures — mostly men — huddled together in basins usually protected by a dome-shaped canopy of the type found in Byzantine art. There are, however, at least two for women — the *sulfutara* (see Figure 23) for gynecological diseases and the Sancte Anastasia.

The physically, if also metaphorically, therapeutic powers of the Pozzuoli baths have their counterpart in the spiritually curative power of the Christian sacrament of baptism. Its universal symbolism is axiomatic. At the point in the *Chemin* when the Sibyl and Christine visit the Muses, as we have noted, they have just set out on their journey; in analogous manner, Christine, after the death of her husband and assumption of the career of a professional writer, starts a new life, casting off her former one as the conventional wife and mother envisioned by her mother, and assuming the "new life" of learning modeled by her father. Conceptually, the visual representation of naked humans in water, especially in the context of late medieval culture, invariably alludes to baptism no matter what other connotations it may also have.[16] The Muses in Harley 4431, shown huddled together, their virginity a counterpart to the pure water in which they are immersed, recall the innocence and vulnerabil-

Figure 23. Balneum Sulfutara. Petrus de Ebulo. From *De Balneis Puteolanis*. Rome, Biblioteca Angelica, MS 1474, fol. 4.

ity of the newborn beginning life. If we keep in mind the various associations I have just discussed, the bath scene in the *Chemin* commingles the classical and the Christian, which are then brought into the contemporary world of 1400 by the telling detail of the Muses' *bourrelets*. Christine, then, brings the three worlds of classical, Christian, and contemporary together in the bath of the Muses.

Christine's proclivity for redefining tropes extends to her involvement with the *Roman de la Rose* and her transformation of its fountain. Her well-known engagement with the *Rose* culminated in the notorious debate over the poem. The height of her involvement spanned the years from 1399 to 1402.[17] Her dossier on the *Rose* was begun on February 1, 1402, and her final letter vehemently defending women in the debate was dated October 2, 1402. The date of this final letter was only three days before Christine began her dream that initiates the *Chemin de long estude*! Having established her authority as female author in the book she constituted from the *Epistres sur le Débat du "Roman de la Rose,"* as Kevin Brownlee ("Discourses" 131–50) has shown, Christine was ready to give a more personal account of her intellectual journey in the allegorical form of the *Chemin*.

The imagery of the *Rose* must have been particularly apposite for Christine while she was writing the *Chemin*, which she began immediately on the conclusion of her part in that dispute. Andrea Tarnowski has pointed out ("Maternity" 119–20) that Christine "remakes the fountain of life into the fountain of knowledge." She has transformed the fountain from the *Rose*—I would add both Guillaume's fountain of Narcissus and Jean de Meun's fountain of life—from a tantalizing erotic site to an inspiring intellectual source. Christine's re-visioning of the fountain can also be thought of as antidote, in the medical sense of curative, to the fountain of the *Rose*. I would also expand and modify Tarnowski's view that Christine refashions the fountain "in order to distance herself from Jean's praise of nature, to set the reader's sights on the study of truth rather than the pleasure of experience" ("Maternity" 120) with the following observations. It is not so much that Christine distances herself from the praise of nature but that she changes the discourse and, in a sense, creates a hybrid being through visual allegory. In effect, what she does is to join the stereotypical idea of the male mind with the female body in the personae of the Muses. The result is a case of what Nadia Margolis ("Poetess" 368) explains as the fusion of two contexts, often disparate and even opposing, into a convincing unity. These two contexts recall the prevalent attitude, dating back to Aristotle and Augustine, that the feminine is to body as masculine is to mind. In the *Bath of the Muses* illumination, as discussed above, Christine has collapsed the binary opposition of that historic discourse, combining female/body and male/mind into one. The text of the *Chemin* establishes the basis for the intellectual tradition associated with the Fountain of Knowledge and its ambient frequented by celebrated male minds. The visual allegory, on the other hand, focuses on the nine nude female bodies immersed in this "water of knowledge." Consequently, they function in a new way. Pictured as chaste virgins clustered together in the fountain, by virtue of their context they are free from traditional erotic connotation; as intellectual inspiration identified with the font of knowledge, they also signify the male world of the mind. Christine has, in effect, transformed canonical male voyeurism into the female authorial gaze. Thus, the female body now carries a new meaning and marks a complete inversion of the prevailing ideology.[18] As Sarah Kay and Miri Rubin aptly point out, "The body, as well as endorsing regimes of power, is also a challenge to dichotomies and hierarchies of established categories" (6).

This kind of mixing or slippage of gender and sex roles is not unique to the *Chemin* in Christine's works. She also uses the female body as a powerful multivalent sign in the text of the *Mutacion de Fortune*, in which she narrates her transformation into a man to guide the family ship after the storm of her husband's untimely death. Analogously, the incipit miniature of the *Livre de la Cité des dames* (Figure 24) depicts Christine and Droiture, albeit in the bodies of women, performing the male role of masons who build the city. With the images of the nude Muses bathing in the Hippocrene spring Christine inscribes male intellectual superiority onto the female body, creating a synchronized, if hybrid, being. Thus, she authorizes women's full assumption of equality in formerly male-only domains without sacrificing the traditional iden-

Figure 24. Christine and Reason, Droiture, and Justice. Incipit to the *Cité des dames*. London, British Library, Harley 4431, fol. 290.

tification of female with nature (body). The visual brings the allegory to concrete realization, combining body and mind before our very eyes.

Notes

For her initial encouragement and subsequent editorial help with this essay I would like to thank Pamela Sheingorn. And for help in translations from the *Chemin* I am most grateful to Leslie Callahan. For help in tracking down bibliography I thank Virginia Budny, and for photographs in Europe I am indebted to Marco Omodarme and Ornella Francisci-Osti. I am also grateful to the staffs of the Biblioteca Angelica in Rome, the Bibliothèque de l'Arsenal and the Bibliothèque Nationale de France in Paris, the Bibliothèque Royale Albert Ier in Brussels, and the Manuscript Room of the British Library in London.

1. Unfortunately, John Fleming's efforts in this direction were canceled out by his summary dismissal of Christine as a minor poet and her part in the Quarrel of the *Roman de la Rose* as "rather inflated . . . by modern feminists and not [to] be taken too seriously." Thus he disregarded the issues he sought to illuminate, that is, the complex questions of text and image in relation to allegory and narrative throughout Christine's numerous works. See Fleming 47.

2. Recognizing Christine's status as an author, Hindman, in her analysis of the *Othea*, shows how the illuminations privilege the political message of the work. With Stephen Perkinson, she demonstrates the part the illuminations play in rewriting the "courtly romance" ("Insurgent Voices"). For other studies of the interaction of text and image in Christine's oeuvre, see Brown-Grant; Zühlke 232–41.

3. Contemporary studies of the body in the Middle Ages is too well known and extensive to be listed here. For Christine, see especially Quilligan, who discusses Christine's metaphorical imagery of the female body in the *Mutacion* and the *Cité des dames*. Christine's most dramatic body imagery occurs in the *Mutacion* when she describes how Fortune turned her body into that of a man so that she could carry out her family responsibilities (lines 1320–97). See also Blumenfeld-Kosinski; Tarnowski, "Maternity," esp. 121–22.

4. A number of scholars have written of Christine's efforts to establish her authority, among whom are Quilligan; Brownlee, "Structures"; Dulac, "Authority"; Krueger, chapter 2 in this volume.

5. The following scholars deal thoroughly with these issues: Hindman, *Christine* 61–63; Laidlaw, "Publisher's Progress" 35–67; Ouy and Reno, "Identification" 221–38; Willard, "Autograph Manuscript" 452–57.

6. For Christine and the figure of the Sibyl, see Hindman, *Christine* 58–59; Margolis, "Poetess as Historian"; Krueger, chapter 2 in this volume; Solterer. An illuminating article, although it does not discuss Christine, is Dronke.

7. Schaefer gives a list, locations, descriptions, and illustrations of the various illuminations, which can be found in the Bibliothèque Nationale de France, Paris, and Bibliothèque Royale Albert Ier, Brussels (119–20).

8. See Brink and Hornbostel for a summary of the Muses' appearance in poetry (18). They were not represented in the medieval period probably because of their pagan origin. Boethius, one of Christine's favorite texts, in his *Consolatio philosophiae*, calls them "stage harlots"! Christine's proclivity for inverting her sources is again apparent here. The Muses were revived by Dante and Petrarch, where Christine knew them, and one finds them frequently later in the Renaissance, but in the visual arts they are commonly represented on Mount Parnassus (conflated with Helicon) accompanied by Apollo, as in the well-known Raphael fresco in the Vatican, and clothed in diaphanous garments, *not* nude bathing.

9. A comparison of the details of Harley 4431 and BNF MS 836, which is similar to Harley 4431, with BNF MS 871 (Figure 22, the *Ovide moralisé*) and the two Brussels manuscripts (10982 and 10983) of the bath further underscores the extent to which Christine

foregrounds the Sibyl, Christine, and the Muses. Brussels, MSS 10982 and 10983 vary some-what from each other. Brussels, MS 10982, not a close-up as the other two, resembles the *Ovide moralisé*'s extensive setting, which delineates the whole mountain and minimizes considerably the figures of the Muses and Pegasus. Brussels, MS 10983 is closer, at least in the relationship of figures to setting, to BNF MS 836 and Harley 4431. Both of the Brussels manuscripts, like the BNF MS 871 *Ovide moralisé*, show the Muses bathing in a natural rather than a man-made pool, downplaying any reference to civilization's artifacts.

10. Pegasus, the child of Poseidon and Medusa, who looms so large in the miniature, was from the Roman period on the symbol of "eternal source of wisdom and poet's flight into the realm of imagination and inspiration." He was essential to the Muses because he provided the waters that they needed to help in passing on truths to poets and philoso-phers (Brink and Hornbostel 18, 34).

11. In the *Cité des dames* Droiture explains to Christine apropos of her relation to her father vis-à-vis her mother: "Your father, who was a great scientist and philosopher, did not believe that women were worth less by knowing science, rather as you know, he took great pleasure from seeing your inclination to learning. The feminine opinion of your mother, however, who wished to keep you busy with spinning and silly girlishness, fol-lowing the common custom of women, was the major obstacle to your being more in-volved in the sciences" (Curnow, "*Cité*" 2.36.4).

12. Kauffmann's monographic study of this subject is informative and profusely illus-trated. I thank Jonathan Alexander for directing me to this valuable reference.

13. See Boccaccio, *Fiametta*; Petrarch lines 1975–85.

14. Increasingly, Christine concerned herself in her writing with the political prob-lems of France. The last half of the *Chemin*, which takes place at the court of Reason, is devoted to this subject. Christine herself is given the task of trying to persuade the feud-ing nobles to establish a peaceful government.

15. According to Kauffmann, there are twenty manuscript versions of the poem and twelve printed editions. The earliest illuminated one, Angelica 1474 in Rome, dates to the third quarter of the thirteenth century; five date to the fourteenth century and four to the fifteenth (20–21). At present, there is no way of knowing whether Christine could have seen the 1392 French translation or any of the other illuminated manuscripts of Peter of Eboli's poem. However, since childhood Christine frequented Charles V's palace at Saint Paul, where he had installed "Roman" baths (Willard, *Christine* 24) and where she con-sulted his extensive library.

16. Infant baptism had replaced adult immersion in the early days of the church, but the ritual of baptism eventually became a sacrament of the church, and its symbolism was embodied visually in the continually repeated scene of John baptizing Christ. Mar-garet R. Miles discusses baptism in the fourth century, with particular emphasis on naked-ness in that context (24–52). Miles quotes Caesarius of Arles who wrote: "Men and women have been redeemed equally by Christ's blood, have been cleansed by the very same bap-tism. . . . with God there are no distinctions of male and female" (Sermon 42, *Corpus Chris-tianorum, Series Latina* 32, 537; quoted in Miles 24).

17. Willard (*Life and Works*) summarizes the history of Christine's involvement in the *Rose* debate (chap. 4). For the details see *Le Débat*, critical edition by Eric Hicks; *Quer-relle*, translations in Baird and Kane.

18. Another instance where the visual allegory inverts established tradition occurs in Christine's treatment of Diana in the *Othea* (chap. 23), where females have been substi-tuted for males. As Marilynn Desmond and Pamela Sheingorn point out, "Christine . . . in-troduces the Creed with a miniature that depicts women reading books; she inscribes fe-male authority in the very place where male authority was usually ensconced" and effectively "erases male Christian authority from visual memory." For further reading on Diana, see especially Vickers; Simons.

❖

CHAPTER 8

"Traittié tout de mençonges"
The *Secrés des dames,* "Trotula," and Attitudes toward Women's Medicine in Fourteenth- and Early-Fifteenth-Century France

Monica H. Green

In a brief exchange with Lady Reason early in the *Livre de la cité des dames,* Christine de Pizan turns to one of the common themes in medieval misogynistic rhetoric: the vile or deformed nature of the female body. So defective is the female body that Nature herself is ashamed at having created it. Christine locates these views in one particular text, what she calls *Du secret des femmes* (which I shall refer to for the moment by both its Latin and French titles, *Secreta mulierum/Secrés des dames).* Christine's opinion of this work is unambiguous: it is a "traittié tout de mençonges," "a treatise composed of lies":

> "Un autre petit livre en latin vi, dame, qui se nomme *Du secret des femmes* qui dit de la composicion de leur corps naturel, moult de grans deffaulx." Responce: "Tu puez congnoistre par toy meismes sans nulle autre preuve, que celluy livre fu fait a voulenté et faintement coulouré: car se tu l'as leu, ce te puet estre chose magnifeste que il est traittié tout de mençonges." (Curnow, *"Cité"* 1.27, p. 649)

> ["I have seen another small book in Latin, my lady, called *The Secret of Women,* which discusses the constitution of their natural bodies and especially their great defects." She replied, "You can see for yourself without further proof, this book was written carelessly and colored by hypocrisy, for if you have looked at it, you know that it is obviously a treatise composed of lies."
> *(City,* trans. Richards [modified], 1.9.2)[1]

Christine's response to the "pure fabrications" and "true lies" ("pures bourdes" and "droittes mençonges") of the *Secreta mulierum/Secrés des dames* is first to ridicule its claims to authority (both Aristotle and the pope are allegedly connected with the text) and then to draw on theological arguments to assert that the female body was created not in some vile place but in Paradise itself, not from mud but from God's highest creation, Adam. Christine was drawing here on common arguments in support of women's "privileges" (Blamires, *Case*). Yet in choosing to follow tradition, Christine foreclosed an opportunity to shift the debate about the female body in a new direction. Nowhere does this physician's daughter draw on any natural philosophical (what we would call "scientific") or medical arguments to claim the similar character of the male and female body, to assert the awesome generative properties of the womb, to plead, as the author of a contemporary English gynecological text did, that the alleged "defects" of living women's bodies are no different from those of women "who now are saints in heaven."[2]

Throughout several years of studying the history of the most widely circulating Latin (and later, vernacular) compendium on women's medicine in later medieval Europe, the so-called *Trotula* texts, I have been haunted by the question of how medieval women might have felt about both these texts and their allegedly feminine author, "Trotula" of Salerno.[3] Did medieval women, for whom sexual modesty was deemed the highest virtue, take comfort in these precepts on the care of their most intimate diseases because they were (apparently) offered by a woman? Was "Trotula," in other words, a heroine for them? To this day, this question has met with only intractable silence: despite the *Trotula's* subject matter, only in a few rare instances do these texts seem to have passed through the hands of women, and I have as yet found no direct testimony to women's attitudes toward the texts or their alleged female author.[4]

Why the silence surrounding "Trotula" extends to Christine's great assembly of heroines, the *Cité des dames*,[5] may be due to any variety of factors, from Christine's attitudes toward history or her range of immediate literary sources (none of which mentioned "Trotula") to the particular rhetorical strategies of the *Cité des dames*. Perhaps Christine simply never heard of "Trotula." Yet I should like to argue that this physician's daughter's silence on one of the most widely known female authors in thirteenth- through fifteenth-century Europe is indeed notable. The *Trotula* were still circulating in late-fourteenth- and early-fifteenth-century France, and Christine would have had access to a copy of the texts in the royal library where, aside from the Sibyl, "Trotula" stood as the sole female author in a collection of more than nine hundred volumes.[6] Christine would have found reference to "Trotula" if she looked at one of the Old French translations of Ovid's *Ars amatoria* available in the libraries of the ducal families of Berry and Burgundy, and perhaps in the royal library as well. Christine would have also found reference to "Trotula" if she had looked at a certain natural-philosophical encyclopedia, the *Placides et Timéo*, three copies of which could be found on the shelves of Charles V's library.

I think it likely that Christine did in fact know something of "Trotula," but that what she knew about her was likely to have made her appear thoroughly *un*suitable for inclusion in the *Cité*. Christine would not, I believe, have thought of "Trotula" favorably as a "mistress of women" (*domina mulierum*, as she was described in the Latin copy at the royal library), nor (as other manuscripts described her) as "the Salernitan woman healer" (*sanatrix Salernitana*) or "Mistress Trotula, the Salernitan" (*magistra Trotula salernitana*; see Figure 25). On the contrary, Christine's image of "Trotula" would more likely have been shaped by a different, less attractive representation that she would have found in certain literary traditions. Here, "Trotula" was lauded not as a compassionate expert on women's medicine so much as a revealer of "women's secrets" to curious, even prurient male clerics. This negative image of the authoress "Trotula" would, in turn, have found further validation in new manipulations of the *Trotula* texts that were being made in the fourteenth and fifteenth centuries, with the result that the authority of both "Trotula" and the *Trotula* was seen to reside in the information they offered on "women's secrets" rather than women's diseases.

Christine's silence on "Trotula" takes on a particular resonance when it is juxtaposed to her articulate and hostile reaction, quoted earlier, to that other widely circulating text on women's bodies, the so-called *Secreta mulierum/Secrés des dames*. Although the *Secreta mulierum/Secrés des dames* is often called a gynecological text (e.g., *City*, trans. Richards, p. 261), such a designation collapses two textual traditions that were in origin quite distinct. While physicians turned to the anatomy, physiology, and pathologies of the female body with the ultimate goal of maintaining health and treating diseases, natural philosophers, beginning in the twelfth century, also expended considerable thought on the workings of the human body, although for them knowledge of sexual difference and generation was pursued for its own sake, for philosophical enlightenment only. Natural philosophical and medical approaches were not necessarily antithetical, and they might be pursued by the same individual, but they were distinct nonetheless. It was more out of the natural philosophical tradition of theorizing generation—its causes and processes—than a medical tradition concerned with therapy that the *Secreta mulierum/Secrés des dames* originated.[7] By the fourteenth century, however, the practical, medical tradition of the *Trotula* texts and the theoretical, natural-philosophical tradition of the *Secreta mulierum/Secrés des dames* began to move toward each other, ultimately becoming so closely allied as to be often indistinguishable. By the time Christine was writing in the early fifteenth century, it would have been very easy for a reader to associate both "Trotula" and the *Trotula* not with therapeutic traditions to *help* women in their diseases, but with the theoretical and downright misogynistic traditions of the *Secrés des dames* and similar texts that mercilessly scrutinized the female body, damning women for their "great defects." Given her silence on "Trotula" and the *Trotula*, we can never know exactly how or even if Christine viewed this feminine figure and her attributed work. However, by delineating the edges

Figure 25. A depiction of "Trotula" from an early-fourteenth-century French manuscript of the *Trotula* ensemble. The orb she holds in her hand is no doubt intended to signify her status as *domina mulierum*. London, Wellcome Institute for the History of Medicine, MS 544, p. 65. By permission of the Wellcome Institute Library.

of Christine's silence on "Trotula" and the *Trotula*, we see that the out-
line fits all too neatly with the jagged form of Christine's harsh response
to that other treatise claiming to discourse on the "corps naturel" of
women, the *Secreta mulierum/Secrés des dames*. Christine's silence on
"Trotula" and the *Trotula* may, therefore, not be a matter of ignorance
at all, but a deliberate silencing of a female authority who, like Heloise,
represented a kind of learning about women that Christine could not
condone.

The *Secreta mulierum/Secrés des dames*

Christine's discussion of the *Secreta mulierum/Secrés des dames* in the
Cité is far more loaded with historical meaning than has hitherto been
realized. Although Christine refers to the *Secrés* as a Latin work and
claims to have herself seen it ("un autre petit livre en latin vi"), it is de-
batable whether she knew the Latin version or the French. Often attrib-
uted to the Dominican theologian Albertus Magnus (d. 1280), who had
taught at the University of Paris from 1245 to 1248 and then at the Do-
minican *studium generale* in Cologne, the Latin *Secreta mulierum* was
probably composed in Germany in the last quarter of the thirteenth cen-
tury, perhaps by a student in Albert's circle.[8] Heavily influenced by the
new Aristotelian learning that Albert had helped to domesticate for Chris-
tian use, the *Secreta* discussed such questions as the process of concep-
tion, astrological influences on the developing embryo, the nature of the
menses, and determination of the sex of the fetus. It focused obsessively
on menstruation, going into great and repetitious detail to describe the
menses' noxious properties.[9] The author of the *Secreta* was apparently
conscious of the potentially illicit use to which the text might be put
(by which he apparently meant prurient if not outright erotic uses), for
he included in the original Latin treatise a warning that it should not be
shown to those who were still children "either in age or in morals."[10] Il-
licit or not, the *Secreta* proved immensely popular throughout Germany
and beyond, circulating widely (first in manuscript and later in print)
both in Latin and in several vernacular translations.[11]

 The Latin *Secreta mulierum* seems to have had limited circulation in
medieval France.[12] Nevertheless, two French translations contributed to
the text's popularity there. The earlier one, called by its editors the *Se-
crés des dames*, is a creative abbreviation and adaptation of its Latin
source.[13] While much of the scholastic posturing of the Latin original
has been eliminated here, the French *Secrés* firmly situates itself in a
learned tradition by expanding its litany of "authorities": Pliny, Solinus,
Pythagoras, and even "Trotula" all expound on the many "secrets" of
the bodies of women. The core of the text, as in the Latin, revolves around
questions of generation: what the material contributions of the parents
are (semen for men, menstrual blood for women), how the fetus devel-

ops in the womb, how the different planets and astrological houses influence the embryo, and so forth. Framing this general discussion are "data" on the nature of the female body and female sexuality. Although not as detailed as its Latin source, the French text perpetuates such misogynistic topoi as the characterization of menstrual blood as poisonous in its effects: it discolors mirrors, drives dogs rabid, kills trees, and can generate within itself "vile, horrible, poisonous creatures" ("mauuaises bestes horibles et enuenimees"). Menstrual blood is so noxious, in fact, that a menstruating woman can harm a child simply by glancing at it. Women who no longer menstruate are even more dangerous, for the evil humors that used to be purged as menstrual blood are now retained in the body.[14] Women are portrayed as sexually voracious: whether menstruating or pregnant (and thus in neither case capable of conception, the natural purpose of heterosexual intercourse), women nevertheless have an insatiable desire for sex.

The intended audience and the didactic purpose of the *Secrés* are not immediately clear. Whereas the Latin text is presented as a dialogue among men, the French text is rather contradictory in its indications of intended audience. On the one hand, the *Secrés des dames* incorporates extended instructions on childbirth drawn from the *Liber de natura rerum* of the Dominican preacher Thomas of Cantimpré. These are presented as the teachings of Cleopatra to her daughter; the instructions are couched in direct second-person address to an intended female audience that includes not only midwives but parturient women themselves who are urged not to let their shame get in the way of proper medical care.[15] Moreover, the text (so the author claims) was composed at the behest of a beloved *damoiselle*. Although she is referred to only in the third person (and therefore not addressed directly), the author still constructs her as a reader by expressing hope that she will not be offended upon reading the text.[16] These hints of an intended female audience are nevertheless contradicted by the other parts of the text that evince a pronounced male orientation: men are instructed on how they can ensure the generation of sons; defloration of virgins is discussed from the male perspective; it is the man who is responsible for ensuring that the woman experiences full satisfaction in heterosexual intercourse since conception cannot take place without it. In a perverse way the text could be read as a kind of *Ars d'amours*: although depicting the female body as full of noxious fluxes and ravenous sexual appetites, the *Secrés* is also an apologia for the necessity of men's continued encounters with the opposite sex. Indeed, men are portrayed as being practically heroic in sacrificing themselves for the sake of women. Unlike women, who cannot get enough of sex, men are depleted by it,[17] yet they must offer themselves to women therapeutically. In discussing uterine dislocation, the *Secrés* asserts that "Galen says that the best remedy for this is the game of love, for the [male] member puts the womb back in its proper place."[18]

151

Thus the French *Secrés*, although it does not engage in the vitriolic excesses of such blatantly misogynistic excursuses as Matheolus's *Lamentations*, nevertheless paints a picture of women that is far from flattering. While the female body is at times almost incidental to the central discussion of generation, the *Secrés des dames* could quite well be described, as Reason described it in the *Cité*, as "a little book...which discusses the constitution of [women's] natural bodies and especially their great defects." Despite its formulaic invocation of the *damoiselle*'s inspiration and the obstetrical instructions addressed to midwives, the *Secrés* appears ultimately intended to educate men about women's bodies. Like the French tradition of *Ars d'amours*,[19] the *Secrés* attempts to preclude a female audience, although in this case that foreclosure is not in the least subtle: the *Secrés* opens with a spurious papal decretal that threatens excommunication to any man who reveals it to a woman.[20]

In mentioning the work she calls *Du secret des femmes*,[21] Christine was, I believe, referring not to the original Latin *Secreta mulierum* (as suggested by Curnow, "*Cité*" 223–24 and, following her, Richards, *City* 261, and "Search" 283) but to this French translation/adaptation.[22] The translation clearly dates far earlier than the specious *terminus a quo* of 1418 proposed by its nineteenth-century editors, Colson and Cazin.[23] Colson and Cazin had based their claim solely on the two references to "Valezius" within the text.[24] They assumed that these referred to Valescus de Tarenta (d. 1418), a Portuguese physician who had studied at Paris and Montpellier and whose medical compendium, the *Philonium*, appeared in the year of his death. The internal references to "Valezius"/ Valescus were, they argued, meant to allude to material in the sixth book of the *Philonium*, which was devoted to the diseases of women.[25] Comparison of the French *Secrés* with its Italian and Dutch counterparts (both of which clearly predate 1418), however, shows that what Colson and Cazin have read as "Valezius" is in fact a corruption of the name "Galenus," that is, the great second-century Greek physician Galen, who in these references is being credited with fairly generic views on human variation and female anatomy.[26] Proper names are badly mutilated throughout the French text, whence for example "Trotula" becomes "Tuilles" or "Tulles" and Cleopatra becomes "Alex Patrix" (Colson and Cazin 13, 36).[27] The 1418 *terminus* that has prevented Christine scholars from connecting the *Secrés* to Christine thus turns out to be based on nothing more substantive than a scribal error.

While it is true that only fifteenth-century manuscripts of this *Secrés des dames* survive,[28] there are several considerations that would push its composition back into the fourteenth century, perhaps even the first half of the century. First, all the extant French copies display pronounced divergences one from the other, which, together with the extensive number of corruptions, would seem to locate their common ancestor at a significant remove from their own dates of composition. Second, the Italian translation, which derives from the French text, exists in a manuscript from the beginning of the fifteenth century, suggesting that the date of composition of the French *Secrés* must be pushed back at least into the late fourteenth century.[29] Third, comparison of the French *Secrés* with its Dutch cousin, *Der Vrouwen Heimelykheid,* points to an even earlier fourteenth-century origin. This Dutch verse text is now extant in two complete copies plus one fragment.[30] According to the Dutch scholars van Doorn and Kuiper, the two different versions of *Der Vrouwen Heime-lykheid,* the "didactic" and the "idyllic," are later redactions of an ear-lier common text, perhaps in prose, which they estimate was written in the mid–fourteenth century. This original Dutch version probably de-rives from the French text when it was at an earlier, much less corrupt stage of development.[31] If, then, the French version is prior to the Dutch, then it must have been composed in the first half of the fourteenth cen-tury. Clearly, a re-edition of the French translation and comparison with the Italian and Dutch versions will be necessary to settle this question definitively, but it is obvious even now that Colson and Cazin's *termi-nus a quo* is without foundation and that the textual relationships just proposed place the composition of the French *Secrés* probably several decades and possibly as much a century earlier than previously believed.

It is, then, more than likely that the French *Secrés des dames* was available in 1405 when Christine was writing the *Cité des dames.* Sev-eral elements of Christine's reference to the text, moreover, point to her use of this translation rather than the Latin original. First, although she clearly knows that the text was originally composed in Latin, Christine could have obtained this information from the French translation itself. Four of the eight copies of the *Secrés,* including all three of northern French origin, state explicitly in the opening rubric that the work has been "translatés de latin en franchois."[32] Second, Christine refers to a papal decretal at the head of the text: "It says at the beginning that who knows what pope excommunicated any man who would read it to a woman or give it to her to read" ("il dit a son commancement que ne sçay quel pappe escommenia tout homme qui le liroit a femme ou a lire luy bailleroit"). In the extant northern French manuscripts, the *Secrés* reads, "And it is forbidden in the decretal *Ad meam doctrinam* by our Holy Father the pope on pain of excommunication to reveal [this book] to a woman" ("Et est deffendu de reveler a femme par nostre saint pere le Pappe sur paine descumement en la decretale Ad meam doctrinam"). Christine has captured the gist of the *Secrés* prohibition: the pope in question is unspecified, excommunication is unambiguously threatened. Her only embellishment is to assert that men are forbidden "to read this to a woman or to give it to her to read," whereas the *Secrés* had more vaguely prohibited men from "revealing" the text to women. This fictitious papal decretal has nowhere been documented in the Latin tra-dition of the *Secreta mulierum.*[33] It thus seems reasonable to conclude that Christine was in fact referring to the French *Secrés des dames*. Why, then, does she claim to have seen the Latin text? Why, in fact, are there several discrepancies between the *Secrés des dames* I have described above and the text Christine pretends to describe in the *Cité des dames*?

Maureen Curnow (who, as I pointed out, believed Christine was referring to the Latin *Secreta mulierum*) was the first to recognize several incongruities in Christine's discussion of the text ("*Cité*" 1048–49). The first and most central of these is Aristotle's alleged authorship: "Some people say that this was made by Aristotle" ("aucuns dient que ce fist Aristote"). Noting Christine's use of the phrase "I remember" ("il me souvient"), Curnow suggested that Christine's attribution of the text to Aristotle was an error induced by faulty recollection. Perhaps this is true: none of the French (nor, for that matter, Latin) manuscripts known to me credit the *Secreta mulierum/Secrés des dames* to Aristotle. Perhaps, as Curnow suggests, Christine confused the *Secreta mulierum* with the immensely popular *Secretum secretorum*, which was commonly attributed to Aristotle. The second major discrepancy, Curnow rightly notes, is that neither of the two assertions about women's bodies that most trouble Christine are actually found in the *Secreta mulierum/ Secrés des dames*. The first—that Nature is ashamed at having formed such an imperfect creature as woman—most probably comes from Matheolus's *Lamentations*, that notorious misogynistic diatribe that was at once the impetus and a major source for Christine's *Cité des dames*. The second—the assertion that the female child is formed when there is impotence and weakness in its mother's womb ("l'impotence et foyblesce qui est cause de fourmer le corps femenin ou ventre de la mere")— echoes Aristotle's assertions in the *Generation of Animals*.[34] These discrepancies thus confirm, according to Curnow, that Christine's faulty recollection has caused her to confuse several different texts, misremembering both their authorship and their content.

I would agree with Curnow that all these are indeed important discrepancies, but I would like to suggest an alternative explanation of their cause: these discrepancies point not to Christine's confusion but to a deliberate rhetorical strategy. In particular, Christine's attribution of the text to Aristotle—or rather, her intimation that other people ("aucuns") say that it was made by him—may reflect not her misremembering the text but her specific concern to deauthorize it. Christine's objective, I propose, was to exonerate Aristotle from the charge of authorship. If the *Secrés* is not the work of the Philosopher, it—and all the beliefs Christine has associated with it—can then be dismissed outright as "mençonges."

Why, if the *Secreta/Secrés* was not really attributed to Aristotle, bring him into the picture at all? One reason may be that, although not assigned authorship of the text, Aristotle's name was in fact intimately associated with the *Secrés des dames*. In the text, generic "masters" (*les maistres*) are cited first and most frequently, yet Aristotle is the first named authority to be cited (as he had been in the Latin original), and, after Hippocrates, it is his authority that is most frequently called on.[35] In fact, whereas the Latin text had frequently referred to him as "the Philosopher" (philosophus), the French translation usually uses his personal name, thus eliminating any possible ambiguity. True, the Aristotelian view about the malgeneration of the female in her mother's womb that Christine situates in the Secrés is not, as I noted above, actually found there. But it would not have been very difficult for any informed reader to see the connection between the views attributed to Aristotle here in the Secrés and those found in his authentic works, particularly the Generation of Animals.

Jeffrey Richards ("Search") has recently examined the role of Aristotelian philosophy in Christine's arguments about the genesis of women in Cité des dames 1.27a. He suggests that Christine's counterargument for the equality of the sexes at the Creation (or at least the equality of their souls) is a learned and subtle critique of the discussion of women in Thomas Aquinas's Commentary on Aristotle's Metaphysics (a text with which Christine was clearly familiar) and in his Summa theologiae.[36] Christine may, Richards concludes, have been returning to a more purely Aristotelian position that, given the identity of the soul in men and women, gender differences are ultimately accidental.

Richards's implication that Christine's critical reading of Aquinas derived from her simultaneous reading of Aristotle's views on the soul is indeed intriguing. I do not, however, believe that Christine could have found Aristotle as recuperable in his views on the bodies of women as Richards implies. While Aristotle was indeed clear in the Metaphysics that men and women did not constitute separate species, he was equally clear in his Generation of Animals that women are in their very essence defective. They are created only when Nature's inherent striving for perfection has failed. They are "mutilated" males who are created when the male principle "does not bear sway and cannot concoct the nourishment [i.e., the menstrual blood] through lack of heat nor bring it into its proper form, but is defeated in this respect" (Aristotle, Gen. anim. 2.3, 737a 27, and 4.1, 766a 17–20). These Aristotelian tenets had been carried over into the medieval Latin West virtually unchanged. Indeed, if anything, Albertus Magnus, Aquinas's teacher, had reasserted the "strong" form of the Aristotelian views, writing, for example, that woman is created "because of a certain impediment of the matter and not because of the intention of nature," for, just as Aristotle says, "the female is by nature a deformed male [mas occasionatus], just like the incomplete development of the fifth finger of the hand or paralysis of a limb happens because of an accidental defect of a [generative] principle" (Albertus Magnus, lib. 3, tract. 2, cap. 8 [ed. Stadler 1:347]).[37] Aquinas, for his part, attempted to rehabilitate the more problematic theological consequences of Aristotle's pagan philosophy, yet in the end his scholastic resolution

155

of the question "On the production of woman" (*Summa theologiae*, book 1a, quaestio 92) retains the core of Aristotle's views.[38] It is little wonder that Matheolus, after having asserted explicitly that the female body is a monstrosity and claimed that Nature is ashamed at having created "a thing so imperfect," credits Aristotle ("le philosophe") with the belief:

> Le philosophe en l'escripture
> Le tesmoingne assés clerement,
> En son livre, et dit telement:
> Lors que nature s'envaïst
> A ouvrer, elle s'esbaïst
> Forment quant son erreur regarde.
> (*Lamentations*, bk. 2, lines 4120–26)

> [The Philosopher in his book witnesses this clearly enough, saying: "Thus Nature, overcome with her labor, is greatly ashamed when she sees her error."]

The argument against women from natural philosophy proves to be the last straw for Christine in *Cité* 1.1c as she realizes how pervasive and unanimous are the opinions of "tous trattiez philosophes, pouettes, tous orateurs": "Being in such thought, a great dissatisfaction and failure of courage overcame me as I began to detest myself and the whole feminine sex, as if it were a monstrosity of nature" ("monstre en nature").[39] And it is precisely this question of the allegedly imperfect creation of woman that prompts Christine's subsequent lament to God. The argument against women from natural philosophy therefore forms the keystone in the edifice of arguments from authority that Christine will soon disassemble one by one (see Curnow, "*Cité*" 1038, 1048). Aristotle, on this matter, was not only in agreement with all the other philosophers who "speak with one mouth" ("parlent par une meismes bouche"; Curnow, "*Cité*" 1.1a, p. 618). Aristotle *was* the authority.

Whether Christine actually read the *Generatio animalium* herself[40] or only Aquinas's summation of it in quaestio 92, Aristotle's association with these profoundly misogynistic views must have deeply troubled her. The Philosopher had, after all, been elevated to a level of new prominence during the reign of Charles V, who, as part of his extensive translation program, had had Nicole Oresme translate several of Aristotle's principal texts into French for the first time (see Sherman). Christine held the Philosopher in similarly high regard. In the *Cité des dames* alone, she refers to him seven times, always deferentially. His authority may not be unassailable (he, too, is subject to criticism by other philosophers; 1.4) and he may not be omniscient, capable of answering every question (1.40), nor can even his teachings, "which have greatly profited human intelligence," outshine the contributions of such women as Ceres, Minerva, and Carmentis (1.106a). Yet he remains the archetypical example of how useful acquired knowledge is to humankind (1.115b). He is still, for Christine, the prince of philosophers. In fact, although Christine had used the argument of physical deformity to explain why some men become misogynous (1.17), she later cites Aristotle's physical deformity to explain why his intellect was so exceptionally well developed (1.51).[41] Christine's kid-glove treatment of Aristotle is particularly striking when compared with her criticism of other misogynous authorities in 1.25–39. Christine discredits Matheolus by stating that he was a bitter old man, Ovid by claiming that he led a dissolute life, Cecco d'Ascoli by implying that his death at the stake was due to his "horrible wickedness" and hatred of women. Cicero she names even if she does not explicitly criticize him, and Cato she indulgently recuperates by saying that, pagan though he was, he "spoke truer than he knew," as she turns his arguments against women into positive truisms. All the remaining "authorities" are consigned to anonymity: "some authors" ("aucuns aucteurs"), "these men" ("ces hommes"), "another author" ("un aucteur"), a Latin proverb ("un prouverbe en latin"), "someone, I don't know who" ("ne sçay qui"), "some men" ("aucuns hommes") and "some foolish preachers" ("aucuns folz sermonneurs"; Curnow *"Cité"* 1.31–34, pp. 654–61).[42] Only in the case of Aristotle and the *Secrés des dames* does Christine assert that the misogynous text in question is misattributed.

Aristotle was too deeply implicated in Charles V's project of *translatio studii*, to which Christine also subscribed, and in her own concept of the virtues of the philosophical enterprise for her to dismiss him as a common misogynist.[43] By simultaneously contesting the attribution of the *Secrés des dames* to Aristotle and locating the offensive views about women's bodies within this now discredited text, Christine has effectively exculpated Aristotle from the charge of authorship and dissociated him from all problematic assertions of women's physical deformity. These assertions, relegated to the same realm of anonymity to which other petty misogynists have already been consigned, can now be rejected outright as "pures bourdes" and "droittes mençonges," lies so blatant that any woman reading the work would immediately criticize it and mock it. And it is perhaps to foreclose any further reading of this text that Christine refers to it as existing only in Latin. As I said earlier, we cannot be sure that Christine did not see the Latin *Secreta mulierum*, but her description (whether from memory or not) of the spurious papal decretal suggests that she did see the French *Secrés des dames*. Her claim that this is "un autre petit livre en latin" — her denial, in effect, that the French translation exists — may thus be yet another feint, another deliberate attempt to deny this text any claim to belong to the intellectual patrimony that has now passed from Rome to France and from Latin into French.

All the "discrepancies" in Christine's allusion to the *Secreta mulierum/ Secrés des dames* thus point to a calculating and deliberate recasting of both Matheolus and Aristotle. But more than demonstrating her attempt to recuperate Aristotle from his own misogyny, Christine's "erroneous" reference to Aristotle and her discussion of women's alleged deformities here in the *Cité des dames* reflects her awareness of a discourse on women's bodies broader than the narrow confines of the *Secrés des dames* or even Aristotle alone. That larger discourse about women's bodies was to be found not only in the moral and literary texts (including Matheolus) that Christine most commonly cited, but also, and more extensively, in scientific works, both natural-philosophical and medical. Another key player in that larger realm of discourse was the *Trotula*, and although Christine may have been silent on both it and its alleged author, it is unlikely that she could have long stayed ignorant of its existence or its significance in late-fourteenth- and early-fifteenth-century discourses on the female body.

"Trotula" and the *Trotula*

The *Trotula* was a compendium of three treatises of different authorship written in the twelfth century, probably at the southern Italian medical center of Salerno. All three texts address women's medicine: the first, *Liber de sinthomatibus mulierum* (Book on the conditions of women), discusses gynecology and obstetrics; the second, *De curis mulierum* (On treatments for women), deals with gynecology, obstetrics, and cosmetics; and the third, *De ornatu mulierum* (On women's cosmetics) treats cosmetics alone. The first and the third texts were almost certainly written by men, yet because these authors' names were not attached to the texts, when all three works were brought together late in the twelfth century they were ascribed to the famous Salernitan healer named Trota, to whom the middle text was (in essence, correctly) attributed. The compendium at first went under the title *Trotula* ("the little Trota"), although the term was soon misunderstood as a personal name—hence the genesis of the authoress "Trotula," whose existence and femininity were hardly ever doubted during the medieval period (M. Green, "Development").

The *Trotula*, either independently or fused into an ensemble, were the most widely circulating specialized texts on women's medicine from the early thirteenth to the mid-fifteenth centuries. In France, the earliest Latin copies appear around the turn of the thirteenth century, and we find "Trotula" referred to by such medical writers as Gerard de Berry (fl. 1220–30) and the Paris-trained Petrus Hispanus (later Pope John XXI, d. 1277). Many copies of the *Trotula* are found in manuscripts of French origin, where the work is situated amid the most popular medical texts of the day. By the end of the fourteenth century, at least three copies of the *Trotula* (plus a fourth text misattributed to "Trotula") could be found at the Sorbonne, and there was probably at least one each at the cathedrals of Laon and Reims.[44] Even the king owned a copy: the inventories of the royal library from 1373 up through 1424 listed a modest collection of Latin works (valued in 1424 at a mere six *sous*) which contained as its opening text *Trotula, domina mulierum*: "Trotula, the mistress of women."[45] As Charles V could appreciate, the utility of the *Trotula* was not limited to Latinate physicians. He himself had had a French copy of the text: "a small, fat volume" containing, in addition to "le petit et le grant Trotole," the surgical treatise of Lanfranc, a book of compound medicines, and medicines for conditions of the eyes (Paris, BNF, MS fr. 2700, fol. 5r; cf. Delisle, item 828 [2:*135]).[46] There were more medieval translations of the *Trotula* into French than into any other European vernacular,[47] and it is indicative of the utility of these vernacular versions that Charles should have given away his copy of "Trotole" to a certain Pierre, surgeon from Montpellier.[48] Indeed, "Trotula" was such an authority that works of entirely different origin came to bear her name, such as the text *Trotula de secretis mulierum*, which could be found in Paris at both the Abbey of Saint Victor and the Sorbonne.[49]

The *Trotula* was, then, by no means an obscure or little-known text in late-fourteenth- and early-fifteenth-century Paris. Although not on the official medical curriculum of the University of Paris, nor even often cited by medical masters when they came to write their own disquisitions on women's diseases (in that context they preferred much more authoritative works like Avicenna's *Canon*), the *Trotula* continued to be incorporated into practicing physicians' handbooks of works essential to daily therapeutic demands, while the alleged authoress "Trotula" continued to be credited as the leading authority on women's medicine.[50]

Whether Christine, the daughter of a physician, would have automatically known of "Trotula" and the *Trotula* is not clear. It is, first of all, possible that Tommaso da Pizzano himself was unacquainted with the learned Salernitan magistra and her attributed opus: if the limited number of later medieval northern Italian manuscripts of the *Trotula* is any indication, the texts' influence may have already been waning there during Tommaso's tenure at Bologna. Moreover, Christine seems to have been somewhat less influenced by her father's medical insights than she was by his astronomical knowledge. While she certainly makes use of medical metaphors in her writings, these rarely display a particularly detailed knowledge of medicine.[51] Christine's failure to mention "Trotula" may thus be attributable more to her lack of interest in medicine than a deliberate omission.

Still, it seems to me inevitable that Christine would at some point have come across at least the name of "Trotula"—the only woman, besides the notorious Cleopatra, who was claimed as the author of any medical texts commonly circulating in medieval France.[52] For not only (as just noted) were copies of the *Trotula* (clearly attributed to "Trotula" as author) available in a variety of fourteenth- and early-fifteenth-century French libraries, both personal and institutional, but Christine is also likely to have encountered the figure of "Trotula" in two nonmedical texts. In both of these works, "Trotula" appears as an authority on the nature of women in a way that could not have but caught Christine's eye.[53]

"Trotula" had first been summoned as an authority on women in an early-thirteenth-century French translation-cum-commentary of Ovid's *Ars amatoria*. Here, "Trotula," "who teaches the nature of women," is cited as the source for the assertion that although women pretend to be simple and modest, they really want to be courted and seen by men:

> Selonc ce que Troculeus [sic], qui enseigna la nature des femmes dist, ja soit ce que les femmes se facent simples et honteuses, si veullent elles bien c'om les prie et qu'on les esgart.... Et ne vont elles aux jeux ne mais pour ce que aussi voulentiers veoient elles les hommes comme les hommes elles. Et ce puet on veoir appere-ment, car aussi volentiers y vont les laides commes les belles. (*L'Art d'amours*, ed. Roy, 81)

> [According to Troculeus, who taught about the nature of women, although women pretend to be unpretentious and bashful, they ac-tually want men to court them and to look at them.... Women go to the games because they want to see men as much as men want to see them. This is quite obvious, because the ugly go there as willingly as the beautiful.]
>
> (Trans. Blonquist, 13)[54]

The discussion of women's shame that one finds in the *Trotula* itself (at the beginning of the *Liber de sinthomatibus mulierum*) is quite different:

> Quia ergo mulieres debilioris sunt nature quam uiri, ideo plus uiris in partu molestantur angustia, hinc etiam quod in eis frequentius habundant egritudines quam in uiris, et maxime circa membra of-ficio nature deputata. Et quoniam ipse sue condicionis fragilitatem uerecundia et rubore fatentur egritudinum suarum que circa partes secretiores eueniunt, medicis non audent angustias reuelare. Earum ergo miseranda calamitas et maxime cuiusdam mulieris gratia ani-mum meum sollicitat ut contra predictas egritudines earum pro-uideam sanitati. (Oxford, Magdalen 173, fol. 246v)

> [Because, therefore, women are of a weaker nature than men, so more than men they are afflicted, [especially] in childbirth. It is for this reason also that more frequently diseases abound in them than in men, especially around the organs assigned to the work of na-ture. And because only with shame and embarrassment do they confess the fragility of the condition of their diseases that occur around their secret parts, they do not dare reveal their distress to

(male) physicians. Therefore, their misfortune, which ought to be pitied, and especially the sake of a certain woman, moved me to provide some remedy for their above-mentioned diseases.]

Whereas the *Liber de sinthomatibus mulierum* (which figured as the opening piece of the *Trotula* ensemble) had stressed that women's shame at revealing their bodies to men was both real and truly debilitating, in effect posing a threat to their well-being, the author of the Old French Ovid perverted that assertion into its exact opposite: women love to be seen by men. The authority of this (allegedly) female expert on women, "Trotula," is thus being invoked to damn and not to defend women.

Christine might well have known this translation of Ovid, since copies of it could be found in the library of the duke of Berry (at least until 1402, by which point he had given his copy to Jean de Bourbon) and perhaps also in the library of the dukes of Burgundy and the royal library (Roy 17–19).[55] Of course, it is possible that even having looked at this translation of Ovid, Christine missed the allusion to the *Liber de sinthomatibus mulierum*. Indeed, what must have been the original feminine form "Trotula" may have already been corrupted in the copy Christine saw to "Troculeus" or "Troculet," which she may not have understood to refer to a feminine author.[56] There is, however, another literary reference to "Trotula" that Christine is also likely to have seen and that could have left no doubt in her mind about the gender of this figure "Trotula."

In the royal library, among the natural-philosophical tracts that Christine would have drawn on repeatedly for her didactic encyclopedism (see Ribémont), she would have found three copies of the *Placides et Timéo ou Li secrés as philosophes*. This encyclopedic work, set in dialogue form between a master Timéo (from Plato's dialogue of that name) and his princely pupil, Placides, covers the creation of the world, reproduction of the human species, meteorology, prodigies of nature, and the history of civilization. Questions surrounding embryology, female physiology, and sexuality make up nearly one-third of the whole text.[57] In a section describing women's allegedly insatiable sexual desire (even during pregnancy), Christine would have found "Trotula" cited as an authority on "the nature of women." Although mentioned alongside "Hermafrodites," a man who dressed in women's clothing and passed amid the company of women to learn their "private natures," and Sirenis, "another *sage femme*," "Trotula" is clearly the leading authority on female sexuality. It was to this much-experienced *femme-philosophe* that "all women disclosed their thoughts more willingly than to a man." She, in turn, "looked in her books and found confirmation of all that nature revealed to her and, from that, she knew most of the nature of women."[58] "Trotula's" learnedness and authority are magnificently reinforced by the depiction of her in the oldest extant manuscript of the *Placides et Timéo*, which dates from 1304. Under the rubric "How the woman reads to the

clerk the secrets of nature" ("Come la fame lit as clers les secres de na-
ture"), "Trotula" appears seated before a large book with her right hand
raised in the classic gesture of instruction (Figure 26).[59] One of the copies
of the *Placides et Timéo* in the royal library was in a volume described
as having a "grant quantité d'istoires" (Delisle, 2:*90); if its iconographic
series was anything like that in Rennes, MS 593, then it is conceivable
that Christine was familiar with both textual and visual portraits of this
highly accomplished *femme-philosophe*.

As with the French Ovid, the views that are actually attributed to
"Trotula" here in the *Placides et Timéo* are nowhere found in the *Tro-
tula* texts themselves.[60] In neither case, however, does that really mat-
ter. In both the French Ovid and the *Placides et Timéo*, the figure of

Figure 26. An illustration of "Trotula" expounding on the nature of women from the
earliest extant copy of the *Placides et Timéo*. The rubric above the illumination reads in
full, "How the woman reads to the clerk the secrets of nature" ("Come la femme lit as
clers les secres de nature"). Rennes, Bibliothèque Municipale, MS 593, an. 1304, fol. 532r.

"Trotula" has been invoked to serve whatever purpose the author wished. "Trotula" has been co-opted—or, as Barbara Newman has recently argued in the case of Heloise, appropriated—to serve as a feminine mouthpiece for misogynistic views on women (Newman). Either text, I believe, would have been enough to induce Christine to turn away from "Trotula" as a source of inspiration. Yet there is more. The way in which the *Trotula* texts themselves came to be used in the fourteenth and fifteenth centuries may have added further "real-life" confirmation to Christine's image of "Trotula" as a traitor to her sex—and of gynecological writings as offering more occasion for slandering women than of aiding them.[61] And it is at this point that the *Secrés des dames* tradition and that of the *Trotula* intersect.

Mistaken Identities

I said earlier that the natural-philosophical and the medical traditions were distinct in the ways they approached the human body. Yet several issues—for example, the primacy of the heart, the nature of digestion, and, above all, generation—elicited the attention of both natural philosophers and physicians. In that both texts dealt with aspects of reproduction, both the *Secreta mulierum* (essentially natural-philosophical in focus) and the *Trotula* (strictly medical in focus) came to be appropriated by wider audiences than those for which they were originally intended.

The majority of copies of the Latin *Secreta mulierum* are found in natural-philosophical or "clerical" contexts: surrounded by works of Aristotle or Albertus Magnus, tracts on astrology or alchemy, treatises on consanguinity, or even sermons. Nevertheless, while the Latin text is not a medical treatise in the sense that it concerns itself with therapy for women's diseases, it was drawn into the ambit of medical discourse, being found in medical contexts in about 29 percent of the manuscripts.[62]

The French *Secrés des dames* has the same bivalent capacity as its Latin progenitor: it can be read as either medicine or natural philosophy. The French translation pushes the associations with medicine further, adding features that draw it more readily into a medical tradition, specifically the extended discussion of childbirth addressed directly to midwives. Seven out of the eight known copies of the *Secrés* appear in surgical codices, confirming that it was indeed perceived as a work with medical utility.[63] In this context, the French *Secrés des dames* might actually be mistaken for a gynecological text; it might be assumed to be a medical text devoted to the description of women's unique afflictions with the specific goal of treating and, ideally, curing them. The eighth copy of the *Secrés des dames*, in contrast, places it next to the encyclopedic *Placides et Timéo*, thus drawing it back into its original ambit of natural-philosophical discussions of generation. The fact that one and the same text could function in these two very different codicological and intellectual milieux demonstrates a mutability, not of the text itself, but of the assumptions and expectations that readers brought to it.

Just as the *Secrés des dames* came to be seen as a quasi-medical text, so, too, the *Trotula*, for its part, came to be seen as a quasi-natural-philosophical one. Beginning in the thirteenth century and gaining momentum in the fourteenth, a transformation occurred in the uses made of gynecological literature, especially the *Trotula*. What had originally functioned as a general compendium covering all of women's diseases was now employed as a narrowly focused source for information on generation: the basic physiological processes involved in generation, the means to ensure conception and to ensure that, once conceived, the fetus was brought out into the world alive. The focus, in other words, has shifted from women and their sufferings to the product that comes out of women's generative organs. Notably, it is precisely when the *Trotula* begins to be pared down and repackaged for these new "generational" uses that it takes on the epithet "the secrets of women."

This shift, exhibited in other parts of Europe in the Latin *Trotula*, is in France most distinctive in the vernacular traditions.[64] The label *Secrés de femmes* is first applied to the *Trotula* in the thirteenth century, when an anonymous redactor created what is in effect a little vernacular sermon on generation by extracting the passages on fertility, contraception, and aid in childbirth from an early version of the *Liber de sinthomatibus mulierum* (Cambridge, Trinity, MS O.1.20). A similar reductionism can be seen in a heavily abbreviated French adaptation of the *Trotula* made perhaps in the late fourteenth or early fifteenth century. Using an earlier, complete French translation of the *Liber de sinthomatibus mulierum* as his or her base, the adaptor leaves largely intact the opening chapters on female physiology and problems of menstruation, but then abbreviates the rest of the text (e.g., the discussions of uterine suffocation[65] or prolapse, lesions, and cancers) in such a way as to view these diseases only insofar as they affect fertility. Most emphasis is placed on fertility problems, contraceptives, and aids for difficult and normal birth. Moreover, in both of the two manuscripts still extant this abbreviated *Trotula* is framed in such a way as to highlight its "generational" character.

In one instance (Kassel, 4° MS med. 1), the *Trotula* is preceded by an account of the creation of Adam, thus situating the following medical discussion of generation within the larger framework of the Creation. In the other manuscript (Lille, MS 863), the *Trotula* now looks more like the pseudo-Albertan *Secreta mulierum* than a text on therapeutics. After copying out the first few sentences of the prologue to the *Trotula*, the compiler introduces a brief dialogue between master and student on the "secrets of women": how long it takes for the embryo to develop, why women are more lusty than men, why people who have suitably hot and moist temperaments cannot generate, why prostitutes ("foles femmes") rarely conceive, why some women incur miscarriages. The text is twice introduced as the "Book of the Secrets of Ladies" (*Livres [sic] des secrés as dames*) and, as in the *Placides et Timéo*, a female authority is set side by side with the traditional male ones: "Here begins the book of the secrets of ladies that Constantine, Galen, and Hippocrates made. And it was made, too, by Helen, the mother of Constantine, who knew all of nature and understood all the properties of herbs." Helen's special credentials are later restated: "Helen, the mother of Constantine, who knew the ways of women."[66] Moreover, a second female authority is added: a certain queen Aelis is said to have proven the efficacy of a contraceptive.[67] Although none of these French adaptations of the *Trotula* emphasize or manipulate the female authorship of "Trotula" (the texts are in every case anonymous),[68] an attribution of these *Secrés as dames* to "Trotula" would have been in no way inconsistent with the image of her already constructed by the Old French Ovid and the *Placides et Timéo*.

Other French adaptations of the *Trotula*, even if they do not bear the title *Secrés des dames*, nevertheless suggest a similar narrowing of focus on issues of generation. One abbreviated (and untitled) version, very similar in content to the two manuscripts just described, is found within a volume comprising not simply medical texts but astrology and computus as well. The *Trotula* is followed first by some additional French recipes to test for fertility, and then by a Latin dialogue on human generation (Paris, BNF, MS nouv. acq. lat. 693). A fourteenth-century Anglo-Norman verse adaptation (also untitled) appeals gratuitously to the authority of Aristotle and situates the *Trotula* amid French and Latin texts on geomancy, prognostications according to the month of birth, tracts on astronomy and natural philosophy, and not one but two additional tracts on human generation (Cambridge, Trinity, MS O.2.5). Yet another French translation bears the title "A Treatise on the Many Diseases Which Afflict Women, and on Their Secret Diseases" ("Un traictié de plusieurs maladies qui peuent avenir aux femmes, et de leurs maladies secretes," Turin, MS L.IV.17). Here, the *Trotula* has been simultaneously pared down to a narrow range of topics revolving around generation and amplified by additional material on female anatomy (which was nowhere described in the original *Trotula*), as well as by citations from "Master Albert of Cologne who was a great naturalist" ("Maistre Albers de Coulongne qui fust un grant naturien").[69] This radically transformed *Trotula* is found within a massive compendium of French astronomical and surgical texts that also comprises, notably, that "treatise composed of lies," the *Secrés des dames*.

The *Trotula*, therefore, like the *Secrés des dames*, now straddled the border between medicine and natural philosophy, sometimes appearing (as it had always done) in juxtaposition to texts of exclusively therapeutic content, but occasionally also next to works of largely natural-philo-sophical interest. If both the *Trotula* and the *Secrés des dames* circulate in the same codicological contexts and if both of them bear similar titles (*Secrés des dames/Secrés des femmes*), does there not arise the possibility that they will be confused? The possibility that, despite their almost complete difference in content, they will be assumed to be similar?

Let us suppose that a medieval reader picks up a manuscript like Paris, Bibliothèque Nationale de France, MS fr. 631. Here, she or he would find the *Secrés des dames* situated between the *Chirurgia* of Lanfranc and a tract on anatomy, on one side, and a brief collection of gynecological recipes on the other. He or she then picks up a manuscript like Paris, Bibliothèque Sainte-Geneviève, MS 1037, where he or she finds the *Livre de Trocule* alongside, again, Lanfranc's *Chirurgia*, as well as a book of compound medicines and a variety of surgical recipes including those of Jean Picart and Henri de Mondeville, which were compiled at the request of Charles of Valois. Would such a reader not be justified in assuming that both these texts on the female body contained similar information? Or let us suppose this reader picks up a manuscript like Glasgow, Ferguson 241, where the *Secrés* appears just after the *Placides et Timéo*.[70] In the former text, "Trotula" could be found revealing women's "secrets" to men, while in the latter those "secrets" could be found spelled out in all their alternately fascinating and appalling detail. Or let us suppose that this reader, him- or herself denied access to the library of the Sorbonne, asks a scholar there whether that library owned a copy of "Trotula." He would reply that it owned four: two entitled "On the Diseases of Women According to Trotula" (*De passionibus mulierum secundum Trotulam*), a third entitled "The Practica of Lady Trota on the Secrets of Women" (*Practica domine Trote de secretis mulierum*), and a fourth, which was kept chained for reference in the *magna libraria*, entitled (albeit spuriously) "Trotula on the Secrets of Women" (*Trotula de secretis mulierum*).[71] Were this reader later to find a copy of the *Trotula* itself, would she or he not open it up with an expectation of finding something akin to what the *Secrés des dames* offered, some kind of discourse on female sexuality and "women's secrets" like that intimated in the *Placides et Timéo*? Would he or she not assume that medical and natural-philosophical discussions about women were essentially identical, that both traditions discussed women's bodies in the same reductionist and narrowly teleological way, that both "spoke with one mouth"? If that reader were Christine, would she not believe that neither "Trotula" nor what passed as women's medicine could be trusted as sympathetic advocates of women's concerns?

Just as in "attributing" the *Secrés des dames* to Aristotle Christine was doing something quite different than simply confusing authorship, so, too, in damning the *Secrés des dames* she was taking aim not simply at that individual text, but at the ways in which male intellectuals in general discoursed on the bodies of women. Just as the *Lamentations* of Matheolus was used to stand for a much broader array of misogynistic texts (many of which, in origin, had not been antifeminist), so, too, the *Secrés* may have stood for a larger phenomenon: that of the appropriation by clerics and natural philosophers of medical discourses on women's bodies and the consequent narrowing of perspective from larger issues of women's pain to more limited problems of women's sexuality and capacity to reproduce. As the *Trotula* were drawn slowly yet ineluctably into the ambit of the "secrets of women" tradition, both they and their alleged author were increasingly compromised and distanced from their original role as aides to women. Had Christine only been a physician's daughter, she might have come to know "Trotula" and the *Trotula* as a fund of knowledge on women's diseases not readily accessible in most general medical textbooks. But as a broadly educated *savante*, Christine may have seen more of the female authority "Trotula" that was represented in natural-philosophical and misogynistic traditions than the Salernitan healer sympathetically attempting to alleviate women's sufferings. The image of "Trotula" as a mouthpiece for misogynistic traditions may have colored, and perhaps even precluded, any engagement with the text of the *Trotula*, which in its original form had been only slightly related to the *Secrés des dames* in content and quite antithetical to it in intent.

Closing the Doors to the *Cité des dames*

I mentioned earlier Barbara Newman's arguments about the appropriation of Heloise's voice by Jean de Meun and others, who thereby rendered her repellent to Christine. I believe the parallels between Heloise and "Trotula" can in fact be extended. Both of them, of course, are absent from the *Cité des dames*. Curnow ("*Cité*"), and now more emphatically Newman and Jeffrey Richards ("'Seulette'"), have suggested why Heloise—whose story Christine certainly knew well—should have been omitted. The omission of "Trotula" from the *Cité des dames* is equally significant, given that she as well as Heloise would have ranked among the most renowned learned women of recent history. Being herself not only a learned woman but also engaged on a mission to show women's general capacity for learning, why would Christine not embrace these two intellectual forebears?

Christine did not embrace them—and perhaps felt she could not—because both, though learned, were learned in a way that Christine would have found profoundly disturbing. It might be supposed from the "coilles" theme in the Debate of the *Rose* that Christine reacted negatively to the *Secrés des dames*, and by extension also to the *Trotula* and its alleged author, because of the explicitness of its language. But simply to be associated with sexuality did not invalidate other women's claims to entry into the *Cité des dames.* Christine is able to recuperate other women of questionable sexuality, such as Semiramis. Heloise and "Trotula," unlike other women, however, share a common feature in the way they were portrayed: their sexuality and their learning are intimately connected. There is a striking parallel in the manner each woman is described, "Trotula" in the *Placides et Timéo,* Heloise in the *Roman de la Rose:*

> Premierement vous di que une femme fu, qui fu philosophe, le quelle fu apelee Trotula, qui moult vesqui et moult fu belle en se jonesche, de le quele les fusiciens qui riens sevent, tiennent moult d'auctorités et de bons enseignemens, la quelle nous dist une partie des natures as femmes. L'unne partie nous en peut elle bien dire, tant comme elle en senti de soy, tant comme elle estoit femme; l'autre partie, pour ce que elle estoit femme: toutes femmes descouvroient a li leur consail plus volentiers que a nul homme et li disoient leur natures; et celle regardoit en ses livres et trouvoit concordance en ce que nature lui en devisoit et, par ce, elle savoit grant partie des natures as femmes. (*Placides et Timéo* 133–34)

> [First I tell you that there was a woman, a philosopher, whose name was Trotula, who lived a long time and who was very beautiful in her youth. From her, physicians who know things gather much authoritative knowledge and good teaching. She tells us something of the nature of women. One part she can tell us well because she feels it in herself, because she herself was a woman. The other part [she knows] also because she was a woman: all women disclosed their thoughts to her more readily than to any man, and they told her of their condition. And she looked in her books and found there concordance with that which Nature had revealed to her, and by means of this she knew the great part of the natures of women.]

> bien antendanz et bien letree
> et bien amanz et bien amee, . . .
> car les livres avoit veüz
> et estudiez et seüz,
> et les meurs feminins savoit,
> car tretouz en soi les avoit. . . .
> . . . .
> Mes je ne croi mie, par m'ame,
> c'onques puis fust nule tel fame;
> si croi je que sa lestreüre
> la mist a ce que la nature
> que des meurs femenins avoit
> vaincre et donter mieuz en savoit.
> (*Roman de la Rose* lines 8735–36, 8743–46, 8795–800)

[well-educated and well-read, and most loving and beloved.... For she had looked at books and studied them and knew them well, and she understood women's ways, for she had them so much within herself....

But I don't believe, by my soul, that there was ever another such woman; I suspect that her learning taught her how best to vanquish and subdue the woman's ways she knew by nature.]

Both women are not simply learned, but they have a kind of knowledge that no man (with the partial exception of "Hermaphrodite") ever could: they have themselves inhabited a female body and "know the nature/ ways of women" ("Trotula" "savoit grant partie des natures as femmes," Heloise "les meurs feminins savoit"). Heloise is later said to have used her book learning "to vanquish and subdue the woman's ways she knew by nature." Jeffrey Richards ("'Seulette'") has suggested that this "denatured" Heloise is repugnant to Christine because she makes learning and femininity seem incompatible. Yet Heloise becomes the misogynists' darling precisely because she is a woman and "knows the ways of women." So, too, with "Trotula." She, indeed, is credited with having accumulated *additional* experiential knowledge from the testimony of women who have told her "leur natures." What is most distinctive about both women, though, is that they combine their knowledge of "women's nature/ways" with what they have found in their books. For misogynistic traditions, therefore, their authority is, in its own way, supreme. For Christine, who is herself attempting to claim validity both for what she knows of herself and her "ways as a natural woman" ("je pris a examiner moy meismes et mes meurs comme femme naturelle") and for what she has learned from women she knows (Curnow, *"Cité"* 1.1b, p. 618), these two learned female predecessors need to be not embraced but repudiated, not lauded but silenced for having turned their learning against women.[72]

Kevin Brownlee has recently demonstrated Christine's technique of recuperating Boccaccian heroines for inclusion in her *Cité des dames.* One of her maneuvers was to deeroticize them, to suppress or omit any negative associations with adultery or sexual promiscuity they may have had (Brownlee, "Canonical Authors").[73] Lynne E. Dickson has similarly shown Christine's uneasiness about the female body; even as Christine refocuses the patriarchal gaze on the female body, she is unable to rethink the female body itself, with the result that her images of that body are vexed and ambiguous (Dickson). "Trotula," with her ineluctable associations with the female body—and specifically her "authority" on female sexuality (as developed by the *Placides et Timéo* and construed by the manipulations of the *Trotula* texts themselves)—may have been as unrecuperable as Heloise. It is perhaps not an accident, therefore, that Christine should be silent about both "Trotula" and Heloise at the same time that her English contemporary, Chaucer, is listing both the Salernitan healer and the abbess of the Paraclete among the named authorities, and the only female authorities, in Jankyn's "Book of wikked wyves" (*Canterbury Tales, The Wife of Bath's Prologue* III [D], 669–85). For Christine, the only medieval learned woman deemed worthy of entry into her *Cité* is Novella, the Italian scholar who, while she was lecturing, decorously hid her beauty—and her female body—behind a curtain so as not to distract her male audience.[74]

The irony, of course, is that had Christine ever looked at the central text of the *Trotula* ensemble, the *De curis mulierum*, which derived from the historic Trota's own work, she would have found perhaps the closest approximation known in medieval Europe to a "treatise composed of truths," a treatise that reflected women's bodies as a woman herself described them.[75] It is unlikely, however, that Christine ever had that opportunity, for the *De curis mulierum* seems to have stopped circulating as an independent text in France in the thirteenth century (M. Green, "Development"). Just as the *De curis mulierum* was subsumed into the *Trotula* ensemble, thereby compromising its distinctly woman-centered cast, so too was the historic Trota subsumed into the malleable and manipulable identity of the textually generated authoress "Trotula." Both the feminine figure of "Trotula" and the whole gynecological tradition had, by the late fourteenth and early fifteenth centuries, been compromised by clerical and medical concerns so as to make them reveal the "secrets" of women and generation. For Christine, the associations of "Trotula" with the "secrets of women" made her into an authority who, despite her learnedness, was too inextricably tied to the sexualized female body as it was construed by learned traditions for "Trotula" herself to be deemed admissible to Christine's citadel for the defense of women.

Notes

It is my pleasure to acknowledge the incisive comments I received on an earlier draft of this paper from Luke Demaitre, Catherine Peyroux, and Helen Solterer. Very special thanks go to Nadia Margolis, who has been equally generous in sharing her endless knowledge of Christiniana and in encouraging the hesitating steps of this historian into the wilderness of interdisciplinarity.

1. I have modified slightly Richards's translation, which gives the title of the work as *Secreta mulierum, The Secrets of Women.* No manuscripts of the *Cité* employ the Latin title, and, as I argue later, the distinctions between the Latin text and the French translation are important, as is the fact that Christine claims to have *seen* ("vi") the text.

2. London, Addit. MS 12195, *Knowyng of Womans Kynde and Chyldyng*, fol. 157v: "And vnderstend that they haue non other evellis that now ben on lyve than tho womenn haden that now be seyntys in hevene." The text, an adaptation of the *Trotula*, was probably composed in the late fourteenth century. See M. Green, "Obstetrical," and "Handlist," part 2.

3. I use the term "Trotula" in quotation marks throughout this chapter to refer to the alleged author of the three most important texts on women's medicine to come out of twelfth-century Salerno, only one of which can be connected with the historic woman

healer Trota. *Trotula* (in italics) is used as a generic title for the three texts when circulating as an ensemble.

4. Neither the extant manuscripts nor evidence from wills, inventories, and other medieval records of book ownership have yet yielded any proof of female ownership of the *Trotula*. There are, however, a few vernacular translations that are addressed to women, and in several cases, given the codicological context of the texts in the extant manuscripts, female ownership is not implausible. For the Middle English manuscripts, see M. Green, "Obstetrical." Even with these vernacular translations there is no proof of female authorship or annotation by female readers, so the question of women's reactions to the texts remains inaccessible.

5. That the great Pizanist Charity Cannon Willard should have once asserted that "Trotula" did appear in the *Cité des dames* (Willard, Introduction 11 [miscited as 13 by Curnow 26]) is indicative of precisely the paradox I wish to address: why should a female figure who, from our perspective, seems so obviously to merit inclusion, be omitted?

6. The volume is described in Gillet's inventory of 1373 as "Medicina Trotula domina mulierum. Sinonima & Rogerina" (Paris, BNF, MS fr. 2700, fol. 24r). Although "Trotula" was indeed often understood as a title, here I take *medicina* to stand as a label for the contents of the volume; the phrase *domina mulierum* serves as an epithet modifying the personal name "Trotula." From the second folio incipit ("parcium postea"), it is most probable that the manuscript in question was a copy of the full *Trotula* ensemble.

7. For general overviews, see Jacquart and Thomasset; and Cadden.

8. See Thorndike; Bosselman-Cyran; Schleissner, "Pseudo-Albertus"; Schleissner, "'Secreta mulierum'"; Schleissner, "Attitude"; and Lemay. Neither Schleissner nor Lemay comments on the locus of origin of the *Secreta*, although a German origin seems likely not least because the earliest (and indeed most) manuscripts are of German provenance. No critical edition of the *Secreta* has yet been attempted; Thorndike's article suggests that the many manuscripts and editions demonstrate considerable textual variation.

9. Set in dialogue form, the *Secreta*, as Margaret Schleissner has pointed out, was very much a male-to-male conversation. Even though the presumed author, Albert, was described in at least one commentary tradition as "having been informed by women," the author of the prologue makes clear that the "we" of the dialogue itself does not include women. See Schleissner, "Pseudo-Albertus," 35–41.

10. *Secreta mulierum*, Munich, Clm 22297, fol. 22r: "Roga etiam vestram conscientiam ut in hoc opere aut negotio constans et celans sitis ne alicui puero tam in etate quam in moribus ad presentiam veniat" (Be sufficiently alert and guarded when you are engaged in this work or business that no one who is a boy either in age or in morals should come into your presence).

11. For Latin manuscripts, vernacular translations, and the later publishing history of the *Secreta*, see Schleissner, "Pseudo-Albertus," "'Secreta mulierum,'" and "Attitude." In her several studies, Schleissner has thus far listed ninety-five manuscripts of the Latin *Secreta*. I have been unable to confirm four of these citations, although I have found six more manuscripts to add to the list. There is also a Czech translation in Brno, MS A 112, fols. 1r–27v, 31r–76r.

12. Of the ninety-seven manuscripts of the Latin *Secreta mulierum* whose existence I have confirmed, only seven are now in French libraries. Paleographical studies have not yet been done to confirm provenance.

13. I have used the copy of the *Secrés des dames* in Glasgow, Ferguson 241, as my reference rather than the patchwork text published by Colson and Cazin. See n. 28 for a full list of manuscripts. The text needs to be reedited. The second French translation of the *Secreta* is far more literal, omitting only the astrology; as yet unedited, it is extant in three copies. See Fery-Hue, "*Secrets*," but note that the Dutch, English, and German texts she mentions have no relation to this second French translation.

14. On the "evil eye" and its connections with menstruation, see the comprehensive study of Salmon and Cabré i Pairet.

15. The excerpts ultimately derive from an abbreviated version of Muscio's *Gynaecia,* a late antique Latin translation of Soranus of Ephesus's Greek *Gynecology* (Hanson and Green). The attribution to Cleopatra occurred because the Muscio text, *Non omnes quidem,* from which this material derives, often circulated with the *Gynaecia Cleopatrae* and was thought to be part of the same text.

16. Glasgow, Ferguson 241, fol. 66r: "Au commenchement vne damoisielle me pria par loialle courtoisie que ie dicasse ou escrisisse aucune chose profitable....Je prie a cheste amoureuse damoiselle que quant elle lira le liure que elle ne se courouche point a moy ne mains ne men ayme de che que ie a conte les secres delles au plus vraiement que ie puis" (At the beginning a young woman begged me by loyal courtesy that I say or write something profitable.... I beg this loving young woman that when she reads it she not be angry with me, neither my hand nor my intention(?), because I have recounted the secrets of women as truthfully as I could).

17. Glasgow, Ferguson 241, fol. 73r: "Et se .j. homme en giette hors plus quil ne doit il seche et pert sa coulleur naturelle et estaint tant quil ne puet viure longuement, car quant il pert sperma il pert sa vie et sa sante" (And if a man ejects more [semen] than he ought to, he dries out and loses his natural color, and he looks as if he will not live long, for when he loses his seed he loses his life and his health). Cf. Colson and Cazin, 72.

18. Glasgow, Ferguson 241, fol. 73r: "Femmes sont bien mallades aucunefois pour che que la marris se depart de son lieu. Et tant quelle cuide creuer et morir Gallien dist que sur che la milleur medecine qui soit cest le jeu damours. Car le membre remet la marris en son droit point" (Women are sometimes very sick because the womb leaves its place. And when such a woman began to waste away and to die, Galen said with assurance that the best medicine was the game of love. For the [male] member puts the womb back in its proper place). The passage in fact goes into even greater detail on the therapeutic virtues of heterosexual intercourse: "Aussy dist il quil est grant profit a femme de faire le jeu damours. Car quant la maris est souuent hurtee nulle malladie ny puet ariester et est plus saine. Et on voit souuent que quant une femme acomplist et fet ycelui mestier, elle est plus belle, plus crasse, plus et mieux coulouree et plus lie que deuant. Pour che est grant pitie quant femme a partie a lui plaisant et on lui blasme ny oste, et espesialment mary. Car quant elle a homme qui lui plaist, elle en est plus aise. On a bien veu morir femmes pour en oster leur parties" (Also he said that it is of great profit for a woman to play the game of love. For when the womb is often knocked about, no sickness is able to stop it and she is healthier. And one often sees that when a woman has undertaken and done this business, she is more beautiful, plumper, more and better colored, and more content than before. Therefore, it is a great pity when a woman has a mate who pleases her yet she reproaches him or fights with him, especially her husband. For when a woman has a man who pleases her, she is more at ease. People have seen women die for fighting with their mates). The *Art d'amours* aspect of the French *Secrés* is taken to an even higher level in what van Doorn and Kuiper call the "idyllic" version of the Dutch text, where the redactor has added numerous asides addressed to or invoking his lady love. By the end of the text, the author confirms that his lady has in fact now "comforted" him.

19. An early-thirteenth-century French translator of Ovid's *Ars amatoria* enjoins his readers under no circumstances to allow a woman to read his book. In discussing the issue of love potions, he says that he who trusts a woman enough to let her read this book "lui baillera le glaive dont elle fera dommage a lui et maint autre vaillant homme" ("gives her the sword whereby she will do damage to him and to many another valiant man") (*L'Art d'amours,* ed. Roy, 167; *L'Art d'amours,* trans. Blonquist, 79). Other French arts of love, like the *Secrés des dames,* bore addresses or dedications to women, although as Roberta Krueger explains, these could have the effect of foreclosing rather than inviting a female readership (Krueger, *Women Readers* 194–96).

20. Admittedly, this decretal may not have been an original part of the text (cf. the Dutch translation discussed below, where the decretal does not appear). Nevertheless, as I

have pointed out, even without the decretal the overall male orientation of the *Secrés des dames* is clear.

21. All known manuscripts of what Colson and Cazin called the *Secrés des dames* pluralize "secrés." "Femmes," found in five of the eight known manuscripts, is probably the earlier reading; "dames" is found only in three manuscripts, all of southern French origin, which present a more abbreviated, later text.

22. I make this argument about Christine's use of the French *Secrés* not, of course, on the assumption that Christine could not have read the Latin. Dulac and Reno's study of Christine's humanism has now confirmed her notable command of the language (Dulac and Reno, "L'Humanisme"). Rather, as I argue here, certain characteristics of the text that Christine describes have only been found in the French tradition of the *Secrés*.

23. Colson and Cazin postulated a composition date between 1418 and 1453, the latter (correctly, 1454) being the date of the earliest dated manuscript.

24. The references to "Valezius" appear on pages 28 and 43 of Colson and Cazin's edition. Although I have not consulted the other extant manuscripts on this question (see n. 28 for a full list), in Glasgow, Ferguson 241, the name is, in its first appearance, clearly "Valerius," not "Valezius." It seems that the "G" initial was misread as "V," and the "n" as "ri." In the second instance, the Glasgow manuscript reads "Pulinus" (cf. the similar reading in Paris, BNF, MS 631, "Volinus," as cited by Colson and Cazin 43 n. 131).

25. On Valescus, see Wickersheimer (772) and Jacquart (276). The section of the *Philonium* on women's diseases is quite traditional, with no originality. Valescus's *Chirurgia*, however, according to Jacquart, devotes particular attention to obstetrics.

26. Two references to Galen later in the text are spelled properly in the Glasgow manuscript (fol. 73r).

27. On the reference to Cleopatra (which comes via Thomas of Cantimpré's *Liber de natura rerum*), see Hanson and Green (1058). Colson and Cazin were stumped by many of the corrupted names, not recognizing, for example, that "Solnis" was a reference to the second-century author Solinus (10 and 13), that "Vincenal" (or as Colson and Cazin transcribe it, "Lulceual," 27) was an error for Avicenna, or that "Maistre Pleing" referred to Pliny (35).

28. In addition to the four manuscripts used by Colson and Cazin for their edition (i.e., Colson's own private copy [whose current whereabouts are, to my knowledge, unknown]; Paris, Bibliothèque Nationale de France [hereafter BNF], MSS fr. 631, 2027, and 19994), these are: Chantilly, Musée Condé, MS 330 (s. xv), fols. 101r–109r; Glasgow, Ferguson 241 (s. xv), fols. 66r–73r; BNF, MS nouv. acq. fr. 11649 (s. xv med.), fols. 150r–160v; and Turin, Biblioteca Nazionale, MS L.IV.17, fols. 539–48 (s. xv med.), which was destroyed by a fire in 1904. Although the Glasgow manuscript was dated by Neil Ker as late fifteenth century (Ker 2:897–98), Françoise Fery-Hue suggests that it may instead have been copied in the first half of the century (Fery-Hue, "Review" 145). On the "twin" surgical manuscripts BNF, fr. 19994 and nouv. acq. fr. 11649, see de Tovar.

29. The Italian translation is found in Florence, MS Palat. 557. Comparison shows that this is a very literal translation of the French; it conforms to the French, for example, in the corruption of proper names, such as "Solio" and "Ulmis" for Solinus, and "Uincinale" for Avicenna. My thanks to Christopher Celenza for doing a preliminary examination of this manuscript for me in 1993, and to Ron Witt for sharing with me his microfilm copy. See also Corsi, esp. 55–56.

30. My thanks to Luke Demaitre for preparing a draft translation of this text for me. Blommaert made his edition from Ghent, MS 444, which may date from 1405. Since then, a second complete copy has been identified, Berlin, MS germ. oct. 187; see van Doorn and Kuiper. An excerpt (= Blommaert ed., lines 823–925, i.e., the obstetrical material) is found in Brussels, MS 19308, which dates from the fourteenth century.

31. Personal communication with van Doorn and Kuiper; my thanks to both these scholars for responding so generously to my queries. The text of *Der Vrouwen Heimelykheid* in the Ghent version alludes frequently to Latin traditions (ed. Blommaert, lines 37, 91,

103, 120, 123, 183, 306, 618, 631, 1286, 1462, 1581), yet the very frequency of these references raises the suspicion that this is a rhetorical ploy reflecting little more than the author's desire to add authority to his text.

32. Paris, MS Colson; Glasgow, Ferguson 241; BNF, MS fr. 631; and Turin, MS L.IV.17. Colson's manuscript has certain linguistic and codicological features that situate its composition in the region of Toulouse; the others, however, have northern French associations.

33. Contrary to Curnow ("*Cité*" 1048), Colson and Cazin do not assert that the decretal is found in the Latin text. The Italian translation preserves an echo of the spurious French decretal: "Quin a presso sono iscritti i segreti delle femine, traslatato di latino in uolgare. E sono uietati per la sancta madre ecclesia che non si lascino leggiere a omgni maniera di gente" (Here now are written the secrets of women, translated from the Latin into the vernacular. And it is prohibited by the Holy Mother Church that any manner of person whatsoever be allowed to read them).

34. The only explanation of the genesis of the two sexes found in the *Secrés* is the theory of the seven cells of the womb. Males are created in the four cells on the right side of the womb, females in the three (colder) cells on the left. In other words, the sex of the embryo is determined solely by the location in which the seed situates itself, not by the character of the seminal or menstrual contributions themselves.

35. In the Glasgow manuscript, "les maistres" are cited eight times, Hippocrates six, and Aristotle five.

36. Richards ("Search") implies that Christine knew the *Summa theologiae*, although he offers no specific evidence for this. That said, I would agree with him that her knowledge of the text seems likely.

37. My thanks to Irven Resnick for bringing this passage to my attention.

38. For a comprehensive summary of Aristotle's, Albert's, and Aquinas's views on the physical nature of women, see Allen.

39. "Adonc moy estant en ceste penssee, me sourdi une grant desplaisance et tristesce de couraige en desprisant moy meismes et tout le sexe feminin, si comme ce ce fust monstre en nature" (Curnow, "*Cité*" 1.1c, p. 620). For Christine, it was only "la mauvaise femme dissolue et perverse" who was a real "monstre en nature"; the *true* natural condition of woman is "simple, coye et honneste" (Curnow, "*Cité*" 1.16a, pp. 642–43).

40. Although there were several copies of Aristotle's collected works in the royal library, it is not clear whether any of these contained *Generatio animalium*; to my knowledge, there was no medieval French translation of this work.

41. Curnow notes ("*Cité*" 1058) that this deformity should be correctly attributed to Aristotle's pupil, Alexander, and not Aristotle himself. Another reference to Aristotle occurs in 1.85, where he is referred to in passing as Plato's pupil.

42. Compare 1.16a–23, where the various types of misogynist are treated anonymously.

43. My thanks to Nadia Margolis for pointing out to me the relevance of Christine's attitudes toward the *translatio studii*. Christine also cites Aristotle frequently in her biography of Charles V and the *Avision-Christine*.

44. A list of medieval owners of the *Trotula* will be found in M. Green, *Women*.

45. Delisle (item 838 [2:*136]) miscited the price as "6 l[ivres]." Cf. *Inventaire*, 115. My thanks to François Avril for bringing this latter citation to my attention.

46. Although the catalog does not explicitly say that the text is in French, several factors suggest that it was: (1) the titles of all the contents of this volume are in French (elsewhere in the catalog, with but four exceptions, Latin medical books are cited by Latin titles); (2) French translations of most of the contents, including the *Trotula*, are known from this period; (3) of the ten surgical books in the library, nine were in French; (4) conversely, surgery made up more than half the French medical codices as a whole (ten out of sixteen), indicating that the kings' interests in vernacular texts focused particularly around surgery; (5) the other book borrowed by Pierre (item 800) is in French. Delisle suggests that this Pierre is to be identified with Master Pierre Fromont, active (according to Wick-

ersheimer, 2:634) in the mid–fourteenth century, who was author of a French surgical text also in Charles's collection (Delisle item 829), but this is not certain.

47. There are at least seven medieval French translations of the *Trotula* (three of which are currently found only in Anglo-Norman versions, although they may be of Continental origin), five into English, three into Dutch and German, two into Italian, and one into Hebrew and Irish. See part 2 of M. Green, "Handlist."

48. What the later fate of this volume was is unclear; although Pierre later returned another volume he had borrowed, the manuscript with the French *Trotula* never again appears in the library's inventories.

49. This text is an adaptation of a late antique Latin gynecological tract by Muscio. One copy is attested at the Sorbonne in the mid-fourteenth-century catalog of Master Adalbertus Ranconis de Ericinio; see Lehmann 24. The other copy (and the only one now extant) is Paris, BNF, MS lat. 15081, which dates from the turn of the fourteenth century; it belonged from at least the late fourteenth century to the Abbey of Saint Victor. Cf. the fourteenth-century Middle English translation, "On the Nature of Women"; transcription in M. Green, "Obstetrical."

50. Although the height of the popularity of the *Trotula* in France occurred in the thirteenth and the turn of the fourteenth century, a few later copies give evidence of its continued utility. See M. Green, "Handlist," Latin manuscript nos. 17, 34, 85, 88, and 89.

51. Picherit, "Références," and more generally, *Métaphore.* On Christine's interest in astrology, see Willard, "Astrologer's Daughter," and Boudet.

52. There are twenty-three copies of the *Gynaecia Cleopatrae* still extant, of which at least four are of French provenance. Copies were also to be found in the medieval period at the Abbey of Saint Victor in Paris, Saint Amand (near Valenciennes), and Amiens. An adaptation of the pseudo–Albertus Magnus *Secreta mulierum* found in a fifteenth-century manuscript was ascribed to Cleopatra, although here for some reason Cleopatra is construed as a masculine name (Paris, BNF, MS lat. 7106, s. xv, *inc.*: Hic oriuntur plura dubia erga mulierum secreta . . . ; *expl.*: . . . Explicit tractatus de secretis mulierum editus a Cleopatra summo medico [Here begin many questions regarding the secrets of women. . . . Here ends the treatise edited by Cleopatra, the great physician]). The medical writings of the twelfth-century Benedictine nun, Hildegard of Bingen, in contrast, seem to have been known only in areas near the Rhine and, in one unique instance, in York, England. See Moulinier, "Fragments"; Moulinier, *Manuscrit* 170–72; Humphreys 110.

53. I have deliberately omitted Rutebeuf's satirical account of Dame Trote ("Dit de l'herberie") from the following discussion. Rutebeuf (who was clearly referring, in my opinion, not to the textually generated "Trotula," but to the historic woman Trota, whose fame was spread independently from the *Trotula* texts by the Normans in the twelfth century) does not implicate Trota specifically as *an authority on women;* he makes no allusion to her association with gynecology, nor does he credit her with any particular knowledge of "women's nature." Dame Trote also appears as a frequently cited authority in a thirteenth-century Anglo-Norman cosmetic text (*Ornement*), which seems to be a pastiche drawn from a variety of Salernitan sources. While in this latter context she is clearly associated with women's matters, there is no gynecological material here, nor is there any implication that Trota is a revealer of "women's secrets" (a term that, in my research, applies to matters of generation, never to cosmetics).

54. My thanks to John Baldwin for bringing this reference to "Trotula" to my attention.

55. The dukes of Burgundy may also have had four different copies of the text in the latter part of the fifteenth century.

56. The orthography of "Trotula" varies considerably in the four extant manuscripts (all of which date from the fifteenth century, some two centuries after composition of the text): "Troculeus," "Theocule," "Troculet," and "Trocule." Roy notes that copyists introduced considerable orthographical errors, particularly of proper names, in the course of transmission. Confusions of gender were particularly common (24, 30, and 36).

57. See Thomasset's introduction to his edition of the *Placides et Timéo* and also his exhaustive analysis, *Vision.* The *Placides et Timéo* enjoyed a healthy circulation throughout the later Middle Ages. It now exists in eight manuscripts ranging in date from 1304 to the end of the fifteenth century; to the seven manuscripts listed by Thomasset, add Glasgow, Ferguson 241, fols. l–65r. The *Placides et Timéo* was also printed numerous times in the sixteenth century.

58. *Placides et Timéo,* para. 291 (ed. Thomasset 134): "et celle regardoit en ses livres et trouvoit concordance en ce que nature lui en devisoit et, par ce, elle savoit grant partie des natures as femmes."

59. Rennes, MS 593 (an. 1304), fol. 532r. For other examples of female figures instructing male clerks, see Solterer.

60. "Trotula's" authority is invoked twice in the *Placides et Timéo:* once for the view that women desire sex even during pregnancy and again for views of the nature of the uterine mole. The latter topic never appears in any version of the *Trotula.* The former appears in only one peculiar subfamily, the *Meretrices* Group (see M. Green, "Development"), where in an added passage discussing the nature of the uterus, it is said that "pregnant women desire intercourse more intensely, because the [male] semen is not able to fall into the uterus to assuage the desire" ("Vnde pregnantes ardentius appetunt coitum, quia semen non potest cadere in matricem ad libidinem temperandam"). The circulation of the *Meretrices* Group seems to have been limited to Germany, the Low Countries, and, in one fifteenth-century instance (which can almost certainly be attributed to transmission by a German student), Italy. It is unclear whether, even if he had had access to a copy of the *Meretrices* version, the *Placides et Timéo* author would have taken the trouble to search the whole text for this one small passage. As his completely fictive biography of "Trotula" makes clear, he has no need for textual precedents for all his views.

61. This notion of slander and the potential offensiveness of gynecological texts to women is also found in Middle English and Dutch texts on women's medicine.

62. Of the 93 copies whose contents I have checked, 27 codices have predominantly medical contents, 32 have predominantly natural-philosophical contents, 23 have predominantly religious texts, and 5 have mostly grammatical texts. In 6 instances, the *Secreta* is the sole contents.

63. Three manuscripts (Chantilly, MS 330; BNF, fr. 19994; and BNF, nouv. acq. fr. 11649), all from southern France, begin "Si commence le livre des secrés des femmes, lequel est deffendu a reveler sur paine d'excomiement a nulle femme, ne a nul homme si n'est de l'office de cirrugie" (Here begins the book of the secrets of women, which is prohibited to be revealed on pain of excommunication to any woman, and to any man unless it is for a medical purpose). All the known owners were surgeons or barbers, with the exception of Ferguson 241, which was owned in the late 15th century by a certain Charles de Beaulieu, whose identity has not yet been established. Chantilly, MS 330; BNF, fr. 19994; BNF, nouv. acq. fr. 11649; and Turin, MS L.IV.17, all have gynecological material in addition to the *Secrés.* The association in France of the "secrets of women" tradition with medicine is also seen in the case of the second French translation. In Paris, MS Arsenal 2889, the *Secrés des femmes* (fols. 63r–82r) is accompanied by vernacular medical handbooks for the use of "simple clercs" or "simple gens": the *Tresor de Maistre Arnault de Ville Noeue catellain sur l'art de medecine et cyrurgie* (fols. lr–62r), translated (according to the text) by Maistre Guillem de Tholouse "pour les simples clers sur l'art et science de medicine et de cyrurgie" (fol. 11r); and the *Erbier de maistre Arnault de Ville Noue* (fols. 83r–138r), which claims to have been translated out of the Latin at the request of "la tres souueraine dame, dame Ysabel de bauieres, jadis royne de france" (fol. 83r–v). On fols. 138v–139v several other hands have added miscellaneous recipes in French, including several on fertility and childbirth.

64. On all these French translations of the *Trotula,* see M. Green, "Handlist," part 2. The only Latin copy of the *Trotula* produced in France to bear the label "secrets of women" is Reims, MS 1002, fols. 251ra–257vb, which ends "Explicit Trotula maior et minor de se-

cretis mulierum." The reductionist trend in adapting the *Trotula* to conform to more narrowly defined concerns with generation is not a phenomenon peculiar to France. In fourteenth- and fifteenth-century manuscripts from all across Europe, the *Trotula* is abbreviated with this same "generational" focus, renamed "The Secrets of Women," and, in Germany, physically juxtaposed to the pseudo-Albertan *Secreta mulierum.*

65. Uterine suffocation is a condition where, in the most common medieval medical traditions, menstrual blood or the woman' s own semen (sic) is retained beyond measure within the uterus and eventually causes epileptic-like fits, fainting, heart palpitations, and occasionally even death.

66. Lille, MS 863, fols. 122v–125v, 127r, at fol. 123v: "Chi commence li liures des secres as dames que Constentins, Galijens et Ypocras fisent. Et fu au faire Helaine qui fu mere Constentin, qui sent toute le nature et cognent toutes les forces des herbes....Et fu au faire Helaine li mere Constentin qui des dames sauoit la manere. " In Kassel, 4° MS med. 1, Helen is said to know "les secrez de nature et les forces et vertus des herbes a ce apartenans," but no mention is made of any special feminine knowledge. This text is the first occasion I have found where the eleventh-century Benedictine monk Constantine the African is mistaken for the Roman emperor Constantine, hence the reference to Helen.

67. It is ironic that a female voice authenticates this contraceptive, for contraceptives were eliminated from most of the vernacular translations of the *Trotula* addressed to women.

68. This is for the simple reason that the *Liber de sinthomatibus mulierum*, on which both this French translation and the earlier one discussed were drawn, was rarely attributed to "Trotula" when it circulated independently. See M. Green, "Development."

69. Regrettably, this manuscript was destroyed in a fire in 1904. From the description provided by Camus, the topical contents seem to have been limited to descriptions of female anatomy, menstruation, conception, lactation, uterine suffocation, signs of conception, and the functions of the midwife. The author claims that because women are "ashamed to name [their diseases] in the manner in which we are accustomed to name them in French" ("ellez ne soient honteuses de nommer en telle maniere que nous lez nommons communement en romant"), he will use various technical terms to make women feel more at ease in referring to their anatomy. Portions of this text are also embedded in a copy of the *Placides et Timéo* under the heading "A Little Treatise Compiled by Albert of Trapizond" ("ung petit traitié compilé par Albert de Trapesonde"). Here, the text has been recast for male readers, and the redactor now claims that the euphemisms will allow *him* to "speak under cover" ("je voeul en parler en couvert," *Placides et Timéo* 265). See also M. Green, "Handlist," pt. 2.

70. Both Paris, BNF, MS fr. 631, and Glasgow, Ferguson 241, may postdate 1405, of course, but their codicological makeup may reflect longer-term patterns of transmission and use. Notably, not only are both of northern French origin, but they also are more similar to each other in their text of the *Secrés* than to any other extant copies of the treatise.

71. As I noted in n. 49, this text, despite its title, is not the *Trotula*, although for the present discussion it is significant that it should have been believed to be the work of "Trotula."

72. Christine's powerful sense of the ethical obligations attendant on learning, as Helen Solterer has now shown, could only have reinforced the critique-by-silence that I am positing here.

73. My thanks to Professor Brownlee for kindly providing me with a copy of his article prior to publication.

74. Cf. Curnow, *"Cité"* 19–20, 26; 1.185, p. 875: "Et adfin que la biauté d'elle n'empeschast la penssee des ouyans, elle avoit une petite courtine au devant d'elle."

75. The only other woman known to have written on aspects of women's medicine was the Benedictine nun Hildegard of Bingen (1098–1179), whose medical works do not seem to have circulated in France; see n. 52. On Trota's connection to the *De curis mulierum*, see M. Green, *Women. De curis mulierum* offers a distinctive perspective on women's

medical conditions, one that reflects an independence from learned traditions and a greater sensitivity to the physicosocial world as twelfth-century Italian women may have experienced it (see M. Green, *Diseases*).

Manuscripts Cited

Berlin, Staatsbibliothek Preussischer Kulturbesitz, MS germ. oct. 187 (s. xv)
Brno, Knihovny Augustiniánu na St. Brne, MS A 112 (IV.Z.d.14)
Brussels, Bibliothèque Royale, MS 19308 (s. xiv)
Cambridge, Trinity College, MS O.1.20 (1044) (s. xiii², England)
Cambridge, Trinity College, MS O.2.5 (1109) (s. xiv med., England)
Chantilly, Musée Condé, MS 330 (s. xv)
Florence, Biblioteca Nazionale Centrale, MS Palat. 557 (s.xv in.)
Ghent, Universiteitsbibliotheek, MS 444 (an. 1405?)
Glasgow, University Library, Ferguson 241 (s. xv)
Kassel, Murhardsche Bibliothek der Stadt und Landesbibliothek, 4° MS med. 1 (ca. 1430–75)
Lille, Bibliothèque Municipale, MS 863 (s. xv med., probably Tournai)
London, British Library, Additional MS 12195 (s. xv²)
London, Wellcome Institute for the History of Medicine, MS 544 (s. xiv in., France)
Munich, Bayerische Staatsbibliothek, Clm 22297 (Winberg 97) (an. 1325, Erfurt)
Oxford, Magdalen College, MS 173 (s. xiv in.)
Paris, Bibliothèque de l'Arsenal, MS 2889 (s. xv)
Paris, Bibliothèque Nationale de France, MS fr. 631 (s. xv, N. France)
Paris, Bibliothèque Nationale de France, MS fr. 2027 (s. xv)
Paris, Bibliothèque Nationale de France, MS fr. 2700 (an. 1373).
Paris, Bibliothèque Nationale de France, MS fr. 19994 (an. 1454, S. France)
Paris, Bibliothèque Nationale de France, MS lat. 7106 (s. xv, France)
Paris, Bibliothèque Nationale de France, MS lat. 15081 (ca. 1300, France)
Paris, Bibliothèque Nationale de France, MS nouv. acq. fr. 11649 (s. xv med., S. France)
Paris, Bibliothèque Nationale de France, MS nouv. acq. lat. 693 (ca. 1300)
Paris, Bibliothèque Sainte-Geneviève, MS 1037 (s. xv, N. France)
Paris, private library of Alexandre Colson, MS Colson (s. xv med.); current whereabouts unknown
Reims, Bibliothèque Municipale, MS 1002 (s. xiii med., N. France)
Rennes, Bibliothèque Municipale, MS 593 (an. 1304).
Turin, Biblioteca Nazionale Universitaria, MS L.IV.17 (s. xv med); destroyed by fire in 1904

PART III

✤

Engendering Authorship

*Ains volt que par lengendrement destude et des choses veues
nasquissent de moy nouvelles lettures.*

*[Indeed, she wished to bring forth new books from me through the
engendering of study and things seen.]*

—Christine, *Avision 3*

CHAPTER 9

❖

Transforming Ovid
The Metamorphosis of
Female Authority

Judith L. Kellogg

The standard view of Ovid in the Middle Ages was that he was love's inspired clerk. Chaucer describes him as "Venus clerk, Ovide, / That hath ysowen wonder wide / The grete god of Loves name" ("House of Fame" lines 1487–89).[1] Christine de Pizan, however, voices an exasperated counterview that saw Ovid as love's degraded and conniving clerk. She says, for instance, of his *Ars amatoria*, "Homs qui veult selon ce livre faire / N'amera ja" (whoever seeks to learn from this book will never know how to love) (*Epistre au dieu d'Amour* lines 374–75).[2] In a subsequent elaboration of this view, she describes Ovid's ideas as "la perverse doctrine, et le venin engoisseux" (perverse, poisonous doctrine) (Hicks, *Débat* 138). She further laments that if women had written the books such as Ovid's on which traditions concerning women were based, then those traditions would look very different. In this spirit she seeks throughout her works to counter Ovid's denigration by consistently developing an alternate view of women as fiercely loyal in their personal commitments, steadfastly sincere in their virtue, and actively dedicated to the building of society and civilization generally. In developing her ideas, Christine ranges widely in her sources, but of particular interest here is the fact that many of her most suggestive and powerful examples used to counter Ovidian tradition are borrowed from Ovid's *Metamorphoses*, largely transmitted via the medieval *Ovide moralisé*.

Christine's use of the Ceyx and Alcyone myth provides an illuminating context for exploring the process by which she uses Ovidian tradition to counteract Ovid's misogynist legacy. In this way Christine demonstrates an adept facility with what has been termed poaching, which involves, as Laurie Finke describes, "appropriations of the dominant social order [that] deflect its power without challenging it overtly. Poaching is neither straightforward conformity nor rebellion, but a dialogic and destabilizing encounter between conflicting cultural codes" (10). Specifically, Christine uses the Ceyx and Alcyone story in both the *Epistre Othea* (1400) and the *Livre de la mutacion de Fortune* (1400–1403) to expose and manipulate the cultural assumptions embedded in her traditional material for the purpose of reclaiming discursive authority for herself and women generally. Particularly in the *Mutacion de Fortune*, we see personal, intertextual, and ideological threads converge, intersect, and realign with startling gender implications. By examining Christine's transformation of one traditional Ovidian source, we can then better appreciate the genesis of her ideas concerning women's place in the building of civilization and the process by which she developed the feminine authorial stance that takes full form in the *Livre de la cité des dames* (1405).

Christine's outspoken criticism of Ovid's misogynist legacy begins quite early in her career. She first explores this problem in the *Epistre au dieu d'Amour* (1399), an allegory in which the God of Love responds to the complaint of outraged and despondent ladies concerning dishonest and disloyal treatment by men. Cupid's final judgment is that all deceitful and false lovers should be banished. Before reaching his verdict, in his lengthy consideration of male irresponsibility to women,[3] he singles out several writers who are especially culpable, notably Jean de Meun and Ovid. Concerning Ovid's *Remedia amoris*, he accuses the poet of having said, "Assez de maulz, dont je tiens qu'il meffist" (many evil things about women—and, I think, wrongly) (line 282). Ovid has characterized women as leading immoral lives, full of "villaines mours, / Ordes, laides, pleines de villenie" (filth, ugliness, and wickedness) (lines 284–85). Ovid, he says, held a grudge against women because he was "maddened by lust," and so "set out to slander them." Cupid suggests that "out of the deep pity he felt" for lusty and thwarted men like himself, he composed the *Ars amatoria*

> ... car pour la grant pitie
> Qu'il ot de ceulz compila il un livre,
> Ou leur escript et enseigne a delivre
> Comment pourront les femmes decevoir
> Par faintises et leur amour avoir;
> Si l'appella livre de l'Art d'amours;
> Mais n'enseigne condicions ne mours
> De bien amer, main aincois le contraire.
> ....
> Et pour ce est li livres mal nommez,
> Car c'est livre d'Art de grant decevance,
> Tel nom li don, et de fausse apparence.
> (lines 366–73, 376–78)

[... to teach them how to trick women into bestowing their favors on them. He called it the *Art of Love*, but far from teaching the code and traditions of noble love, he teaches the exact opposite. So this book is badly named: it is rather a book of the art of sheer deceit and dissimulation—that's the name I give it.]

Christine further develops her attitude toward Ovid in the *Roman de la Rose* debate. Although Christine's primary target was, of course, Jean de Meun, whom she accused of advocating hypocrisy, duplicity, avarice, lust, blasphemy, and most important for her, a slanderous attitude toward women, Christine well understood that criticisms of Jean de Meun's views on women must in large part also be directed at "Ovide que il prant" (Ovid from whom he borrowed) (Hicks, *Débat* 138).[4] Ovid, after all, was the primary source for Jean's crass and denigratory views, represented largely in the *Roman de la Rose* by two of his most conniving and self-interested characters, La Vieille and Ami. La Vieille's views on women's devious manipulation of marriage and her open advocacy of promiscuity for the right price sordidly discredited women's virtue, and Ami's cynical advice on how to entrap women for men's sexual amusement degraded and victimized them.[5] La Vieille is modeled on Ovid's corrupt old bawd, Dipsas, and much of her advice is from the *Ars amatoria*. And as Gerard Paré says of the predatory Ami, "Si Raison savait bien son Aristote, lui connait parfaitment son Ovide" (136). Christine describes the *Ars amatoria* as a major source for this tawdry and sordid outlook, being a work that she says might as well have been titled the "art de faulse malicieuse industrie de decepvoir fanmes" (the art of falsely and maliciously deceiving women) (138–39).

Christine's indignant view of Ovid as so-called love poet was shaped early in her career, and this attitude remained consistent in later works. But as Christine continues to write, her anger at the abuses against women is balanced by a commitment to articulating an alternative view that emphasizes their achievements, contributions, and moral fiber. This validation of women is implicit in her first major prose work, the *Epistre Othea,* in which she identifies the dynamic forces at work in shaping human history.[6] She does this in a sophisticated, extended work of mythography, addressed to a young knight and meant to teach him ideal moral and spiritual conduct. Here she gathers one hundred separate "story moments" (Tuve 34) retold from classical mythology, her major source being the influential *Ovide moralisé.*[7] Christine unfolds three textual levels from each of her stories: (1) text (the literal story, often with euhemeristic interpretation), (2) gloss (moral, and often specifically chivalric, application), and (3) allegory (the Christian truth revealed). Two significant thematic threads emerge: first, the importance of chivalric values for shaping and preserving the ideal social structure, and, second, the active place of women in this process.[8] In this work, over half of Christine's mythic retellings focus on women, and these stories are reworked to support her overriding vision of women's intelligence, virtue, and initiative.

It is in this richly symbolic exegetical context that Christine uses the Ceyx and Alcyone fable. Briefly, the Ovidian version of the story recounts the tragic separation of a loving couple, King Ceyx and his wife, Alcyone, by his death at sea after Alcyone had pleaded that he not undertake such a perilous voyage. The couple is eventually reunited when the gods transform them into seabirds. Christine reworks significant details so that Alcyone is transformed from a peripheral figure into an impressive centerpiece of the story. A close examination of this segment of the *Othea* illustrates how Christine thus uses Ovid, the masterful writer of classical myth, to counter Ovid, the disseminator of misogynist misconception.

Before we deal with Christine's version, we should note the exegetical treatment in the *Ovide moralisé*. As is typical of the *Ovide moralisé*, there is first a long, detailed recounting of the story (11.2996–3787), which follows Ovid closely. Very little of this story is later picked up in the allegory (lines 3788–4117), which treats a single part of the story in minute detail — the storm in which Ceyx drowns. So much attention is given to the details of peripheral physical background that the players in the story are lost. There is no final reference back to Ceyx's suffering and his moving final thoughts about his wife, or to Alcyone's subsequent sorrowing. The mythographer seems so caught up in allegorizing such details as the mast, the sail, the anchor of the ship, and the different sins represented by the winds that he forgets the human context and even the symbolic logic of his material. He surely does not want to suggest that Holy Church (which is Ceyx's ship) in the end fails to protect its innocent pilgrim from the evils of the world. And then at the end of his allegorization, almost gratuitously, the transformed lovers who have submitted to so much battering from earthly trials become negative symbols of those who delight too much in this world.

Christine's version is much more finely focused. Instead of letting elements really peripheral to the emotional center of the story carry the symbolic weight, Christine moves the center back to the human drama, providing unity by focusing upon the commitment and courage of the female figure. At the moral level, she sees Alcyone as embodying the essence of the loving devotion that one finds in the secular realm among loyal friends who wish to draw others from the dangers of misguided "voyages" by their sincere counsel. At the spiritual level, that devotion is matched by the Church, whose counsel, offered in the spirit of purest charity, should be heeded. By changing the vehicle for Holy Church from the ship to Alcyone, Christine associates the idea of the Church with loving female actions rather than an inanimate object.

Certain of Christine's changes in detail further suggest the consequence of female agency. When Ceyx departs, Alcyone tries to join him in his ship, a fact that certainly enhances the idea of her devotion, especially since the tempest has already begun (also Christine's detail). Alcyone insists (although unsuccessfully) on being with her husband, even though the danger is clear. The desire for union and the determination to share her beloved's fate is further developed in Christine's reworking by having Alcyone cast herself into the sea and die with Ceyx after she learns that her husband has drowned. Christine's source, in contrast, shows Alcyone attempting to cast herself into the sea, but being immediately transformed into a seabird instead. The fact that in Christine's version both Ceyx and Alcyone actually die and are then resurrected reinforces the Christian suggestion that eternal salvation is only attained after death, and after a life of self-sacrifice, of loving another more than oneself, as Alcyone has done. She, by her spirit of charity, thus becomes an appropriate and satisfying emblem for the Church.

Christine's subsequent use of the Ceyx and Alcyone story in the *Mutacion de Fortune* indicates the care with which Christine refashions her borrowed detail to focus on the power and consequence of female action. Whereas in the *Othea* she uses Alcyone as an emblem for the dignified, steadfast, and generous spirit of the Church, here she uses the story in a deeply personal way to dramatize the emotional turmoil surrounding her own husband's death. As in the *Othea,* the wife and her situation are central to the passage, but here the narrative emphasis moves to the storm and its aftermath, and the thematic emphasis to the concept of metamorphosis and its consequences.

The *Mutacion de Fortune* is a universal history describing events that are memorable or influential because of unexpected turns of circumstance. Christine opens with her own lengthy autobiographical narration, establishing her firsthand familiarity with the subject of change. In fact, the most central event in her life was an abrupt turn of fortune, which created a "mutacion / Comment de femme devins homme" (transformation, how from being a woman, I became a man) (lines 52–53).[9] She is fully aware that she is recounting "une aventure...a plusieurs impossible a croire" (an occurrence...to some impossible to believe) (lines 51–53), and so the narration of her life is offered to explain how this "grant merveille" (61) came about. She recounts her childhood, her education (which she calls the "treasure" given her by her father),[10] her marriage at fifteen, and the happy years at the court of Hymen. The final tragic episode that precedes her extraordinary transformation is the metaphorical sea journey from Hymen's court with her husband as captain (le Patron) and the terrible storm in which he is lost.[11]

Christine's autobiographical narrative becomes clearly reminiscent of Ovid's tale of Ceyx and Alcyone as the weather turns foul and the seas rise.[12] At the climactic moment when her husband is plunged into the water, she wants to act just as Alcyone had done by jumping in after him and so sharing his fate. She recounts, when she learned that her husband was swept away:

Me lieve com femme enragiee,
Hault m'en monte et en mer plungiee
Je me fusse, et ja n'y faillisse,
Qui ne me tenist, je y saillisse,

185

N'onc Alchyonie ne sailli
Plus tost en mer, quant lui failli
Ceys, que tant souloit amer,
Que je fusse tumbee en mer,
(Lines 1253–1260)

[I raised myself up like a mad woman. I climbed high and would have plunged myself into the sea and came close to doing so. If someone hadn't held me, I would have jumped. For never did Alcyone jump any sooner into the seas when Ceyes, whom she had long loved, was lost to her than I would have fallen into the sea.]

She intensely desires to follow Alcyone's lead, but is restrained by her responsibility to her household, which she describes as running to her, weeping, to share her grief and console her. However, the story, modeled as it is on Ovid, demands a miraculous transformation of some kind. So, after Christine resists suicide and grieves at length, Fortune takes pity. Christine begins to feel herself changing into a man. She can feel her body hardening and strengthening, her voice deepening, her tears drying, and her courage resolving. Christine's transformation thus allows her a symbolic death, inasmuch as her life as a woman has ended. She is thus able to rebuild the damaged boat and to learn to captain it, taking over her husband's form as a man and his role as head of the household. She can in that limited sense experience life in tandem with his.

The symbolic power of this extraordinary sequence has often been commented upon, representing as it does the many ways Christine's loss of her husband marked the point at which she was forced to find her place as head of a household and her voice as a writer.[13] But her experience of establishing her autonomy and finding her authorial voice exposed unsettling intersections between her personal situation and the cultural assumptions encoded in the tale of Ceyx and Alcyone. These convergences can be appreciated if we look at specific elements in the Ovidian tale that have been destabilized by Christine's gender transformation.

First, the adaptation whereby Christine takes control of her husband's ship rather than join him in death shifts assumptions from the source about the balance between masculine and feminine power and authority. The woman in Christine's version is no longer simply a mirror for responding to the tragedy of male circumstance—and thus left with no role except to follow her husband in his fate. The Ovidian solution, that Alcyone simply fly out of the tale with Ceyx as a seabird works in a narrative where the male is the subject and the woman functions as "other." As "other" she is erased from the tale once the central player, the subject, has died.

But in Christine's narrative, she must become the central player, the subject of her own story. She cannot be erased so easily. However, negotiating her reentry into the tale is not easy either. She is, after all, emotionally at sea. The chaotic, violent, and alienating imagery suggests profound personal disruption. The immediacy with which Christine sees her gender identity ruptured and displaced with the loss of her husband resonates with mingled grief, longing, love, rage, confusion, and ultimately strength.

In the midst of the emotional confusion, Christine is quick to respond to the tough realization that she must act as a man if she hopes to weather the storms of the world alone. And acting as a man involves some complex social adjustments, for she is wrenched from the status of wife or widow, where she has necessarily been defined by her relationship to a man (as wife she is identified socially with a husband; as widow she is defined socially by the absence of a husband). Whereas the Ovidian transformation skirts any problems of a widow's social readjustment by taking Alcyone out of the world of human activity altogether, Christine's metamorphosis forces the Alcyone figure from the margins of society to the center, as she sails toward public productive activity.[14]

However, before she can set sail, she must first rebuild the ship, wielding the hammer and pounding the nails herself. In a dramatic image of energetic activity, she sets to work:

> ...a clous et a mortel
> Rejoing les ais et fort martel;
> Mousse vais cueilant sus les roches,
> Es fentes la fiche, a grans troches,
> Tant qu'estanche la feis assez
> Et rejoigny les bors cassez.
> La çantine je fay vuider.
> (Lines 1377–83)

> [Hammer in hand, with mortar and nails,
> I rejoined the planks; then where snails
> Swell, under rocks, I gathered moss
> To cover leaks, I spread it across,
> And made the hull watertight, then
> I drained the bilge: she floats again!]

By her own labor, she must develop the only economic resource she has, the "ship" of learning and language that will keep her afloat in the world.[15] With great effort, she must fabricate the means of production that will allow her to provide for her family, suggesting that the exchange of her female body for a male body is at a fundamental level an economic exchange, a "business" decision that allows her entry into the intellectual marketplace.

However, in order to survive economically as a writer, Christine must be allowed to speak and be heard, and discursive authority is conferred

187

by gender in medieval society. Given the unsettling cultural signification attached to the female body, considered a grotesque sign of a woman's base and irrational nature, it is not surprising that a male body would become a necessary symbolic vehicle for admittance into the public, economically driven world of patriarchal discourse.[16]

This moment of transformation in the *Mutacion de Fortune* offers a powerful and dramatic image of a woman corporeally breaking out of the literary paradigm she has inherited from Ovid's telling of the Ceyx and Alcyone story. Although the critic Trinh Minh Ha writes about the colonized female, I find her terms for describing female assertion of discursive authority suggestive here. Christine's metamorphosis can be described as the extraordinary moment when she is transformed from being a written woman to become a writing woman; that is, from being a body only capable of being inscribed upon to one capable of inscribing. She is, after all, writing her own symbolic autobiography, and has written herself as Alcyone until the moment when, instead of flying into oblivion with her husband, she independently takes command of his ship. In a man's body, she can no longer return to the Ovidian myth of Ceyx and Alcyone. She can only sail out of the original story, in command of a vehicle that she has reconstructed herself. She must continue recreating the story, that is, refashioning and inscribing herself, on her own terms, and testing her own authoritative voice.

Layers of irony, even paradox, are implicit in Christine's transformation of Ovidian metamorphosis. The moment that Christine breaks out of the Ovidian paradigm marks the beginning of her forced independence as a woman. But to assert a feminine authorial identity, she must be transformed into a male. By armoring herself with the cover of patriarchal discursive privilege, she can explore the relationship between her personal and cultural construction as a woman, which will take full shape in the *Cité des dames*. Although she takes on a masculine form as she describes her corporeal change, she continues to write from a female subject position. Her experience here highlights "the paradox of female subjectivity" discussed by Roberta Krueger, that textually and culturally "'woman' is cast as a non-being, but that historical *women* may be conscious of their condition" (*Women Readers* 15). Given her own consciousness of her condition, "Christine sees authorship as masculine performance, and in the *Mutacion* she fashions her authorial identity accordingly" (Desmond, *Reading Dido* 195). Ultimately, however, she yearns to have her subject position and authorial identity mesh, "to return as a woman and be heard" (line 1397), a desire realized, of course, in her most developed defense of women, the *Livre de la cité des dames*.

Although Christine does not use the Ceyx and Alcyone myth in the *Cité des dames*, she continues to reformulate many of the issues she has confronted in her two previous renditions of the story. As she had in the *Othea*, she refashions traditional stories to highlight women's active role and fundamental contribution to society generally. And she does this using a female authorial voice discovered and honed as part of the general process of finding her public voice described in the *Mutacion de Fortune*. The important difference is that she now is able "to return as a woman and be heard."

If Ceyx and Alcyone do not specifically figure in the *Cité des dames*, Ovidian influences are still prevalent. She uses a number of other Ovidian sources, and she continues to point to Ovid as a major source of misogynist misconception. Christine reinforces her disdain by repeating the apocryphal story that Ovid was "castrated and disfigured" for his dissipation, and she attributes his exile to his licentious and degenerate sexual behavior. She posits that he "prist a blasmer les femmes par ses soubtilles raisons et . . . de les faire aux autres desplaire" (began to attack women with his subtle reasoning . . . and make women unattractive to others) (Curnow, *"Cité"* 1.9.2) only when he became incapable of indulging in sexual pleasure.[17]

Christine is particularly troubled by the claim of Ovid and those following his lead that "ce qu'ilz en mettent en leurs livres, tant des meurs decevables d'elles comme de leurs mauvaistiez, qu'ilz le font pour le bien publique et commun, adfin de adviser les hommes de leurs cautelles" (everything contained in his books regarding women's deceptive manners was for the benefit of the common good, in order to warn men about women's ruses) (Currow, *"Cité"* 2.54.1). But, she asks, how can Ovid be concerned with common good unless "chascun, tant femmes comme hommes, participent ou ont part" (all members, women as well as men, participate and take part) (Curnow, *"Cité"* 2.54.1)? In fact, the *Cité des dames* is Christine's insistent depiction of women's significant contribution to the common good. In building and populating her allegorical city, Christine draws a powerful collective portrait of women that represents them as essential to the formation of the institutions and values of civilized life.[18]

After the allegorical edifice is completed and populated, Christine turns her attention at the end of her work from her city of "compensatory history" (Schulenburg, "Clio's European Daughters" 35) to her actual society, addressing the issues concerning Ovid she had explicitly raised in the *Roman de la Rose* debate. In that debate, Christine had indignantly asked:

Est ce dont tout gaaingnié que de bien decepvoir ces fames? Qui sont fames? Qui sont elles? Sont ce serpens, loups, lyons, dragons, guievres ou bestes ravissables devourans et ennemies a nature humainne, qu'il conviengne fere art a les decepvoir et prandre? Lisés donc l'*Art*: aprenés a fere engins! Prenés les fort! Decevés les! Vituperés les! Assallés ce chastel! Gardés que nulles n'eschappent entre vous, hommes, et que tout soit livré a honte! Et par Dieu, si sont elles vos meres, vos suers, vos filles, vos fammes et vos amies; elles sont vous mesmes et vous meesmes elles. (Hicks, *Débat* 139)[19]

[Is then everything gained by deceiving women well? Who are women? Who are they? Are they serpents, wolves, lions, dragons, monsters, or ravishing, devouring beasts and enemies to human nature that it is necessary to make an art of deceiving and capturing them? Read then the *Art*. Learn then how to make traps, capture the forts, deceive them, condemn them, attack this castle, take care that no woman escape from you men, and let everything be given over to shame! And, by God! these are your mothers, your sisters, your daughters, your wives, and your sweethearts: they are you yourselves and you yourselves are they.]

In the *Livre de la cité des dames*, Christine responds to Ovid's tactics by addressing the prey itself, the mothers, sisters, daughters, wives, and sweethearts that men have so miserably failed to protect from "poisonous" Ovidian assumptions about women and love.[20] Whereas in the *Roman de la Rose* debate she accuses men of creating "traps" in order that "no woman escape" from them, in the *Cité des dames*, using complementary language and images,[21] she urges:

O! mes dames, fuyés, fuyés la folle amour dont ilz vous admonnestent. Fuyez la! Pour Dieu, fuyez! Car nul bien ne vous en pueent venir. Ains soyés certaines que, quoy que les aluchemens en soyent decepvables, que tousjours en est la fin a vos prejudices; et ne croyés le contraire; car autrement ne puet estre. Souviengne vous, chieres dames, comment ces hommes vous appellent frailles, legieres et tost tournees; et comment toutesvoyes ylz quierent tous engins estranges et decepvables a grans paines et travaulx pour vos prendre, si que on fait les bestes aux laz. Fuyez, fuyez, mes dames, et eschevez telz acointances, soubz lesquelz ris sont envelopez venins tres angoisseux et qui livrent a mort. (Curnow, *"Cité"* 3.19.6)

[Oh my ladies, flee, flee the foolish love they urge on you! Flee it, for God's sake, flee! For no good can come to you from it. Rather, rest assured that however deceptive their lures, their end is always to your detriment. And do not believe the contrary, for it cannot be otherwise. Remember, dear ladies, how these men call you frail, unserious, and easily influenced but yet try hard, using all kinds of strange and deceptive tricks, to catch you, just as one lays traps for wild animals. Flee, flee, my ladies, and avoid their company — under these smiles are hidden deadly and painful poisons.]

Throughout her career, Christine confronts Ovid in ways that effectively, often wittily, interweave her previous interactions with Ovidian

190

material. Furthermore, the *Cité des dames*, as did the *Epistre Othea*, illustrates that in addition to passion and polemics, [22] her counter also involves an alternate depiction of women that essentially reverses and defuses Ovid's uncomplimentary portrayal. We can thus see the ramifications of one of Christine's own most interesting speculations. In the *Epistre au dieu d'Amour* she remarks that if women were able to write the stories that established intellectual traditions, then the picture her age inherited of women would be far different.[23] After pointing to the common view that women are by nature "flighty, fickle, changeable, guileful, and unreliable," Christine remarks:

Et s'on me dit li livre en sont tuit plein,
C'est le respons a maint dont je me plain,
Je leur respons que les livres ne firent
Pas les femmes,
. . . .
Mais se femmes eussent les livres fait
Je sçay de vray qu'autrement fust du fait.
(Lines 407–10, 417–18)

[And if anyone tells me that books are full of women like these, this very reply is what causes me to complain. My answer is that women did not write these books. . . . But if women had written these books, I know full well the matter would have been handled differently.]

And indeed the matter is handled differently in the tradition Christine rewrites, both in the *Othea* and in the more fully developed *Livre de la cité des dames*. For her, virtue is associated with agency, and so Christine replaces the gullible, and sometimes complicitious, woman with an enlightened women who refuses to be taken in by "foolish love," the seduction game whose rules were largely articulated by Ovid. In addition, she also takes the scope of women's virtue well beyond chaste sexual behavior, for she describes women as fundamental to the building of a strong, just, and enlightened society.[24] Her *Cité des dames* is among other things a bold rewriting of human history that shows women not only as models of moral uprightness, but also as active creators, builders, and guardians of the institutions, intellectual traditions, social structures, and beliefs cherished by the medieval world.

   Although this feminist rewriting of human history took its most developed and elaborate form in the *Cité des dames*, it was evolving early in her career. And clearly, interaction with Ovidian tradition was an important catalyst. Although Ovid's is certainly not the only misogynist voice reverberating through the medieval world, it insistently represented that legacy for Christine, consistently goading her to react to it and spurring her to revise its assumptions. Her use of the Ceyx and Alcyone story illustrates the ways that Christine was able to respond, devising innovative ways to poach from Ovid, to use Ovid's own legacy as masterful storyteller and stylist to negotiate and reconfigure the constricting paradigms that she felt he was so instrumental in creating. So against the degenerate "Ovide menteur" (Pinet, *Christine* 68) she utilized Ovid the mythmaker, whom she described as "homme soubtil en l'art et science de poisie" (a man skilled in the learned craft of poetry), who "moult ot grant et vif engin et entende ment" (possessed great wit and understanding) (Curnow, "*Cité*" 1.9.2), tailoring his own words to provide an authoritative discursive voice for herself and the women in her society.

Notes

1. Ann Moss marks 1531 as the point at which the "less censorious attitude toward the *Ars* and the *Remedia*" (2) was reversed in France.

2. Translations from this poem and from the debate on the *Roman de la Rose* are from Baird and Kane.

3. In much of her early poetry, Christine explores the courtly ideal from a woman's perspective, revealing the ways that it is, as Helen Finkel remarks, "a pretext designed to serve the intentions and pleasures of a man.... While the experience of courtly love remains a beautiful creation for the man, it devastates the woman by the disillusion she must inevitably encounter" (144–45). Charity Willard further suggests, "What troubled [Christine] particularly, on practical as well as on moral grounds, was the veneer of nobility that served to disguise illicit love, all too frequently providing a snare for unsuspecting or inexperienced women" (*Christine* 87). In Christine's courtly poetry the development of this idea can be traced through the *Cent Ballades*, *Le Livre du duc des vrais amans*, and *Le Débat de deux amants*. *Le Dit de la Rose* provides a fictive remedy for the deplorable state to which male honor has fallen by gathering together those who, swearing loyalty in love, form a new Order of the Rose. See also Thelma Fenster, "Did Christine Have a Sense of Humor?"

4. Kevin Brownlee discusses Jean's indebtedness to Ovid in his excellent treatment of the ways Christine modifies the courtly and clerkly discourses embodied in the *Roman de la Rose* as an act of self-legitimation. He states, "Both the *Ars amatoria* and the *Rose* are viewed as practical manuals of how to deceive women, with the French poet being authorized by the Latin one, whose work he continues" ("Discourses" 239).

5. L. P. Wilkinson notes that "in all, Ovid contributed about 2,000 lines to the poem" (329). This represents almost 10 percent of the poem's total.

6. The only modern edition of the French text of the *Epistre Othea* available at the time of this writing is contained in a dissertation by Halina Loukopoulos. However, a new edition edited by Gabriella Parussa is forthcoming.

7. When Christine cites Ovid as a source for her mythology, she is referring explicitly to the *Ovide moralisé*, as amply demonstrated by P. G. C. Campbell (*"L'Epître" Othéa*). The *Ovide moralisé* is a lengthy work (more than 72,000 lines of octosyllabic couplets). It is based primarily on Ovid's *Metamorphoses*, with occasional additions from classical and medieval sources. The text of the medieval work is available in C. de Boer's edition.

8. For fuller discussion, see Judith Kellogg "Christine"; also, for an excellent discussion of the *Othéa* that takes into account the exquisite and important illuminations, see Sandra L. Hindman, *Christine*.

9. Translations of the *Mutacion de Fortune* are from Willard, *The Writings of Christine de Pizan*, except for lines 1253–60 (my translation, since not in Willard).

10. For an interesting discussion of the "family jewels" in the form of the *science* Christine aspired to inherit from her father, and the ways that this inheritance of "learning is inextricably linked to virility" (120–21), see Andrea Tarnowski, "Maternity."

11. In fact, he died of a fever while away in Beauvais on royal business.

12. Christine has prepared for this episode with a cluster of other explicit references to Ovid. She remarks that if it seems hard to believe that "de femme homme devins," one need only be reminded that Fortune is able to create even greater miracles, a point that she illustrates by recounting several other metamophoses, two of which involve explicit gender change: men changed into swine by Circe; Tiresias, transformed into a woman and back into a man; and Iphis, turned into a man at her marrige so that her lifelong male disguise would never be discovered. These will prepare us, she says, for "la moye transmutacion." For a good discussion of this cluster of Ovidian fables, see Renate Blumenfeld-Kosinski.

13. The diversity of responses to this passage is illustrated by those of Gottlieb and Margolis ("Poetess"). Beatrice Gottlieb remarks on the feminist implications of being turned into a man: "At the very least it suggests that widowhood revealed resourcefulness in women that was ordinarily hidden, and that only outside their tightly confined 'normal' roles could women find opportunities to develop wider skills" (353). But she also reminds us not to forget that "turning into a man . . . was a misfortune" for her, whatever the strength it brought. Nadia Margolis demonstrates how the change of sex reflects a transformed range of activities and, ultimately, a transformed mode of writing. Just as Tiresias's transformation expands the range of his prophetic powers, Christine's "real-life misfortunes transformed and enabled her to know more" ("Poetess" 369). Not only was this a change from a passive to an active role, but "her metamorphosis can also be seen to represent her bursting forth from the more passive, decorative — and therefore more 'feminine' — genres of courtly poetry" (370) to the more "masculine" genre of historiography, masculine because the central focus was typically power and the interrelationships of power.

14. Christine's ongoing concern with the problems faced by widows in her society is discussed by Liliane Dulac, "Mystical Inspiration."

15. What Hindman says for the central metaphor of building in the *Cité des dames* applies also to Christine's ship reconstruction in the *Mutacion*, for here too we see Christine "reinforcing the association between the enterprises of authoring and building" ("With Ink" 465).

16. For good discussions of medieval attitudes toward the female body, see Carolyn Walker Bynum; chap. 3 ("The Grotesque Mystical Body: Representing the Woman Writer") in Finke; Lomperis and Stanbury; and Burns.

17. Christine's source for this tradition is Jean Le Fèvre's *Livre Leesce*. Quilligan relates this story to "a castration anxiety that may be said to be the originary moment for the misogyny in the texts of both the *Rose* and the *De claris*" (42). She further comments that "the argument about Ovid was, of course, conventional, but in the context of the *Cité*'s rejection of the whole misogynist tradition, Christine anticipates a series of modern feminist critiques of Freudian theories about the oedipal complex and female sexuality" (42 n). See also Hélène Cixous and Luce Irigaray.

18. See Kellogg, "*Le Livre*."

19. This passage suggests that Christine sees Ovid's influence extending beyond Jean's misogynist attitudes to his formulation of allegory. Ovid's hunting, trapping, and war images are translated into Jean's representation of the seduced woman as a successfully assaulted castle. Christine insists that the shameful ludicrousness of Jean's view is that those women who are the targets of this assault are those very women whom men should take the greatest care to protect, leading in the *Cité* to Christine's extensive development of her own fortress image.

20. Solterer provides a useful discussion of the dynamics of these assumptions, derived from the *Ars amatoria* and the *Remedia amoris*. At base is a mode of domination derived from "an Ovidian model of mastery [by which] a woman's opposition functions as the preface to her succumbing" (35).

21. The striking repetition of imagery in the prologue to her later work, the *Livre de trois Vertus*, translated as *The Treasure of the City of Ladies*, suggests that this work too

represents, in part, Christine's ongoing response to Ovid. Here Christine reverses the idea of the trap and snare, for at the beginning of this work, the three luminous ladies—Reason, Droiture, and Justice—return to Christine and urge her to disseminate her teaching in the world so that more ladies may be lured into the "cage of our glorious city," and so presumably be protected from the traps and snares of foolish love. The allegorical ladies tell her: "We hope that the wise birdcatcher readies his cage before he may take his birds, so, after the shelter of honoured ladies is made and prepared, devices and traps may be set with your help as before. You will spread fine and noble nets and snares that we will provide you throughout the land in the places and localities and in all the corners where ladies and generally all women pass and congregate, so that those who are wild and hard to tame can be grabbed, taken and snared in our nets so that no one or very few who get caught can escape and all or the largest part of them may be installed in the cage of our glorious city" (*Treasure,* trans. Lawson, 31–32).

22. In describing her city, she managed in this work more than any other to outline the terms of the feminist debate that would be influential well into the Renaissance. As Joan Kelly notes, Christine "defined what was to become the modern feminist sensibility" (9).

23. Christine's statement reminds one of Chaucer's Wife of Bath, who also speculates about the negative treatment women have received from learned scholars. She remarks: "Who peyntede the leon, tel me who? / By God, if wommen hadde writen stories, / As clerkes han withinne hire oratories, / They wolde han writen of men moore wikkednesse / Than al the mark of Adam may redresse" (lines 692–95). The difference here is that the Wife speculates that if women were to write, they would turn the portrayal of "wikkednesse" against men. Christine does suggest men's moral shortcomings, but also demonstrates that women have more profound and complex concerns than simple recrimination against the opposite sex.

24. Helen Finkel also makes clear that Christine's notion of virtue is not one of passive self-effacement. As she argues, "The word Christine so frequently uses, *vertu,* encompasses the active force of moral courage" (150).

❖

CHAPTER 10

What Is a Patron?

Benefactors and Authorship in Harley 4431, Christine de Pizan's Collected Works

Deborah McGrady

Around 1411, Christine de Pizan presented the queen of France, Isabeau of Bavaria, with an exquisite manuscript copy of her courtly and didactic works (British Library, Harley 4431). Containing thirty texts and decorated with 130 miniatures, this anthology constitutes the most complete extant collection of Christine's works. The manuscript opens with a dedication addressed to the queen, along with a frontispiece depicting the presentation scene (Figure 27). This liminary material reproduces the traditional components of a medieval gift-giving scene; through word and image, the writer subordinates herself to the queen, and the patron functions as inspiration for and judge of the creative enterprise. In harmony with the aim of courtly literature to entertain, the dedication situates the queen's pleasure as the driving impetus behind the book's fabrication:

Si l'ay fait, ma dame, ordener
Depuis que je sceus qu'assener
Le devoye a vous, si qu'ay sceu
Tout au mieulx et le parfiner
D'escripre et bien enluminer,
Dès que vo command en receu...
(Christine, *Oeuvres*, vol. 1, dedication, lines 49–54)

[I had [this book] compiled, my lady, as soon as I knew that I was to address it to you, and I knew all the better to finish it, to write it and to illuminate it nicely, as soon as your request was received...]

Yet, there exists evidence discrediting Christine's claims that the patron's desire dictated the fabrication of this manuscript. First, all of the works contained in Harley 4431, except for the dedication, had already been offered to other patrons prior to 1411. Second, the workshop responsible for the Harley compilation presumably based the layout and most of the miniature cycle on an earlier collection prepared around 1408 for Louis of Orléans (Bibliothèque Nationale de France, MSS fr. 835, 606, 836, 605 and 607, or MS D).[1] Moreover, Sandra Hindman questions Christine's claim that the queen's request launched the collection's fabrication. Hind-

Figure 27. Dedication frontispiece. London, British Library, Harley 4431, fol. 3.

man contends that Harley 4431 may contain texts already written and decorated, which were subsequently bound together for the queen ("Composition" 99).[2]

Why would Christine and her bookmakers evoke a conventional patronage system in the margins of an anthology whose composition challenges the premises of that system? For although Isabeau may figure as judge of the anthology, she cannot claim to be the inspiration, the subject, or the original recipient of the works found in the collection. I contend that Harley 4431 contains written and visual evidence of a changing patronage economy in which the benefactor's authority over the text is subverted in the name of the author's. In both her historical and fictional dealings with patrons, Christine reconceptualizes the literary artifact as an object intimately associated with the author. The dedication and several incipit miniatures in the Harley compilation disclose how the author and her bookmakers manipulate conventional patronage topoi and iconography to enhance the author's identity. In the specific case of the Harley opening miniatures to the *Complainte amoureuse* and the *Livre du duc des vrais amans,* the artists altered the MS D prototypes to explore authorial involvement in literary creation.

When defining medieval patronage, scholars usually refer to court artists as entertainers, who are selected by royalty to amuse and sometimes to educate their audience. In exchange, artists often receive from the patron food, lodging, clothing, money and sometimes, a stable position at court. Richard Green stresses that a "reciprocal obligation" occurs between poet and patron within the confines of court culture (63). Douglas Kelly also concentrates on the intimacy between poet and benefactor, and defines their ideal relationship as one in which the artist submits to the patron's desires, becoming a scribe "to record the thoughts and sentiments of the prince" (77). Natalie Zemon Davis and Claude Macherel nuance the remarks of Green and Kelly by examining patronage dynamics as a social structure. They argue that poet-patron relations are based on an archaic gift-exchange economy. Marcel Mauss defines this exchange as a linear system in which a gift offered must be reciprocated with a countergift of equal or greater value. According to Mauss, once a gift is offered the giver relinquishes all control over that gift. Therefore, if the poet-patron relationship exemplifies the gift-exchange economy, then once an author presents her work to a patron, she relinquishes her authority over the literary object.

The patronage culture underwent substantial modifications in the late Middle Ages. The rise of the book trade, the availability of cheaper materials, and the demand for manuscripts by multiple courts from the fourteenth century onward facilitated a wider dissemination of manuscripts (Febvre and Martin 17–37). Likewise, historical shifts in the cultural priorities of French nobility prompted writers and bookmakers to distribute their manuscripts to a larger buying audience. If Charles VI abandoned the artistic agenda promoted by his father, who had supported the arts as a national treasure, the dukes of Berry, Orléans, and Burgundy aggressively sought to enhance their own libraries by obtaining copies of works already in circulation or by commissioning new works. Their increased interest in manuscript acquisition challenged the king's role as patron of the arts. The wider dissemination of texts to multiple patrons, however, had a secondary impact on patronage dynamics, not mentioned by scholars, in that it encouraged noble figures to collect examples of diverse writers, rather than support the literature of a select few. Consequently, many writers, especially Christine, lacked a source of consistent and substantial support from a single patron. As a result, she shifted her fidelities and her literary inclinations according to interest in her poetic endeavors (Willard, *Christine* 157). Instead of remaining exclusively involved with a single patron, she redistributed works to other royal figures for supplemental countergifts, as was the case for the compilation offered to Queen Isabeau. Indeed, Christine's literary patronage led to her concurrent association with both the royal court and the antiroyalist factions of Burgundy, Orléans, and Berry.

A brief survey of Christine de Pizan's activities from 1406 to 1412, when she was ostensibly working for the Burgundian court, shows Christine accommodating the "thoughts and sentiments" of several patrons. Christine's patronage history depicts a radically different system from the gift-exchange economy discussed earlier. In this new system, Christine undertakes concurrent projects intended for individual patrons and then disseminates copies of these same works to multiple members of nobility. During the time of the fabrication of Harley 4431, Christine was not a member of the queen's court, but was apparently working for the Burgundian court. Her dealings with the Burgundians began in 1401 with the request of Philip the Bold that Christine write the *Livre des fais et bonnes meurs de Charles V.* However, the duke died before she completed the work, but the duke's son, John the Fearless, paid the author one hundred *ecus* in 1406 for this book (Willard, *Christine* 170). Subsequently, Christine composed many works dedicated to the duke, including the *Avision-Christine* (1405), the *Sept Psaulmes allégorisés* (1409), the *Livre des fais d'armes et de chevalerie* (1409), and the *Lamentacion* (1409). Although details of the duke's payment for these texts and others written by Christine are sparse, Burgundian records indicate that money was given to Christine for books as late as December 3, 1412 (Doutrepont 278). In fact, John the Fearless was Christine's most faithful patron; inventories of his property in 1420 show that he possessed seven volumes of her works, making Christine the most represented author in his library (Doutrepont 478). Yet, despite the substantial patronage of John the Fearless, Christine continued to disseminate her works throughout France. While producing works for the duke, Christine also offered MS D to the duke of Berry around 1408, books to the duke of Brabant and Philip of Nevers around 1407–8, and the Harley manuscript to Isabeau of Bavaria around 1411. Throughout Christine's career, she offered copies of her texts to many other royal figures, such as Charles VI, Jean of Berry, Marguerite of Burgundy, Louis of Guyenne, Marie of Berry, the seneschal of Hainaut, John of Bourbon, the duke of Milan, the earl of Salisbury, King Richard II, and King Henry IV. In the specific case of the *Epistre Othea,* the author rededicated this work to at least four different patrons during her lifetime. It was packaged with a different prologue for Louis of Orléans in 1401, Philip the Bold in 1403, and both Jean of Berry and Henry IV of England in 1404.[3] The patronage pattern that we find here suggests that Christine's texts are not circulating as gifts offered to an individual who can lay exclusive claim to them. Instead, they function as artifacts associated primarily with their creator, who masterminds their continued distribution.

In the *Avision-Christine,* the author's pseudoautobiography, additional evidence shows that the precepts of the gift-exchange economy were being manipulated by Christine de Pizan and her readers to valorize her authorship. First, she claims that her audience desires her books because of their interest in the author, rather than in the designated patron or in the story line. The narrator remarks on two occasions that her gender substantially contributes to the success of her works. She writes that princes present to other royal figures her literature "plus... pour la chose non usagee que femme escripse comme pieca ne avenist que pour dignete qui y soit" (more so because of the unusual and rare event that a woman should write than because of the quality found therein).[4] Later, she remarks that her works disseminate throughout Europe because they represent "chose nouvelle venue de sentement de femme" (new things deriving from a woman's perspective) (166). In the eyes of her readers, Christine's enterprising stance increases in value because of her precarious position as a woman in a man's domain. Furthermore, restricted by functions she could perform within the court system as a woman and exclusively dependent on the gifts of noble figures, Christine emphasizes her gender to maintain a certain level of mastery over her literary corpus (Quilligan 5–6). Contrary to Foucault's understated speculation that it matters little "who is speaking" (101), Christine identifies her personal history of patronage and gender as essential to a correct reading of her works.

Christine also challenges our understanding of medieval patronage as a gift-exchange economy by revealing in the *Avision-Christine* that she bartered her books for future services. Underscoring the value of her literature, the narrator discusses the exchange of her books for the services of various royal figures. She offered works to King Richard II of England so that he would take her son into his court (165). Later when the king died, she sent more copies of her literature to the new king of England as ransom for the return of her son (165–66). Again, she sent manuscripts to Philip, duke of Burgundy, to request that he subsequently govern her child (167). These examples spotlight the value of Christine's books, thereby exposing the author's and her audience's perception of her books as commodities. At least in this pseudoautobiography, Christine de Pizan proposes a variation of the gift-exchange economy, as she establishes sometimes in advance the countergift anticipated. If her works are initially presented as gifts, they sometimes circulate as commodities. Nowhere is this more apparent than in Harley 4431, in which Christine and her bookmakers rework conventional scenes of patronage to underscore the intimacy between poet and book.

Harley 4431 documents Christine's challenge to the traditional patronage system by exposing Isabeau's lack of control over literary production in the dedication. In her address to Isabeau, Christine de Pizan asks the queen to ignore weaknesses in her works because she has only tried to please people in producing them:

Ne vueillez pas, dame sensible,
Pour tant prendre garde au deffail,
Mais a ce que je me travail
Voulentiers de ce que possible

M'est a faire en chose loisible
Qu'a haulte gent voulentiers bail.
(Lines 79–84)

[Would you, sensible lady, ignore the mistakes [in this book] and instead, notice that I willingly do my best to compose pleasant works that I then offer to worthy people.]

Disrupting the traditional image of patronage, this passage evokes a past that challenges Isabeau's own association with literary creation. By referring to "haulte gent," Christine breaks with her earlier statement that Isabeau inspired the collection (cited earlier, lines 49–54); instead, she acknowledges that the compiled texts were written to please others. On the larger scale of the anthology, several works identify individuals other than the queen as the patron. For instance, the *Livre du duc des vrais amans*, the *Dit de la pastoure*, and *Cent ballades d'amant et de dame* identify unnamed princes as dictating the works' contents. By designating additional noble figures as potentially controlling different aspects of the work, Christine fragments Isabeau's command over literary creation. With the dispersement of the patron's authority in the Harley manuscript and the dissemination of Christine's works to multiple royal figures, it is the author, not the patron, who emerges as master of the artistic object. As I will show presently, the references to Christine's patronage history in Harley 4431 establish an overarching authorial identity, who claims control of the literary enterprise.

By interweaving her personal history into the fabric of the Harley anthology via the dedication, Christine situates herself at the center of the literary enterprise. The sizable half-page frontispiece reinforces the centrality of the author-figure in the written text. Here, the *Cité des dames* master prioritizes Christine's gender by depicting the unprecedented scene of a woman writer, who displays the coveted book amid a circle of ladies and the queen.[5] The exclusively female audience surrounding Christine validates her specifically as a woman writer. The artist reconceptualizes the traditional patronage scene as a uniquely female enterprise, thereby stabilizing her previous persona as a "curiosity" in a man's world. Thus, the miniaturist manipulates audience to construct an authorial identity.

Authorship also constitutes the central theme of the dedication accompanying this illumination. Rather than restrict her discussion to the conventional precepts of a formal dedication by presenting a laudatory portrait of Isabeau, Christine calls on the queen to contemplate the writer's extraordinary participation in the literary enterprise. The collection opens with the detailed record of the author's responsibilities concerning the composing, ordering, transcribing, and decorating of the Harley manuscript (cited earlier, lines 49–54).[6] This passage redefines the dynamics of the medieval poet-patron relationship by evoking the textual artifact in terms of the author's control over its creation. The narrator stresses that she invests her "pouoir, force et sceu" (line 59; power, strength, and knowledge) to create what she identifies in its final form as "mon euvre" (line 63; my work), and "mon labour et lonc travail" (line 73; my labor and hard work). Furthermore, she underscores her position as an accomplished author through an extended discussion of her impressive and diverse collection of works:

> ... ce livre cy que je tiens
> Vous presenter, ou il n'a riens,
> En histoire n'en escripture,
> Que n'aye en ma pensée pure
> Pris ou stile ...
>
> Et sont ou volume compris
> Plusieurs livres es quieulx j'ay pris
> A parler en maintes manieres
> Differens, et pour ce l'empris
> Que on en devient plus appris
> D'oÿr de diverses matieres,
> Unes pesans, aultres legieres.
> (Lines 16–31)

[This book, which I intend to present to you, in which there is not a single thing, neither in stories nor in learned writings, that I have not, with my pure thought, adopted or fashioned.... And included in this volume are many books in which I undertook to speak in many different styles because one can learn more in hearing varied material, some profound, others light.]

Christine transforms the queen's gift into a treasure-house testifying to the author's learnedness, poetic versatility, and prolific production. Although the frontispiece and dedication unify the diverse prose and poetic pieces in the anthology by announcing the benefactor's authority over literary creation, they also explicitly identify every facet of the book's creation with the author.

The dedication also subordinates the queen to the writer by reconfiguring the patron's relationship with the text. Christine undermines the patron's traditional role as judge and instead fashions Isabeau as student of the writer's "diverses matieres." Christine more discreetly shapes her royal reader as student through remarks that associate the desire to read with the attainment of wisdom:

> ... les sages tesmoignent
> En leurs escrips, les gens qui songnent
> De lire en livres voulentiers,

Ne peut qu'aucunement n'eslongnent
Ygnorence....

(Lines 37–41)

[Wise men witness in their writings that people who think of reading books willingly can often avoid ignorance.]

By designating the queen's relationship to the book in didactic terms, Christine transforms her courtly identity as entertainer into the more prestigious identity of teacher. However, Christine's references to the educational value of books may signal the queen's ultimate influence over the anthology, as the author may be repackaging her collection according to Isabeau's predilection for didactic books.[7] The designation of the patron as student also may derive from the medieval *miroir des princes* genre, but Christine uses the tradition to her advantage. This genre concerns itself with providing advice to its primary reader on how to lead a correct life. Thus, the reader is called upon to submit to the writer's wisdom. By incorporating the *miroir* theme in the dedication, Christine enhances her own authorial identity by implementing a didactic model in place of the master/servant dichotomy evoked in the opening illumination. She symbolically "unseats" the queen who resides in judgment over the author in the frontispiece. In addition to redefining the queen's relationship to the book and its author, Christine's comments on the educational quality of her works simultaneously transform the book from otiose luxury item, as presented in the illumination, into a collection of serious texts. In the dedication, the presentation of Isabeau as student attributes an uncommon prestige to a collection of courtly texts and to the female author.

Christine develops the potential impact that the queen could have on the author's fame in the final lines of the dedication, where she calls on Isabeau to remember her always:

Prendre en gré, qui loyale et voire
Est et sera, et si notoire
Ceste mienne posicion
Vous soit qu'a tousjours mencion
Soit de moy en vostre memoire,
Si que vostre grace m'avoire
Qu'ayés a moy affection.

(Lines 90–96)

[She, who is and always will be loyal, true, and noteworthy, accept my proposition that you always have a place for me in your memories, if your grace would have me and that you feel affection for me.]

Whereas the conventional *locus* would designate the written artifact as key to the benefactor's eternal glory, this closing comment instead solic-

202

its the benefactor to perpetuate the author's memory. Since these clos-
ing lines show scarce concern for the queen's own future reputation and
eternal survival, they effectively distance the patron from the literary
artifact and even supplant her with the poet. In Christine's system, the
benefactor neither fully controls inspiration and production, nor profits
from its creation through poetic immortality. Instead, it is the author who
gains from the process, as she is duly designated as gifted poet, teacher,
and even master of the anthology. Harley 4431 carefully fashions the pa-
tron into a vehicle of authorial valorization.

Christine and the bookmakers of Harley 4431 appear to be less con-
cerned with acknowledging the queen than with valorizing the author.
The anthology makes no allusion to the queen's involvement in its cre-
ation beyond her initial request. Moreover, apart from the dedication, the
poet explicitly refers to the queen on only two other occasions in Harley
4431: once to wish her a happy New Year in ballade 18 of *Autres ballades*
(*Oeuvres* 1:227) and later to identify her as one of France's respected
women in the *Livre de la cité des dames* (2.68.1). In contrast, several texts
identify in word and image the active involvement of other patrons in
the creation and reception of the same texts. Apart from the portrait of
Isabeau as patron in the frontispiece, five out of seventeen opening minia-
tures in Harley 4431 depict another individual accepting the book or dis-
cussing some aspect of the literary enterprise with the writer. For exam-
ple, the artist depicts Christine offering her works to Louis of Orléans in
the incipit miniature to the *Epistre Othea* (1399–1400) (fol. 95) (Figure
28) and to Charles VI in the opening image to the *Livre du chemin de
long estude* (1403) (fol. 178).[8] The miniature to the *Débat de deux amans*
(fol. 58v) shows Christine introducing Louis of Orleans to the two fic-
tional lovers of the poem, and the image to the *Livre des trois jugemens*
(fol. 71v) presents her between the seneschal of Hainaut and the three
fictional couples he is to judge.[9] The last two images replace the book
with the fictional couples whom Christine presents to the patron. Finally,
at the head of the *Livre du duc des vrais amans* (fol. 143), an unidenti-
fied prince and the author-figure carry on a discussion in the poet's
study (Figure 29). This incipit illumination, which will be discussed in de-
tail later, replaces the typical image of the author offering her book to
the patron with one that portrays the benefactor's initial request.

Evidence of Christine's extensive patronage in the Harley manuscript
conflicts with the queen's identity as inspiration and recipient of the lit-
erary text, as suggested in the opening material. Even if we recognize the
opening frontispiece to function as a "self-celebratory mark of visual
ownership" for Isabeau, as Brigitte Buettner has suggested of presenta-
tion miniatures in general ("Profane Illuminations" 76), we must also
acknowledge the competing "self-celebratory marks" of various princes
in Harley 4431. Indeed, who figures as owner of the book? No single
royal figure portrayed in Harley 4431 can exclusively claim possession

Figure 28. *Epistre Othea.* London, British Library, Harley 4431, fol. 95.

of literary creation, for the book seems to be appropriated by multiple benefactors. Instead, the liminary illuminations to the various poems in the Harley anthology systematically depict the author's possession of the text, whether she is firmly holding the book or discussing its contents. Whereas the author-figure's portrait remains strikingly consistent in every

Figure 29. *Livre du duc des vrais amans.* London, British Library, Harley 4431, fol. 143.

image, the patron-figure differs in every miniature. With the dispersement of the patron's authoritative role in the literary enterprise, a more consistent image of authorship develops. The six poet/patron portraits brought together in the Harley anthology usurp the authority commonly bestowed on the patron and attribute it to the author. Additionally, Christine's claim of authority is reinforced by this series of presentation images, as they situate her alongside the major noble figures of her time. These many scenes of patronage in Harley 4431 challenge Isabeau's control over the literary enterprise. Concomitant to the fragmentation of the patron's control in the Harley anthology is the establishment of a cohesive and powerful author-figure.

The author-figure's construction in Harley 4431 consists of a complex process that involves both Christine de Pizan and the bookmakers. An examination of two incipit illuminations in the Harley anthology brings to light the miniaturists' participation in reconceptualizing patronage dynamics to spotlight the author. The incipit miniature to the *Complainte amoureuse*, although not depicting a presentation scene, confronts the conventional relationship between poet and prince by incorporating evidence of the author's participation in literary creation. Even though the narrative is absent of any reference to the author-figure, the opening miniature to the *Complainte amoureuse* arguably depicts her in the scene, thereby transforming a courtly work that exclusively records the prince's words into a discreet commentary on authorship. The second image to be studied here, the incipit illumination to the *Livre du duc des vrais amans*, provides a faithful visual rendition of the text's prologue, resulting in a controversial image of patronage dynamics. These two images take on even greater importance when they are compared with their presumed prototypes in MS D. Based on the differences between the opening miniatures to the *Complainte amoureuse* and the *Livre du duc des vrais amans* in Harley 4431 and in MS D, we can conclude that Christine de Pizan and her bookmakers reconceptualize patronage so that references to patrons become valuable components in the construction of Christine's authorial identity. In altering the scenes that introduce these two works, the Bedford Trend master, responsible for the opening image to the *Complainte amoureuse*, and the *Cité des dames* master, responsible for the incipit miniature to the *Livre du duc des vrais amans*, challenge the traditional performance of gift exchange in which the prince typically takes center stage. These two miniatures transform the courtly works they enhance into complex discourses on authorship.

Harley 4431 is recognized by some Christine scholars as a copy of an earlier anthology owned by the duke of Berry. Nonetheless, the queen's anthology has been inaccurately identified by Millard Meiss as identical in contents and layout to MS D (*Limbourgs* 1:293–96). Although MS D contains illuminations similar to the five presentation miniatures depicting various princes, it lacks liminary material that would unify the anthology under the aegis of a single patron. However, MS D includes internal references to its intended recipient, the duke of Orléans. He is identified and portrayed as the patron of the *Epistre Othea* (Figure 28) and the *Débat des deux amans*, which are also included in the queen's anthology. Moreover at the very least, even the duke of Berry, who acquired the manuscript after Louis of Orléans's death, could identify with the many visual and written references to unnamed princes. When the narrator in the *Livre du duc des vrais amans* speaks of "un seigneur / A qui doy bien obeïr" (lines 12–13; a lord whom one must obey) or when the narrator in the *Dit de la pastoure* (1400) refers to a "Bon chevalier, vaillant, plein de savoir" (*Oeuvres*, vol. 3, line 1; good, knowledgeable and courageous knight), the duke could easily assume the role of the unidentified prince. If it were not for the collection's accommodation of its female audience in Harley's liminary material, such a perspective would not be as easily adapted in Isabeau's reading of her collection. Nevertheless, Christine and the Harley workshop retained the many references in the anthology to an otherwise exclusively male patronage. The question that arises then is to what end do Christine and the Harley bookmakers include so many references to Christine's patronage history?

The Harley incipit illumination to the *Complainte amoureuse* presents the lover-protagonist, who kneels before his lady. Behind and to the right of the lady, two unidentified female characters observe the scene (fol. 48) (Figure 30). Contrary to Meiss's claim that this miniature is an exact replica of its MS D counterpart, the opening miniature to the *Complainte amoureuse* in MS D does not include the two female characters. Instead, MS D depicts the lover offering a written text to the lady, who accepts it (fol. 50) (Figure 31). The two unidentified women in the Harley miniature announce an important disjunction between text and image, as they are never mentioned in the text. Although they may represent ladies-in-waiting, the observer depicted in a three-quarter view stands out because of her attire, which calls to mind the author-figure depicted elsewhere in the Harley anthology. I contend that this unidentified observer is the author-figure. Although difficult to see in a black-and-white photo, the blue dress and the *cotehardie* (a simple headdress and wimple worn by the upper class) donned by this woman duplicate the costume of the easily identifiable author-figure in the only two miniatures preceding it, the frontispiece and the miniature introducing *Cent ballades*.[10] Moreover, the lady in blue, situated as a bystander who views the events to be developed in the text, brings to mind the *Dit de Poissy*, in which the narrator also performs as a bystander who records the story of her fellow travelers: "m'ont enchargié / Lui dui amant que tost fust abrigié / De leur affaire" (lines 2061–64; the two lovers requested that I retell their story). Reinforcing the narrator's statement in the *Dit de Poissy*, the incipit illumination to the poem shows her on horseback riding behind the two men and two women whose story she is to transcribe. In this miniature, like the one heading the *Complainte amoureuse*, she is attired in a blue dress and *cotehardie*.[11] Thus, if the lady in blue is, in fact, intended to be the author-figure, the opening illumination to the *Complainte amoureuse* signals an authorial presence with terms used by Christine de Pizan on other occasions. However, the two female characters in the Harley miniature to the *Complainte amoureuse* might also

Figure 30. *Complainte amoureuse.* London, British Library, Harley 4431, fol. 48.

allude to the female audience of the anthology. If so, this visual reference may anticipate Christine's call to her female audience in *Cent ballades d'amant et de dame,* in which the female protagonist requests that her women readers consider her fate as potentially their own:

> Ha! mirez vous, dames, en mon dommage,
> Pour Dieu mercy! ne vous laissiez attraire
> Par homme nul, tous sont de faulx plumage.
> > (Ballade 94, lines 17–19)

> [Helas! See yourselves, ladies, in my suffering. I beg of you, do not let yourself be attracted by any man, they are all deceptive.]

Figure 31. *Complainte amoureuse.* Paris, Bibliothèque Nationale de France, MS fr. 835, fol. 50.

The written address in *Cent ballades d'amant et de dame* to women readers and the possible visual depiction of a female audience in the Harley miniature to the *Complainte amoureuse* might represent efforts to reconstruct texts that prioritize princes so that women can be included.

Should we understand the incipit illumination to the *Complainte amoureuse* in Harley 4431 as supplementing the narrative? Even though it is impossible to ascertain who exactly the two additional female figures represent, their presence in the miniature echoes Michael Camille's remarks on the visual register of medieval books as sometimes representing "disagreement and juxtaposition" with the written word (21). The image contradicts the narrative through the incorporation of other players in the literary game and transforms a poem that only speaks of the prince's sentiments into one dominated by women.

In the *Livre du duc des vrais amans*, we find an even more explicit example of the visual construction of the author-figure based on manipulating the patron's identity in the margins of the text. The *Duc des vrais amans* recounts the tale of a man who seduces and must eventually abandon his lady. It combines their poetic correspondence with verse dialogue during their occasional encounters. In addition, it includes a secondary correspondence between the lady and an older woman, Dame de la Tour. An elaborate paratextual frame, including six miniatures, a prologue, an epilogue, and a collection of love poems, surrounds the story.[12] Whereas the *Complainte amoureuse* is silent regarding the circumstances surrounding the poem's creation, the prologue to the *Duc des vrais amans* underscores the poet's resistance to the imposed subject:

> Combien que occupacion
> Je n'eusse ne entencion
> A present de dictiez faire
> D'amours, car en autre affaire,
> Ou trop plus me delictoie,
> Toute m'entente mettoie,
> Vueil je d'autrui sentement
> Commencier presentement
> Nouvel dit, car tel m'en prie
> Qui bien peut, sans qu'il deprie,
> Commander a trop greigneur
> Que ne suis.
> (Lines 1–12)

[Although I had no desire or intention at this point in time to compose a love poem, because I was occupied by other things that pleased me more, I want to now begin a new poem for someone else, for he could easily ask someone more powerful than myself.]

The prologue succeeds in evoking complex interconnections with the other texts in the anthology by alluding to works that are more pleasing to the poet. Christine's reference to these other works calls attention to her prolific production, which she already mentioned in the dedication ("unes pesans, autres legieres," line 31). In addition, by detailing the poet's begrudging acquiescence and opposing her desire to the patron's request, the prologue to the *Duc des vrais amans* constructs an authorial identity that challenges the patron's authority.

A comparison of the incipit miniatures to the *Livre du duc des vrais amans* in Harley 4431 and MS D reveals how the *Cité des dames* master manipulated the visual register with the intent to validate as well as valorize the author-figure. In their recent study of this text, Sandra Hindman and Stephen Perkinson acknowledge that the opening miniature to the *Duc des vrais amans* in Harley 4431 clearly "emphasizes the priority of Christine's voice" by manipulating the representation of the opening scene proposed in the MS D prototype (225). In MS D, the scene transpires in the traditional setting of a presentation scenario, with the patron seated on a throne and "Christine" kneeling before him, but apparently she only listens to his request, rather than offer him the book (BNF, MS fr. 836, fol. 65) (Figure 32). Although no book transference occurs in

Figure 32. *Livre du duc des vrais amans.* Paris, Bibliothèque Nationale de France, MS fr. 836, fol. 65.

MS D's miniature, the location and characteristic poses of poet and prince replicate the dynamics of the traditional donation scene in which the writing subject is portrayed as subservient to the royal figure.

In comparison, the Harley version of the opening scene to the *Livre du duc des vrais amans* offers a striking rereading of patronage dynamics, for the poet does not kneel before her prince, but stands, while he appears to bow toward her (Figure 29). Although as a court author Christine de Pizan was unquestionably dependent on the patron, the miniature introducing the *Duc des vrais amans* in Harley 4431 complements the prologue's presentation of the patron's need for the poet. The Harley scene develops Christine's identity by situating the poet and prince in the private space of the poet's chambers rather than in the benefactor's public sphere, as its counterpart in MS D does. The scene in the Harley miniature fills the room with evidence of her literary profession: two books are located on an upper shelf behind the poet, and she stands before a chair and a desk on which lies a large bound red book. Even though the miniature presents the prince as an imposing presence, it strips the patron of visual signs of his authority and depicts his dependence on the author.[13] Finally, the visual rendition of the *Duc des vrais amans* in Harley 4431, unlike its counterpart in the duke's copy, captures the sentiments of the poem's earlier-quoted opening lines. The miniaturist depicts the author on the sidelines, hedged in by her chair and the prince. The additional characters effectively bar the doorway. The author-figure, with her body slightly bent backward, appears to make every effort to distance herself from the patron-figure and the unwanted assignment. Unlike the author-figure's subservience to the system evoked in the narrative's prologue and developed in MS D's incipit illumination, the opening miniature to the *Duc des vrais amans* in Harley 4431 reconfigures the exchange and prioritizes the message of the poet's resistance to the patron's request.

I began this essay under the aegis of a loaded question—What is a patron?—a question that already insinuated the intricate function performed by the patron in constructing the author-figure. Harley 4431 communicates a revamped vision of medieval patronage. Christine's corpus challenges traditional views that the patron constituted the source, subject, and recipient of the medieval text by referring to an overarching author-figure responsible for the entire corpus of composed works as well as their manuscript fabrication.[14] Inevitably, the author's increased authority over the text coincides with the recession of the patron's conventional power. Indeed, the visual and verbal references to her various benefactors subvert the patron's authority over literary creation. As a result, the patron-figure sustains Christine's authorial identity. Enhancing the vast majority of her texts with visual and verbal references to the events surrounding production, Christine de Pizan, in collaboration with the Harley workshop, transforms courtly works into discourses on authorship.

The manipulation of late medieval patronage in Harley 4431 challenges not only poet-patron dynamics, but contemporary theories of authorship as well. Michel Foucault's seminal essay "Qu'est-ce qu'un auteur?" ("What Is an Author?") demonstrates the extent to which the term "author" goes beyond biographical details of the writer to embrace a series of strategies that lead to the construction of an author-figure inextricably associated with the book. Foucault limits his discussion to the study of how the text points to the author-figure and ignores strategies used by authors and bookmakers to construct a coherent image of authorship. By reversing Foucault's approach and examining the process by which writers and bookmakers infuse a text with an authorial presence, I have shown that at least for Christine de Pizan and the Harley miniaturists, the questions of who is speaking and who is reading were central to their strategy. Possibly recognizing the impact of her personal history on her audience, Christine infused her literary corpus with multiple references to her gender and to her literary status. In both instances, Christine and the workshop used the audience to reinforce her authorship.

The powerful role attributed to Christine de Pizan in Harley 4431 is unprecedented. Furthermore, Daniel Poirion refers to Christine as France's "first author," a status he attributes to her making "a cause of the feminine condition and her personal experience be[coming] a system and a style" (*Littérature* 206; trans. Willard, *Christine* 223). However, the authority of Christine's literary identity goes beyond the personal to engage social structures. By reconceptualizing the poet-patron relationship, Christine de Pizan and the Harley workshop transformed the patron's traditional power over literary creation into evidence of the writer's authority and, as a result, replaced the image of a court entertainer with that of an author.

Notes

1. On the similarity between the two anthologies, see Laidlaw, "Publisher's Progress," and Millard Meiss, *Limbourgs* 1:293–96.

2. The idea that Harley 4431 represents reconstituted sections was first suggested by Gianni Mombello (*Tradizione*). James Laidlaw questions Mombello and Hindman's suppositions on the organizing of the collection, arguing that the anthology was created as a whole ("Publisher's Progress" 61–62).

3. James Laidlaw names and dates the recipients of the *Epistre Othea* in "Publisher's Progress" 41. He speaks of Henry IV in "Earl of Salisbury" 138.

4. Christine de Pizan, *L'Avision-Christine*, ed. Towner, 165. All subsequent references are to this edition and are cited parenthetically in the text.

5. In "Iconography," Sandra Hindman provides a detailed analysis of the Harley frontispiece. She argues that the highly realistic nature of the miniature suggests that it may depict the presentation scene as it truly occurred.

6. Recent codicological studies have enhanced our appreciation of Christine's claims that she supervised the fabrication of this manuscript. In "Identification," Gilbert Ouy and Christine Reno designate the author as scribe of the entire anthology, arguing that she transcribed the texts, added rubrics, and even corrected mistakes in the margins.

7. Records of Queen Isabeau's library clearly point to her pronounced interest in religious works intended to fortify the reader; out of thirty-three books, only eight, including Christine's volume, were of a nonspiritual nature (S. G. Bell, "Medieval Women" 750).

8. Reproduction of the miniature to the *Livre du chemin de long estude* is found on the cover plate to Castel's *Damoiselle Christine de Pizan*.

9. The miniature from the *Débat de deux amans* is found in Castel pl. 42, and the opening image of the *Livre des trois jugements* is also in Castel pl. 43.

10. Hindman provides a copy of this incipit in "Composition" 95. See Laurie Rinaldi Dufresne for an extensive analysis of authorial costume in the miniatures decorating Christine's manuscripts.

11. The miniature is found in Castel pl. 48.

12. All six miniatures decorating Harley 4431 can be found in Thelma Fenster's edition of the work (46, 49, 52, 65, 73, 79).

13. The patron seeking out the poet is not a novel concept. Vincent de Beauvais's *Speculum historiale* includes two examples: in the first case, Saint Louis, king of France, stands before the author-figure, and, in the second, Queen Jeanne de Bourgogne gives orders for the translation to the author-figure (Martin, *Miniaturistes* 2: fig. 26, p. 124).

14. See Sylvia Huot's recent study of single-author anthologies in the Middle Ages, in which she extensively examines the use of author-centered imagery in manuscripts to give cohesion to these collections (*Song*).

Manuscripts Cited

London, British Library, Harley 4431
Paris, Bibliothèque Nationale de France, MS fr. 605
Paris, Bibliothèque Nationale de France, MS fr. 606
Paris, Bibliothèque Nationale de France, MS fr. 607
Paris, Bibliothèque Nationale de France, MS fr. 835
Paris, Bibliothèque Nationale de France, MS fr. 836

CHAPTER 11

The Reconstruction of an Author in Print

Christine de Pizan in the Fifteenth and Sixteenth Centuries

Cynthia J. Brown

In 1488, Antoine Vérard published the *Livre des fais d'armes et de chevalerie*, the first of Christine de Pizan's texts to be printed in France. The author, however, would not have recognized her own work at first glance. Not only was the title altered to read the *Art de chevalerie selon Vegece*,[1] but Christine's name as author was replaced by the name Vegetius, one of her acknowledged sources. In addition, the first-person speaker had disappeared from the text in Vérard's version. Christine's female narrator had originally been identified from the start, since the speaker defended her status as a woman discussing warfare in the opening prologue; in Vérard's version, all such references were either excised or carefully replaced by a male voice.[2] Certainly Vérard, one of the most enthusiastic — and aggressive — book entrepreneurs of late-fifteenth- and early-sixteenth-century France (see Macfarlane; M. B. Winn, "Treasures," *Vérard*), often overshadowed the authors of his editions, in part because he consciously promoted his association with the volumes he published. At the end of the 1488 *Art de chevalerie*, for example, he advertised the fact that this volume had been printed for him, offered his address as bookseller, and had his mark prominently displayed.[3] But, as it turns out, Vérard was not responsible for the disappearance of Christine's authorship and narrative voice from this edition, since they are already missing in fifteen of the twenty-four extant manuscripts of the *Fais d'armes*, one of which had served as the basis of his version.[4] Nonetheless, purchasers of Vérard's *Art de chevalerie* thought they were reading a translation of Vegetius instead of a vernacular work by Christine de Pizan.

This misrepresentation of Christine's writing and disinterest in her full identity typify the publications of the first generation of French printers. It was later French publishers, however, who restored Christine's image. Like Vérard, they exploited Christine's works to market their editions, especially those that would appeal to a female audience. But by providing a more comprehensive advertisement of her authorship and works, their rehabilitation of Christine was not so self-centered. By contrast,

Christine's reputation in England took an opposite trajectory.[5] Whereas her name and works were attentively promoted in the last decades of the fifteenth century, a second generation of English printers failed to publicize or even acknowledge her authorship. It is these divergent patterns that I will examine through a close study of the presentation of Christine de Pizan's early printed works (see accompanying publication list).

One year after the appearance of Vérard's misattributed and mistitled edition of her *Fais d'armes*, William Caxton printed *The Fayttes of Armes and of Chyvalrye*. Although Caxton's 1489 edition lacks a title page—a feature of print that was not exploited as rapidly in England as in France (Hirsch)—Caxton's edition, unlike Vérard's, not only provided a literal translation of Christine's original title, but also carefully promoted her authorship, Italian heritage (see n. 39), and relationship to her sources. The name "Crystyne" first appears on the opening folio, whose table of contents announces the prologue in which she defends herself:

> The fyrst chapitre is the prologue in which *Crystyne* excuseth her to have dar enterpryse to speke of so hye matere as is conteyned in thys sayd book. (my emphasis)

Her full name is found in the rubric that precedes the beginning of the text, which repeats many of the same details:

> Here begynneth the Book of Fayttes of Armes and of Chyvalrye. And the first chapytre is the prologue, in whiche *Chrystyne of Pyse* excuseth hir self to have dar enterpryse to speke of so hye matere as is conteyned in this sayd book. (Fol. A1; my emphasis)

We again discover the author's name in a rather lengthy colophon, in which Caxton details how King Henry VII transmitted to him a manuscript of the work, and asked him to translate and print it. It begins:

> Thus endeth this boke whiche *Chrystyne of Pyse* made and drewe out of the boke named Vegecius De Re Militari and out of Th'Arbre of Bataylles [by Honoré Bouvet] wyth many other thynges sett in to the same requisite to werre and batailles. (Fol. S5; my emphasis)

Whether or not he knew of Vérard's earlier French edition of Christine's work,[6] Caxton clearly relied on a different source than the French publisher. Neither he nor Henry VII questioned the fact that a female had authored *The Fayttes of Armes*, as some French scribe or editor had apparently done.[7] Moreover, in contrast to the common loss of authorial signatures in translations at this time (see Brown 184–87), Caxton's translations of two of Christine de Pizan's works are all the more remarkable because they call attention to her authorship. With this and his earlier

**Printed Editions of Christine de Pizan's Works
in the Fifteenth and Sixteenth Centuries**

France	England
	1478: *The Morale Proverbes of Cristyne* Westminster, William Caxton
1488: *L'art de chevalerie selon vegece* Paris, Antoine Vérard	
	1489: *The Fayttes of Armes and Chyvalrye* Westminster, William Caxton
1497: *Le tresor de la cite des dames selo[n] dame cristine* Paris, Antoine Vérard	
1499/1500: *Les cent histoires de troye* Paris, Philippe Pigouchet	
1503: *Le tresor de la cite des dames de degre en degre: et de tous estatz selon dame cristine* Paris, Michel Le Noir	
*ca. 1518: *S'ensuyt l'epistre de Othea deesse de Prudence moralisee… par Christine de Pisan* Paris, Widow Trepperel	
[ca. 1521: Paris, Widow Trepperel?]	1521: *Here begynneth the booke whiche is called the body of Polycye…* London, John Skot
	Here begynneth the boke of the Cyte of Ladyes… London, Henry Pepwell
1522: *Les cent hystoires de troye* Paris, Philippe Le Noir	
	1526: "Morall Proverbes of Christyne" (fols. e4–e5), in *Here begynneth the boke of Fame made by Geffray Chaucer…* London, Richard Pynson
1527: *L'Arbre des batailles Et fleur de chevalerie selon Vegece…* Paris, Philippe Le Noir	
before 1534: *L'Epistre de Othea deesse de Prudence moralisee…* Rouen, Raulin Gaultier	
1536: *Le tresor de la Cite des dames, selon Dame Christine de la Cité de Pise…* Paris, Jehan André/Denis Janot	1536–45: *Here foloweth the .C. Hystoryes of Troy* Charing Cross, Robert Wyer
1549: *Le Chemin de long estude de Dame Christine de Pise…* Paris, Estienne Groulleau	
N.p., n.d.: *Contre rommant de la rose*	

*1518: *O espelo de Christine*
Lisbon, Hernao de Campos

edition of Christine's *Morale Proverbes,* dating from 1478, Caxton played a critical role in introducing to the middle-class English public the works of Christine de Pizan; she already had a readership among the nobles since her own association with the English court earlier in the century and the duke of Bedford's acquisition of important manuscripts from French royal libraries in 1425.[8]

Had she been alive at the time, Christine de Pizan, whose search for an authorizing audience has been well documented by her many manuscript dedications,[9] would have probably responded favorably to the multiple possibilities for textual transmission that print offered, at least based on the example of Caxton's versions of her works. However, her fortune in France would not appear, at first glance, to have emphasized her identity as author. Having been deceased for nearly sixty years when Vérard's edition of her *Fais d'armes* appeared in 1488, Christine was not, of course, in a position to challenge the misattribution of authorship and removal of her narrator's voice from his *Art de chevalerie.*[10] Nevertheless, a preliminary examination of evidence in several French manuscripts and early editions of her writings suggests that Christine received increasing attention as an author as a result of the publication of her works. By contrast, paratextual details in later English editions of Christine's works indicate that her image as author increasingly diminished across the Channel.[11]

Evidence of the reconstruction of Christine in France is offered by an inscription in the margins of a fifteenth-century manuscript of Christine de Pizan's *Fais d'armes* that provides a historical context for the poet that was absent from the manuscript itself. BNF, MS fr. 1241 identifies "Christine" as narrator throughout the text, without, however, advertising her authorship paratextually; the following information is written on folio 1 by a sixteenth-century hand: "Composé par Dame Christine qui vivoit soubz Charles 6ᵉ de laquelle le Champion des dames parle ainsy..." (written by Lady Christine, who lived during the reign of Charles VI, about whom the Champion of Ladies speaks in this way...), with reference made to the preceding page. The verses alluded to from Martin Le Franc's poem are penned by the same hand on the opposite leaf. They praise Christine's virtue, eloquence, wisdom, and knowledge of Latin and Greek. These verses, which date from shortly after Christine's death (ca. 1440) and are here entitled "De Dame Christine" (About Lady Christine), read:

Aux estranigers [sic] pouvons la feste
Faire de la vaillant Christine,
Dont la vertu est manifeste
En langue grecque aussi latine...
Mais celle fut Tulle et Caton:
Tulle, car en toute eloquence

Ell'eust la rose et le bouton;
Caton aussi en sapience.[12]

[Before foreigners we can celebrate the valiant Christine, whose virtue is manifest in both the Greek and Latin tongues.... But she was a Tulius (Cicero) and a Cato: Tulius because in eloquence she possessed the rose and the bud; Cato also in wisdom.]

While these notes prove that their author, Nicolas Le Febvre, possessed historical and literary knowledge about Christine de Pizan,[13] the fact that he made the effort to pen these rather extensive details into the margins of the *Fais d'armes* manuscript suggests that Christine's was not a "household name" by the late sixteenth century.[14] In a dialogue with future readers of manuscript 1241, he was literally filling in the unknown biographical gaps about the author of this work. Le Febvre may well have obtained this information about her from earlier printed publications. It is possible, for example, that he had read the verses about Christine in the circa 1485 Lyons edition of Le Franc's *Champion des dames*, or Pierre Vidoue's 1530 edition of the work may have been the source of these lines.[15]

This kind of reference appeared elsewhere, as an examination of the three extant editions of Christine's *Trésor de la cité des dames* corroborates.[16] Unlike the *Fais d'armes* editions, the author's name appears on the title page of this imprint, published for the first time by Vérard in 1497. It reads: *Le Tresor de la cité des dames selon Dame Cristine* (The treasure of the city of ladies according to Lady Christine). Since contemporary imprints did not always advertise the identity of a vernacular writer, Vérard, ever the entrepreneur, may have consciously displayed Christine's name in this prominent space to attract book purchasers, especially women, to the unusual phenomenon of a female author. And yet, one wonders if the publisher and average contemporary reader were familiar with just who "Dame Christine" was. The author and fictional narrator are never referred to in this edition as more than "Christine" or "Dame Christine" (fols. A2, A3, 2, 73). While Christine de Pizan's status as a female author may have been as remarkable in the late fifteenth century as it had apparently been during her own time,[17] her manuscripts had circulated during her life among nobles who knew her or knew about her. With the passage of years and the development of a means of book reproduction that expanded French readership beyond royal circles, Christine de Pizan's literary fame in France seems to have diminished. A late-fifteenth-century manuscript of the *Trésor*, for example, BNF, MS fr. 1180, bears a hand-scripted Middle French addition on the inside flyleaf that reads: "L'instruction des Princesses des Dames de Court et d'aultres femmes. Composee par une Dame nommee Christine" (The instruction of princesses, of court ladies and of other women, written by a lady named

Christine).[18] The use of the indefinite article confirms that the mid-six-teenth-century reader of this manuscript did not really know who Chris-tine was.[19] Few late medieval writers, for example, many of whom in-corporated poetic tributes to their French predecessors in their writings, made reference to Christine as an author before her works were printed.[20] This suggests that her notoriety among French literati at this time, in comparison with Alain Chartier's, for example, had declined after her death. Although Charity Cannon Willard ("Anne de France") has convinc-ingly traced many of the *Trésor* manuscripts to an aristocratic female audience of the late fifteenth century, assumptions that Christine de Pizan had a wide middle-class following at the time are more difficult to measure and substantiate.[21] Even the hand-penned addition of the words "de pisan" after "Dame Christine" on the title page of one copy of Vér-ard's 1497 edition of the *Trésor* (BNF, Rés. Y² 186) does not imply an informed perspective about Christine de Pizan as a fifteenth-century author.[22] However, the appearance in printed form in later publications of Christine's works of the information found in the handwritten inscrip-tions described above and references to her authorship by later French writers (see n. 37) suggest that the advent of print played a critical role in the introduction of Christine de Pizan to a noncourtly French public during the early modern period. I would argue, moreover, that her repu-tation owed a greater debt to the later printers of her works than to her first publishers. The infamous Vérard provides a case in point.

It may have been Vérard's association with the French queen, adver-tised in his opening dedicatory prologue to Anne of Brittany, that at-tracted a clientele to his first printing of the *Trésor de la cité des dames,* rather than interest in "Dame Christine."[23] Indeed, Vérard's replacement of the writer's voice with his own through his appropriation of a tradi-tionally authorial role, namely an address to a (potential) royal patron, may have overshadowed the author's presence. His dedication echoes Christine's original dedication of this same work to Marguerite de Bour-gogne nearly a century earlier;[24] this pseudoauthorial relationship that Vérard tried to establish with the *Trésor* and other works he had printed is reinforced by the absence of information about the writer and by his self-advertisement as publisher in the colophon (73).[25] Moreover, while crediting "Dame Christine" in his dedication with having "made and composed" the *Trésor,* he claims to have "made," or produced, the work as well, profiting from the polyvalent meanings of the verb "faire:" "je ... ay fait le *Livre des trois dames de vertus* ... lequel livre fist et composa Dame Christine" (I ... have made the Book of the Three Ladies of Virtue ... the book which Lady Christine made and wrote) (A2).

The ambiguity about Christine de Pizan and Vérard's relationship to her is expressed by a miniature specially made for the vellum copy the publisher offered to Queen Anne of Brittany (Vienna, ÖNB, Inc.3.D.19, fol. 1v) (Figure 33).[26] Divided into two frames, this illumination portrays

Figure 33. Upper register: Dame Christine conversing with the Three Virtues. Lower register: Antoine Vérard offers his edition of the *Trésor de la cité des dames* to Queen Anne of Brittany. Vienna, Österreichische Nationalbibliothek Inc.3.D.19, fol. 1v.

"Dame Christine" in the upper register, not, however, as an author seated at her desk or dedicating her work to a patron, as was characteristic of many of the earlier illuminated manuscripts of her time, but rather as one of the female protagonists of the *Trésor*. Dressed in a nun's habit, she lies in bed conversing with the Three Virtues at her side, a direct depiction of the events outlined in her prologue. In the lower register, however, the publisher's dedication is visually rendered: a kneeling Vérard has assumed an authorial pose as he presents his edition of the *Trésor* to the enthroned French queen, who is presented in a triumvirate arrangement (although Anne of Brittany's noble dress differentiates her from her two attendants) that may consciously echo the Three Virtues in the image above. A comparison of this lower illustration with one decorating fol. 114 of manuscript BNF, MS fr. 1177 (Figure 34), which contains Christine's *Trésor* and dedication to Marguerite de Bourgogne, visually confirms that Vérard has used the iconography of authorial dedication miniatures in an attempt to appropriate the role of a pseudoauthor.[27] The illustration in Vérard's edition emphasizes the female character of the narrative, perhaps to entice Anne to respond positively to the publisher's donation by becoming his sponsor.[28] But the image, like the text, lacks any representation of Christine's authorship. As publisher, Vérard has stepped into her shoes to become donor of her book. In the end, he blatantly uses Christine's work about women to market himself to a female patron.[29]

Vérard, however, was not ultimately as successful in gaining the queen's patronage as he had been with her first husband, King Charles VIII, and her contemporary Louise de Savoie (M. B. Winn, "Treasures"). Anne of Brittany was not apparently won over by his tactics, but other book purchasers appear to have been influenced by his public relations strategy. Despite the vague acknowledgment of Christine de Pizan's identity in Vérard's 1497 edition of her *Trésor de la cité des dames*, it appears to have been a successful printing venture, since Michel Le Noir decided in 1503 to publish a second edition, which closely follows Vérard's.[30] Yet the third known edition of the *Trésor*, dating from 1536, differs significantly from Vérard's and Le Noir's versions, especially in its paratextual apparatus, which promotes Christine de Pizan in a much more conscious fashion. Before comparing the 1536 edition of the *Trésor* with the two earlier versions, however, I would first like to examine briefly the French editions of Christine's *Epistre Othea*, because their paratextual features may have influenced the design of the 1536 *Trésor*.

Although the narrator of the *Othea*, "nommee Chrestienne" (named Christine), is introduced in the opening lines (a1v) of Philippe Pigouchet's edition of the work, published around 1500, the printer, like Vérard before him, provided no prominently advertised details about the author herself.[31] The title was rearranged and ultimately changed to the subtitle *Les Cent histoires de Troye* (The hundred stories of Troy), which ap-

Figure 34. Christine de Pizan dedicates her *Trésor de la cité des dames* to Marguerite de Bourgogne. Paris, Bibliothèque Nationale de France, MS fr. 1177, fol. 114.

pears in bold letters on the title page. Below the printer's mark, which occupies most of the folio, the title that more directly evokes Christine's work appears in much smaller letters: *L'epistre de Othea deesse de Prudence envoyee a l'esperit chevalereux Hector de Troye, avec cent hystoires* (The epistle of Othea, goddess of Prudence, sent to the chivalric

spirit Hector of Troy, with a hundred stories).[32] Yet a careful reading of
the opening passage, which contains Christine's dedication to Louis d'Or-
léans found in a number of manuscripts (Mombello, *Tradizione*), pro-
vides some biographical data about the work's narrator, with reference
made to Christine's father, Thomas de Pizan. Moreover, the handwritten
comments of the reader of one particular copy of this edition (BNF, Rés.
Ye 286) suggest that there were those besides Pigouchet who possessed
and wished to publicize a more informed view of the work's author.
First, the words "De Chrestienne de Pise" (by Christian[?] of Pisa) are
written after the title on the first folio; second, descriptions of Christine
and her father in the opening prologue are underlined (a1v) by the same
commentator; and finally, on the flyleaf hand-penned verses copied from
the *Jardin de Plaisance* place Christine de Pizan in the august company
of celebrated male French writers, including her son. They are introduced
by the announcement: "L'autheur du Jardin de Plaisance ... parle de ceste
Chretienne de Pise fort honnorablement, la nommant entre plusieurs
poetes et rheteurs en ces vers" (The author of the Garden of Pleasure ...
speaks of this Christian[?] of Pisa most honorably, naming her among
several poets and rhetoricians in these verses).[33] Significantly, the lines
written on the opposite leaf had appeared in Regnaud Le Queux's *Jardin
de Plaisance* verse anthology, published by none other than Vérard in
1501, confirming that Christine's reputation as a revered French poet
had entered the world of print toward the turn of the century and had
begun to reach a middle-class public at least by the mid–sixteenth cen-
tury. They read:

> Par Maistre Alain à qui Dieu pardon face
> Cest art icy [se] monstre et verifie,
> Et Maistre Arnoul Greban bien suit sa trace,
> Christine aussy noblement metrifie,
> Mesmes Castel qu'elle eut à fils pour sien,
> Qui de puis fut grand Rhetoricien.[34]

> [This art is demonstrated and verified here by Master Alan [Chartier],
> may God grant him pardon, and Master Arnoul Greban follows his
> path well; Christine too versifies nobly, even Castel, whom she had
> as her own son, who, since that time, became a great rhetorician.]

Thus, although Pigouchet virtually ignored the author in designing the
paratext of his edition of the *Epistre Othea* around 1500, later readers of
this edition, at least in one instance, went to lengths to emphasize bio-
graphical details about Christine de Pizan both by underlining relevant
passages in the text itself and by penning additional information about
her into the volume by hand.

Philippe Le Noir's 1522 edition and Raulin Gaultier's pre-1534 publi-
cation of the *Cent Histoires* also failed, like Pigouchet's, to acknowl-

edge or to elaborate upon Christine de Pizan's authorship.[35] Nevertheless, one now untraceable version, published around 1518 by the widow of Jean Trepperel, made some dramatic modifications. Its title page read:

> S'ensuyt l'epistre de Othea deesse de Prudence moralisee en laquelle sont contenuz plusieurs bons et notables enseignemens pour toutes personnes voulant ensuivir les vertus et fuir les vices par Christine de Pisan...[36]
>
> [Here follows the Moralized Epistle of Othea, goddess of Prudence, in which many good and notable teachings for all persons wishing to follow virtues and flee vices are found, by Christine de Pizan...]

We will never know if it is a complete coincidence or not that a female publisher printed the one known edition of the *Othea* that carefully identifies the author and offers the *Epistre Othea* rather than the *Cent Histoires* as its principal title. Widow Trepperel's announcement, which suggests she had read Christine's prologue more carefully than Pigouchet or Le Noir (or copied someone else who had carefully read it) certainly offers evidence that by 1520 or so, Christine's full identity as a French author of moral subjects had become an integrated feature of title pages and other paratextual spaces. Jean Bouchet's remarks about Christine's poetic talents in his 1516 *Temple de bonne renommee* complement this growing public acquaintance with Christine de Pizan,[37] and both acknowledgments likely had a bearing on her elaborate reconstruction in the 1536 edition of the *Trésor de la cité des dames*, to which I would now like to return.

An examination of Jean André's 1536 *Trésor* reveals that the biographical information that sixteenth-century readers had penned in the margins of earlier manuscripts and editions of Christine de Pizan's *Fais d'Armes*, *Trésor de la cité des dames*, and *Epistre Othea* appeared in the printed paratext of her publications by the third decade of the sixteenth century.[38] Because most of these handwritten notations actually postdated the publication of the 1536 edition of the *Trésor*, they conceivably derived from the information provided in the 1536 *Trésor* paratext. Compared with Vérard's and Le Noir's editions of 1497 and 1503, respectively, the changes found in André's edition of the *Trésor* are quite dramatic. First of all, the title page offers more information about the author, her writing, and her potential readership: "Le Tresor de la Cité des dames, selon Dame Christine de la Cité de Pise, Livre tresutille et prouffitable pour l'introduction des Roynes, Dames, Princesses et autres femmes de tous estatz, auquel elles pourront veoir la grande et saine Richesse de toute Prudence, Saigesse, Sapience, Honneur, et Dignité dedans contenues" (The treasure of the city of ladies, according to Lady Christine of the city of Pisa, a very useful and very profitable book for the introduction of queens, ladies, princesses and other women of all classes, in which they will be able to see the great and wise wealth of all prudence, wisdom, knowledge, honor and dignity contained therein). Despite the incorrect association of Christine with "Pise" instead of "Pizan,"[39] André has identified "Dame Christine" more fully than in the first two editions of the *Trésor* not only on the title page, but also in the prologue (fol. a3) and in certain rubrics (fol. 1, for example) where he has added "de Pise" to Vérard's text, which had only identified "Dame Christine."

In addition, in a sixteen-verse description conspicuously printed on folio 2, André advertises the *Trésor*'s direct association with Christine's earlier *Livre de la cité des dames*, praises her words as models for virtuous, noble ladies, and exhorts all to read this work that celebrates womanhood:

Christine, aiant bien au long recité
Les bastimentz et lieux de la Cité
Faicte en l'honneur de toutes nobles Dames
Qui ont aymé Vertu de corps et d'ames,
Veult cy aprés l'enrichir d'ung Tresor
Non transitoire, ainsi qu'argent et or,
Mais immortel, plein de richesse et gloire.
C'est ung tresor qu'on doibt mettre en memoire,
Pource qu'en luy sont toutes les vertus
Dont nobles cueurs foeminins sont vestus.
Ce livre cy tant honnore et celebre
La qualité de l'estat muliebre,
Qui bien merite estre veu de tous yeulx:
Voiez le donq d'ung voulloir gracieux,
Donnant louenge au grand Dieu tout parfaict,
Remerciant la Dame qui l'a faict.

(a2)

[Christine, having described at length the buildings and sites of the City, constructed in honor of all noble ladies who have loved physical and spiritual virtue, wishes to enrich the latter with a treasure, one that is not transitory like silver and gold, but one that is immortal, full of richness and glory. It is a treasure that must be remembered, because all the virtues of which noble, feminine hearts are clothed are found in it. This book honors and celebrates the quality of being a woman so much, it fully merits being seen by all eyes. Look at it, therefore, with gracious will; praise our great, all-perfect God, and thank the lady who wrote it.]

Echoing the description of his expected audience of women of all ranks on the title page, he directly appeals to his readers in an "Advertissement aux lecteurs" (Notice to the readers).[40] While the publisher prominently advertises his own commercial enterprise in this edition,[41] the character of Christine's potential readership has grown from Queen Anne of Brittany and a vague, unidentified general public to "queens, ladies, princesses, and ladies of all estates." Likewise, the identity of Christine as author of moral subjects has become a matter of more intense concern for André than for Vérard or Le Noir, and these changes doubtless represent significant marketing factors in the sale of this volume. Like Vérard and other publishers of the day, André used Christine for his own personal gain, but to profit from her work he had to develop the author's image at length as well as the profile of a growing female public. In the end, it was print technology that best ensured that the *Trésor de la cité des dames* would reach the very social classes Christine had addressed in the work.

Estienne Groulleau's 1549 publication of Christine de Pizan's *Chemin de long estude,* the last-known sixteenth-century edition of any of her works, likewise prominently publicized the poet's authorship along with biographical and literary history. As in the 1536 *Trésor* publication, the author of the *Chemin* is again identified as "Dame Christine de Pise" (Lady Christine of Pisa). In his address "Au Lecteur" (to the reader) (A3v–A4v), the "translator" of this prose adaptation, Jan Chaperon, alerts readers to "l'intention de Dame Cristine de Pise" (Christine of Pisa's intention), her dedication of the work to King Charles VI, and her moralistic aims in writing. Furthermore, the praise she received from kings, coupled with her ability to both practice and write about the virtuous ways of living, justifies his contention that her words are profitable not only to women but "à toute maniere de gens, principalement aux Roys, princes et chevaliers" (to all kinds of people, principally to kings, princes, and knights) (A3v). Taking responsibility for any errors in his translation, Jan Chaperon pointedly credits the talents of "Dame Christine" with all the pleasure and profit his audience might find in reading the work. The publication of the *Chemin* reveals both that Christine de Pizan's authorship and literary reputation had become firmly reestablished by the mid–sixteenth century and that French publishers were directing her work to a male and female audience.[42]

What might explain this interest in the details and history of Christine de Pizan's authorship, an emphasis that contrasts sharply with that of her first publishers, who focused very little on her life and works? I would argue that Christine's enhanced literary profile can be traced to the heightened awareness about authorship that gradually developed out of writers' challenges to printers and publishers concerning their legal rights as authors to their words during the first decades of the sixteenth century, a sensitivity that had not yet reached England.[43] As I have shown elsewhere (Brown), a number of French vernacular writers at the time, including André de la Vigne, Pierre Gringore, and Jean Lemaire de Belges, took conscious steps to take control of the publication of their works and promotion of their name and image in association with their texts. Their actions led to a new legal and literary acknowledgment of their authorship. By the 1520s and 1530s, in response to the reading public's heightened awareness of their new status, the advertisement of authors on the title page and recognition of their contributions had become a standard publication feature. It is not a coincidence, in my opinion, that Jean Bouchet and Clément Marot, writers particularly attuned to the self-promotional potential print offered authors like themselves, were among the earliest French vernacular authors to promote Christine de Pizan in a more comprehensive way than their predecessors (see nn. 20 and 37).

The decline in Christine de Pizan's popularity as an author in England can be measured by the fact that although seventeen of her manuscripts eventually made their way into British collections, only one of the five English editions of her works was ever reedited. By comparison, all but one of the first editions of her works were reprinted in France (but see n. 42). Despite the developed use of title pages and other paratextual material in England by the second decade of the sixteenth century and despite Caxton's careful authorial advertisement some forty to fifty years earlier, Christine de Pizan's authorship was not publicized in John Skot's version of her *Body of Polycye* nor in Henry Pepwell's edition of Christine's *Cyte of Ladyes*, both printed in 1521.[44] Although the narrative voice of "Christine" is present in these edited texts, sixteenth-century English book purchasers would not have easily identified Christine de Pizan as the author; they would have been even less likely to know about the extraordinary role she had played in early-fifteenth-century French literary history.

While Christine's greater anonymity in the English editions of her works can be attributed in part to the fact that the identity of authors often disappeared in translations, Caxton's early translations of Christine de Pizan's works had not, in fact, followed this pattern. It is all the more surprising, therefore, that Richard Pynson's 1526 reedition of the *Morale Proverbes* all but ignored the identity of the author by reducing what had been eight pages of Caxton's text into two condensed pages of a double-columned, smaller-typed format; in addition, he couched the *Morale Proverbes*, which had been a single edition of her work in Caxton's 1478 version, in the middle of an anthology of Geoffrey Chaucer's works. The author's first name, at least, is maintained in the title, which reads "Morall prouerbes of Christyne," although it is eliminated from the running head.[45] By the third decade of the sixteenth century, it is likely that Robert Wyer, who printed his own translation of Christine's *Epistre Othea*, or *C Hystoryes of Troy*, had no idea who the work's French author was. He advertised nothing whatsoever about her in his edition, but actively promoted his role as publisher and translator in the colophon and elsewhere.[46] As his title and the appearance of the subtitle in French on the first folio of this volume suggest, Wyer followed his source, one of the French editions of the *Othea* that had not promoted Christine's authorship;[47] his edition is the only known evidence of a French-English print connection in the publication of Christine's works during the fifteenth and sixteenth centuries. Ironically, at a time when the reconstruction of Christine's authorial image was increasingly detailed in France, the one example of any direct borrowing from a French imprint of her work enabled its London publisher to continue the English trend of diminishing if not virtually erasing her literary reputation. In the end, the authorization of a woman writer may have appealed less to readers in England, since Christine de Pizan's English imprints had strong affiliations with male endorsers and a male public throughout this entire period,[48] while her French editions were increasingly associated with a female constituency.[49]

In France, interest in Christine de Pizan's writings apparently waned during the second half of the sixteenth century, presumably because medieval literature was becoming increasingly passé. If print played a critical role in rehabilitating Christine's image during the early decades of the sixteenth century, it seems to have played an equally dramatic role in the disappearance of her voice following the publication of the *Chemin de long estude* in 1549. This was the only early French edition of Christine's that was not reprinted in the early modern period. While a knowledge about Christine de Pizan's reputation did not immediately die with this temporary halt to the publication of her works,[50] her expanding public and literary presence was diminished with the cessation of the printing of her large corpus. The first printed page of the long-term reconstruction of Christine de Pizan had thus been turned.

Notes

1. In this and all other passages cited directly from fifteenth- and sixteenth-century manuscripts and editions, abbreviations have been expanded, capital letters have been added to mark the beginning of a proper name, the use of *i* and *j*, *u* and *v* has been modernized, apostrophes have been used to indicate elided vowels, and accents and punctuation have been added or modified when necessary.

2. Christine de Pizan's name and narrative voice are likewise absent in Philippe Le Noir's 1527 edition, whose title was expanded to read: "L'Arbre des batailles Et fleur de chevalerie selon Vegece avecques plusieurs hystoires et utilles remonstrances du fait de guerre par luy extraictes de Frontin, Valere et de plusieurs aultres aucteurs comme pourrez veoir cy apres" (The tree of battles and flower of chivalry according to Vegetius, with several stories and useful warnings about warfare by him, drawn from Frontinus, Valerius and several other authors, as you can see hereafter). Wareham (139–40) shows that Le Noir made additional changes in his version to reflect the fact that Spain, rather than England, had since become France's enemy.

3. The colophon on fol. n4r reads: "Explicit le livre de droit d'armes subtilité et cautelle ad ce serva[n]s selon Vegece de l'art de chevalerie. Imprimé le xxvi[e]. jour de juing Mil. CCCC.quatrevings et huit par Anthoine Verard Libraire demourant a Paris sur le pont Nostre Dame a l'ymage sainct Jehan l'evangeliste ou au palaiz enprés la chapelle ou on chante la messe des messeigneurs les presidens" (Here ends the book about the power of arms, [and the] craft and cunning helping attain it, according to Vegetius in the Art of Chivalry. Printed the 26th day of June 1488 by Antoine Vérard, bookseller living in Paris

on the Notre Dame Bridge at the sign of Saint John the Evangelist or at the Palace near the chapel where the mass of the presiding lords is sung).

4. See Byles (Introduction xv–xvi) for a discussion of the two groups of manuscripts of the *Fais d'armes*, one acknowledging Christine and the other in which all references to her and her female narrator are missing. He claims that "Vérard follows exactly a MS. of the anonymous group" (Introduction xxvii). Wareham mistakenly attributes the disappearance of Christine de Pizan's authorship to Vérard himself.

5. Teague (32), who examines the *Fais d'armes*, suggests that Christine de Pizan was more popular in English than in French.

6. The possibility of some intercultural influence existed, since Henry VII was apparently one of Vérard's royal patrons (Macfarlane xiv) and Caxton had had associations with Burgundy from 1453 to 1473 (Teague 33).

7. Twenty copies and two fragments of Caxton's edition of *The Fayttes of Armes*, from which he apparently eliminated Christine de Pizan's uncomplimentary references to England (Byles, Introduction liii), are still extant (Teague 32).

8. See Campbell ("Angleterre" 659–60, 663). In February 1478, the earl of Rivers, Anthony Woodville, had commissioned Caxton to print his — Woodville's — translation of *The Morale Proverbes of Cristyne*. Although advertising only her first name in the title and the colophon, Caxton again promoted Christine's authorship in this edition: "Of these sayyinges Cristyne was aucteuresse / Whiche in makyng hadde suche Intelligence / That therof she was mireur and maistresse / Hire werkes testifie thexperience..." Campbell shows how the French manuscripts that Bedford acquired, including the famous Harley manuscript, were inherited in 1483 by Woodville from his mother, Jacquette de Luxembourg, second wife of Bedford.

9. See Deborah McGrady's discussion of this issue in chapter 10 of this volume.

10. She was probably also unaware of the pseudoanonymous manuscript versions of her *Fais d'armes*.

11. See Genette (*Seuils*) for a discussion of the paratext.

12. Verses 4 and 5 are slightly different in the manuscript version of the *Champion des dames*, cited by Thomassy (96). The comment — "Bien est vray que l'Adversaire des Femmes dit que ce n'estoit elle qui composoit les livres, ains Chastel son filz" (It is true that the Adversary of Women states that it wasn't she who wrote the books, but Castel, her son) — is followed by eight verses pronounced by the Champion des Dames (Champion of Ladies) in the *Champion des dames*: "Certes je croy que soit cas tel / De toutes, l'aultre luy redit / Que de Christine a qui Chastel / Son filz faisoit ou livre ou dit. / Puis les seigneurs sans contredit / Luy en eut donné la louange. / Car volontiers on ne desdit / Femme, ne contr'elle on calange" (Indeed I believe that such is the case; of all of them, the other repeats to her that it's only a question of Christine, whose son was Castel, in the book or poem. Then, the nobles without doubt gave her praise; for one does not willingly contradict [the] woman, nor challenge her). A second inscription on the flyleaf informs the reader that many other works by Christine can be found in old bookshops: "Elle a fait plusieurs aultres oeuvres qui voient ez vieilles librairies" (She wrote several other works that can be seen in old bookstores).

13. Byles (Introduction xxii) stated that both inscriptions in this manuscript (see n. 12) were penned by sixteenth-century hands. I am grateful to François Avril, head of the Département des Manuscrits at the Bibliothèque Nationale, who has identified the hand of the long citation as that of the tutor of Louis XIII as a boy (personal communication, October 24, 1995). Nicolas Le Febvre lived at the end of the sixteenth century and died in 1612.

14. This runs counter to much scholarship, which, relying on scattered references, has not really taken into account her printed editions. For example, Richards ("Medieval" 103) argues not only that her potential audience was above all "specialists able to read medieval French manuscripts," but that her reception throughout the Renaissance is well known, as Marot's (he doesn't specify which Marot) references to her confirm. See n. 37.

15. See Le Franc (vii–viii) for a description of these editions. It is also possible that Le Febvre had read one of the extant manuscripts of the *Champion des dames* (see Le Franc, vii, for their listing).

16. Compare with the other titles of this work: "L'instruction des Princesses des dames de court et d'aultres femmes" (BNF, MS fr. 1180); "Le Livre des Trois Vertus de Christine pour le gouvernement des Princesses, des dames et damoiselles, des bourgeoises et femmes de bas estat" (BNF, MS fr. 1177).

17. Even though Christine describes how her uniqueness as a female author attracted interest in the early fifteenth century (*Avision-Christine*, ed. Towner, 164–65), she nevertheless had difficulties finding and maintaining patronage (Willard, *Christine* 155–71). Vérard's edition makes an interesting gender slip on fol. a2, which reappears in Michel Le Noir's 1503 and Jean André's 1536 editions as well, when the plural male subject pronoun, instead of the plural female subject pronoun, is used in the opening lines of the text: "[C]y commence le livre que fit Dame Christine pour toutes roynes, haultes dames et princesses. Et premierement comment *ilz* doyvent aymer et craindre Dieu..." (Here begins the book written by Lady Christine for all queens, noble ladies and princesses. And first how they [masculine plural] must love and fear God) (fol. a2; my emphasis).

18. François Avril dates this inscription about 1550–60 and suggests that it may have been penned by Mellin de Saint Gelais (personal communication, October 24, 1995). I am grateful to him for this information. The hand-penned details about Christine de Pizan in BNF, MS 1241 and in one BNF copy of the ca. 1500 edition of her *Epistre Othea* were made by more informed contemporaries. See also n. 37.

19. A second hand has added "de pisan."

20. The late medieval references to Christine de Pizan (see Willard, *Christine* 219–20) either appeared after printed versions of her works, did not circulate widely in manuscript form, remain too vague to confirm a knowledge of her as an author, or refer to other aspects of her character. Octavien de Saint-Gelais, for example, celebrated Christine's son, Jean Castel, but not Christine de Pizan herself in his *Séjour d'honneur* of 1490–93 (see Thomassy 97 n. 1). Georges Chastellain, Jean Molinet, André de la Vigne, Pierre Gringore, and Jean Lemaire de Belges figure among the prominent writers of the time who never mentioned Christine.

21. Willard ("Manuscript Tradition") assumes in several places (436, 437, 439–40) that the large number of paper manuscripts indicates middle-class ownership of the *Trois Vertus*, especially in northern France and the Netherlands from the second quarter of the fifteenth century on. While a number of scholars refer to Curnow's work for evidence that middle-class readers owned books of Christine de Pizan's writings (Bornstein, Introduction; Rooks; etc.), Curnow refers to the middle-class readers of the *Cité des dames* without, however, providing any details.

22. I am grateful to Ursula Baurmeister, curator in the Réserve des Livres Rares at the Bibliothèque Nationale, who informs me that this hand dates from the first decades of the sixteenth century (personal communication, October 25, 1995).

23. According to Mary Beth Winn, this is the only known dedication Vérard ever wrote to Anne of Brittany. He apparently never wrote a prologue in the work of a living author (personal communication, October 20, 1995). See also Winn, *Vérard*.

24. For example, where Christine had identified herself as "Je Cristine, vostre humble servante" (I, Christine, your humble servant), Vérard describes himself as "Je vostre treshumble et tres obeissant serviteur" (I, your very humble and very obedient servant) (A2). For the full text of these dedications, see BNF, MSS fr. 1177 and 25294, and Brussels, Bibl. Roy., MS 10973, or the recent edition of the work by Charity Cannon Willard and Eric Hicks, entitled the *Livre des trois Vertus* (2–4). Willard ("Manuscript Tradition" 437) indicates that Christine dedicated the *Trois Vertus* to Marguerite de Bourgogne in 1405.

25. It reads: "Cy finist le Tresor de la Cité des Dames selon Dame Christine, Imprimé a Paris le .viii. jour d'aoust Mil quattre cens quattre vingtz et xvii. Pour Anthoine Verard, libraire demourant a Paris sur le pont Nostre Dame, A l'ymaige sainct Jehan l'evangeliste

ou au palais au premier pillier devant la chappelle ou l'en chante la messe de messieurs les presidens" (Here ends the *Treasure of the City of Ladies* according to Lady Christine, printed in Paris the 8th day of August 1497 for Antoine Vérard, bookseller living in Paris on the Notre Dame Bridge, at the sign of Saint John the Evangelist or at the Palace at the first pillar in front of the chapel where the mass of the presiding lords is sung). See Tchémerzine (201) for a copy of the title page and colophon.

26. For a detailed description of this image and copy, see Pächt and Thoss (175–76) and M. B. Winn ("Treasures" 669–76).

27. The arms at the bottom of the folio have not been identified but are thought to have been added at a later time. See Willard ("Manuscript Tradition" 439) for details about this manuscript, which contains the *Cité des dames* (fols. 1–112) and the *Trésor* (fols. 113–207), and was made for Louis of Bruges.

28. It is unclear whether or not Anne of Brittany knew who Christine de Pizan really was and whether or not she actually commissioned Vérard to reproduce the work.

29. For an example of a similar displacement of author by "editor" in a manuscript reproduction, see Brown-Grant (265) and Hindman (*Christine* 138–42), who discuss the dedication miniature of Jean Miélot presenting his reworking of the *Epistre Othea* to Philip the Good. See also n. 31.

30. Le Noir's version follows Vérard's so closely—he even copied the very same dedication to Anne of Brittany—that it would be redundant to study it here. The texts of these two versions are considered as one variant by Willard and Hicks (*Livre des trois Vertus* xxi). Michel Le Noir expanded the title to read (changes emphasized) "Le tresor de la cité des dames *de degre en degre: et de tous estatz* selon Dame Christine" (The treasure of the city of ladies, by rank and including all estates, according to Lady Christine) and added a woodcut on the title page. But Vérard's shorter title is reiterated in the colophon. The format of Le Noir's edition is in-quarto compared with Vérard's in-folio. See also Willard ("Portuguese Translation") and Bernard for information about a Portuguese translation and edition of the *Trésor*.

31. Pigouchet, who published the earliest editions of Pierre Gringore's works, his *Chasteau de labour* (1499) and *Chasteau d'amour* (1500), did not publicize Gringore's authorship, either (see Brown 79–85). Campbell ("Angleterre" 665) explains how two of the *Othea* dedications in manuscripts brought to England did not contain the author's name.

32. See Brown-Grant's enlightening study of Jean Miélot's reworking of Christine de Pizan's *Epistre Othea* (Brussels, Bibl. Roy., MS 9392), in which Miélot, translator and scribe, takes on the role of author-continuator at times, and the work becomes more male-oriented. See also Tchémerzine (203) for a copy of the title page and colophon of the Pigouchet edition.

33. These hand-penned comments date from the second half of the sixteenth century. I am grateful to Ursula Baurmeister for this information.

34. As in the inscription in BNF, MS 1241, cited earlier (see n. 12) and in the prologue of this edition, Christine de Pizan is associated with a male family member. See also nn. 44 and 48.

35. See Mombello (*Tradizione* 359–70) for a discussion of all the printed editions of the *Othea*. Le Noir's title page prominently features his printer's mark, and the colophon provides many details about his function. See Tchémerzine (204) for a copy of the title page and colophon. Like Le Noir, Gaultier advertises his name and address on the title page and in the colophon. It is interesting to note, however, that his title differs considerably from Pigouchet's and Le Noir's, offering a version closer to the manuscripts and to Widow Trepperel's edition. It reads: "L'Epistre de Othea Deesse de prudence moralisee, en laquelle sont contenus plusieurs bons et notables enseignemens pur toutes personnes voulans ensuyvir les vertus et fuyr les vices, nouvellement imprimé a Rouen. Pour Raulin Gaultier" (The moralized epistle of Othea, goddess of Prudence, in which many good and notable teachings for all persons wishing to follow virtues and flee vices are found, recently printed in Rouen for Raulin Gaultier) (cited from Mombello, *Tradizione* 369). The original

dedicatory letter to the duke of Orleans that it contains is announced in a rubric as having been written not by Christine, but by "la deesse de prudence" (the goddess of Prudence).

36. Quoted by Mombello (*Tradizione* 362) from Jacques-Charles Brunet (*Manuel du libraire et de l'amateur de livres, Supplément,* 1:259 [Paris: Dorbon-Ainé, 1878]). See also Tchémerzine (205). There may have been another Widow Trepperel edition dating from around 1521. See n. 35, where evidence that Raulin's edition bears a similar title to that of the Widow Trepperel edition is provided.

37. Jean Bouchet describes Christine in his 1516 *Temple de bonne renommee,* where she is placed after famous Roman women: "Et les suyvoit Christine l'ancienne, / Qui fut jadis grant rethoricienne, / Et mere aussi de l'orateur Castel, / Qui fit si bien que onc ne viz ung cas tel" (And following them was Christine the ancient, who was once a great poet and mother of the orator Castel, who did so well that one never saw such an example) (fol. k1). Bouchet also praises Christine in his 1538 *Jugement poetic de l'honneur feminin:* "Je ne scauroye oublier les epistres, rondeaux et ballades en langue françoyse...de Christine, qui [s]avoit la langue greque et latine, et fu mere de Castel, homme de parfaicte eloquence" (I could not forget the French letters, rondeaus, and ballads of Christine, who knew Greek and Latin, and was the mother of Castel, a man of perfect eloquence) (fol. bbv). Le Febvre may have based his reference to Christine's knowledge of Latin and Greek in his inscription in MS fr. 1241 on Bouchet's text. Symphorien Champier apparently acknowledged Christine in his *Nef des dames* of 1503 (cf. Willard, *Christine* 220, who gives no specific details, however), but I have not been able to locate the relevant passage in that text. In 1523, Pierre de Lesnauderie wrote about Christine in his *Louenge de mariage* in the following manner: "Maintenant me vient en memoire Dame Christine de Pise laquelle fut tresexperte en l'art de rhetorique et composa plusieurs beaulx doctrinaux et volumes. Et entre les autres elle composa la *Cité des dames,* en laquelle *Cité* elle ramentoit et ramaine a memoire moult de dames vertueuses et bien renommees, lequel livre est tresbeau et bon a veoir et estudier pour les dames, attendu qu'il est composé par une femme" (Now I remember Lady Christine of Pisa who was most expert in the art of poetry and wrote several fine books of learning and volumes. And among the others she wrote the *City of Ladies,* in which she brought and brings to mind many virtuous and very famous ladies. This book is very beautiful and good for ladies to see and study, given that it was written by a woman) (fol. 28). Jean Marot's praise of Christine in his *Vray-Disant Advocate des dames* comes at a relatively late date (ca. 1520) (Marot, *Poésies*); moreover, placing her in the same context as references to Ceres, Ysis, Pamphille, Sappho, Deborah, Thamar, and Dido and praising her for her great wisdom, Jean Marot's allusion tends to mythologize and decontextualize Christine in a rather abstract way, without acknowledging her reputation as an author: "Lisez de Debbora la saige, / Lisez de Thamar la Paintresse, / Qui fust souveraine maitresse / De vivifier ung ymaige; / De Christine la grande sagesse; / Et puis de Dido la largesse." (Read about Deborah the wise; read about Thama the female painter, who nobly mastered the art of giving life to an image; the great wisdom of Christine; and then about the generosity of Dido). Curiously, the eighteenth-century edition in which this citation appears, Lenglet Du Fresnoy's *Poésies de Jean Marot et de Michel Marot,* volume 5 of the six-volume *Oeuvres de Clément Marot* (302), provides information about Christine in a footnote ("Christine de Pisan fort célèbre dans L'Histoire Littéraire du XV siècle" (Christine de Pizan very renowned in the literary history of the fifteenth century), confirming that she was not well known in the eighteenth century. The poem printed in this edition appears to have come from a manuscript in the duke de Bourbon's library. Coustelier's 1723 edition of the Marots' works did not contain the *Vray-Disant Advocate,* nor did it appear in Clément Marot's edition of Jean's works (1532). Clément Marot's reference to Christine in a rondeau to Jeanne Gaillard (dating from before 1527, according to Gérard Defaux) does acknowledge Christine as an important female writer: "A Jeanne Gaillard, Lyonnoise / D'avoir le prix en science et doctrine / Bien merita de Pisan la Christine / Durant ses jours; mais ta plume doree / D'elle seroit a present adoree, / S'elle vivoit par volunte divine / Car pour ainsi que le feu l'or affine, / Le temps a

faict nostre langue plus fine / De qui tu as l'eloquence asseuree / D'avoir le prix" (To Jean Gaillard, woman of Lyon, for her outstanding knowledge and learning. Christine de Pizan merited well [this praise] in her time, but your golden pen would be admired by her now if she lived by divine grace. For just as fire refines gold, so time has refined our language, from which you have the assured eloquence to take the prize) (*Oeuvres*, ed. Guiffrey, 136). Some critics have tried to show that certain authors, such as Antoine de la Sale and Marguerite de Navarre, must have known Christine de Pizan's works, even though these writers never mention her (Willard, "Antoine de la Salle"; Sommers).

38. Unlike any of the earlier editions, accents and punctuation appear in this edition, and rubrics are carefully spaced vis-à-vis the text, often in attractive geometric formations. A sign of the contemporary interest in orthography, silent *e*'s are crossed out as well. See Tchémerzine (202) for a copy of the title page and colophon.

39. They are reminiscent of the additions written on the title page of one of Pigouchet's *Cent Histoires* editions, discussed earlier. See Willard (*Christine* 16–17), who confirms the ties of Christine de Pizan's father with the village of Pizzano, although she herself was born in Venice and lived there until age four. Caxton's association of Christine with Pisa ("Pyse") in 1489 appears to be the earliest.

40. The entire passage reads: "Cueurs vertueux de foeminine grace, / Qui desirez toute perfection, / Appreciez ce tresor d'efficace, / Car vous n'avez richesse d'or ne mace / De si grand pris ne d'exaltation. / Mirez vous doncq en l'explanation / Des beaux propos, et louables sentences. / Car de leurs fleurs aurez sans fiction / Le fruict entier en l'augmentation / De tous honneurs, loz, et magnificences. / Or avez vous en veue maintenant / Ung grand tresor qui vous est mis en vante / Pour peu d'argent; Jehan André le presente / Qui l'a ouvert à ung chascun venant" (Virtuous hearts of feminine grace that desire all perfection, appreciate this treasure with efficacy, for you have not richness of gold nor mace of great worth or of exaltation. Look at yourselves therefore in the explanation and praiseworthy thoughts of beautiful expression, for from their flowers you will have in truth the entire fruit in its amplification of all honors, praises, and magnificence. Now you have in view a great treasure which is put on sale for you at a low cost. John André who opened it for anyone offers it to you) (a2v).

41. The bookseller's address, either that of Denis Janot or that of Jean André, which appears at the bottom of the title page, and André's privilege, announced on its verso side, are prominently displayed in this edition. The mark of Denis Janot appears in the BNF edition (Rés. Y² 2073) on folio 8v.

42. Other signs that Christine's audience was apparently expanding at this time include the gradually decreasing size of her works from Vérard's in-folio *Trésor* of 1497 to André's in-8° *Trésor* of 1536 to the in-12° edition of the *Chemin* in 1549. Presumably the smaller the volume, the more affordable it was. See Tchémerzine (205) for a copy of the title page and colophon. Kennedy (*Christine* [1984] 78) lists another printed work of Christine de Pizan, the eighteen-folio *Contre rommant de la Rose* (lacking date, publisher, and place of publication), but he did not examine the copy. Roy (Introduction 2:ix), on whom Kennedy based his information, claimed that the only known copy of this early printed edition of the *Epistre au dieu d'Amours*, which had been held by the Biblioteca Colombina in Seville from 1510–39, was bought by Baron Pichon in 1884. I am grateful to Nadia Margolis for calling my attention to this now seemingly lost or inaccessible edition.

43. Campbell ("Angleterre" 669) attributes the lack of knowledge in England about Christine's life to a greater interest at the time in the work, not the author.

44. Skot not only fails to advertise Christine's authorship on the title page of his *Body of Polycye*, but makes no mention that the work was even a translation. Nevertheless, the text itself does bear signs of Christine's authorship and narrative voice. A female narrator defends her book about a more male-oriented topic in the opening prologue, and a rubric announces when "Christine cocludeth [*sic*] her booke" (fol. p3). The narrator makes reference on the second-to-last folio to "the wrytynges of [the] humble creature Christine." Bornstein (Introduction xiii) suggests that Woodville may have translated this work. Al-

though the name "Christine" appears repeatedly in the table of contents of the *Cyte of Ladyes*, no mention is ever made of Christine de Pizan's authorship either on the title page, in the printer's prologue, or in the colophon at the end. In his prologue Pepwell speaks of spreading the royal fame of "ladyes (abrode)" but does not mention Christine de Pizan. In fact, he refers to "This foresayd boke by Bryan Anslay." Rooks (85) confirms the absence of any mention of Christine and suggests that the ideas added to this English version of her work were to attract a public of male Renaissance readers. Bornstein (Introduction xxi) suggests a connection between Anslay's translation of the *Cité des dames* and the literary activities of Anthony Woodville, who had translated Christine's *Morales Proverbes*.

45. See the British Library copy G. 11584 (2), fols. e4–e5.

46. The title page reads: "Here foloweth the .C. Hystoryes of Troy." Below a woodcut of two armored jousting knights appears the following French title: "L'epistre de Othea, deesse de Prudence, envoyee a l'esperit chevalereux Hector de Troy avec cent Histoires, nouvellement imprimee." The colophon, followed by Wyer's mark, reads: "Thus endeth the C. Hystories of Troye, translated out of Frenche in to Englysche, by me. R. W. Imprynted by me Robert Wyer, dwellyng in S. Martyns parysche, at Charyng Crosse at the sygne of S. Johann Evangelist besyde the Duke of Suffolkes place. Cum privilegio, ad imprimendum so[?]um."

47. Presumably either Pigouchet's ca. 1500 edition or Philippe Le Noir's 1522 edition.

48. A *Fais d'armes* manuscript was given by the earl of Shrewsbury to King Henry VI and Margaret of Anjou in 1445 (see Michel-André Bossy's discussion of this manuscript in chapter 12 of this volume), and Caxton subsequently translated the work for Henry VI. Pepwell dedicated the *Cyte of Ladyes* to the earl of Kent, whose uncle, Anthony Woodville, owner of a manuscript copy of the *Cyte* (but not the same one used by Ansley) had translated Christine's *Proverbes*. Campbell ("Angleterre" 669) lists the male nobles associated with her manuscripts in England. For other details, see Rooks and n. 44.

49. See Bornstein (Introduction xviii), who discusses contemporary English views about women.

50. See Richards ("Medieval"), who examines some fifty references to Christine de Pizan between 1545 and 1795.

Manuscripts, Incunabula, and Early Printed Books Cited

Brussels, Bibliothèque Royale, MS 9392
Brussels, Bibliothèque Royale, MS 10973
London, British Library, copy G. 11584 (2)
Paris, Bibliothèque Nationale de France, MS fr. 1177
Paris, Bibliothèque Nationale de France, MS fr. 1180
Paris, Bibliothèque Nationale de France, MS fr. 1241
Paris, Bibliothèque Nationale de France, MS fr. 25294
Paris, Bibliothèque Nationale de France, Rés. Y^2 186
Paris, Bibliothèque Nationale de France, Rés. Y^2 2073
Paris, Bibliothèque Nationale de France, Rés. Ye 286
Vienna, Österreichische Nationalbibliothek, Inc.3.D.19

❖

CHAPTER 12

Arms and the Bride

Christine de Pizan's Military Treatise as a Wedding Gift for Margaret of Anjou

Michel-André Bossy

Manuscript Royal 15.E.VI in the British Library is a gift that Queen Margaret of Anjou received in 1445 from John Talbot, first earl of Shrewsbury, on the occasion of her marriage to Henry VI of England. The book is a compilation of narrative texts and treatises, all in French, and the crowning piece close to the end is Christine de Pizan's military treatise, the *Livre des fais d'armes et de chevalerie*, which she wrote in 1410. What did Talbot with his scribes and illuminators have in mind when they selected the *Fais d'armes* for special display in the gift anthology? And how were Margaret and Henry meant to respond to the large illustrated volume bestowed on them by a great field commander? These are intertwined questions. To answer them we will look for connections between the anthology's plan of compilation, several of its illuminations, and the court politics that shaped the manuscript. We will examine first what the donor meant to impress on the royal newlyweds and second how he wanted them to respond to Christine's war treatise.

The marriage between Henry and Margaret was a diplomatic maneuver toward peace. By taking the hand of a French princess, Henry was sealing a truce with his Valois adversary, who was also his maternal uncle, Charles VII. Such a truce was in Henry's best interest: English power in France had been steadily eroding for a decade and a half. Henry, whose reign over Lancastrian England and France had begun in early infancy (1422), was seven years old when Joan of Arc lifted the siege of Orléans and crushed the English army at the battle of Patay, capturing one of its chief commanders, John Talbot (1429). By Henry's fifteenth birthday, the Anglo-Burgundian alliance woven by his father and Philip the Good had unraveled, Philip had crossed over to the French side, and the city of Paris, where Henry had once been crowned ruler of the dual monarchy, now belonged to Charles VII. In 1445, the twenty-three-year-old Lancastrian king desired peace, and for its sake he was more than willing to marry the French queen's niece, even without a dowry.[1]

Many in England looked askance at the match Henry had made: Margaret of Anjou was a pennyless bride, costly to the English royal purse (Lee 190; Griffiths 315–16). Her father, "le bon roi René," held many titles—

Duke of Anjou, Bar and Lorraine, Count of Provence, Lord of Majorca and Minorca, King of Naples, Sicily, and Jerusalem. In fact, he ruled no estates outside of France, for he had lost his Italian throne to Alfonso V of Aragon in 1441. Before that, he had been Philip the Good's prisoner for the better part of five years. René offset these political and military reverses by becoming an inspired patron of poetry and the fine arts. He was himself a man of letters—the author of two allegorical narratives—and his love of elegantly produced books is well attested. For instance, he appears to have closely overseen the sumptuous program of illuminations for the allegorical romance, the *Livre du cuer d'amours espris,* which he composed in 1457.[2]

Talbot probably surmised that Margaret shared her father's fondness for books and would be pleased by the gift of a beautiful codex. In fact, he may have taken note of her literary tastes during February and March 1445, when he and his wife accompanied Margaret on her journey westward from Nancy to Rouen, which she reached on the eve of her fifteenth birthday, and then onward to England (Pollard 61).[3] In any case, his decision to offer Margaret an anthology as a wedding gift is not surprising: books were frequently offered as wedding gifts, especially to brides who were sent to a foreign country (S. G. Bell, "Medieval Women" 763–65). Talbot had spent over twenty years in France, enough time to acquire a set of French manuscripts, of which at least one provided the major portions of a text that Talbot's scribes copied into the book presented to Margaret.[4] That text is a version of the *Chanson d'Aspremont* belonging to a manuscript originally owned by the counts of Laval and then looted by Talbot when he took their castle and town in 1428 (Mandach, "Wedding-Present" 69; Pollard 13, 105, 126).[5]

Margaret and her retinue reached England in April 1445. By then Talbot had perhaps already drawn up agreements with two workshops in order to assemble the gift anthology. One was located in Canterbury and provided drafts for several texts (Mandach, "L'Anthologie" 318–22, 331–35). The other workshop was in Rouen; there the texts assembled by Talbot and his helpers were copied and illustrated. It is doubtful that the book could have been ready in time for the wedding ceremony, which was celebrated on April 22 at Titchfield Abbey (Griffiths 488). Yet a box of folios might have been presented to the royal couple by Talbot either in Titchfield or five weeks later in London, where Margaret was crowned at Westminster Abbey (May 30). In fact, the scene depicted by the book's opening illumination strongly suggests a court festivity following the coronation, since Margaret is both wearing her crown and holding her scepter.

Upon opening the large vellum codex containing the Queen Margaret Anthology we find a table of contents (fol. 1r) and then a richly ornamented frontispiece with a verse dedication (fol. 2v, Figure 35). The facing page, to the right, displays a genealogical table studded with portraits in roundels (fol. 3r, Figure 36). The frontispiece shows Talbot kneeling before Queen

Figure 35. Talbot presenting his anthology to Queen Margaret. London, British Library, MS Royal 15.E.VI, fol. 2v.

Figure 36. Genealogical table of Henry VI. London, British Library, MS Royal 15.E.VI, fol. 3r.

Margaret, who is holding hands with Henry VI. The earl wears a red robe decorated with the insignia of the Order of the Garter. Behind him struts a Talbot hound with characteristic white coat and drooping ears. A curtain behind the royal couple is checkered with the leopards of England and the lilies of France, for the queen is a French princess. Over the roof turrets fly the banners of France, Saint George, England, and Anjou. The margins are strewn with marguerites or daisies, the queen's emblem.

Our attention is drawn to the book that Talbot is handing to the queen, which is in fact none other than the codex open before us. Two columns of verse inform Margaret about the general contents and intent of the book. Between its covers she will discover

> ... maint beau conte
> Des preux qui par grant labeur
> Vouldrent acquerir honneur
> En France, en Angleterre
> Et en aultre mainte terre.
> (Lines 4–8)

[... many beautiful tales of heroes who through their great labors strove to win honor in France, England, and many other lands.]

Speaking on Talbot's behalf, the narrator anticipates that those noble tales will accomplish several things. First, they will be a pleasant pastime and chase away Margaret's boredom,

> Esperant qu'a vostre loisir
> Vous vueillez prendre plaisir
> En passant temps pour y lire
> Pour oster ennuy qui nuire
> Peult a toute creature.
> (Lines 9–13)

[hoping as I do that you might there, at your leisure, find it enjoyable to pass time in reading, so as to banish tedium, which is so harmful to all beings.]

Second, these French readings will keep her from forgetting her native tongue:

> Et que lors que parlerez anglois
> Que vous n'oubliez le françois.
> (Lines 37–38)

[And when you will be speaking English, may this book keep you from forgetting French.]

Third, the anthology will make her more knowledgeable about history and more eloquent about noble deeds and chivalry. The rewards thus promised by the preface form an ascending scale: first pleasurable pastime, then personal benefit (i.e., French language practice), and finally full-fledged instruction.

The ordering of texts in the compilation follows that scheme by and large (the contents are cataloged in Warner 2:176–79; see also Conlon 16–19). The Queen Margaret Anthology begins with enjoyable narratives, rich in marvels, then it moves into increasingly didactic territory. The book first presents a copiously illustrated prose *Roman d'Alexandre* (fols. 4v–24r). From there it progresses into a series of heroic narratives, mostly (but not exclusively) in verse (fols. 25r–292v), followed by a series of military and political treatises (fols. 293r–438v); later on we will itemize the constituent works. The anthology's closing text lists the statutes of the Order of the Garter (fols. 439r–440v). The crucial penultimate slot is reserved for the *Fais d'armes* (fols. 405r–438v). The compiler's selection of Christine de Pizan's work is interesting: a treatise written by a woman holds the place of honor in a book offered to a queen, and it is apparently chosen as the culminating lesson about the arts of war. Yet the manuscript's program of illustrations tells a different story (Warner 2:179). As we shall see, the place of honor awarded to the treatise does not mean that the author herself will be acknowledged by the illumination that introduces her work.

In the dedicatory frontispiece Talbot poses as the book's maker. According to fifteenth-century conventions of preface illuminations, the gesture of handing over a book from a kneeling position, adopted here by Talbot, may signify that the donor is a writer presenting his own work to a patron. Indeed, we find such illuminations later in the Queen Margaret Anthology: one shows Honoré Bouvet presenting his treatise, entitled *L'Arbre des batailles*, to Charles VI of France (fol. 293r, Figure 37);[6] another depicts Giles of Rome (Egidio Colonna) giving his *De regimine principum* to a king—possibly Philip the Bold, father of the dauphin for whom Giles wrote his treatise (fol. 327r). Alternatively, the kneeling figure in a book presentation may be a man of letters who has directed the work of *other* writers on behalf of his patron. That second possibility is illustrated, for instance, by the well-known frontispiece of the *Chroniques de Hainaut* in Brussels (Bibliothèque Royale, MS 9242, fol. 1r). The man kneeling there before Duke Philip the Good of Burgundy is probably *not* Jean Wauquelin, the writer and editor of the *Chroniques*, but rather a very eminent member of the duke's court, the councillor Simon Nockart (Delaissé, "'Chroniques'" 37). The initial frontispiece of the Queen Margaret Anthology falls in this second category of images. The kneeling man presenting the gift volume is not the writer of one of the texts collected in the volume. He is Talbot himself.

Figure 37. Honoré Bouvet offering his book to Charles VI. London, British Library, MS Royal 15.E.VI, fol. 293r.

The Queen Margaret Anthology is an artifact shaped by many hands: the numerous writers who composed its sundry parts, as well as the several scribes who copied and illustrated them in two separate scriptoria (Mandach, "L'Anthologie" 318–35). One belonged to the Abbey of Saint Augustine in Canterbury and furnished preliminary drafts for many of the book's sections. The other scriptorium, as recent scholarship has revealed, was located in Rouen. Its chief artist was the illuminator now often called the Talbot master, for he illustrated both the Queen Margaret Anthology and three books of hours for Talbot and his wife, Margaret Beauchamp (Plummer 17; Avril and Reynaud 170–71; Avril, in Tesnière 95–96 n. 34).[7] The Talbot master's hallmarks include firmly etched court scenes in bright, monotone colors, human figures in solid hieratic postures, stylized backgrounds evenly studded with stars or tapestry motifs, and floral borders with spiraling, highly filigreed tendrils (see Figures 35, 38, and 39).

Talbot's frontispiece stance is clear: although many hands have contributed to the book, Talbot positions himself in the foreground, designat-

Figure 38. Frontispiece of *Roman d'Alexandre*. London, British Library, MS Royal 15.E.VI, fol. 4v.

ing himself the chief planner and producer of the book.[8] Kneeling but holding his chin very high, he offers the red-covered volume to the royal couple as an enduring reminder that he is their loyal and devoted servant. He is not merely the person who commissioned the book: he is the one who brought it into existence. It bears his image at the outset and, as we shall see, also toward the end, above the *Fais d'armes.* The book and the ceremony in which Talbot gives it away are bonded together by the dedicatory image. He shapes both and puts his stamp on them.

On closer inspection of that page, we find that Talbot even contributes to the book a tiny text authored by him. The bottom margin features a scroll, flanked on the right by a bouquet of daisies and on the left by the arms of Talbot and his wife (fol. 2v, Figure 35). The scroll bears these lines:

Mon seul desir
Au Roy et vous
E[s]t bien servir
Jusqu'au mourir.
Ce sachent tous:
Mon seul desir
Au Roy et vous.

[My single desire for the King and you is to serve you well until death. Let everyone know: my single desire for the King and you.]

This poem is a shaky rondeau: having committed a barbarism in the second line ("au roy" instead of "por le roy"), it stumbles grammatically in the third line and forgets to repeat the refrain in the middle of the poem. Talbot's modern biographer comments that the verse is "so execrable that one cannot help feeling that he composed it himself" (Pollard 128).[9] One might almost think that the blemishes were intentionally left in, as if to convince the queen and others that those are truly Talbot's words, in his own version of French. The theme of royal service appears also on the facing page (Figure 36), whose genealogical table shows how Henry VI descends from both Saint Louis and Edward I. This genealogical table was apparently a copy of one made by Lawrence Calot in 1423, at Bedford's request, who had it put on display in Paris at Notre-Dame in order to convince the inhabitants that the infant Henry VI was the rightful heir of France as well as England (Rowe 77–83; McKenna 151–55).

In the anthology, the principle of dual monarchy is literally held aloft by the two princes of the blood: the king's uncle, Humphrey, duke of Gloucester, stands on the right side of the family tree, bracing the Plantagenet branch, while Richard, duke of York, the king's second cousin once removed, props up the Valois branch on the left. The middle branch traces the Capetian line, from Saint Louis down to its last male descendant, Charles IV. The pictorial message is clear: Henry VI restores central dynastic unity by having a Plantagenet father and a Valois mother.

Gloucester and York are pictured as foremost supporters of Henry's lineage.[10] They are next in line for the throne, and they will remain so until Henry and Margaret produce an offspring. Historical hindsight lends considerable irony to the picture of the dukes, as one scholar well notes: within a few years both of them would be enemies of Margaret and Henry (Teague 26).[11]

But where is Margaret in the genealogical table? We find her neither named nor pictured on the family tree—although in the verses of the facing page the narrator tells her how confident he is that she too is a descendant of Saint Louis:

> ...le roy nostre souverain...
> (De vostre affye que Dieu y gart)
> Est venu de si noble part
> Comme du bon Roy saint Louys;
> Si estes vous, certain en suys.
> (Lines 18–22)

[The king our sovereign (may God uphold your faith in it) comes from the very noble stock of the good king Saint Louis, and so do you, I am certain.]

On the genealogical page Margaret is no longer portrayed on center stage. She is translated into emblems. In the right margin, a royal antelope holds up her banner. In the middle, we may discern her concealed monogram: the three branches of the family tree, which resemble a fleur-de-lis, also form an inverted *M*. The vertical and horizontal alignments of portrait roundels suggest yet another inverted *M* combined with an *H* for Henry. In the center of the bottom margin, in symmetrical position to the scroll proclaiming Talbot's service to the queen, stands a bouquet of marguerites. A pointed appendage beneath the portrait of Henry VI suggestively penetrates the parted flowers. Talbot and his illustrator, had they taken part in the great debate about the *Roman de la Rose* at the turn of their century, would have clearly sided with the callow admirers of Jean de Meun rather than with Christine de Pizan. In any case, their iconographical message is unmistakable: the queen's function in this table of lineage is procreative—she is to produce a son and heir for Henry VI.

The next folio leads us to the anthology's first narrative text, the *Roman d'Alexandre* (fols. 4v–24r), which begins with the hero's miraculous conception and birth. The text is a thirteenth-century French prose adaptation of Julius Valerius's *Historia de proeliis* (in turn a fourth-century translation of Pseudo-Calisthenes' second-century Alexander legend). In the anthology, the *Roman d'Alexandre* is by far the most lavishly illustrated work: the twenty folios of text also contain eighty-four illuminations. The first occupies a full page (fol. 4v, Figure 38). It shows on the right Nectanebus, the Egyptian prince and magician, who as a guest of King Philip of Macedonia cured Queen Olympias of her sterility by subjecting her to an enchantment and becoming her lover. Olympias then gave birth to Alexander, whom Philip adopted as son. Nectanebus is pictured seated in the City of Babylon, near the Castle of Cairo and the Garden of Balm. Toward the bottom, three water mills churn under gables that suggest smiling human faces: their tiny windows look like eyes, the white barge-boards lining their roofs resemble kerchiefs.[12] Perhaps their turning wheels allude to cycles of life and procreation.[13] In the left border (not shown in Figure 38), a herald wearing Shrewsbury arms on his tabard holds Margaret's banner, as a reminder that this illumination and the book that it introduces are specifically directed by Talbot to her.

One may be surprised to find Nectanebus so prominently featured right at the front of the anthology. This conniving seducer of a queen is an odd figure to thrust before royal newlyweds. Is there a humorous intent? An allusion to the procreative services rendered by the Egyptian enchanter to the royal family of Macedonia may have been Talbot's idea of a risqué marriage joke for Henry and Margaret. An impish visual detail hints at such mirth: on the left side of the page one can see a musician who is wearing a turban and leaning over a crenellated castle wall. The instrument in his hands is a straight bugle, from which hangs a pennant emblazoned with a white Talbot hound. He points and blows this horn with its Talbot insignia straight toward Nectanebus, seated on the right. The line of sight from this elongated instrument eventually reaches the king's abdomen. Midway, it passes through a double arched window, where it grazes the tip of a tracery cusp projected between the arches. This cusp recalls the pointed appendage seen earlier beneath the portrait of Henry VI in the genealogical table (fol. 3r, Figure 36), and its shape is even more blatantly phallic.

The *Alexandre* frontispiece thus slyly recalls the lechery of Nectanebus and the vulnerability of the royal Macedonian couple. The impudent little joke is unlikely to have amused the pious and prudish Henry (Gillingham 53–54; Griffiths 249–50). In years that followed the wedding, the jest may have become downright embarrassing, since it took Henry and Margaret a full eight years to produce an offspring.[14] However, the story of Nectanebus and Olympias also lends itself to an allegorical reading: Nectanebus could be interpreted as a wise counselor who "inseminates" the minds of his sovereigns with useful knowledge. In this perspective, the trumpet and its insignia would proclaim Talbot's role as an instructor of the royal couple and perhaps also their future heir.

The anthology could be used to educate a young prince. Alexander's exotic adventures and their numerous illustrations would have made the opening section of the anthology particularly appealing to a child. Fifteenth-century noblewomen were expected to teach their children the alphabet and introduce them to psalters and books of hours (S. G. Bell,

"Medieval Women" 755–57). Talbot may have envisioned that the queen would instruct her future son by reading to him from the anthology—or perhaps she would have it read aloud to the two of them by a court secretary (Mandach, "Wedding-Present" 59). She would teach him in her native language, which he as future heir of the dual monarchy ought to master. By sharing the anthology with the young prince, she would sharpen his interest in the feats of Alexander and other youthful heroes, thus helping him to develop noble ambitions.

The *Roman d'Alexandre* is followed by three *chansons de geste* identified in a rubric as a Charlemagne Book ("le lieuvre du roy Charlemane," fol. 25r).[15] The first two *chansons* offer a tacit salute to Margaret's lineage, for they are set respectively in Apulia (*Simon de Pouille*, fols. 25r–42v) and Calabria (*Chanson d'Aspremont*, fols. 43r–69v), two regions claimed by Margaret's family—her father, René, was titular king of Naples and overlord of Apulia, while her brother John was duke of Calabria. A third *chanson*, *Fierabras* (fols. 70r–85v), completes the anthology's Charlemagne cycle—the emperor himself is the protagonist. *Ogier le Danois* (fols. 86r–154v) and *Renaut de Montauban*, also called *Les Quatre Fils Aymon* (fols. 155r–206v), feature two other very popular heroes. *Ogier* is a *chanson de geste*, in alexandrines like *Fierabras*. The version of *Renaut* selected for the anthology is a prose adaptation of the *chanson*. It is followed by three prose romances: *Ponthus et Sidoine* (fols. 207r–226v), a late-fourteenth-century adaptation of the *Roman de Horn*, set in England, as are also *Gui de Warrewik* and its sequel, *Herolt d'Ardenne* (fols. 227r–272v). The final narrative work (before the treatise section) is *Le Chevalier au cygne* (fols. 273r–292v), a branch of the epic crusade cycle that connects the Swan-Knight legend to the adventures of Godfrey of Bouillon. Two competing principles of organization may be found in this section: geography (Italy, England) and the verse/prose distinction.

In his youth, Henry VI had received a verse *Renaut de Montauban* as a gift from Philip the Good's secretary, and Mandach speculates that the king's fondness for that heroic poem may have prompted the makers of the Queen Margaret Anthology to recruit a prose *Renaut* ("L'Anthologie," 330, 338, 347). Actually, the inclusion of this text requires little explanation: the tales of Renaut de Montauban were highly popular, from the Netherlands to Italy. More singular is the selection of *Gui de Warrewik*, since that romance was little known beyond the confines of England. It must, however, have appealed to Talbot for personal reasons: in 1433 he had married Margaret Beauchamp, eldest daughter of Richard, earl of Warwick (Conlon 22–25). Moreover, Warwick had been a companion at arms, with whom he had defended Lancastrian Normandy from 1437 until the earl's death in 1439 (Griffiths 453–55; Pollard 51). It is possible, in fact, that Talbot himself commissioned the prose version of the romance that appears in the anthology (Mandach, "L'Anthologie" 331–32).

We can picture Talbot as a patron who actively guides the work of his scriptoria. He orders *Gui de Warrewik* modernized from verse to prose, perhaps to make it look more like an authoritative ancestral chronicle than like a poetical fiction.[16] His scribes in Canterbury plan to copy the *Chanson d'Aspremont* from two manuscripts owned by their abbey; he furnishes them a third model, a version of *Aspremont* found in a book that he seized as booty in 1428, the Laval-Middleton Anthology (Mandach, "Wedding-Present" 56–69).

The choice of the *Arbre des batailles* (fols. 293r–326v) to open the anthology's treatise section is significant. It was Talbot's intent to instruct the queen and her future son in the rules and theory of warfare. *L'Arbre* would afford them a useful overview of universal history (book 2) and introduce them to the laws of war, which the author, Honoré Bouvet, exposes in books 3 and 4.[17] They would return to the subject of warfare on a broader scale in the anthology's final treatise, Christine de Pizan's *Fais d'armes et de chevalerie* (fols. 405r–438v), which draws many of its materials from *L'Arbre*, as well as from Vegetius, John of Legnano, and Frontinus (Willard, "Treatise," "Pilfering Vegetius"). Indeed books 3 and 4 of the *Fais d'armes* are framed as a dialogue between Christine and an interlocutor highly reminiscent of Honoré Bouvet, who appears to her in a dream vision.

In short, the *Arbre* opens a cycle of treatises that closes with the *Fais d'armes*. Talbot's compilers doubtless perceived the strong affinities between the *Arbre* and the *Fais d'armes*, especially on the issue of the just war, and they must have recommended stationing those two works symmetrically at either end of the treatise section. That section (fols. 293r–438v) comes on the heels of the earlier corpus of heroic narratives, which extends from the *Roman d'Alexandre* to the *Chevalier au cygne* (fols. 4–292). The heroic cycle anticipates the treatise cycle through the simulation of genealogical historiography in the prose *Gui de Warrewik*.

After finishing the *Arbre des batailles*, Margaret and her future son discover the *De regimine principum* by Giles of Rome (Egidio Colonna, Aegidius Romanus), in Henri de Gauchy's French translation (*Le Livre de politique*, fols. 327r–362v). This political primer, written in 1279 for an eleven-year-old dauphin, the future Philip the Fair, had become an influential mirror of princes. In the anthology's sequential plan, the *De regimine* acquaints Margaret with the basics of political theory and social psychology. Certain chapters can teach her the conduct expected of a queen (Egidio 160–68); others can guide her in the education of children (188–230), the management of a noble household (257–67), the principles royal government (314–69), and the art of war (369–427).

Political philosophy is followed by history. The *Chroniques de Normandie* (fols. 363r–402v), a prose reworking of Wace's *Roman de Rou*, introduce Margaret to the legends and annals of her husband's lineage — from Duke Rollo (d. 933) to William the Conqueror (d. 1087) and his royal descendants in England, down to Richard Lion-Heart (d. 1199)—and invite her to pass this lore on to the future Prince of Wales. Next comes Alain Chartier's *Bréviaire des nobles* (fols. 403r–404v), a cycle of thirteen ballades that was a fifteenth-century "best-seller" (extant in fifty-three manuscripts). In the *Breviaire* a company of allegorical personifications— *Noblesce* and twelve chivalric Virtues—each declaim a ballade in their own praise. This little verse cycle would provide a high-minded interlude before Margaret tackled the thirty-four folios of the *Livre des fais d'armes et de chevalerie* (fols. 405r–438v).

In sum, the underlying pedagogical aim of Talbot's compilation is to instill martial qualities and principles in the royal family, and Christine's treatise provided an admirably clear, thorough exposition of those values. In fact, the *Fais d'armes* was designed as a textbook for royalty. It had been commissioned in 1410 by John the Fearless for a purpose very similar to Talbot's: as Charity Cannon Willard has demonstrated, the duke of Burgundy wanted to educate the young dauphin of France, Louis of Guyenne, in military matters, and he asked Christine de Pizan to write a book that would provide such instruction (Willard, "Pilfering Vegetius," "Treatise" 184–88).[18] Talbot must have relished the parallel situations: he was offering his new queen a treatise that the mighty duke of Burgundy had originally ordered as a gift for the dauphin, a prince under his tutelage and also his son-in-law (Willard, *Christine* 116–17, 176). Philip had been the regent of France; Talbot was the great defender of the Lancastrian dual monarchy in France. It must also have pleased Talbot that the *Fais d'armes* in his gift anthology was a copy derived from a manuscript in the very library of John the Fearless, now owned by his son, Philip the Good—for that is where the master copy for the anthology was probably borrowed, as Mandach reasons ("L'Anthologie" 324–25).[19] In short, Talbot must have hoped that a treatise prized by the dukes of Burgundy would also appeal to Margaret of Anjou. If she took an interest in it perhaps Henry might follow suit, in spite of his benign, peace-loving temperament.

Six of the fifteen extant manuscripts of the *Fais d'armes* erase Christine's name and imply that the text comes from an anonymous male author (Byles, Introduction xv–xvi).[20] The Queen Margaret Anthology is not one of them. Talbot and his scribes keep intact Christine's prologue, whose stately eloquence dramatically underscores that, after listening to so many male narrators and thinkers, we are now hearing the voice of a learned woman. To be sure, the twelve female personages in the *Bréviaire* (only Honneur is masculine, for grammatical reasons) already set the stage for Christine's entrance into the anthology. Yet this does not diminish the impact of her appearance as a woman writer in a book created for a young queen. Christine is no allegory. She identifies herself as an author who is undertaking a difficult task, and she beseeches Minerva for assistance, stressing to the goddess that they are both Italian women: "tant te plaise me estre favorable..., je suis comme toy femme ytalienne" (may it please you to be favorable to me: like you, I am an Italian woman) (fol. 405v, *Fayttes of Armes* 8). The compilers must have been pleased that the appeal to Minerva alludes to Apulia and Calabria, regions associated with Margaret's family and for that reason highlighted earlier in the anthology, as we have seen. However, the full resonance of this passage in the anthology is that it heightens the implicit woman-to-woman exchange between narrator and royal reader. Minerva counsels Christine, and Christine counsels Margaret — in a way that seems prophetic, given the active role later played by Margaret during the War of the Roses in mustering armies and ordering general maneuvers (Gillingham 106–47, 195–208).

Talbot and his compilers interfere but occasionally with Christine's text. They excise a few anti-English passages from the original, such as a paragraph in book 1, chapter 5, where Christine erroneously states that the Black Prince had put to death envoys of Charles V in 1369.[21] On the whole, these are minor alterations, and one senses that Talbot heartily endorsed many sections of Christine's treatise. He must have approved of her additions to Vegetius, notably the chapter in which she describes fifteenth-century tactics and "modern" ways of deploying armies on battlefields with examples drawn from two battles fought in her own lifetime (1.23).[22]

He must also have applauded her recommendation to monarchs that they should appoint capable soldiers as constables and marshals, and that major decisions on the field of battle should be entrusted to them rather than to less expert princes.[23] Being a conscientious field commander, unflagging even after setbacks, he must have approved of Christine's insistence on orderly planning and discipline (Pollard 68–101, 138–39). He probably thought that her portrait of the ideal constable was a close match to himself. A good constable, says Christine, should possess qualities of self-restraint, dignity, generosity, and good speech: "Et large soit es cas qui le requierent; son commun parler soit d'armes et fais de chevalerie et de proesses des bons; bien se garde de vantise; il soit raisonnable, aime son prince et feal lui soit; soit secourable aux vesves et aux orphenins et aux povres" (And let him be munificent when circumstances require; let him commonly speak of arms, feats of chivalry, and the mighty deeds of great men; he should carefully refrain from boasting; let him behave wisely, love his prince, and serve him loyally; he should protect widows, orphans, and the poor) (1.7). In sum, the constable must be conversant with the very literature compiled in the Queen Margaret Anthology, and he must impart that literature to others, as Talbot shows himself doing in the opening illumination and poem of dedication.

Talbot uses the *Fais d'armes* as his own pedestal, and that intent is vividly revealed by the illumination that introduces the treatise (fol. 405r, Figure 39). We might expect to see Christine portrayed there, just as

Figure 39. Frontispiece of Christine de Pizan's *Fais d'armes:* Henry VI giving Talbot his sword of office. London, British Library, MS Royal, 15.E.VI, fol. 405r.

Honoré Bouvet and Giles of Rome (Egidio Colonna) were shown in the small illuminations introducing their treatises (fol. 293r, Figure 37; fol. 327r). But Christine is entirely absent from the scene. The omission is striking: as Willard tells us, the earliest manuscripts of the *Fais d'armes* depict Christine counseled in her study by Minerva ("Treatise"). The Queen Margaret Anthology offers us instead a tableau in which Talbot receives the sword of constable — or more precisely of marshal of France. His position recalls the anthology's dedicatory frontispiece (fol. 2v, Figure 35): once again he kneels and is shown in profile, but his position is reversed — he faces toward the left. His face is less awkwardly tilted as he looks at the seated king, who hands him the sword of office. The setting has shifted from a palace chamber to a sumptuous dais placed in a meadow. The spectators include courtiers on the left and men-at-arms gathered on the right around Talbot's banner. The queen and her ladies, so prominent in the dedicatory frontispiece, are not featured here. In this picture Talbot substitutes his effigy for that of Christine de Pizan: her text is subordinated to his image. This covert switch enables Talbot to highlight another exchange: in return for his initial gift of a book to the queen, the kneeling Talbot now obtains a sword of office from the king. The man-to-man exchange now holds the stage. Women are excluded from this scene; even the marguerite emblems in the margins are pruned severely back.

Taking a look at the whole final third of the anthology, we find only two illuminations showing female figures. One is the frontispiece of the

Bréviaire des nobles, which depicts the allegorical group of chivalric Virtues in that cycle of ballades (fol. 403r, Figure 40). Eleven of those twelve female Virtues are shown. The second illumination is the book's very last picture (fol. 439r, Figure 41). In it we see a female figure standing close behind Saint George: it is the princess whom he has rescued from the dragon. The threesome of Saint George, the princess, and the dragon form a dumb show at a banquet of the Order of the Garter. The princess is a silent actress, just as the virtues of the *Bréviaire des nobles* are abstract personifications. These ladies are all mute figures in a court pageant; although they stand on center stage, they are not protagonists.

Yet the initial illumination of Margaret receiving Talbot's book represented the queen as an active, leading figure in the court (Figure 35). Later events and legends of the Wars of the Roses confirmed that image of an influential queen (Lee 191–210). Historical records show that Margaret was perceived by many of her contemporaries as an energetic and enterprising woman, who was not likely to sit demurely on the sidelines.[24] Even before her marriage she may have been considered a strong-minded princess, and Talbot had been for several weeks in her entourage, as we have seen. One might almost be tempted to speculate that this reputation alarmed Talbot and his illuminator in Rouen, causing them to downplay the role of all women in the anthology, including Christine de Pizan. It is more likely, however, that Talbot simply wanted to promote his own standing as military commander and courtier. Christine de Pizan's treatise was a good and useful piece of writing on the art of war, but the

Figure 40. Frontispiece of Alain Chartier's *Bréviaire des nobles.* London, British Library, MS Royal 15.E.VI, fol. 403r.

Figure 41. Chapter of the Order of the Garter. London, British Library, MS Royal, 15.E.VI, fol. 439r.

king needed to know that such a work was not as profitable as Talbot's actual mastery and execution of the art.

In conclusion, the Queen Margaret Anthology does not excise Christine de Pizan's name and authorial presence from her war treatise, as do six other manuscripts. Yet her text is made ancillary to a male exchange of gifts between monarch and donor. In that way, it becomes absorbed within circuits of prestige and emulation between English and French courts, and it enters the barter economy that surrounds fifteenth-century marriages. Talbot purports to offer his gift to the queen as a token of admiration for her culture. Margaret is the daughter of a prince renowned for his patronage of the arts, and Talbot prides himself on having acquired an appreciation for French book culture. Having campaigned in France for several decades, he belongs to a group of fifteenth-century English war commanders who collect French literary manuscripts—the duke of Bedford and Sir John Fastolf are two other notable examples (Durrieu; Delisle 1:399–402; Harris 170, 180–81, 186, 196).[25]

The *Fais d'armes* is one of the texts that Talbot collects as a discerning patron of culture and that he gives away in order to increase his prestige and leverage in the Lancastrian court. For him, as for his manuscript artists, the circuit of relations between king and soldier eclipses a woman's writings, just as the principle of lineage recasts a queen's initial effigy into daisy petals and emblems of fertility painted around margins.

Notes

1. Margaret's mother was Isabel of Lorraine, who married René of Anjou in 1420. Her sister Marie wed Charles VII in 1422—and in that same year both Charles VI and Henry V died.

2. Vienna, Österreichische Nationalbibliothek, Cod. 2597. For a brief overview of René's role in shaping the program of illuminations, see Alexander, *Medieval Illuminators* 145, 148, 178.

3. Talbot's wife, the countess of Shrewsbury, even took over Margaret's role during the ceremonial entry into Rouen, because Margaret was ill: see Griffiths 487. We have no literary texts from Margaret, but she dictated precise, lively letters—seventy-three of them are edited by Monro.

4. The dates of Talbot's campaigns in France are 1420–23, 1427–29, 1433–45, 1447–49, and 1452–53 (Pollard 9–61, 135–39). He was captured by the French at Patay in June 1429 and released in the spring of 1433.

5. The Laval-Middleton Anthology (Nottingham University Library, MS Mi.LM.6) contains, among other things, the only extant copy of the *Roman de Silence.*

6. Honoré Bouvet is mistakenly named Bonet in most manuscripts, including the Queen Margaret Anthology (Willard, "Treatise," n. 11).

7. The Talbot master, who may have been trained in Paris, was active in Rouen during the 1440s (Rabel 48–49, 59). After the French retook Rouen (1449), the city councillors commissioned him to illuminate a sumptuous anthology of writings by Cicero, Giles of Rome, and Alain Chartier (Paris, Bibliothèque Nationale de France, MS fr. 126); many visual and decorative aspects of the codex strongly recall the Queen Margaret Anthology (Avril, n. 34). Two of the books of hours that this same master produced for Talbot and his wife are now in Cambridge (Fitzwilliam Museum, MSS 40-1950 and 41-1950), and the third is in Edinburgh, at the National Library of Scotland (Avril and Reynaud 170). André de Mandach surmised that the Queen Margaret Anthology was compiled and illustrated not in English-held Rouen but in Mons (capital of Burgundian Hainaut), at the scriptorium of Jean Wauquelin, who, as a writer and maker of books, served Philip the Good and members of his entourage ("L'Anthologie" 323–31). Mandach's 1973 hypothesis, albeit intriguing, cannot match the much stronger case put forward since then by art historians in favor of the Talbot master of Rouen.

8. This frontispiece and the table of contents and genealogical tables were not included in the manuscript's original pagination (Mandach, "L'Anthologie" 329); this reveals that they were added after the workshop in Rouen had completed the main body of the anthology.

9. We may note, parenthetically, that Talbot kept his promise of serving the king until death: in 1452 he did not side with Richard of York against Somerset and the king, even though he had been one of York's officers for many years. Instead he led an expedition to Gascony on behalf of Henry. Having recaptured Bordeaux and other towns, he perished the following year at Castillon, the last major battle of the Hundred Years' War.

10. As marshal of France since 1436, Talbot had close dealings with both men. For example, he was the godfather of York's daughter Elizabeth, who was christened at Rouen in September 1444 (Pollard 61). Around the time of the royal wedding, he purchased from Gloucester a lordship title in Normandy, in order to end a dispute between them about rights of revenue (Pollard 108).

11. Gloucester clashed with the royal couple over their plans to surrender Maine and Anjou to France. In February 1447 he was be arrested on a charge of treason and subsequently died (Griffiths 495–99). York fell out of favor later that same year; bitter feuding followed, leading to the Wars of the Roses (1455–85), in whose military and political turmoil Margaret played a most prominent role.

12. These water mills recall pumps built by Saladin to supply the fortress of Cairo with water (Ross 82–86). In this illumination, however, the river flows out from the fortress down to the mills.

13. We may think here of the saw invoked by Jean de Meun's Old Woman in the *Roman de la Rose* in defense of female promiscuity: "et qui ne peut a un moulin, / hez a l'autre tretout le cours!" (If you can't grind at one mill, hustle right away to another!) (Guillaume de Lorris and Jean de Meun 2:149, lines 13118–19).

14. The royal couple's inability to have a child provoked gossip (Griffiths 255–56). Their son Edward was finally born in October 1453, yet Yorkist rumors claimed that Henry was not the real father (Griffiths 771).

15. A summary of the entire narrative contents of the anthology can be pieced together in Ward 1:129–30, 627–29, 508–600, 615–19, 604–10, 469–70, 487–89, 708–10.

16. On the political aims of the Picard and Flemish nobility in switching from verse to prose narratives, see Spiegel.

17. Interestingly, Honoré Bouvet had been a counselor of Margaret's grandfather, Louis II of Anjou. However, that could not have been known by the anthology's compilers, who completely garbled his name, spelling it as "Honnore Lone" (Warner 178).

18. As Charity Cannon Willard further observes in chapter 1 of the present volume, Christine de Pizan had strong ties to the Burgundian court from 1403 to 1410. She had placed her young son, Jean de Castel, in John the Fearless's household and had composed a grateful ballade praising the Burgundians (1403). Duke Philip the Bold (John's father) had commissioned her to write a biography of his brother, Charles V, *Le Livre des fais et bonnes meurs du sage roy Charles V* (1404). See Willard, *Christine,* 115–18, 155–56, 167–93.

19. Having campaigned at the side of Philip the Good in 1433 and 1434, Talbot probably had good friends at the court of Burgundy—even though circumstances had also obliged him to fight against Philip in late 1437 (Pollard 19–20, 49).

20. The printer Antoine Vérard in his 1488 edition of the *Fais d'armes* also omits Christine's name, making it look like his own French translation of Vegetius (see Willard, chapter 1 in this volume).

21. The episode led to the collapse of the Brétigny Treaty signed in 1360. The treaty had provided ransom for John II (captured at Poitiers in 1360) by ceding to Edward III Aquitaine plus other territories and vast sums of money. Christine alleges in particular that the Black Prince had slain the envoys sent to him by Charles V in order to summon him to Paris to answer the complaints of Gascon lords, as if Charles were "lord paramount" of Gascony (Byles, Introduction xliv). In fact, the prince imprisoned the envoys but did not harm them.

22. The 1382 victory of Charles VI over Flemings at Roosebeke (1382) and the victory of John the Fearless over the Liégeois at Hasbain (1408). See Byles, Introduction xli–xlvi.

23. "For it shold be a thyng moche to be repreued to chese one of hye blood beyng ygnoraunt and to sette hym in the offyce in whiche subtylte, wysedom and long vsage hath ofte more grete nede than the quantite of peple or ony other strengthe" (1.7, Caxton's translation, *Fayttes of Armes* 22).

24. A London letter writer describes her in February 1456 as "a grete and strong labourid [intensively active] woman, for she spareth noo peyne to sue hire thinges to an intent and conclusion to hir power" (*Paston Letters* 3:75, John Blocking to Sir John Fastolf, quoted in Lee 196). See also the report by the Milanese ambassador Raffaelo de Negra to Bianca Maria Visconti, in Hinds 1:18–19.

25. On John Fastolf's French books, see Schofield 28; Harris 186; Meale 208, 229. Talbot and Fastolf may have shared an interest in French books, but they were on very bad terms after the 1429 Battle of Patay (Pollard 123). Talbot accused Fastolf of having fled from the battle instead of coming to his rescue. The stigma of cowardice attached itself to Fastolf's comic literary avatar, Shakespeare's Falstaff.

Manuscripts Cited

Brussels, Bibliothèque Royale, MS 9242
Cambridge, Fitzwilliam Museum, MS 40-1950

Cambridge, Fitzwilliam Museum, MS 41-1951
Nottingham, Nottingham University Library, MS Mi.LM.6
London, British Library, MS Royal 15.E.VI
Paris, Bibliothèque Nationale de France, MS fr. 126
Vienna, Österreichische Nationalbibliothek, Cod. 2597

Works Cited

❖

Manuscripts

See under individual chapters.

Primary Sources

Albertus Magnus. *De animalibus libri XXVI nach der Cölner Urschrift*. Ed. Hermann Stadler. 2 vols. Münster: Aschendorff, 1916.

Agrippa von Nettesheim [Heinrich Cornelius]. *Declamatio de Nobilitate et Praecellentia Foeminei Sexus*. Opera 2. Darmstadt: Olms, 1970.

Aquinas, Thomas. *Summa theologiae*. Trans. Edmund Hill. N.p.: Black Friars, 1964.

Aristotle. *The Complete Works of Aristotle: The Revised Oxford Translation*. Ed. Jonathan Barnes. Princeton, N.J.: Princeton University Press, 1984.

——. *The Metaphysics*. Trans. Hugh Tredennick. 2 vols. Loeb Classical Library. London: Heinemann, 1933.

L'Art d'amours (The Art of Love). Trans. Lawrence B. Blonquist. New York: Garland, 1987.

L'Art d'amours: Traduction et commentaire de l'Ars amatoria d'Ovide. Ed. Bruno Roy. Leiden: Brill, 1974.

Augustine. *The City of God against the Pagans*. Trans. G. E. McCracken. Loeb Classical Library. Cambridge: Harvard University Press, 1957–72.

Baird, Joseph, and John Kane, trans. *La Querelle de la Rose: Letters and Documents*. North Carolina Studies in Romance Languages and Literatures 199. Chapel Hill: University of North Carolina Press, 1978.

Blank v. Sullivan and Cromwell. 418 F. Supp. 1 (S.D.N.Y. 1975).

Boccaccio, Giovanni. *Concerning Famous Women*. Trans. Guido Guarino. New Brunswick, N.J.: Rutgers University Press, 1963.

——. *Elegia de Madonna Fiammetta*. Ed. Maria Pia Mussini Sacchi. Milan: Mursia, 1987.

Boethius. *The Consolation of Philosophy*. Trans. V. E. Watts. Harmondsworth, England: Penguin, 1969.

——. *Philosophiae Consolationis Libri Quinque*. Ed. Walter Berschine and Walter Bulst. Editiones Heidelbergenses 11. Heidelberg: Winter, 1977.

Bouchet, Jean. *Le Jugement poetic de l'honneur femenin et sejour des illustres, claires et honnestes Dames*. Poitiers: Marnef, 1538.

——. *Le Temple de bonne renommé*. Paris: Vidoue, 1516.

Bouvet, Honoré. *The Tree of Battles of Honoré Bouvet: An English Version with Introduction*. Liverpool: Liverpool University, 1949.

Bradwell v. Illinois. 83 U.S. 130. 1872.

Cereta, Laura. "Letter to Bibulus Sempronius." In King and Rabil Jr., 81–84.

——. "Letter to Lucilia Vernacula." In King and Rabil Jr., 85–88.

Champier, Symphorien. *La Nef des dames vertueuses*. Lyon: Arnollet, 1503.

Chaucer, Geoffrey. *The Riverside Chaucer*. Ed. Larry Benson. 3rd ed. Boston: Houghton Mifflin, 1987.

Christine de Pizan. *Lavision-Christine.* Ed. Mary Louis Towner. Washington, D.C.: Catholic University of America, 1932. Reprint, New York: AMS, 1969.

———. *The Body of Polycye.* London: John Skot, 1521. Reprint, New York: Da Capo, 1971.

———. *The Boke of the Cyte of Ladyes* (London: Henry Pepwell, 1521). In *Distaves and Dames: Renaissance Treatises for and about Women,* ed. Diane Bornstein. Delmar, New York: Scholar's Facsimiles and Reprints, 1978.

———. *The Book of Fayttes of Armes and of Chyualrye Translated and Printed by William Caxton from the French Original by Christine de Pisan.* Ed. A T. P. Byles. London: EETS, 1937. Reprint of *The Book of Fayttes of Armes and of Chyvalrye,* trans. William Caxton, ed. A. T. P. Byles. London: Oxford University Press, 1932.

———. *The Book of the City of Ladies.* Trans. Earl Jeffrey Richards. New York: Persea, 1982.

———. *Le Chemin de longue etude.* Ed. and trans. Andrea Tarnowski. Paris: Librairie Générale Française, 1998.

———. "Christine de Pisan to Isabelle of Bavaria." In *Anglo-Norman Letters and Petitions from All Souls Ms. 182,* ed. M. Dominica Legge, 144–49. Anglo-Norman Text Society 3. Oxford: Blackwell, 1941.

———. *Christine's Vision.* Trans. Glenda K. McLeod. New York: Garland, 1993.

———. *The Debate Poems of Christine de Pizan.* Ed. Barbara Altmann. Gainesville: University of Florida Press, 1998.

———. *Enseignemens moraux.* In *Oeuvres poétiques de Christine de Pisan,* ed. Maurice Roy. Vol 3. Paris, 1886–96; Reprint, New York: Johnson Reprint, 1965.

———. *The Epistle of Othea.* Ed. Curt F. Bühler. Trans. Stephen Scope. Early English Text Society 264. London: Oxford University Press, 1970.

———. *L'Epistre au dieu d'Amours.* In *Oeuvres poétiques de Christine de Pizan,* ed. Maurice Roy, 1–27. Vol. 2. Paris: Didot, 1981.

———. *Epistre Othea.* Ed. Gabriella Parussa. Geneva: Droz, 1998.

———. *L'Epistre Othea.* See Loukopoulos (under Primary Sources).

———. *The Fayt of Armes & of Chyualrye.* Westminster: William Caxton, 1489. Reprint, New York: Da Capo, 1968.

———. "The Hours of Contemplation on the Passion of Our Lord." In *The Writings of Christine de Pizan,* ed. Charity Cannon Willard, 346–47. New York: Persea, 1993.

———. "La Lamentacion sur les maux de la France de Christine de Pisan." Ed. Angus J. Kennedy. In *Mélanges de langue et littérature françaises du Moyen Age et de la Renaissance offerts à Charles Foulon,* I. 177–85. Rennes: Université de Haute-Bretagne, 1980.

———. "Letter to Jean de Montreuil, Provost of Lille." In *Medieval Women Writers,* ed. Katharina M. Wilson, trans. Charity Cannon Willard. Athens: University of Georgia Press, 1984.

———. *Le Livre de la cité des dames.* Trans. Eric Hicks and Thérèse Moreau. Paris: Stock, 1986.

———. *Le Livre de la cité des dames/La citt'delle dame.* Ed. Earl Jeffrey Richards. Italian translation by Patricia Caraffi. Milan: Luna editrice, 1997.

———. *Le Livre de la cité des dames.* See Curnow (under Primary Sources).

———. *Le Livre de l'Advision Cristine.* Ed. Christine Reno and Liliane Dulac. Paris: Champion, forthcoming.

———. *Le Livre de la mutacion de Fortune.* Ed. Suzanne Solente. 4 vols. Paris: Picard, 1959–66.

———. *Le Livre de la paix.* Ed. Charity Cannon Willard. The Hague: Mouton, 1958.

———. *Le Livre des fais et bonnes meurs du sage roy Charles V.* Ed. Suzanne Solente. 2 vols. Paris: Champion, 1936–40.

———. *Le Livre des faits et bonnes moeurs du roi Charles V le Sage.* Trans. Eric Hicks and Thérèse Moreau. Paris: Stock, 1996.

———. *Le Livre des trois Vertus.* Ed. Charity Cannon Willard and Eric Hicks. Bibliothèque du XVe siècle 50. Paris: Champion, 1989.

------. *Le Livre du chemin de long estude.* Ed. Robert Püschel. Berlin, Paris, 1881.

------. *Le Livre du chemin de long estude.* Ed. Robert Püschel. Rev. ed. Berlin, 1887. Reprint, Geneva: Slatkine, 1974.

------. *Le Livre du corps de policie.* Trans. Angus Kennedy. Forthcoming.

------. *Le Livre du corps de policie.* Ed. Robert H. Lucas. Geneva: Droz, 1967.

------. *Le Livre du duc des vrais amans.* Ed. Thelma S. Fenster. Medieval and Renaissance Texts and Studies 124. Binghamton, N.Y.: Center for Medieval and Early Renaissance Studies, 1995.

------. *The Morale Prouerbes of Christyne.* Westminster: William Caxton, 1478. Reprint, New York: Da Capo, 1970.

------. *Oeuvres poétiques de Christine de Pisan.* Ed. Maurice Roy. 3 vols. Paris, 1886–96. Reprint, New York: Johnson Reprint, 1965.

------. *Proverbes moraux.* In *Oeuvres poétiques de Christine de Pisan,* ed. Maurice Roy. Vol. 3. Paris, 1886–96. Reprint, New York: Johnson Reprint, 1965.

------. *The Treasure of the City of Ladies.* Trans. Sarah Lawson. New York: Penguin, 1985.

C[olson], Al., and Ch.-Ed. C[azin], eds. *Ce sont les Secrés des Dames deffendus à réveler.* Paris: Rouveyre, 1880.

Conlon, Denis J., ed. *Le Rommant de Guy de Warwick et de Herolt d'Ardenne.* Chapel Hill: University of North Carolina Press, 1971.

Curnow, Maureen Cheney, ed. "The *Livre de la cité des dames* of Christine de Pisan: A Critical Edition." Ph.D. diss. Vanderbilt University, 1975.

Dante. *The Divine Comedy.* Trans. Charles S. Singleton. Princeton, N.J.: Princeton University Press, 1970–75.

de Pure, Michel. *La Prétieuse ou le mystère des ruelles.* Paris, 1656–58.

Deschamps, Eustache. *Oeuvres complètes de Eustache Deschamps publiées d'après le manuscrit de la Bibliothèque Nationale.* Ed. Auguste De Queux de Saint-Hilaire and G. Raynaud. 11 vols. Paris: Société des anciens textes français, 1878–1903.

E.E.O.C. v. Sears, Roebuck. 839 F.2d 302. 7th Cir. 1988.

Egidio Colonna [Giles of Rome, Aegidius Romanus]. *Li Livres du gouvernement des rois.* Trans. Henri de Gauchy. Ed. Samuel Paul Molenaer. New York: Macmillan, 1899.

Enguerrand de Monstralet. *Chroniques.* Ed. J. A. C. Buchon. Paris: Desrez, 1836.

Fenster, Thelma S., and Mary Carpenter Erler, eds. *Poems of Cupid, God of Love: Christine de Pizan's* Epistre au dieu d'Amours *and* Dit de la Rose; *Thomas Hoccleve's* The Letter of Cupid; *with George Sewell's* The Proclamation of Cupid. Leiden: Brill, 1990.

Froissart, Jean. *Chronicles.* Trans. G. Brereton. Harmondsworth, England: Penguin, 1968.

------. *Oeuvres de Froissart.* Ed. Kervyn de Lettenhove. 24 vols. Brussels: Victor Devaux, 1871.

Gerson, Jean. *Lectiones duae contra curiositatem studentium.* In *Oeuvres,* ed. Pierre Glorieux, 3:224–29. Paris: Desclée, 1966.

------. *La Montaigne de Contemplation.* In *Oeuvres,* ed. Pierre Glorieux, 7:16–55. Paris: Desclée, 1962.

------. *Oeuvres complètes.* Ed. Pierre Glorieux. 10 vols. Paris: Desclée, 1960–1973.

Gervase of Tilbury. *Le Livre des merveilles: Divertissement pour un empereur (troisième partie).* Ed. Annie Duchesne. Paris: Belles Lettres, 1992.

------. *Otia imperiala ad Ottonem IV imperatorum: Scriptores rerum Brunsvicensium.* Ed. G. W. Leibnitz. Vol. 1. Hanover, 1707.

Gower, John. *Confessio Amantis.* Ed. Russell A. Peck. New York: Holt, 1968.

Guillaume de Lorris and Jean de Meun. *Roman de la Rose.* Ed. Félix Lecoy. Classiques Français du Moyen Age. 3 vols. Paris: Champion, 1965–70.

Guillaume le Clerc. *Bestiary.* Trans. George Claridge Druce. Ashford, Kent: Invicta, 1936.

Hicks, Eric, ed. *Le Débat sur le "Roman de la Rose."* Bibliothèque du XVe siècle 43. Paris: Champion, 1977.

Inventaire de la Bibliothèque du Roi Charles VI fait au Louvre en 1423 par ordre du Régent Duc de Bedford. Ed. Douët d'Arcq. Paris: Société des Bibliophiles, 1867.

Jean de Montreuil. *Opera*. Ed. N. Grévy et. al. Vol 2. Turin: Giappichelli, 1975.

John of Legnano. *Tractatus de bello, de represaliis et de duello*. Ed. T. E. Holland. Trans. J.: Oxford University Press, L. Brierly. Oxford: Oxford University Press, 1917.

Kempe, Margery. *The Book of Margery Kempe*. Ed. Sanford Brown Meech and Hope Emily Allen. Early English Text Society, n.s., 212. London: Oxford University Press, 1940.

——. *The Book of Margery Kempe*. Trans. Barry A. Windeatt. Harmondsworth, England: Penguin, 1985.

King, Margaret L., and Albert Rabil Jr., eds. *Her Immaculate Hand: Selected Works by and about the Women Humanists of Quattrocento Italy*. Rev ed. Binghamton, N.Y.: Center for Medieval and Renaissance Studies, 1992.

Le Franc, Martin. *Le Champion des dames*. Ed. A. Piaget. Lausanne: Payot, 1968.

Lesnauderie, Pierre de. *La Louenge de mariage et recueil des hystoires des bonnes, vertueuses et illustres femmes*. Paris: Regnault, 1523.

Loukopoulos, Halina Didycky. "Classical Mythology in the Works of Christine de Pisan, with an Edition of *L'Epistre Othea* from the Manuscript Harley 4431." Ph.D. diss., Wayne State University, 1977. Ann Arbor: UMI, 1977.

Macrobius. *Commentary on the Dream of Scipio*. Trans. William Harris Stahl. New York: Columbia University Press, 1952.

Marot, Clément. *Oeuvres*. Ed. G. Guiffrey. Vol. 5. Paris: Plattard, 1931.

——. *Oeuvres poétiques complètes*. Ed. Gérard Defaux. Vol. 1. Classiques Garnier. Paris: Bordas, 1993.

Marot, Jean. *Poésies de Jean Marot et de Michel Marot*. Ed. N. Lenglet Du Fresnoy. Vol. 5 of *Oeuvres de Clément Marot*. The Hague: Gosse, 1731.

Matheolus. *Les Lamentations de Matheolus et le livre de leesce de Jehan le Fèvre*. Ed. A.-G. van Hamel. 2 vols. Paris: Bouillon, 1892.

Monro, Cecil, ed. *Letters of Margaret of Anjou and Bishop Beckington and Others*. London: Camden Society, 1863.

Montaigne, Michel de. "On Some Verses of Virgil." In *The Complete Essays*, trans. Donald Frame. Palo Alto, Calif.: Stanford University Press, 1965.

L'Ornement des Dames (Ornatus mulierum): Texte anglo-normand du XIIIe siècle. Le plus ancien recueil en français de recettes médicales pour les soins du visage, publié avec une introduction, une traduction, des notes et un glossaire. Ed. Pierre Ruelle. Brussels: Presses Universitaires de Bruxelles, 1967.

Ovide moralisé, poème du commencement du quatorzième siècle. Ed. Cornelis de Boer. Amsterdam: Johannes Muller, 1915–38.

Petrarch, Francesco. *Letters on Familiar Matters*. Trans. Aldo Bernardo. 3 vols. Baltimore, Md.: Johns Hopkins University Press, 1975–85.

Pico della Mirandola, Giovanni. "Oratio de Dignitate Hominis." In *The Renaissance Philosophy of Man*, ed. Ernst Cassirer et. al., trans. Paul Oskar Kristeller, 223–54. Chicago: University of Chicago Press, 1950.

Placides et Timéo ou Li secrés as philosophes: Edition critique avec introduction et notes. Ed. Claude Thomasset. Geneva: Droz, 1980.

Rutebeuf. *Oeuvres complètes de Rutebeuf*. Ed. Michel Zink. 2 vols. Paris: Bordas, 1990.

Der Vrouwen Heimelykheid: Dichtwerk der XIVe eeuw. Ed. Ph. Blommaert. Ghent: Annoot-Braeckman, 1846.

Secondary Sources

Ahern, John. Review of *The Inferno of Dante: A New Verse Translation*, trans. Robert Pinsky. *New York Times Book Review*, Jan 1, 1995, 3, 21.

Alexander, Jonathan J. G. "Art History, Literary History, and the Study of Medieval Illuminated Manuscripts." *Studies in Iconography* 18 (1997): 51–66.

——. *Medieval Illuminators and Their Methods of Work*. New Haven, Conn.: Yale University Press, 1992.

Allaire, Gloria. "The Chivalric 'Histories' of Andrea de Barberino: A Re-evaluation." Ph.D. diss., University of Wisconsin–Madison, 1993.

Allen, Prudence. *The Concept of Woman: The Aristotelian Revolution, 750 BC–AD 1250.* Montreal: Eden, 1985.

Altmann, Barbara. "L'Art de l'autoportrait littéraire dans les *Cent ballades* de Christine de Pizan." In Dulac and Ribémont, 327–36.

Ashley, Kathleen. "Medieval Courtesy Literature and Dramatic Mirrors of Female Conduct." In *The Ideology of Conduct: Essays on Literature and the History of Sexuality*, ed. Nancy Armstrong and Leonard Tennenhouse, 25–37. New York: Methuen, 1987.

Autrand, Françoise. "La Culture d'un roi: Livres et amis de Charles V." *Perspectives Médiévales* 21 (1995): 99–106.

———. "Les Livres des hommes de pouvoir: De la Pratique à la culture écrite. Pratique diplomatique et culture politique au temps de Charles V." In Ornato and Pons, 193–204.

Avril, François, and Nicole Reynaud, eds. *Les Manuscrits à peintures en France, 1440–1520.* Paris: Flammarion, 1994.

Badel, Pierre-Yves. *Le Roman de la Rose au XIVe siècle.* Geneva: Droz, 1980.

Bal, Mieke. "Scared to Death." In *The Point of Theory: Practices of Cultural Analysis*, ed. Mieke Bal and Inge E. Boer, 32–47. New York. Continuum, 1994.

Barnard, Mary E. *The Myth of Apollo and Daphne from Ovid to Quevedo: Love, Agon, and the Grotesque.* Duke Monographs in Medieval and Renaissance Studies 8. Durham, N.C.: Duke University Press, 1987.

Baroin, Jeanne, and Josiane Haffen, ed. *"Des Cleres et Nobles Femmes" (Ms. Bibl. Nat. 12420).* Annales littéraires de l'Université de Besançon 498. Paris: Belles Lettres, 1993.

Batany, Jean. "L'Amère maternité du français médiéval." In *Approches langagières de la société médiévale*, 95–105. Caen: Paradigme, 1992.

Beaune, Colette. *The Birth of an Ideology: Myths and Symbols of Nation in Late-Medieval France.* Ed. Frederic L. Cheyette. Trans. Susan Ross Huston. Berkeley: University of California Press, 1991. Originally published as *Naissance de la nation France* (Paris: Gallimard, 1985).

Belenky, Mary Field, Blythe McVicker Clinchy, Nancy Rule Goldberger, and Jill Mattuck Tarule. *Women's Ways of Knowing: The Development of Self, Voice, and Mind.* New York: Basic Books, 1986.

Belin, Théophile. "Notice sur quelques mss., remarquables . . ." Paris, 1926.

Bell, David N. *What Nuns Read: Books and Libraries in Medieval English Nunneries.* Cistercian Studies Series 158. Kalamazoo, Mich.: Cistercian Publications, 1995.

Bell, Derrick. *Faces at the Bottom of the Well.* New York: Basic Books, 1992.

Bell, Susan Groag. "Christine de Pizan (1364–1430): Humanism and the Problem of a Studious Woman." *Feminist Studies* 3 (1976): 173–84.

———. "Medieval Women Book Owners: Arbiters of Lay Piety and Ambassadors of Culture." *Signs* 7 (1982): 742–68.

Benveniste, Henriette. "Les Enlèvements: Stratégies matrimoniales, discours juridique et discours politique en France à la fin du Moyen Age." *Revue historique* 283 (1990): 13–35.

Bérier, François. "La Traduction en français." In Biermann and Tillman-Bartylla, 219–65.

Bernard, Robert B. "The Intellectual Circle of Isabel of Portugal, Duchess of Burgundy, and the Portuguese Translation of *Le Livre des Trois Vertus (O Liuro dos Tres Vertudes).*" In McLeod, 43–56.

Berriot-Salvador, Evelyn. "Les Femmes et les pratiques de l'écriture de Christine de Pisan à Marie de Gournay: 'Femmes Sçavantes et Savoir Féminin.'" *Réforme, Humanisme, Renaissance* 9, no. 16 (1983): 52–69.

Biddick, Kathleen. "Humanist History and the Haunting of Virtual Worlds: Problems of Memory and Rememoration." *Genders* 18 (1993): 47–66.

Biermann, Armin, and Dagmar Tillman-Bartylla, eds. *La Littérature française aux XIVe et XVe siècles.* Grundriss der romanischen Literaturen des Mittelalters 8/1. Heidelberg: Winter, 1988.

261

Blamires, Alcuin. *The Case for Women in Medieval Culture.* New York: Oxford University Press, 1997.

Blamires, Alcuin, Karen Pratt, and C. W. Marx, eds. *Woman Defamed and Woman Defended: An Anthology of Medieval Texts.* Oxford: Clarendon, 1992.

Blanchard, Joël. "Christine de Pizan: Une Laïque au pays des clercs." In *"Et c'est la fin pour quoy sommes ensemble": Hommage à Jean Dufournet; Littérature, histoire et langue du Moyen Age,* ed. Jean-Claude Aubailly et al., vol 1, 215–26. Paris: Champion, 1993.

———. "Christine de Pizan: Les Raisons de l'histoire." *Le Moyen Age* 92 (1986): 417–36.

———. "Christine de Pizan: Tradition, expérience et traduction." *Romania* 111 (1990): 200–35.

———. "L'Entrée du poète dans le champ politique au XVe siècle." *Annales ESC* 1 (1986): 43–61.

Bloch, R. Howard. "Medieval Misogyny." *Representations* 20 (1987): 1–24.

Blumenfeld-Kosinski, Renate. "Christine de Pizan and Classical Mythology: Some Examples from the 'Mutacion de Fortune.'" In Zimmermann and De Rentiis, 3–14.

———. "Christine de Pizan and the Misogynistic Tradition." *Romanic Review* 81, no. 3 (1990): 279–92.

Blunt, Wilfred, and Sandra Raphael. *The Illustrated Herbal.* London: Lincoln, 1994.

Bolter, Jay David. *Writing Space: The Computer, Hypertext, and the History of Writing.* Hillsdale, N.J.: Erlbaum, 1991.

Born, Lester Kruger. "The Perfect Prince: A Study in Thirteenth- and Fourteenth-Century Ideals." *Speculum* 3 (1928): 470–504.

Bornstein, Diane. "The Ideal of the Lady of the Manor as Reflected in Christine de Pizan's *Livre des trois vertus.*" In Bornstein, *Ideals,* 117–128.

———. Introduction to *Distaves and Dames: Renaissance Treatises for and about Women,* ed. Bornstein, v–xx. Delmar, New York: Scholar's Facsimiles and Reprints, 1978.

———, ed. *Ideals for Women in the Works of Christine de Pizan.* Medieval and Renaissance Monograph Series 1. Ann Arbor: Michigan Consortium for Medieval and Early Modern Studies, 1981.

Bosselman-Cyran, Kristian. Introduction to *"Secreta mulierum" mit Glosse in der deutschen Bearbeitung von Johann Hartlieb,* ed. Kristian Bosselman-Cyran. Würzburger medizinhistorische Forschungen 36. Pattensen/Hannover: Horst Wellm, 1985.

Boudet, Jean-Patrice. "Prévision de l'avenir et connaissance du passé: Les Relations entre astrologie et histoire à la fin du Moyen Age." In Ornato and Pons, 299–312.

Bourdieu, Pierre. *Language and Symbolic Power.* Ed. John B. Thompson. Trans. Gino Raymond and Matthew Adamson. Cambridge: Harvard University Press, 1991.

Brabant, Margaret, ed. *Politics, Gender, and Genre: The Political Thought of Christine de Pizan.* Boulder, Colo.: Westview, 1992.

Braunstein, Philippe. "Toward Intimacy: The Fourteenth and Fifteenth Centuries." In *Revelations of the Medieval World,* vol. 2 of *A History of Private Life,* ed. Georges Duby, trans. Arthur Goldhammer. 535–630. Cambridge: Belknap Press of Harvard University Press, 1988.

Brink, Claudia, and Wilhelm Hornbostel, eds. *Pegasus and the Arts.* Munich: Deutscher Kunstverlag, 1993.

Brondy, Rejane, Bernard Demotz, and Jean-Pierre Leguay. *La Savoie de l'an mil à la réforme.* Rennes: Ouest-France, 1984.

Brown, Cynthia J. *Poets, Patrons, and Printers: Crisis of Authority in Late Medieval France.* Ithaca, N.Y.: Cornell University Press, 1995.

Brown-Grant, Rosalind. "Illumination as Reception: Jean Miélot's Reworking of the 'Epistre Othea.'" In Zimmermann and De Rentiis, 260–71.

Brownlee, Kevin. "Christine de Pizan's Canonical Authors: The Special Case of Boccaccio." *Comparative Literature Studies* 32 (1995): 135–52.

———. "Discourses of the Self: Christine de Pizan and the 'Romance of the Rose.'" In *Rethinking the "Romance of the Rose": Text, Image, Reception*, ed. Kevin Brownlee and Sylvia Huot, 234–61. Philadelphia: University of Pennsylvania Press, 1992.

———. "The Image of History in Christine de Pizan's *Livre de la Mutacion de Fortune*." In *Contexts: Styles and Values in Medieval Art and Literature*, ed. Daniel Poirion and Nancy Freeman Regalado, 44–56. Yale French Studies Special Edition. New Haven, Conn.: Yale University Press, 1991.

———. "Structures of Authority in Christine de Pizan's 'Ditié de Jehanne d'Arc.'" In *Discourses of Authority in Medieval and Renaissance Literature*, ed. Kevin Brownlee and Walter Stephens, 131–50. Hanover, N.H.: Published for Dartmouth College by University Press of New England, 1989.

Brownmiller, Susan. *Against Our Will: Men, Women, and Rape*. Toronto: Bantam, 1981.

Brundage, James A. *Law, Sex, and the Christian Society in Medieval Europe*. Chicago: University of Chicago Press, 1987.

———. "Rape and Seduction in Medieval Canon Law." In *Sexual Practices and the Medieval Church*, ed. Vern Bullough and James A. Brundage, 141–48. Buffalo: Prometheus, 1982.

Buchthal, Hugo. *Historia Troiana: Studies in the History of Mediaeval Secular Illustration*. Studies of the Warburg Institute 32. London: Warburg Institute; Leiden: Brill, 1971.

Buettner, Brigitte. "Dressing and Undressing Bodies in Late Medieval Images." In *Künstlerischer Austausch/Artistic Exchange: Akten des XXVIII Internationalen Kongresses für Kunstgeschichte*, ed. Thomas W. Gaehtgens, 383–92. Berlin: Akademie Verlag, 1993.

———. "Profane Illuminations, Secular Illusions: Manuscripts in Late Medieval Courtly Society." *Art Bulletin* 74 (1992): 75–90.

Burns, E. Jane. *Bodytalk: When Women Speak in Old French Literature*. Philadelphia: University of Pennsylvania Press, 1993.

Byles, A. T. P. Introduction to *The Book of Fayttes of Armes and of Chyvalrye, Translated and Printed by William Caxton from the French Original by Christine de Pisan*, xi–lvi. 2nd ed. London: EETS, 1937.

Bynum, Caroline Walker. *Holy Feast and Holy Fast: The Religious Significance of Food to Medieval Women*. Berkeley: University of California Press, 1987.

Cadden, Joan. *Meanings of Sex Difference in the Middle Ages: Medicine, Science, and Culture*. Cambridge: Cambridge University Press, 1993.

Cahoon, Leslie. "Raping the Rose: Jean de Meun's Reading of Ovid's *Amores*." *Classical and Modern Literature* 6 (1986): 261–85.

Calin, William. *Nine Centuries of the Epic in France*. Toronto: University of Toronto Press, 1983.

Camille, Michael. *The Gothic Idol: Ideology and Image-making in Medieval Art*. New York: Cambridge University Press, 1989.

Campbell, P. G. C. "Christine de Pisan en Angleterre." *Revue de littérature comparée* 5 (1925): 659–70.

———. *"L'Epître Othéa": Étude sur les sources de Christine de Pisan*. Paris: Champion, 1924.

Camus, Jules. "La Seconde Traduction de la Chirurgie de Mondeville (Turin, Bibl. nat. L.IV.17)." *Bulletin de la Société des Anciens textes français* 28 (1902): 100–119."

Case, Sue-Ellen. *The Domain-Matrix: Performing Lesbian at the End of Print Culture*. Bloomington: Indiana University Press, 1996.

Castel, Françoise du. *Damoiselle Christine de Pizan, Veuve de M. Etienne de Castel, 1364–1431*. Paris: A. et J. Picard, 1972.

Chance, Jane. "Christine's Minerva: The Mother Valorized." In *Christine de Pizan's "Letter of Othea to Hector,"* trans. Jane Chance, 121–33. Newburyport, Mass.: Focus, 1990.

Chartier, Roger. *Forms and Meanings: Texts, Performances, and Audiences from Codex to Computer*. Philadelphia: University of Pennsylvania Press, 1995.

———. "Libraries without Walls." In *Future Libraries*, ed. R. Howard Bloch and Carla Hesse, 38–52. Berkeley: University of California Press, 1995.

Chaytor, H. J. *From Script to Print: An Introduction to Medieval Literature.* Cambridge: Heffer, 1945.

Chiffoleau, Jacques. *Les Justices du Pape: Délinquance et criminalité dans la région d'Avignon au quatorzième siècle.* Paris: Sorbonne, 1984.

Cixous, Hélène. "The Laugh of the Medusa." *Signs* 1 (1976): 875–93.

Clifford, Gay. *The Transformations of Allegory.* London: Routledge, 1974.

Cockerell, Sydney C., and John Plummer. *Old Testament Miniatures: A Medieval Picture Book.* New York: Braziller, 1975.

Code, Lorraine. *What Can She Know? Feminist Theory and the Construction of Knowledge.* Ithaca, N.Y.: Cornell University Press, 1991.

Colker, Ruth. "Feminism, Sexuality and Self." *Boston University Law Review* 68 (1988): 217–64.

Combes, André. *La Théologie mystique de Gerson: Profil de son évolution.* 2 vols. Rome: Desclée, 1963.

Conlon, Denis J. Introduction to *Le Rommant de Guy de Warwick et de Herolt d'Ardenne,* 13–47. Studies in the Romance Languages and Literatures 102. Chapel Hill: University of North Carolina Press, 1971.

Constable, Marianne. *The Law of the Other: The Mixed Jury and Changing Conceptions of Citizenship, Law, and Knowledge.* Chicago: University of Chicago Press, 1994.

Coopland, G. W. "*Le Jouvencel* (Revisited)." *Symposium* 5 (1951): 143–81.

Copeland, Rita. *Rhetoric, Hermeneutics, and Translation in the Middle Ages: Academic Traditions and Vernacular Texts.* Cambridge Studies in Medieval Literature 11. Cambridge: Cambridge University Press, 1991.

Copleston, F. C. *A History of Medieval Philosophy.* New York: Harper, 1974.

Corsi, Dinora. "'Les Secrés des dames': Tradition, traductions." *Médiévales* 14 (1988): 47–57.

Cosneau, E. *Le Connétable de Richmont.* Paris: Hachette, 1886.

Curnow, Maureen Cheney. "*The Boke of the Cyte of Ladyes,* An English Translation of Christine de Pisan's *Le livre de la cité des dames.*" *Les Bonnes Feuilles* 3 (1974): 116–37.

——— "'La Pioche d'Inquisicion': Legal-Judicial Content and Style in Christine de Pizan's *Livre de la Cité des Dames.*" In Richards et al., *Reinterpreting,* 157–72.

Curran, Leo. "Rape and Rape Victims in the *Metamorphoses.*" In *Women in the Ancient World: The "Arethusa" Papers,* ed. J. Perradotto and J. P. Sullivan, 263–86. Albany: State University of New York Press, 1984.

Davis, Natalie Zemon. "Beyond the Market: Books as Gifts in Sixteenth-Century France." *Transactions of the Royal Historical Society,* 5th ser., 33 (1983): 69–88.

Delaissé, L. M. J. "Les 'Chroniques de Hainaut' et l'atelier de Jean Wauquelin à Mons, dans l'histoire de la miniature flamande." *Miscellanea Erwin Panofsky. Bulletin des Musées Royaux des Beaux Arts* 4, no. 13 (1995): 21–56.

Delany, Sheila. "History, Politics, and Christine Studies: A Polemical Reply." In Brabant 193–206.

——— "'Mothers to Think Back Through:' Who Are They? The Ambiguous Example of Christine de Pizan." In *Medieval Texts and Contemporary Readers,* ed. Laurie A. Finke and Martin B. Shichtman, 177–97. Ithaca, N.Y.: Cornell University Press, 1987.

Delgado, Richard. "The Imperial Scholar." *University of Pennsylvania Law Review* 132 (1984): 561–78.

——— "When Is a Story Just a Story: Does Voice Really Matter?" *University of Virginia Law Review* 76 (1990): 95–111.

Delisle, Léopold. *Recherches sur la librairie de Charles V, roi de France, 1337–1380.* 2 vols. Paris, 1907. Reprint, Amsterdam: van Heusden, 1967.

De Rentiis, Dina. "'Sequere me': 'Imitatio' dans la 'Divine Comédie' et dans 'Livre du Chemin de long estude.'" In Zimmerman and De Rentiis, 31–42.

De Rijk, Lambert Marie. *La Philosophie au Moyen Age.* Trans. P. Swiggers. Leiden: Brill, 1985.

Desmond, Marilynn. *Reading Dido: Gender, Textuality, and the Medieval Aeneid.* Minneapolis: University of Minnesota Press, 1994.

Desmond, Marilynn, and Pamela Sheingorn. "Queering Ovidian Myth: Bestiality and Desire in Christine de Pizan's *Othea.*" Forthcoming.

Dickson, Lynne E. "Embracing the Antifeminist Body: Corporal Ambivalence in the *Cité des dames.*" Paper presented at "Christine de Pizan: Texts/Intertexts/Contexts," Twenty-Ninth CEMERS Conference. Binghamton University, Binghamton, N.Y., Oct. 20–21, 1995.

Dictionnaire du Moyen Français; La Renaissance. Ed. A. Greimas and Teresa Mary Keane. Paris: Larousse, 1992.

Donaldson, Ian. *The Rapes of Lucretia: A Myth and Its Transformations.* Oxford: Clarendon, 1982.

Doorn, Mieke van, and Willem Kuiper. "Der vrouwen heimlicheid." *Spektator* 6, nos. 9–10 (1976–77): 539–51.

Doutrepont, Georges. *La Littérature française à la cour des ducs de Bourgogne.* Geneva: Slatkine, 1970.

Dronke, Peter. "Medieval Sibyls: Their Character and Their 'Auctoritas.'" *Studi Medievali,* 3rd ser., 36 (1995): 581–615.

DuBois, Ellen C., Mary C. Dunlap, Carol J. Gilligan, Catharine A. MacKinnon, and Carrie J. Menkel-Meadows. "Feminist Discourse, Moral Values, and the Law — A Conversation." *Buffalo Law Review* 34 (1985): 11–87.

Dufresne, Laura Rinaldi. "A Woman of Excellent Character: A Case Study of Dress, Reputation, and the Changing Costume of Christine de Pizan in the Fifteenth Century." *Dress* 17 (1990): 104–17.

Dulac, Liliane. "Authority in the Prose Treatises of Christine de Pizan: The Writer's Discourse and the Prince's Word." Trans. Earl Jeffrey Richards. In Brabant, 129–40.

———. "La Figure de l'écrivain dans quelques traités en prose de Christine de Pizan." In *Figures de l'écrivain au Moyen Age: Actes du colloque du Centre d'Etudes Médiévales de l'Université de Picardie, Amiens (18–20 mars 1988),* ed. Danielle Buschinger, 113–23. Göppinger Arbeiten zur Germanistik 510. Göppingen: Kümmerle, 1991.

———. "Mystical Inspiration and Political Knowledge: Advice to Widows from Francesco da Barbarino and Christine de Pizan." In *Upon My Husband's Death: Widows in the Literature and Histories of Medieval Europe,* ed. Louise Mirrer, trans. Thelma Fenster, 223–58. Ann Arbor: University of Michigan Press, 1992.

———. "The Representation and Functions of Feminine Speech in Christine de Pizan's *Livre des Trois Vertus.*" In Richards et al., *Reinterpreting,* 13–24.

Dulac, Liliane, and Christine Reno. "L'Humanisme vers 1400, essai d'exploration à partir d'un cas marginal: Christine de Pizan, traductrice de Thomas d'Aquin." In Ornato and Pons, 160–78.

———. "Traduction et adaptation dans *L'Advision-Cristine* de Christine de Pizan." In *Traduction et adaptation en France à la fin du Moyen Age et à la Renaissance. Actes du colloque organisé par l'Université de Nancy II, 23–25 mars 1995,* ed. Charles Brucker, 121–31. Colloques, congrès et conférences sur la Renaissance X. Paris: Champion, 1997.

Dulac, Liliane, and Bernard Ribémont, eds. *Une Femme de lettres au Moyen Age: Etudes autour de Christine de Pizan. Medievalia* 16 Série, "Etudes christiniennes." Orleans: Paradigme, 1995.

Dunbabin, Jean. "The Reception and Interpretation of Aristotle's *Politics.*" In *The Cambridge History of Later Medieval Philosophy: From the Rediscovery of Aristotle to the Disintegration of Scholasticism, 1100–1600,* ed. Norman Kretzmann, Anthony Kenny, and Jan Pinborg, 723–37. Cambridge: Cambridge University Press, 1982.

Dupuy, R. E., and T. N. Dupuy. *The Encyclopedia of Military History from 3500 B.C. to the Present.* New York: Harper, 1986.

Durrieu, Paul. *Les Souvenirs historiques dans les manuscrits à miniatures de la domination anglaise en France au temps de Jeanne d'Arc. Annuaire-Bulletin de la Société de l'Histoire de France.* Paris, 1905.

Easton, Martha. "Saint Agatha and the Sanctification of Sexual Violence." *Studies in Iconography* 16 (1994): 83–118.

Even, Yael. "Andrea del Castagno's *Eve:* Female Heroes as Anomalies in Italian Renaissance Art." *Woman's Art Journal* 4 (1994): 37–42.

———. "Mantegna's Uffizi *Judith:* The Masculinization of the Female Hero." *Konsthistorisk Tidskrift* 12 (1992): 8–20.

———. "The Heroine as Hero in Michelangelo's Art." *Woman's Art Journal* 11 (1990): 29–33.

Febvre, Lucien, and Henri-Jean Martin. *L'Apparition du livre.* Paris: Albin Michel, 1971.

Fenster, Thelma. "Did Christine Have a Sense of Humor? The Evidence of the 'Epistre au dieu d'Amours.'" In Richards et al., *Reinterpreting,* 37–47.

Ferrante, Joan. "Beyond the Borders of Nation and Discipline." In *The Future of the Middle Ages,* ed. William Paden, 145–63. Gainesville: University Press of Florida, 1994.

Ferrier, Janet. *French Prose Writers of the Fourteenth and Fifteenth Centuries.* Oxford: Pergamon, 1966.

Ferster, Judith. *Fictions of Advice: The Literature and Politics of Counsel in Late Medieval England.* Philadelphia: University of Pennsylvania Press, 1996.

———. "O Political Gower." *Medievalia* 16 (1993): 33–53.

Fery-Hue, Françoise. Review of *Placides et Timeo ou Li secrés as philosophes: Edition critique avec introduction et notes.* Ed. Claude Alexandre Thomasset. *Romania* 105 (1984): 142–54.

———. "*Secrets des femmes.*" In *Dictionnaire des lettres françaises: Le Moyen Age,* ed. G. Hasenohr and M. Zink, 1371. Paris: Livre de Poche, 1993.

Finke, Laurie. *Feminist Theory, Women's Writing.* Ithaca, N.Y.: Cornell University Press, 1992.

Finkel, Helen. "The Portrait of the Woman in the Works of Christine de Pisan." *Les Bonnes Feuilles* 3 (1974): 138–51.

Fleming, John V. *The "Roman de la Rose": A Study in Allegory and Iconography.* Princeton, N.J.: Princeton University Press, 1969.

Foucault, Michel. "What Is an Author?" Trans. Josué V. Harari. In *The Foucault Reader,* ed. Paul Rabinow, 101–20. New York: Pantheon, 1984.

Friedman, Rodger. "Il Codici Spencer 33 Della Public Library di New York." *Studi sul Boccaccio* 22 (1991/92): 3–17.

Gabriel, Astrik L. "The Educational Ideas of Christine de Pisan." *Journal of the History of Ideas* 16 (1955): 3–21.

Garnier, François. *Le Langage de l'image au Moyen Age: Signification et symbolique.* Paris: Léopard d'Or, 1982.

———. *Le Langage de l'image au Moyen Age II: Grammaire des Gestes.* Paris: Léopard d'Or, 1989.

Garrard, Mary. *Artemisia Gentileschi: The Image of the Female Hero in Italian Baroque Art.* Princeton, N.J.: Princeton University Press, 1989.

Gauvard, Claude. "Christine de Pisan a-t-elle eu une pensée politique? A propos d'ouvrages récents." *Revue Historique* 250 (1973): 417–30.

———. "Christine de Pizan et ses contemporains: L'Engagement politique des écrivains dans le royaume de France aux XIVe et XVe siècles." In Dulac and Ribémont, 105–128.

———. "*De Grace especial*": *Crime, état et société en France à la fin du moyen âge.* Paris: Sorbonne, 1991.

———. "Violence citadine et réseaux de solidarité: L'exemple français aux XIVe et XVe siècles." *Annales* 47 (1993): 1113–26.

Gehl, Paul F. *A Moral Art: Grammar, Society, and Culture in Trecento Florence.* Ithaca, N.Y.: Cornell University Press, 1993.

Genette, Gérard. *Palimpsestes: La littérature au second degré.* Paris: Seuil, 1982.

———. *Seuils.* Paris: Seuil, 1987.

Giddings, Paula. *When and Where I Enter: The Impact of Black Women on Race and Sex in America.* New York: Bantam, 1984.

Gillingham, John. *The Wars of the Roses.* Baton Rouge: Louisiana State University Press, 1981.

Gilmore, Leigh. *Autobiographics: A Feminist Theory of Women's Self-Representation.* Ithaca, N.Y.: Cornell University Press, 1994.

Godefroy, Frédérick. *Dictionnaire de l'ancienne langue française et de tous ses dialectes du IXe au XVe siècle.* Paris, 1891–1902. Reprint, Geneva: Slatkine, 1982.

Goreau, Angeline, ed. *The Whole Duty of a Woman: Female Writers in Seventeenth-Century England.* New York: Doubleday, 1985.

Gottlieb, Beatrice. "The Problem of Feminism in the Fifteenth Century." In Kirshner and Wemple, 337–64.

Gournay, Marie de. *Fragments d'un discours féminin.* Paris: José Corti, 1988.

Gravdal, Kathryn. *Ravishing Maidens: Writing Rape in Medieval French Literature and Law.* Philadelphia: University of Pennsylvania Press, 1991.

Grayson, Cecil. *A Renaissance Controversy: Latin or Italian?* Oxford: Clarendon, 1960.

Green, Monica H. "The Development of the *Trotula.*" *Revue d'Histoire des Textes* 26 (1996): 119–203.

———. *"The Diseases of Women According to Trotula": A Medieval Compendium of Women's Medicine.* Forthcoming.

———. "A Handlist of Latin and Vernacular Manuscripts of the So-Called *Trotula* Texts. Part 1: The Latin Manuscripts." *Scriptorium* 50 (1996): 137–75.

———. "A Handlist of Latin and Vernacular Manuscripts of the So-Called *Trotula* Texts. Part 2: The Vernacular Translations and Latin Re-Writings." *Scriptorium* 51 (1997): 80–104.

———. "Obstetrical and Gynecological Texts in Middle English." *Studies in the Age of Chaucer* 14 (1992): 53–88.

———. *Women and Literate Medicine in Medieval Europe: Trota and the "Trotula."* Cambridge: Cambridge University Press, Forthcoming.

Green, Richard. *Poets and Princepleasers: Literature and the English Court in the Late Middle Ages.* Toronto: University of Toronto Press, 1980.

Greilsammer, Myriam. *L'Envers du tableau: Mariage et maternité en Flandre médiévale.* Paris: Colin, 1990.

Greimas, A. J. *Dictionnaire de l'ancien français.* Paris: Larousse, 1968.

Griffiths, Jeremy, and Derek Pearsall, eds. *Book Production and Publishing in Britain, 1375–1475.* Cambridge: Cambridge University Press, 1989.

Griffiths, Ralph A. *The Reign of King Henry VI.* Berkeley: University of California Press, 1981.

Grosz, Elizabeth. "Sexual Difference and the Problem of Essentialism." In *The Essential Difference,* ed. Naomi Schor and Elizabeth Weed, 82–97. Bloomington: Indiana University Press, 1994.

Hanson, Ann Ellis, and Monica H. Green. "Soranus of Ephesus: *Methodicorum princeps.*" In *Aufstieg und Niedergang der römischen Welt,* ed. Wolfgang Haase and Hildegard Temporini, pt. 2, vol. 37, no. 2, 968–1075. Berlin: Walter de Gruyter, 1994.

Haraway, Donna J. "The Actors Are Cyborgs, Nature Is Coyote, and the Geography Is Elsewhere: Postscript to Cyborgs at Large." In *Technoculture,* ed. Constance Penley and Andrew Ross, 21–26. Minneapolis: University of Minnesota Press, 1991.

———. "The Promises of Monsters: A Regenerative Politics for Inappropriate/d Others." In *Cultural Studies,* ed. Lawrence Grossberg, Cary Nelson, and Paula A. Treichler. 295–337. London: Routledge, 1992.

———. *Simians, Cyborgs, and Women: The Reinvention of Nature.* New York: Routledge, 1991.

Harris, Kate. "Patrons, Buyers, and Owners: The Evidence for Ownership and the Role of Book Owners in Book Production and the Book Trade." In Griffiths and Pearsall, 163–99.

Haussherr, Reiner. *Bible moralisée. Faks[imile]-Ausg[abe] im Originalformat des Codex Vindobonesis 2554 der Österr[eichischen] Nationalbibliothek.* Graz: Akademische Druck- und Verlanganstalt, 1973.

Hedeman, Anne D. *The Royal Image: Illustrations of the Grandes Chroniques de France, 1274–1422.* Berkeley: University of California Press, 1991.

———. "Valois Legitimacy: Editorial Changes in Charles V's *Grandes chroniques de France.*" *Art Bulletin* 66 (1984): 97–122.

Hicks, Eric. Introduction to *Le Débat sur le "Roman de la Rose,"* ed. Eric Hicks. Bibliothèque du XVe siècle 43. Paris: Champion, 1977.

———. "Une Femme dans le monde: Christine de Pizan et l'écriture de la politique." In *L'Hostellerie de pensée: Etudes sur l'art littéraire au Moyen Age offertes à Daniel Poirion par ses anciens élèves,* ed. Eric Hicks and Manuela Python, 223–43. Paris: Presses de l'Université de Paris-Sorbonne, 1995.

Hindman, Sandra L. *Christine de Pizan's "Epistre Othéa": Painting and Politics at the Court of Charles VI.* Toronto: Pontifical Institute of Mediaeval Studies, 1986.

———. "The Composition of the Manuscript of Christine de Pizan's Collected Works in the British Library: A Reassessment." *British Library Journal* 9, no. 2 (1983): 93–123.

———. "The Iconography of Queen Isabeau de Bavière (1410–1415): An Essay in Method." *Gazette des beaux arts,* série 6, 102 (1983): 102–10.

———. "With Ink and Mortar: Christine de Pizan's *Cité des Dames* (An Art Essay)." *Feminist Studies* 10 (1984): 457–77.

Hindman, Sandra L., and Stephen Perkinson. "Insurgent Voices: Illuminated Versions of Christine de Pizan's 'Le Livre du Duc des vrais amans.'" In Zimmermann and De Rentiis, 221–31.

Hinds, Allen B., ed. *Calendar of State Papers and Manuscipts Existing in the Archives and Collections of Milan, 1385–1618.* Vol 1. London: HMSO, 1912.

Hirsch, Rudolf. "Title Pages in French Incunables, 1486–1500." *Gutenberg Jahrbuch* 53 (1978): 63–66.

Holzknecht, Karl Julius. *Literary Patronage in the Middle Ages.* Ph. diss., University of Pennsylvania, Philadelphia, 1923; Menasha, Wis.: Collegiate Press, 1923.

hooks, bell. *Teaching to Transgress: Education and the Practice of Freedom.* New York: Routledge, 1994.

Huffer, Lynne. "Christine de Pisan: Speaking Like a Woman/Speaking Like a Man." In *New Images of Medieval Women: Essays Towards a Cultural Anthropology,* ed. Edelgard E. Du Bruck, 61–72. Lewiston, N.Y.: Mellen, 1989.

Huizinga, Johan. *The Autumn of the Middle Ages.* Trans. Rodney J. Payton and Ulrich Mammitzsch. Chicago: University of Chicago Press, 1996.

———. *Herfsttij der middeleeuwen: Studie over levens- en gedachtenvormen der veertiende en vijftiende eeuw in Frankrijk en de Nederlanden.* Haarlem: H. D. Tjeenk Willink, 1928.

Hults, Linda. "Dürer's *Lucretia*: Speaking the Silence of Women." *Signs* 16 (1990): 205–37.

Humphreys, K. W., ed. *The Friars' Libraries.* Corpus of British Medieval Library Catalogues. London: British Library in association with the British Academy, 1990.

Huot, Sylvia. *From Song to Book: The Poetics of Writing in Old French Lyric and Lyrical Narrative Poetry.* Ithaca, N.Y.: Cornell University Press, 1987.

———. *The "Romance of the Rose" and Its Medieval Readers: Interpretation, Reception, Manuscript Transmission.* Cambridge: Cambridge University Press, 1993.

———. "Seduction and Sublimation: Christine de Pizan, Jean de Meun, and Dante." *Romance Notes* 25 (1985): 361–73.

Ignatius, M. A. "Christine de Pizan's *Epistre Othea:* An Experiment in Literary Form." *Medievalia et Humanistica* 9 (1979): 127–42.

Irigaray, Luce. *Speculum of the Other Woman.* Trans. Gillian Gill. Ithaca, N.Y.: Cornell University Press, 1985.

Jacquart, Danielle. *Supplément to Ernest Wickersheimer, Dictionnaire biographique des médecins en France au Moyen Age.* Geneva: Droz, 1979.

Jacquart, Danielle, and Claude Thomasset. *Sexualité et savoir médical au moyen âge.* Paris, 1985. Translated by Matthew Adamson under the title *Sexuality and Medicine in the Middle Ages* (Cambridge: Polity, 1988).

Jardine, Lisa. "Isotta Nogarola: Women Humanists: Education for What?" In *From Humanism to the Humanities: Education and the Liberal Arts in Fifteenth- and Sixteenth-Century Europe,* ed. Anthony Grafton and Lisa Jardine, 29–57. Cambridge: Harvard University Press, 1986.

Jordan, Constance. "Boccaccio's In-Famous Women: Gender and Civic Virtue in the *De mulieribus claris.*" In Levin and Watson, 25–47.

Kaempf-Dimitriadou, Sophia. *Die Leibe der Götter in der Attischen Kunst des 5. Jahrhunderts v. Chr.* Beiheft zur Halbjahresschrift Antike Kunst 11. Bern: Francke, 1979.

Kauffmann, C. M. *The Baths of Pozzuoli: A Study of the Medieval Illuminations of Peter of Eboli's Poem.* Oxford: Cassirer, 1959.

Kay, Sarah, and Miri Rubin. *Framing Medieval Bodies.* Manchester: Manchester University Press, 1994.

Kellogg, Judith. "Christine de Pizan as Chivalric Mythographer: *L'Epistre Othea.*" In *The Mythographic Art: Classical Fable and the Rise of the Vernacular in Early France and England,* ed. Jane Chance, 100–24. Gainesville: University of Florida Press, 1990.

———. "*Le Livre de la Cité des Dames*: Feminist Myth and Community." *Essays in Arts and Sciences* 18 (1989): 1–15.

Kelly, F. Douglas. "Reflections on the Role of Christine de Pisan as a Feminist Writer." *Sub-Stance* 2 (1972): 63–71.

Kelly, Joan. "Early Feminist Theory and the *Querelle des Femmes,* 1400–1789." *Signs* 8 (1982): 4–28.

———. *Women, History, and Theory.* Chicago: University of Chicago Press, 1984.

Kennedy, Angus J. *Christine de Pizan: A Bibliographical Guide.* London: Grant, 1984.

———. *Christine de Pizan: A Bibliographical Guide, Supplement 1.* London: Grant, 1994.

Ker, Neil R. *Medieval Manuscripts in British Libraries.* 4 vols. Oxford: Clarendon, 1969–92.

Keuls, Eva. *The Reign of the Phallus: Sexual Politics in Ancient Athens.* New York: Harper, 1985.

King, Margaret L. "Book-lined Cells: Women and Humanism in the Early Italian Renaissance." In *Beyond Their Sex: Learned Women of the European Past,* ed. Patricia Labalme. New York: New York University Press, 1980.

Kirshner, Julius, and Suzanne Wemple, eds. *Women in the Medieval World: Essays in Honor of John H. Mundy.* Oxford: Blackwell, 1985.

Kittay, Jeffrey, and Wlad Godzich. *The Emergence of Prose: An Essay in Prosaics.* Minneapolis: University of Minnesota Press, 1987.

Koonce, B. G. "Satan the Fowler." *Medievalia* 21 (1959): 176–84.

Krueger, Roberta. "'Chascune selon son estat': Women's Education and Social Class in the Conduct Books of Christine de Pizan and Anne de France." *Papers on French Seventeenth Century Literature* 24 (1997): 19–34.

———. *Women Readers and the Ideology of Gender in Old French Verse Romance.* Cambridge Studies in French 43. Cambridge: Cambridge University Press, 1993.

Krynen, Jacques. *Idéal du prince et pouvoir royal en France à la fin du Moyen Age (1380–1440): Etude de la littérature politique du temps.* Paris: Picard, 1981.

La Curne de Sainte-Palaye, Jean Baptiste. *Dictionnaire historique de l'ancien langage françois.* Hildesheim: Olms, 1972.

Laennec, Christine Moneera. "Prophétie, interprétation et écriture dans *L'Avision-Christine.*" In Dulac and Ribémont, 131–38.

Laidlaw, James. "Christine de Pizan: An Author's Progress." *Modern Language Review* 78 (1983): 532–50.

———. "Christine de Pizan: A Publisher's Progress." *Modern Language Review* 82 (1987): 35–67.

———. "Christine de Pizan, the Earl of Salisbury, and Henry IV." *French Studies* 36 (1982): 129–43.

———. "From Scriptorium to Database and Back Again." *Journal of the Institute of Romance Studies* 1 (1992): 59–67.

Laigle, Mathilde. *Le Livre des Trois Vertus de Christine de Pisan et son milieu historique et littéraire*. Paris: Champion, 1912.

Laird, Judith. "Christine de Pizan's 'The Book of The Deeds and Good Character of King Charles V, the Wise.'" Ph.D. diss., University of Colorado, 1996.

Landow, George P. *Hypertext: The Convergence of Contemporary Critical Theory and Technology*. Baltimore, Md.: Johns Hopkins University Press, 1992.

Lecourt, Marcel. "Une Source d'Antoine de la Sale: Simon de Hesdin." *Romania* 76 (1955): 39–83.

Lee, Patricia-Ann. "Reflections of Power: Margaret of Anjou and the Dark Side of Queenship." *Renaissance Quarterly* 39 (1986): 183–217.

Le Goff, Jacques. *Les Intellectuels au Moyen Age*. Paris: Seuil, 1972.

Lehmann, Paul. "Mitteilungen aus Handschriften VII." *Sitzungsberichte der Bayerischen Akademie der Wissenschaften, Philosophisch-historische Abteilung* 10 (1942): 3–28.

Lejeune, Philippe. *Le Pacte autobiographique*. Paris: Seuil, 1975.

Lemay, Helen Rodnite. Introduction to *Women's Secrets: A Translation of Pseudo-Albertus Magnus' De secretis mulierum with Commentaries*, trans. Helen Rodnite Lemay, 1–58. Albany: State University of New York Press, 1992.

Lengenfelder, Helga, ed. *Christine de Pizan: L'Epistre d'Othéa, Farbmikrofiche-Edition der Handschrift Erlangen-Nürnberg, Universitätsbibliothek, Ms. 2361*. Intro. Helga Lengenfelder. Munich: Ed. Lengenfelder, 1996.

Levin, Carole, and Jeanie Watson, eds. *Ambiguous Realities: Women in the Middle Ages and Renaissance*. Detroit, Mich.: Wayne State University Press, 1987.

Lomperis, Linda, and Sarah Stanbury, eds. *Feminist Approaches to the Body in Medieval Literature*. Philadelphia: University of Pennsylvania Press, 1993.

Lorcin, Marie-Thérèse. "Les Echos de la mode dans *Le Livre des trois Vertus* de Christine de Pizan." *Razo* 7 (1987): 89–94.

———. "Le *Livre des trois Vertus* et le *Sermo ad Status*." In Dulac and Ribémont, 139–149.

———. "Pouvoirs et contre-pouvoirs dans le *Livre des trois vertus*." *Revue des Langues Romanes* 92, no. 2 (1988): 359–80.

Lord, Carla. "Three Manuscripts of the *Ovide moralisé*." *Art Bulletin* 57 (1975): 161–75.

Lucie-Smith, Edward. *Sexuality in Western Art*. London: Thames, 1991.

Lusignan, Serges. "Autorité et notoriété: Langue française et savoir au XIVe siècle." In *Florilegium historiographiae linguisticae: Etudes d'historiographie de la linguistique et de grammaire comparée à la mémoire de Maurice Leroy*, 185–202. Bibliothèque des cahiers de l'Institut de linguistique de Louvain 75. Louvain-la-Neuve: Peeters, 1994.

———. "Le Français et le latin aux XIIIe-XIVe siècles: Pratiques des langues et pensée linguistique." *Annales ESC* 4 (1987): 955–67.

———. "Le Latin était la langue maternelle des Romains: La Fortune d'un argument à la fin du Moyen Age." In *Préludes à la Renaissance*, 265–303. Paris: CNRS, 1992.

———. "Nicole Oresme, traducteur, et la pensée de la langue française savante." In *Nicolas Oresme: Tradition et innovation chez un intellectuel du XIVe siècle*, ed. P. Souffrin and A. Ph. Segonds, 93–104. Paris: Belles Lettres, n.d.

———. *Parler vulgairement*. Paris: Vrin; Montreal: Presses de l'Université de Montréal, 1987.

———. "La Topique de la *translatio studii* et les translations françaises des textes savants au XIVe siècle." In *Traduction et traducteurs au Moyen Age: Colloque international du CNRS*, 303–15. Paris: CNRS, 1989.

Lyotard, Jean-François. *The Postmodern Condition: A Report on Knowledge*. Trans. Geoff Bennington and Brian Massumi. Minneapolis: University of Minnesota Press, 1984.

Macfarlane, John. *Antoine Vérard*. Geneva: Slatkine, 1971.

Macherel, Claude. "Don et réciprocité en Europe." *Archives Européennes de Sociologie* 24, no. 1 (1983): 151–66.

MacKinnon, Catharine. *Feminism Unmodified*. Cambridge: Harvard University Press, 1987.

———. *Toward a Feminist Theory of the State*. Cambridge: Harvard University Press, 1989.

Mahoney, Dhira. "Middle English Regenderings of Christine de Pizan." In *The Medieval Opus: Imitation, Rewriting in the French Tradition*, ed. Douglas Kelly, 405–27. Amsterdam-Atlanta: Rodopi B. V., 1996.

Mandach, André de. "L'Anthologie chevaleresque de Marguerite d'Anjou (B. M. Royal 15 E VI) et les officines Saint-Augustin de Canterbury, Jean Wauquelin de Mons, et David Aubert de Hesdin." *VIe Congrès International de la Société Rencesvals: Actes*, ed. Jean Subrenat, 317–50. Aix-en-Provence: Université de Provence, Imprimerie du Centre d'Aix, 1974.

———. "A Royal Wedding-Present in the Making: Talbot's Chivalric Anthology (Royal E VI) for Queen Margaret of Anjou and the 'Laval-Middleton' Anthology of Nottingham." *Nottingham Medieval Studies* 18 (1974): 56–76.

Marcus, Sharon. "Fighting Bodies, Fighting Words: A Theory and Politics of Rape Prevention." In *Feminists Theorize the Political*, ed. Judith Butler and Joan W. Scott, 385–403. New York: Routledge, 1992.

Margolis, Nadia. "Christine de Pizan and the Jews: Political and Poetic Implications." In Brabant, 53–73.

———. "Christine de Pizan: The Poetess as Historian." *Journal of the History of Ideas* 47 (1986): 361–75.

Martin, Henry. *Les Miniaturistes françaises du XIIIe au XVe siècle*. 2nd ed. Paris, Brussels: van Oest, 1924.

———. *Le Térence des ducs*. Paris: Plon, 1907.

Matsuda, Mari. "Public Response to Racist Speech: Considering the Victim's Story." *Michigan Law Review* 87 (1989): 2320–81.

Maurer, Armand A. "Some Aspects of Fourteenth-Century Philosophy." *Medievalia et Humanistica*, n.s., 7 (1976): 175–88.

Mauss, Marcel. *The Gift: Forms and Functions of Exchange in Archaic Societies*. Trans. Ian Cunnison. London: Cohen, 1954.

McCash, June Hall. "The Cultural Patronage of Medieval Women: An Overview." In *The Cultural Patronage of Medieval Women*, ed. June Hall McCash. Athens: University of Georgia Press, 1996.

McGinn, Bernard. "The Sibylline Tradition in the Middle Ages." In Kirshner and Wemple, 7–35.

McKenna, J. W. "Henry VI of England and the Dual Monarchy: Aspects of Royal Political Propaganda, 1422–1432." *Journal of the Warburg and Courtauld Institutes* 28 (1965): 145–62.

McLeod, Glenda K., ed. *The Reception of Christine de Pisan from the Fifteenth through the Nineteenth Centuries: Visitors to the City*. Lewiston, N.Y.: Mellen, 1991.

McRae, Laura Kathryn. "Interpretation and the Arts of Reading and Writing in Christine de Pisan's *Livre de la Cité des Dames*." *Romanic Review* 82 (1991): 412–33.

Meale, Carol M. "Patrons, Buyers and Owners: Book Production and Social State." In Griffiths and Pearsall, 201–38.

Meiss, Millard. *French Painting in the Time of Jean of Berry. The Boucicaut Master*. London: Phaidon, 1968.

———. *French Painting in the Time of Jean of Berry. The Limbourgs and Their Contemporaries*. 2 vols. New York: Braziller, 1974.

Meiss, Millard, and Elizabeth H. Beatson. *The Belles Heures of Jean, Duke of Berry*. New York: Braziller, 1974.

Mellinkoff, Ruth. *Outcasts: Signs of Otherness in Northern European Art of the Late Middle Ages*. 2 vols. Berkeley: University of California Press, 1993.

Meyer, P. "Les Anciens traducteurs français de Végèce et en particulier Jean de Vignai." *Romania* 25 (1896): 401–23.

Miles, Margaret R. *Carnal Knowing: Female Nakedness and Religious Meaning in the Christian West*. Boston: Beacon, 1989.

271

Miller, J. Hillis. *Illustration*. Cambridge: Harvard University Press, 1992.

Minow, Martha. "The Supreme Court Foreword: Justice Engendered." *Harvard Law Review* 101 (1987): 10–95.

Mombello, Gianni. "Quelques Aspects de la pensée politique de Christine de Pizan d'après ses oeuvres publiées." In *Culture et politique en France à l'époque de l'humanisme et de la Renaissance*, ed. Franco Simone, 43–153. Turin: Accademia delle Scienze, 1974.

———. *La Tradizione manoscritta dell' "Epistre Othea" di Christine de Pizan: Prolegomeni all'edizione del testo*. Turin: Accademia delle Scienze, 1967.

Monfrin, Jacques. "Humanisme et traductions au Moyen Age." *Journal des Savants*, July–Sept. 1963, 161–90.

———. "Les Traducteurs et leur public en France au Moyen Age." *Journal des Savants*, Jan.–March 1964, 5–20.

Moran, Richard, and Peter d'Errico. "An Impartial Jury or an Ignorant One? North Trial Shows Danger of Panel with No Peer." *Boston Globe*, Feb. 12, 1989, A-18.

Morel, Octave. *La Grande Chancellerie royale et l'expédition des lettres royaux de l'avènement de Philippe de Valois à la fin du XIVe siècle (1328–1400)*. Mémoires et documents publiés par la Société de l'Ecole des Chartes 3. Paris: Picard, 1900.

Moss, Ann. *Ovid in Renaissance France*. London: Warburg Institute, 1982.

Moulinier, Laurence. "Fragments inédits de la *Physica*: Contribution à l'étude de la transmission des manuscrits scientifiques de Hildegarde de Bingen." *Mélanges de l'École Française de Rome. Moyen Age* 105 (1993): 629–50.

———. *Le Manuscrit perdu à Strasbourg: Enquête sur l'oeuvre scientifique de Hildegarde*. Paris: Publications de la Sorbonne; Saint-Denis: Presses Universitaires de Vincennes, 1995.

Nauert, Charles G., Jr. *Agrippa and the Crisis of Renaissance Thought*. Urbana: University of Illinois Press, 1965.

Newman, Barbara. "Authority, Authenticity, and the Repression of Heloise." *Journal of Medieval and Renaissance Studies* 22 (1992): 121–57.

Nicholas, David. *The Domestic Life of a Medieval City: Women, Children, and the Family in Fourteenth-Century Ghent*. Lincoln: University of Nebraska Press, 1985.

Nichols, Stephen G. "Prophetic Discourse: St. Augustine to Christine de Pizan." In *The Bible in the Middle Ages: Its Influence on Literature and Art*, ed. Bernard S. Levy, 51–76. Binghamton, N.Y.: MRTS, 1992.

Noakes, Susan. *Timely Reading: Between Exegesis and Interpretation*. Ithaca, N.Y.: Cornell University Press, 1988.

Nunberg, Geoffrey, ed. *The Future of the Book*. Berkeley: University of California Press, 1996.

O'Donnell, James J. "The Pragmatics of the New: Trithemius, McLuhan, Cassiodorus." In Nunberg, 32–62.

Ornato, Monique and Nicole Pons, eds. *Pratiques de la culture écrite en France au XVe siècle: Actes du Colloque international du CNRS, Paris, 16–18 mai 1992, organisé en l'honneur de Gilbert Ouy par l'unité de recherche "Culture écrite du Moyen Age tardif."* FIDEM, Textes et études du Moyen Age 2. Louvain-la-Neuve: Turnhout, 1995.

Otis, Leah Lydia. *Prostitution in Medieval Society: The History of an Urban Institution in Languedoc*. Chicago: University of Chicago Press, 1985.

Ouy, Gilbert. "Honoré Bouvet (appelé à tort Bonet) prieur de Selonnet." *Romania* 85 (1959): 255–59.

———. "Paris, l'un des principaux foyers de l'humanisme en Europe au début du XVe siècle." *Bulletin de la Société de l'Histoire de Paris et de l'Ile de France* 94/95 (1967–68 [1970]): 71–98.

Ouy, Gilbert, and Christine Reno. "Identification des autographes de Christine de Pizan." *Scriptorium* 34 (1980): 221–38.

Ozment, Steven E. "The University and the Church: Patterns of Reform in Jean Gerson." *Medievalia et Humanistica*, n.s., 1 (1970): 111–26.

Pächt, Otto, and Dagmar Thoss. *Die illuminierten Handschriften des Österreichischen Nationalbibliothek: Französische Schule II.* Vienna: Österreichischen Akademie der Wissenschaften, 1977.

Pannier, L. "Les Joyaux du duc de Guyenne: Recherches sur les goûts artistiques et la vie privée du dauphin Louis, fils de Charles VI." *Revue archéologique* 26 (1873): 209–25.

Paré, Gérard. *Les Idées et les lettres au XIIIe Siècle: Le* Roman de la Rose. Montreal: Bibliothèque de Philosophie, 1947.

Paris, Gaston. "Rapport à l'Académie des Inscriptions et Belles Lettres." *Romania* 9 (1880): 122–24.

Parker, Patricia. *Literary Fat Ladies: Rhetoric, Gender, Property.* London: Methuen, 1987.

Parussa, Gabriella. "Le Concept d'intertextualité comme hypothèse interprétative d'une oeuvre: L'exemple de l'*Epistre Othea* de Christine de Pizan." *Studi francesi* 111 (1993): 471–93.

Pascoe, Louis B. "Jean Gerson: The 'Ecclesia Primitiva' and Reform." *Traditio* 30 (1974): 379–409.

Picherit, Jean-Louis. *La Métaphore pathologique et thérapeutique à la fin du Moyen Age. Zeitshrift für romanische Philologie,* supplement 260. Tübingen: Niemeyer, 1994.

———. "Les Références pathologiques et thérapeutiques dans l'oeuvre de Christine de Pizan." In Dulac and Ribémont, 233–44.

Pinet, Marie-Josèphe. *Christine de Pisan, 1364–1430: Etude Biographique et Littéraire.* Paris: Champion, 1927.

———. *La Montaigne de Contemplation, la Mendicité spirituelle de Jehan Gerson: Etude de deux opuscules français de Gerson sur la prière.* Lyon: Bosc et Riou, 1927.

Pistono, Stephen P. "Rape in Medieval Europe." *Atlantis* 14 (1989): 36–43.

Plummer, John. *The Last Flowering: French Painting in Manuscripts, 1420–1530.* New York: Pierpont Morgan Library, 1982.

Poirion, Daniel. "L'Epanouissement d'un style: Le Gothique littéraire à la fin du Moyen Age." In Biermann and Tillman-Bartylla, 29–44.

———. *Littérature française: Le Moyen Age 1300–1480.* Paris: Arthaud, 1971.

———. *Le Poète et le prince: L'évolution du lyrisme courtois de Guillaume de Machaut à Charles d'Orléans.* Paris: Presses Universitaires de France, 1965.

Pollard, A. J. *John Talbot and the War in France, 1427–1453.* London: Royal Historical Society, 1983.

Porter, Roy. "Rape—Does It Have a Historical Meaning?" In Tomaselli and Porter, 216–36.

Poulain de la Barre, François. *De l'égalite des deux sexes.* Paris: Fayard, 1984.

Prevenier, Walter. "Violence against Women in a Medieval Metropolis: Paris around 1400." In *Law, Custom, and the Social Fabric in Medieval Europe: Essays in Honor of Bryce Lyon,* ed. Bernard S. Bachrach and David Nicholas, 263–84. Kalamazoo, Mich.: Medieval Institute, 1990.

Quilligan, Maureen. *The Allegory of Female Authority: Christine de Pizan's Cité des Dames.* Ithaca, N.Y.: Cornell University Press, 1991.

Rabel, Claudia. "Artiste et clientèle à la fin du Moyen Age: Les manuscrits profanes du Maître de l'échevinage de Rouen." *Revue de l'Art* 84 (1989): 48–60.

Rasmussen, Jens. *La Prose narrative française du XVe siècle: Etude esthétique et stylistique.* Copenhagen: Munksgaard, 1958.

Régnier-Bohler, Danielle. "Imagining the Self." Trans. Arthur Goldhammer. In *Revelations of the Medieval World,* vol. 2 of *A History of Private Life,* ed. Georges Duby, 311–93. Cambridge: Belknap Press of Harvard University Press, 1988.

Reno, Christine M. "Christine de Pizan: 'At Best a Contradictory Figure'?" In Brabant, 171–191.

———. "Feminist Aspects of Christine de Pizan's 'Epistre d'Othea a Hector.'" *Studi Francesi* 24 (1980): 271–76.

———. "The Preface to the *Avision-Christine* in ex-Phillipps 128." In Richards et al., *Reinterpreting,* 207–27.

Ribémont, Bernard. "Christine de Pizan et l'encyclopédisme scientifique." In Zimmermann and De Rentiis, 174–85.

Richards, Earl Jeffrey. "Christine de Pizan and Dante: A Reexamination." *Archiv für das Studium der neueren Sprachen und Literaturen* 222/137–1 (1985): 100–11.

———. "Christine de Pizan and the Question of Feminist Rhetoric." *Teaching Language through Literature* 22, no. 2 (1983): 15–24.

———. "In Search of a Feminist Patrology: Christine de Pizan and 'les glorieux dotteurs.'" In Dulac and Ribémont, 281–95.

———. Introduction to *The Book of the City of Ladies,* by Christine de Pizan, trans. Richards, xiii–li. New York: Persea, 1982.

———. "The Medieval 'femme auteur' as a Provocation to Literary History: Eighteenth-Century Readers of Christine de Pizan." In McLeod, 101–50.

———. "Rejecting Essentialism and Gendered Writing: The Case of Christine de Pizan." In *Gender and Text in the Later Middle Ages,* ed. Jane Chance, 96–131. Gainesville: University of Florida Press, 1996.

———. "'Seulette a part'—The 'Little Woman on the Sidelines' Takes Up Her Pen: The Letters of Christine de Pizan." In *Dear Sister: Medieval Women and the Epistolary Genre,* ed. Karen Cherewatuk and Ulrike Wiethaus, 139–70. Philadelphia: University of Pennsylvania Press, 1993.

Richards, Earl Jeffrey, Joan Williamson, Nadia Margolis, and Christine Reno, eds. *Reinterpreting Christine de Pizan.* Athens: University of Georgia Press, 1992.

Richardson, Lula. *The Forerunners of Feminism in French Literature of the Renaissance: Part 1. From Christine de Pisan to Marie de Gournay.* Baltimore, Md.: Johns Hopkins University Press, 1929.

Riddy, Felicity. "Mother Knows Best: Reading Social Change in a Courtesy Text." *Speculum* 71 (1996): 66–86.

Rigaud, Rose. *Les Idées féministes de Christine de Pisan.* Neuchâtel: Attinger, 1911.

Robertson, D. W. *A Preface to Chaucer.* Princeton, N.J.: Princeton University Press, 1962.

Rooks, John. "*The Boke of the Cyte of Ladyes* and Its Sixteenth-Century Readership." In McLeod, 83–100.

Rorty, Richard. "Feminism and Pragmatism." *Michigan Quarterly Review* 30 (1991): 230–50.

Ross, D. J. A. "Nectanebus in His Palace: A Problem of Alexander Iconography." *Journal of the Warburg and Courtauld Institute* 15 (1952): 67–87.

Rowe, B. J. H. "King Henry VI's Claim to France in Picture and Poem." *Library,* 4th ser., 13 (1933): 77–88.

Roy, Maurice. Introduction to *Oeuvres poétiques de Christine de Pisan,* 2:i–xxi. Paris, 1886–96. Reprint, New York: Johnson Reprint, 1965.

Ruggiero, Guido. *The Boundaries of Eros: Sex, Crime, and Sexuality in Renaissance Venice.* Oxford: Oxford University Press, 1985.

Salmon, Fernando, and Monserrat Cabré i Pairet. "Fascinating Women: The Evil Eye in Medical Scholasticism." In *Medicine from the Black Death to the Great Pox,* ed. R. French, J. Arrizabalaga, A. Cunningham, and L. Garcia Ballester. Aldershot: Scolar Press, forthcoming.

Sandoval, Chela. "New Sciences: Cyborg Feminism and the Methodology of the Oppressed." *The Cyborg Handbook,* ed. Chris Hables Gray, Heidi J. Figueroa-Sarriera, and Steven Mentor, 407–21. London: Routledge, 1995.

Schaefer, Lucie. "Die Illustrationen zu den Handschriften der Christine de Pisan." *Marburger Jahrbuch für Kunstwissenschaft* 10 (1938): 119–209.

Schibanoff, Susan. "Taking the Gold Out of Egypt: The Art of Reading as a Woman." In *Gender and Reading: Essays on Readers, Texts, and Contexts,* ed. Elizabeth A. Flynn and Patrocinio P. Schweickart, 83–106. Baltimore, Md.: Johns Hopkins University Press, 1986.

Schleissner, Margaret R. "A Fifteenth-Century Physician's Attitude Toward Sexuality: Dr. Johann Hartlieb's *Secreta mulierum* Translation." In *Sex in the Middle Ages,* ed. Joyce A. Salisbury, 110–25. New York: Garland, 1991.

————. "Pseudo-Albertus Magnus: *Secreta mulierum cum commento,* Deutsch: Critical text and commentary." Ph.D. diss., Princeton University, 1987.

————. "'Secreta mulierum.'" In *Die deutschen Literatur des Mittelalters: Verfasser-lexikon,* ed. Kurt Ruh, 2nd ed., vol 8., 986–93. Berlin: de Gruyter, 1978.

Schofield, Margaret E. Introduction to *Stephen Scrope: The Dicts and Sayings of the Philoso-phers,* 1–48. Philadelphia: University of Pennsylvania Press, 1936.

Schor, Naomi. "French Feminism Is a Universalism." In *Bad Objects: Essays Popular and Unpopular,* 3–27. Durham: Duke University Press, 1995.

Schulenburg, Jane Tibbetts. "Clio's European Daughters: Myopic Modes of Perception." In *The Prism of Sex: Essays in the Sociology of Knowledge,* ed. Julia Sherman and Evelyn Beck, 33–53. Madison: University of Wisconsin Press, 1974.

————. "The Heroics of Virginity: Brides of Christ and Sacrificial Mutilation." In *Women in the Middle Ages and the Renaissance: Literary and Historical Perspectives,* ed. Mary Beth Rose, 29–72. Syracuse: Syracuse University Press, 1986.

Scott, Joan Wallach. "Experience." In *Feminists Theorize the Political,* ed. Judith Butler and Joan Wallach Scott. New York: Routledge, 1992.

————. Introduction to *Feminism and History,* 1–13. Oxford: Oxford University Press, 1996.

Scott, Margaret. *The History of Dress Series: Late Gothic Europe, 1400–1500.* London: Mills, 1980.

Sherman, Claire Richter. *Imaging Aristotle: Verbal and Visual Representations in Four-teenth-Century France.* Berkeley: University of California Press, 1995.

Simone, Raffaele "The Body of the Text." In Nunberg, 239–51.

Simons, Patricia. "Lesbian (In)Visibility in Italian Renaissance Culture: Diana and Other Cases of *donna con donna.*" *Journal of Homosexuality* 27, no. 1–2 (1994): 81–122.

Skemp, Mary L. "Autobiography as Authority in *Lavision-Christine.*" *Le Moyen Français* 35/36 (1994–95): 17–31.

Snyder, Lee Daniel. "Gerson's Vernacular Advice on Prayer." *Fifteenth-Century Studies* 10 (1984): 161–74.

Solente, Suzanne. "Deux chapitres de l'influence littéraire de Christine de Pisan." *Biblio-thèque de l'Ecole des Chartes* 94 (1933): 27–45.

————. Introduction to *Le Livre des fais et bonnes meurs du sage roy Charles V,* by Chris-tine de Pizan, 1:1–103. Paris: Champion, 1936–1940.

Solterer, Helen. *The Master and Minerva: Disputing Women in French Medieval Culture.* Berkeley: University of California Press, 1995.

Sommers, Paula. "Marguerite de Navarre as Reader of Christine de Pizan." In McLeod, 71–82.

Spiegel, Gabrielle. *Romancing the Past: The Rise of Vernacular Prose Historiography in the Thirteenth Century.* Berkeley: University of California Press, 1993.

Stechow, Wolfgang. *Apollo und Daphne.* Studien den Bibliothek Warburg 23. Leipzig: Teub-ner; London: Warburg Institute, 1932.

Sterling, Charles. *La Peinture médiévale à Paris: 1300–1500.* Paris: Bibliothèque des Arts, 1987.

Tarnowski, Andrea. "Autobiography and Advice in the *Livre des Trois Vertus.*" In Dulac and Ribémont, 151–60.

————. "Maternity and Paternity in 'La Mutacion de Fortune.'" In Zimmermann and De Rentiis, 116–26.

Tavoni, Mirko. "The Fifteenth-Century Controversy on the Language Spoken by the An-cient Romans." In *The History of Linguistics in Italy,* ed. Paolo Ramat, Hans-J. Niederehe, and Konrad Koerner, 23–50. Amsterdam Studies in the Theory and History of Linguis-tic Science, ser. 3, vol. 33. Philadelphia: John Benjamins, 1986.

Tchémerzine, Avenir. *Bibliographie d'éditions originales et rares des auteurs français des XVe, XVIe, XVIIe, et XVIIIe siècles.* Vol. 5. Paris, 1933. Reprint, Paris: Hermann, 1977.

Teague, Frances. "Christine de Pizan's *Book of War.*" In McLeod, 25–41.

Tesnière, Marie-Hélène, ed. *Creating French Culture: Treasures from the Bibliothèque Nationale de France.* New Haven, Conn.: Yale University Press, 1995.

Thomas, Antoine. *Jean Gerson et l'education des dauphins de France.* Paris: Droz, 1930.

Thomasset, Claude. *Une Vision du monde à la fin du XIIIe siècle: Commentaire du Dialogue de* Placides et Timéo. Geneva: Droz, 1982.

Thomassy, Raymond. *Essai sur les écrits politiques de Christine de Pisan.* Paris: Debécourt, 1838.

Thorndike, Lynn. "Further Consideration of the *Experimenta, Speculum astronomiae,* and *De secretis mulierum* Ascribed to Albertus Magnus." *Speculum* 30 (1955): 413–43.

Timmermans, Linda. *L'Accès des femmes à la culture (1598–1715): Un débat d'idées de Saint François de Sales à la Marquise de Lambert.* Paris: Champion, 1993.

Tomaselli, Sylvana, and Roy Porter, eds. *Rape: An Historical and Cultural Enquiry.* Oxford: Blackwell, 1989.

Tovar, Claude de. "Les Versions françaises de la *Chirurgia parva* de Lanfranc de Milan. Etude de la tradition manuscrite." *Revue d'Histoire de Textes* 12–13 (1982–83): 195–262.

Tranøy, Knut. "Thomas Aquinas." In *A Critical History of Western Philosophy,* ed. D. J. O'Connor, 98–123. New York: Macmillan, 1964.

Trinh T. Minh-ha. *Woman, Native, Other: Writing Postcoloniality and Feminism.* Bloomington: Indiana University Press, 1989.

Tuve, Rosemond. *Allegorical Imagery: Some Mediaeval Books and Their Posterity.* Princeton: Princeton University Press, 1977.

Vickers, Nancy. "Diana Described: Scattered Woman and Scattered Rhyme." *Critical Inquiry* 8 (1981): 265–79.

Viriville, Valet de. "La Bibliothèque d'Isabeau de Bavière." *Bulletin du Bibliophile* 14 (1858): 663–87.

Ward, H. L. D. *Catalogue of Romances in the Department of Manuscripts in the British Museum.* 3 vols. London: British Museum, 1883–1910.

Wareham, T. E. "Christine de Pisan's *Livre des Faits d'Armes et de Chevalerie* and Its Fate in the Sixteenth Century." In *Seconda Miscellanea di Studi e Ricerche sul Quattrocento Francese,* ed. Franco Simone, Jonathan Beck, and Gianni Mombello, 137–42. Chambéry: Centre d'Etudes Franco-Italien, 1981.

Warner, George F., and Julius P. Gilson. *British Museum: Catalogue of Western Manuscripts in the Old Royal and King's Collections.* 4 vols. London: British Museum, 1921.

Watson, Paul. *The Garden of Love in Tuscan Art of the Early Renaissance.* Philadelphia: Art Alliance, 1979.

Wayne, Valerie. "Zenobia in Medieval and Renaissance Literature." In Levin and Watson, 48–65.

West, Robin. "Jurisprudence and Gender." *University of Chicago Law Review* 55 (1988): 1–72.

Wickersheimer, Ernest. *Dictionnaire biographique des médecins en France au Moyen Age.* 2 vols. Reprint, Geneva: Droz, 1979.

Wilkinson, L. P. *Ovid Recalled.* Cambridge: Cambridge University Press, 1955.

Willard, Charity Cannon. "Anne de France, Reader of Christine de Pizan." In McLeod, 59–70.

———. "Antoine de la Salle, Reader of Christine de Pizan." In McLeod, 1–9.

———. "An Autograph Manuscript of Christine de Pizan?" *Studi Francesi* 27 (1965): 452–57.

———. "Christine de Pizan as Teacher." *Romance Languages Annual* 2 (1992): 132–36.

———. *Christine de Pizan: Her Life and Works.* New York: Persea, 1984.

———. "Christine de Pizan: The Astrologer's Daughter." In *Mélanges à la mémoire de Franco Simone: France et Italie dans la culture européenne I: Moyen Age et Renaissance,* 95–111. Geneva: Slatkine, 1980.

———. "Christine de Pizan's *Cent ballades d'amant et de dame*: Criticism of Courtly Love." In *Court and Poet,* ed. G. S. Burgess, 357–64. Liverpool: Cairns,1981.

———. "Christine de Pizan's *Livre des Trois Vertus:* Feminine Ideal or Practical Advice?" In Bornstein, *Ideals,* 91–116.

———. "Christine de Pizan's Treatise on the Art of Medieval Warfare." In *Essays in Honor of Louis Francis Solano,* ed. Raymond J. Cormier and Urban T. Holmes, 179–91. University of North Carolina Studies in the Romance Languages and Literatures 92. Chapel Hill: University of North Carolina Press, 1970.

———. "A Fifteenth-Century View of Women's Role in Medieval Society: Christine de Pizan's *Livre des trois Vertus*." In *The Role of Woman in the Middle Ages*, ed. Rosmarie Thee Morewedge, 90–120. Albany: State University of New York Press, 1975.

———. Introduction to *The "Livre de la paix" of Christine de Pisan*, ed. Charity Cannon Willard, 7–54. The Hague: Mouton, 1958.

———. "Jean de Werchin, Seneschal de Hainaut: Reader and Writer of Courtly Literature." In *Courtly Literature: Culture and Context*, ed. Keith Busby and Erik Cooper, 595–603. Amsterdam-Philadelphia: Benjamins, 1990.

———. "The Manuscript Tradition of the *Livre des trois Vertus* and Christine de Pizan's Audience." *Journal of the History of Ideas* 27 (1966): 433–44.

———. "Pilfering Vegetius? Christine de Pizan's *Faits d'Armes et de Chevalerie*. In *Women, the Book, and the Wordly*, ed. Lesley Smith and Jane H. M. Taylor, vol. 2, 31–37. Cambridge: Brewer, 1995.

———. "A Portuguese Translation of Christine de Pisan's *Livre des Trois Vertus*." *PMLA* 78 (1963): 459–64.

———, ed. *The Writings of Christine de Pizan*. New York: Persea, 1993.

Williamson, Marilyn. "Who's Afraid of Mrs. Barbauld? The Bluestockings and Feminism." *International Journal of Women's Studies* 3 (1980): 89–102.

Winn, Colette H. "'Des mères en filles': Les manuels d'éducation sous l'ancien régime." *Atlantis* 19, no. 1 (1993): 23–29.

———. "La *Dignitas mulieris* dans la littérature didactique féminine (du XVe au XVIIe siècle): Les Enjeux Idéologiques d'une appropriation." *Etudes littéraires* 27, no. 2 (1994): 11–24.

Winn, Mary Beth. *Anthoine Vérard, Parisian Publisher, 1485–1512: Prologues, Poems, and Presentations*. Geneva: Droz, 1997.

———. "Treasures for the Queen: Anne de Bretagne's Books From Anthoine Vérard." *Bibliothèque d'Humanisme et Renaissance* 58 (1996): 667–80.

Winter, Patrick Marc de. *La Bibliothèque de Philippe le Hardi, Duc de Bourgogne (1364–1404)*. Paris: CNRS, 1985.

———. "Christine de Pizan: Ses enlumineurs et ses rapports avec le milieu bourguignon." In *Actes du 104e Congrès National des Sociétés Savantes (Bordeaux 1979)*, 335–75. Paris: Bibliothèque Nationale, 1982.

Wisman, Josette A. "Aspects socio-économiques du *Livre des trois Vertus* de Christine de Pizan." *Le Moyen Français* 30 (1992): 27–44.

———. "L'Epitome rei militari de Végèce et sa fortune au moyen âge." *Le Moyen Age* 85 (1979): 13–31.

Wolfthal, Diane. "'A Hue and a Cry': Medieval Rape Imagery and Its Transformation." *Art Bulletin* 75 (1993): 39–64.

Woodmansee, Martha. "On the Author Effect: Recovering Collectivity." In *The Construction of Authorship: Textual Appropriation in Law and Literature*, ed. Martha Woodmansee and Peter Jaszi, 15–28. Durham: Duke University Press, 1994.

Wright, N. A. A. "The Tree of Battles and the Laws of War." In *War, Literature, and Politics in the Late Middle Ages*, ed. C. T. Allmand, 25–26. Liverpool: Liverpool University, 1976.

Zeitlin, Froma. "Configurations of Rape in Greek Myth." In Tomaselli and Porter, 122–51.

Zimmermann, Margarete, and Dina De Rentiis, eds. *The City of Scholars: New Approaches to Christine de Pizan*. Berlin: Walter de Gruyter, 1994.

Zink, Gaston. "La Phrase de Christine de Pizan dans *Le Livre du corps de policie*." In Dulac and Ribémont, 383–95.

Zühlke, Bärbel. "Christine de Pizan: Le 'Moi' dans le texte et l'image." In Zimmerman and De Rentiis, 222–41.

Contributors

❖

Michel-André Bossy is professor of comparative literature and French studies at Brown University. He is the editor of *Medieval Debate Poetry: Vernacular Works,* and is currently working on the compilation of manuscript anthologies and *canzonieri* of the thirteenth to the fifteenth centuries.

Cynthia J. Brown is professor of French at the University of California, Santa Barbara. She is the author of *The Shaping of History and Poetry in Late Medieval France,* a critical edition of André de la Vigne's *Ressource de la Chrestienté,* and *Poets, Patrons, and Printers: Crisis of Authority in Late Medieval France,* which won the 1996 Scaglione Prize for French and Francophone Literary Studies. She is currently engaged in a study of female sovereignty in late medieval Europe.

Mary Anne C. Case is professor of law and Class of 1966 Research Professor at the University of Virginia, where she teaches feminist jurisprudence as well as constitutional and European law. She has written on the early history of arguments for the equality of the sexes, on the regulation of sexuality and of gender, and on feminist uses of sociobiology.

Marilynn Desmond is associate professor of English and comparative literature at Binghamton University. She is the author of *Reading Dido: Gender, Textuality, and the Medieval Aeneid* and the editor of a special issue of *Medievalia* on "Ovid in Medieval Culture."

Thelma Fenster is professor of French at Fordham University. She has edited and translated Christine de Pizan's *Epistre au dieu d'Amours, Dit de la Rose,* and *Livre du duc des vrais amans.* She is the editor of *Arthurian Women: A Casebook.*

Mary Weitzel Gibbons is an art historian who specializes in Italian Renaissance sculpture. She is the author of *Giambologna: Narrator of the Catholic Reformation,* and is currently working on text image studies, particularly of the French fairy Melusine and in the works of Christine de Pizan.

Monica H. Green is associate professor of history at Duke University. She has published on various aspects of women's health care in medieval Europe and is currently completing an edition and general historical study of the so-called *Trotula* texts.

Judith L. Kellogg is associate professor of English at the University of Hawaii at Manoa. She is the author of *Medieval Artistry and Exchange: Economic Institutions, Society, and Literary Form in Old French Narrative.* She has also published on Chaucer, Middle English Romance, the *Chanson de Roland,* Chrétien de Troyes, Christine de Pizan, Arthurian tradition, and the influence of medieval literature on recent fantasy and children's works.

Roberta Krueger is professor of French at Hamilton College and the author of *Women Readers and the Ideology of Gender in Old French Verse Romance.* She is editor of the forthcoming *Cambridge Companion to Medieval Romance* and is working on a book-length project about women's education and the literature of conduct in late medieval France.

Deborah McGrady holds a postdoctoral fellowship at the Medieval Institute at Western Michigan University. Her Ph.D. dissertation is entitled "Constructing Authorship in the Late Middle Ages: A Study of the Books of Guillaume de Machaut, Christine de Pizan, and Jean Lemaire de Belges."

Benjamin M. Semple is assistant professor of French at Yale University. He has published on the *Chanson de Roland* and on the works of Christine de Pizan. He is currently working on the dream visions of Christine de Pizan.

Charity Cannon Willard has edited the *Livre de la Paix* and the *Trésor de la cité des dames* (*Le Livre des trois Vertus*) and is currently working on an edition of the *Fais d'armes et de chevalerie.* She has translated the *Trésor* and has, along with the late Sumner Willard, completed a translation of the *Fais d'armes.* She is also the author of *Christine de Pizan: Her Life and Works,* as well as a collected edition of Christine's texts in English translation.

Diane Wolfthal is assistant professor of art history at Arizona State University. She is the author of *The Beginnings of Netherlandish Canvas Painting: 1400–1530,* and has completed a book manuscript entitled "Images of Rape: The 'Heroic' Tradition and Its Alternatives."

Index

❖

Abelard, Peter, 16; *Historia*, 16
Aegidius Romanus. *See* Giles of Rome
Aeneas, 116–17
Agrippa of Nettesheim, 86 n. 16, 87 n. 20, 87 n. 23
Albertus Magnus, 150, 155, 163, 165
Alcyone. *See* Ceyx and Alcyone
Alexander, legend of, 245–47. *See also* *Roman d'Alexandre*
André, Jean: as editor and printer of Christine's works, 225–27
Andrea, Giovanni (Andreae, Johannes), 12, 24, 80, 86 nn. 14–15. *See also* Novella
Andromache, 21, 36, 38 n. 10
Anne of Brittany, 34, 37, 220–22, 226–27, 231 n. 23, 232 n. 28; in manuscript illumination, 221 fig. 33
Anne of France. *See* Anne of Brittany
Antoine de la Sale, 234 n. 37; *Le Petit Jehan de Saintré*, 100
Apollo, 51–53, 57, 68, 136; in manuscript illuminations, 51 fig. 10, 53 fig. 11, 55 fig. 12. *See also* Phoebus
Aquinas, Thomas, 108, 155–56; *Commentary on Aristotle's Metaphysics*, 92, 94, 155; *Summa theologiae*, 155
Arès, Michel, 57–58
Aristotle, 75, 91, 110–11, 138, 142, 146, 154–58, 163, 165, 166–67, 174 n. 43; *Ethics*, 94–95; *Generation of Animals* (*Generatio animalium*), 154–55, 156; *Metaphysics*, 111, 126 n. 5, 155; *Politics*, 94, 95
Art de chevalerie selon Vegece. *See* Vérard, Antoine
Arthur de Richmont, 14, 15
Astell, Mary, 80, 82–83
Augustine, Saint, 4, 12, 16, 60, 67, 94, 142; *City of God*, 43, 69 fig. 16, 94–95; *Confessions*, 16
Avicenna: *Canon*, 159

Bal, Mieke, 42, 58, 67
Barbauld, Anna Laetitia, 83–84

Bedford Trend master, 206
Bellerophon, 48–49, 51, 58; in manuscript illuminations, 49 fig. 8, 50 fig. 9
Bellerophon's stepmother, 48–49, 58, 59, 67; in manuscript illuminations, 49 fig. 8, 50 fig. 9
Belles Heures, 43, 57
Bible moralisée, 43, 49, 67
Boccaccio, Giovanni, xii, 37, 56, 61, 64, 65–67, 140; *De casibus*, 61; *De mulieribus claris*, 61; *Des cleres femmes* (translation of *De mulieribus claris*), 62–64, 62 fig. 13, 63 fig. 14, 65, 66 fig. 15
Boethius, 22, 105 n. 8; *Consolatio philosophiae*, 144 n. 8
Bonaventure, 108
Boreas, 45–46; in manuscript illumination, 45 fig. 5
Bouchet, Jean, 228; *Temple de bonne renommee*, 225
Boucicaut, 3, 4–5
Bouvet, Honoré, 241, 248, 251; *Arbre des batailles*, 5, 11, 12, 13, 14, 216, 241, 248; in manuscript illumination, 242 fig. 37

Caesarius of Arles, 145 n. 16
Callekin Van Laerne, 68
Carmentis, 29, 30, 157
Cassandra, 20, 30, 35, 36
Catherine of Alexandria, Saint, 35, 78
Cato, 157
Caxton, William, 12, 14, 216, 218, 228; *The Fayttes of Armes and of Chyvalrye* (translation of *Livre des fais d'armes et de chevalerie*), 216; *Morale Proverbes* (translation of *Proverbes moraux*), 216–18. (*see also* Pynson, Richard)
Cecco d'Ascoli, 75, 157
Ceres, 29, 156, 233 n. 37
Cereta, Laura, 80, 82, 83, 84
Ceyx and Alcyone, 38 n. 8, 181, 191–92; in *Epistre Othea*, 183–85; in *Mutacion de Fortune*, 185–88

MEDIEVAL CULTURES

287